22-34

Politics and Policies:
The Continuing Issues

Politics and Policies: The Continuing Issues

Phillip O. Foss

and

Duane W. Hill

Colorado State University

Wadsworth Publishing Company, Inc., Belmont, California

Prologue

In preparing this volume we have attempted to provide students and instructors with an integrated selection of readings that are woven into the fabric of the authors' prose. The resulting continuity should provide the reader with a clear overall picture of the issues and enable him to see how issues are related to each other. Most importantly, the technique helps overcome the problems of transition that readers encounter when moving from one selection to the next in the traditional collections of readings. This approach should make the book a better pedagogical tool.

This volume has been designed for use as a supplementary text in basic political science courses. The readings we have included are brief and clear statements of policy and issues, and we have let the issues and the political gladiators speak for themselves wherever possible. There is little commentary from the sidelines, except for our orienting explanations. Moreover, we go to the places where policies are formulated and issues are fought out. We assume that the politics of education, for example, is not confined to the activities of school boards, legislatures, and other public authorities. It is as fully a matter of action by students, faculties, and school administrators.

Most of the selections in this book are recent statements. A number of statements from out of the past have been included to show that not every problem has appeared, fullgrown, overnight. But our primary purpose in this collection is to give the reader a sense of immediacy and involvement by using current names and events. We have also chosen issues which are not temporary or transient (although we realize that most social issues—racial discrimination for example, or national defense—have existed since the beginnings of organized government). In general, then, our selections are modern versions of age-old policy issues, but they are issues "NOW!"

We are aware that major issues have many facets and that presentation of "both sides" of an issue is ordinarily not enough. Thus, within the limits of space, we have tried to include several significant points of view on each issue. Hopefully, such an offering will give each student something substantive on which he can argue "for" as well as "against."

As we move from one point of view to the next, we are not necessarily presenting arguments that fit into a logical pattern. Rather we are seeking to familiarize the reader with ideas and attitudes of significant segments of the population. Matt Murphy's words to the Southern jury in Selma may make little sense to many readers, but they express the attitudes of many Southerners with tremendous force.

Obviously, the choice of issue areas, the manner in which an issue is stated, and the particular selections presented give direction to analysis and tend to "stack the deck" in favor of the authors' values, no matter how sincerely we have strived for objectivity. That is why we have tried to present as many sides and positions as we can. It is also the reason why we have abstained from attempts to define specific issues. We leave definitions to the reader and instructor.

Hopefully, our technique will leave the instructor free to decide how the policy process is to be analyzed and described and how the issues are to be related to that process. And hopefully, too, the materials in this book will stimulate students and other readers to develop a more critical outlook on public programs and issues and will goad them to construct more refined tools for analyzing the political world.

We are grateful to the authors and publishers for permission to reprint the selections that appear in this book. Appropriate acknowledgements appear throughout the text.

It is a pleasure to acknowledge our debt to Professors Thomas R. Dye of Florida State University, Richard Phipps of the College of San Mateo, and Randall B. Ripley of Ohio State University, as well as Robert J. Gormley of Wadsworth. They reviewed the manuscript in painstaking detail and it has been improved immeasurably thanks to their perceptive suggestions.

Phillip O. Foss
Duane W. Hill

Contents

We decide or debate, carefully and in person, all matters of policy, holding, not that words and deeds go ill together, but that acts are foredoomed to failure when undertaken undiscussed. For we are noted for being at once most adventurous in action and most reflective beforehand. Other men are bold in ignorance, while reflection will stop their onset. But the bravest are surely those who have the clearest vision of what is before them, glory and danger alike, and yet notwithstanding go out to meet it.

Pericles' Funeral Oration—
431 B.C.

Negroes: The Continuing Revolution

Oh deep in my heart I do believe
that we shall overcome some day.

American folk song

Burn the mother down.

Black militant statement, 1968

1

During the past decade, the issues with the highest emotional charge have centered around Negroes; but Negro problems have been with us since 1619, when the first slaves were imported into the Colony of Virginia. By the time the Founding Fathers convened in Philadelphia for the Constitutional Convention, one of the most vexing questions was whether Negroes should be counted as people for the apportionment of members of the national House of Representatives. The issue was finally compromised by allowing each Negro to be counted as three-fifths of one person.

During the first half of the 19th century, when new states were being admitted to the Union, the burning issue was whether they would be admitted as "free" or "slave" states. This issue was thought to have been resolved when the Supreme Court ruled in the Dred Scott decision of 1857 that neither a state nor the federal government could bestow federal citizenship upon native-born Negroes, whether slave or free. This meant that even if a state gave citizenship to a freed Negro, he did not thereby become a federal citizen or a citizen in any other state; a slave did not become free simply by residence in a free state. Instead of resolving the issue, the Dred Scott decision helped trigger the Civil War.

That war was basically a contest over the issue of slavery even though the question of state sovereignty and a state's right to secede from the Union may have been the more immediate issues.

After the North won the War and the Emancipation Proclamation was

4 made meaningful, the 13th, 14th, and 15th Amendments to the Constitution were adopted to legitimatize and stabilize the new status of former Negro slaves. The 13th Amendment (adopted in 1865) provides in part:

Neither slavery nor involuntary servitude, except as punishment for crime whereof the party shall have been duly convicted, shall exist within the United States or any place subject to their jurisdiction.

The crucial part of the 14th Amendment reads:

No State shall make or enforce any law which shall abridge the privileges or immunities of citizens of the United States; nor shall any State deprive any person of life, liberty or property without due process of law; nor deny to any person within its jurisdiction the equal protection of the laws.

And the 15th Amendment guarantees the right to vote in these words:

The right of citizens of the United States to vote shall not be denied or abridged by the United States or by any State on account of race, color or previous condition of servitude.

Immediately following the Civil War, Negroes enjoyed some of the privileges granted them by the 14th and 15th Amendments (a Negro was elected to the United States Senate from Mississippi) but supporters of the old order quickly regrouped and began to devise means and methods to keep Negroes "in their place."

Jim Crow

Possibly the most effective method for maintaining the inferior status of Negroes was a set of practices which came to be called "Jim Crow," meaning that whites and blacks were segregated in schools, theatres, restaurants, transportation facilities, and other public places. Jim Crow practices were acknowledged and accepted by the Supreme Court in the case of *Plessy* v. *Ferguson* in 1896. In that opinion the Court held:

. . . in the nature of things it (the 14th Amendment) could not have been intended to abolish distinctions based upon color, or to enforce social, as distinguished from political, equality, or a commingling of the two races upon terms unsatisfactory to either. Laws permitting, and even requiring, their separation in places where they are liable to be brought into contact do not necessarily imply the inferiority of either race to the other, and have been generally, if not universally, recognized as within the competency of the state legislatures in the exercise of their police power. . . .

If one race be inferior to the other socially, the Constitution of the United States cannot put them upon the same plane. . . .[1]

For the next 58 years, the courts generally upheld the constitutionality of the "separate but equal" doctrine enunciated in *Plessy* v. *Ferguson.* Then, in the case of *Brown* v. *Board of Education of Topeka*[2] in 1954, the Court announced:

We conclude that in the field of public education the doctrine of "separate but equal" has no place. Separate educational facilities are inherently unequal. Therefore, we hold that the plaintiffs . . . are, by reason of the segregation complained of, deprived of the equal protection of the laws guaranteed by the Fourteenth Amendment.

Probably no incident since the Emancipation Proclamation has given greater impetus to the rising expectations of Negroes in "the continuing revolution." Shortly after the *Brown* case, the Court extended the desegregation rule to public recreation facilities[3] and to intrastate public transportation.[4]

The Brown decision and those that followed it caused Negro hopes to soar, but traditional segregation practices changed slowly or not at all. In education, employment, housing, and public accommodations, discrimination against Negroes continued. Each of these areas of dispute will be considered separately.

Education

According to the U. S. Commission on Civil Rights:

Nearly 10 years after the Supreme Court decision in the *School Segregation Cases,* Negro schoolchildren still attend segregated schools in all parts of the Nation.

In the South, most schools continue to be segregated by official policy. But in the North and West, school segregation is widespread

---

[1] 163 U. S. 537 (1896).
[2] 347 U. S. 483 (1954).
[3] *Mayor and City Council of Baltimore City* v. *Dawson,* 350 U. S. 877 (1955).
[4] *Gayle* v. *Browder,* 352 U. S. 903 (1956).

6 because of existing segregated housing patterns and the practice of assigning pupils to neighborhood schools. . . .[5]

Employment

The commission reported that median urban family income for white families was $6,433 as compared with $3,711 for nonwhites, while the unemployed rate for whites was 4.6 percent as compared with 9 percent for nonwhites.[6]

It is significant that discrimination against Negroes in employment is not restricted to the South. According to Congressman William M. Colmer of Mississippi:

I went out in the State of Indiana . . . and I traveled over four counties . . . and I said to my host, "A lot of things remind me of home around here, but there is one thing that is absent. I have not seen any Negroes in the two days I have been traveling over those four counties." I said, "Don't you have any Negroes here?"

He said, "No, we don't have any."

And I said, "You mean to tell me that the town where I spent the last night, a town of about 25,000 population, has no Negroes in it?"

And he said, "No, we don't have any."

I said, "How do you account for that?"

He said, "It is very simple. We just don't give them jobs. That way we keep them out."[7]

Housing

In the words of the U. S. Commission on Civil Rights:

Shelter is the one necessity of life which some Americans, by reason of their color, race, religion, or national origin, cannot purchase freely. From its beginning, this Commission has studied and collected information concerning legal developments in the field of housing. Evaluating these facts in terms of equal protection of the laws under the Constitution, the Commission has concluded that Federal, State, and local governments are still promoters of residential segregation.[8]

---

[5] *Report of the U. S. Commission on Civil Rights, 1963* (Washington, D. C.: U. S. G.P.O. 1964), pp. 53–63.

[6] *Ibid.,* p. 155.

[7] U. S. Congress, House of Representatives, Committee on Rules, 88th Cong., 2d sess., Hearings on H.R. 7152, p. 469.

[8] *Report on the U. S. Commission on Civil Rights, 1963,* pp. 95–96.

In the closing days of the 1963 session, the California legislature passed the Rumford Bill which prohibited discrimination for reasons of creed or race in the rental or sale of most California real property. In the election of the following year (1964), the voters of California rejected the Rumford Act almost 2–1 by passing Proposition 14 and amended the State Constitution to read:

Neither the state nor any subdivision or agency thereof shall deny, limit or abridge, directly or indirectly, the right of any person who is willing or desires to sell, lease or rent any part or all of his real property, to decline to sell, lease or rent such property to such person or persons as he, in his absolute discretion, chooses.

In essence, Californians voted to allow discrimination in housing. The U. S. Supreme Court later disallowed Proposition 14 as unconstitutional, and the Rumford Act still stands.[9]

Public Accommodations

In the words of Roy Wilkins:

It must be remembered that while we talked last week, and while the Congress will be debating in the next weeks, Negro Americans throughout our country will be bruised in nearly every waking hour by differential treatment in, or exclusion from, public accommodations of every description. From the time they leave their homes in the morning, en route to school or to work, to shopping or to visiting, until they return home at night, humiliation stalks them. Public transportation, eating establishments, hotels, lodginghouses, theaters and motels, arenas, stadiums, retail stores, markets, and various other places and services catering to the general public offer them either differentiated service or none at all.[10]

The Civil Rights Act of 1964

On June 11, 1963, in a radio and television address, President John F. Kennedy asked the American people to support his policy proposals for new legislation on Negro rights:

---

[9] *Mulkey* v. *Reitman*, 387 U. S. 369 (1967).

[10] From statement of Roy Wilkins, Executive Secretary, National Association for the Advancement of Colored People, before the Committee on Commerce, U. S. Senate, 88th Cong., 1st sess., Hearings on S. 1732, p. 656.

8   We are committed to a world-wide struggle to promote and protect all of those who wish to be free and when Americans are sent to Viet Nam or West Berlin, we do not ask for whites only. It ought to be possible, therefore, for American students of any color to attend any public institution they select without having to be backed up by troops.

It ought to be possible for American consumers of any color to receive equal service in places of public accommodation, such as hotels and retail stores, without being forced to resort to demonstrations in the street, and it ought to be possible for American citizens of any color to register and vote in a free election without interference or fear of reprisal. . . .

The Negro baby born in America today, regardless of the section of the nation in which he is born, has about one half as much chance of completing high school as a white baby born in the same place on the same day, one third as much chance of completing college, one third as much chance of becoming a professional man, twice as much chance of becoming unemployed, about one seventh as much chance of earning $10,000 a year, a life expectancy which is seven years shorter, and the prospects of earning only half as much.

This is not a sectional issue. Difficulties over segregation and discrimination exist in every city, in every state of the union, producing in many cities a rising tide of discontent that threatens the public safety.

Nor is this a partisan issue in a time of domestic crisis. Men of goodwill and generosity should be able to unite regardless of party or politics. This is not even a legal or legislative issue alone. It is better to settle these matters in the courts than in the streets and new laws are needed at every level, but law alone cannot make men see right.

We are confronted primarily with a moral issue. It is as old as the scriptures and is as clear as the American Constitution. The heart of the question is whether all Americans are to be afforded equal rights and equal opportunities, whether we are going to treat our fellow Americans as we want to be treated.

In the congressional hearings that followed the Kennedy proposals, most of the common positions on Negro rights were set forth and their rationale expounded. Excerpts from these hearings are reproduced below.

Statement of the Hon. Robert Kennedy, Attorney General and brother of the President:

What the President has proposed in this bill is a law which will eliminate one of the most embittering forms of racial discrimination: the denial of free access to places of public accommodation — restaurants, stores, hotels, lunch counters, and other establishments of service or amusement — to a large number of our fellow citizens whose skin is not white.

The law will set no precedent in the field of governmental regulation, nor will it unjustly infringe on the rights of any individual.

The only right it will deny is the right to discriminate — to embarrass and humiliate millions of our citizens in the pursuit of their daily lives.

The places of business covered by this law are public in a very real sense: they are not private homes or clubs. They deal with the general public. They invite and in fact compete for public patronage. . . .

White people of whatever kind — prostitutes, narcotics pushers, Communists, or bank robbers — are welcome at establishments which will not admit certain of our Federal judges, ambassadors, and countless members of our Armed Forces. . . .

If Congress can control the labeling of every bottle of aspirin in every drug store, surely it is no deprivation of anyone's liberty to permit Negroes to shop and eat there.

Senator Thurmond [South Carolina]. Suppose I owned a restaurant and wanted to cater to redheaded secretaries?

Mr. Kennedy. I think if you wanted to make it quite clear that you wanted to cater only to redheaded secretaries, I suppose they would want to inquire as to why you would want to do that, Senator. . . .

Senator Thurmond. I would like to read from the decision in a recent case, *Peterson* v. *City of Greenville*. This is from the concurring opinion of Mr. Justice Harlan and I quote:

> Freedom of the individual to choose his associates or his neighbors, to use and dispose of his property as he sees fit, to be irrational, arbitrary, capricious, even unjust in his personal relations are things all entitled to a large measure of protection from governmental interference.

What do you think of his views of this subject?

Mr. Kennedy. I might express it somewhat differently. I have great respect for Justice Harlan. . . .

Senator Thurmond. You don't feel that this bill goes directly to the Constitution in that it interferes with a man's control and use of his property? . . .

Mr. Kennedy. No more than many, many, dozens of provisions at the present time, Senator. You have a lot of local, state, and federal laws that govern the use of property. Your right to property is not absolute,

10   Senator. This is not the first time anybody has brought in any legislation that deals with your right of property.

All this deals with is when you open your doors to the general public, you ask for the general public. All we say in this bill is that you shouldn't discriminate. You can't refuse somebody just on the basis of the fact they don't happen to be white.[11]

Statement of the Hon. Dean Rusk, Secretary of State:

Mr. Rusk. . . . Let me say, at the very beginning, that I consider [the] foreign policy aspects to be secondary in importance. I should like to emphasize that it is not my view that we should resolve these problems here at home merely in order to look good abroad. The primary reason why we must attack the problems of discrimination is rooted in our basic commitments as a nation and a people. We must try to eliminate discrimination due to race, color, religion, not to make others think better of us but because it is incompatible with the great ideals to which our democratic society is dedicated. If the realities at home are all they should be, we shan't have to worry about our image abroad. . . .

The spiritual sons of the American Revolution are of every race. For let us remind ourselves that the great declaration said "all men are created equal and are endowed by their Creator with certain unalienable rights," it did not say, "all men except those who are not white." . . .

Senator Thurmond. Do you believe that the problems which you have presented here today justify a legislative act which at the very least diminishes freedom in the use of property which each property owner now has?

Mr. Rusk. Well, I could not agree, sir, that such a law would diminish freedom. The purpose of law in a free society is to enlarge freedom by letting each know what kind of conduct to expect from the other. And it is through our laws that personal freedom is not only protected but constantly enlarged, so we can pursue our respective orbits with a minimum of collisions.[12]

Statement of the Hon. Ross E. Barnett, Governor of the State of Mississippi:

---

[11] U. S. Senate, Committee on Commerce, 88th Cong., 1st sess., Hearings on S. 1732, pp. 83, 84, 85, 91, 92, 94, 116, 117.

[12] *Ibid.*, pp. 281, 282, 315.

. . . Gentlemen, we are facing one of the most critical times in the history of our Nation. Minority groups in our country have taken to the streets to agitate, to demonstrate, to breach the peace, and to provoke violence calculated to blackmail this Congress into passing legislation in direct violation of the U. S. Constitution. . . .

Gentlemen, it is the divide, disrupt, and conquer technique. The passage of this civil rights legislation will positively and unmistakably, to my humble way of thinking, provoke more violence, not just in the South, but throughout all areas of this Nation. . . .

The purpose of government should be to protect the individual and to see to it that no one interferes with his private property. The present administration seems to have adopted the very heart of the socialistic philosophy that the private rights of men are to be tolerated only at the suffrage of the State. . . .

Senator Russell has stated and the press has failed to report, I understand:

> Our American system has always rejected the idea that one group of citizens may deprive another of legal rights and property by process of agitation, demonstration, intimidation, law defiance, and civil disobedience. Every Negro citizen possesses every right that is possessed by any white citizen. But there is nothing in either the Constitution or in Christian principles or common sense and reason which could compel one citizen to share his rights with one of another race at the same place and at the same time. Such compulsion would amount to a complete denial of inalienable rights of the individual to choose or select his associates. . . .

Eighty years ago in *United States* v. *Nichols,* entitled the *Civil Rights* cases, 109 U. S. 3, the Supreme Court of the United States held sections 1 and 2 of the Civil Rights Act of 1875 unconstitutional. Said acts provided that all persons in the United States were entitled to the full and equal enjoyment of accommodations, advantages, facilities, and privileges of inns and places of amusement. In holding that Congress had no right to pass such a law under the 14th amendment, the Court said — I am quoting from 109 U. S., page 3. The Court said:

> It is State action of a particular character that is prohibited. Individual invasion of individual rights is not the subject matter of the amendment. . . .[13]

---

[13] Authors' note:

Section 1 of the Civil Rights Act of 1875 (18 Stat. 335) provided in part

> that all persons within the jurisdiction of the United States shall be entitled to the full and equal enjoyment of the accommodations, advantages, facilities, and privileges of inns, public conveyances on land or water, theatres, and other

12   In 1959, you recall, a Howard Johnson Restaurant denied service to Charles E. Williams, a colored attorney for the Internal Revenue Service. He brought suit claiming that such action violated the Civil Rights Act of 1875 and the commerce clause of the Federal Constitution. In this case, *Williams* v. *Howard Johnson Restaurants*, U.S.C.A. 4th, 268 F. 2d 845, the court reaffirmed the doctrine of the *Civil Rights* Cases, and said

> that the amendment did not invest Congress with power to legislate upon the actions of individuals, which are within the domain of State legislation. . . .

. . . Congress does not have the power to enact this legislation under the commerce clause of the Constitution of the United States. . . .

This issue, gentlemen, was raised in *Williams* v. *Howard Johnson Restaurant, supra* — that is, the attempt to take away the rights of the States — and was held not to fall within the commerce clause of the Constitution. The Court said in that particular case:

> The plaintiff makes the additional contention based on the allegations that the defendant restaurant is engaged in interstate commerce because it is located beside an interstate highway and serves interstate travelers.
>
> . . . we do not find that a restaurant is engaged in interstate commerce merely because in the course of its business of furnish-

---

places of public amusement; subject only to the conditions and limitations established by law, and applicable alike to citizens of every race and color, regardless of any previous condition of servitude.

The Civil Rights Cases (109 U. S. 3) arose out of alleged violations of the 1875 Act. Excerpts from Justice Bradley's majority opinion follow:

The first section of the Fourteenth Amendment (which is the one relied on), after declaring who shall be citizens of the United States, and of the several States, is prohibitory in its character, and prohibitory upon the states. . . .

It is State action of a particular character that is prohibited. Individual invasion of individual rights is not the subject-matter of the amendment. . . .

It does not invest Congress with power to legislate upon subjects which are within the domain of State legislation; but to provide modes of relief against State legislation, or State action, of the kind referred to. It does not authorize Congress to create a code of municipal law for the regulation of private rights; but to provide modes of redress against the operation of State laws, and the action of State officers executive or judicial, when these are subversive of the fundamental rights specified in the amendment. . . .

The wrongful act of an individual, unsupported by any such authority, is simply a private wrong, or a crime of that individual. . . .

On the whole we are of opinion, that no countenance of authority for the passage of the law in question can be found in either the Thirteenth or Fourteenth Amendment of the Constitution. . . .

ing accommodations to the general public it serves persons who are traveling from State to State.

. . . Neither the fact that some customers of an establishment may be traveling in interstate commerce nor the fact that some of the goods sold may have been purchased from outside the State constitutes commerce subject to control by Congress. In *Elizabeth Hospital, Inc.* v. *Richardson,* U.S.C.A. 8th, 269 F. 2d 167, the Court held that the treatment of some patients who were traveling in interstate commerce did not destroy the purely local character of the services furnished by the hospital. . . .

Equality in a social sense is attainable only in total slavery. Justice Brandeis, who was a great justice of the U. S. Supreme Court said, and I quote, "one of the inalienable rights of men is to be let alone." And you know so many times the government that serves best is the government that serves least.[14]

Statement of the Hon. George C. Wallace, Governor of the State of Alabama:

I come here today as an American, as a Governor of a sovereign State and as an individual with full respect for constitutional government. I appear to respectfully call upon the Congress of the United States to defeat in its entirety the proposed Civil Rights Act of 1963. . . .

The free and uncontrolled use of private property is the basic and historic concept of Anglo-Saxon jurisprudence. One of the primary reasons our forefathers came from Europe to carve this Nation out of a raw and savage wilderness was for the purpose of using, controlling, and enjoying their private property and to pursue their chosen professions without fear of interference from kings, tyrants, despots, and I might add, Presidents. . . .

I will tell you what this Senate bill 1732 does: It places upon all businessmen and professional people the yoke of involuntary servitude. It should be designated as the "Involuntary Servitude Act of 1963."

Under the provisions of Senate Bill 1732, if you are engaged in any profession where you offer your personal services, you cannot refuse to serve anyone without fear of violating this act. I don't know of any business or profession that does not have some abstract connection with interstate travel or interstate movement of goods. . . .

I will go on and say that the President, the Attorney General, and I

---

[14] U. S. Senate, Committee on Commerce, 88th Cong., 1st sess., Hearings on S. 1732, pp. 359–371.

14   say respectfully, every Member of this Congress who has sponsored this legislation stand indicted before the American people.

This group has invited the Negro to come North to a land of milk and honey. They accepted the proposition, and instead of finding this utopia, they have found unemployment. They have been stacked in ghettos on top of one another, to become a part of every city's Harlem. Thereby social and economic problems have been compounded.

The end result is that this gross hypocrisy has brought guerrilla warfare and insurrection to every large city of the United States endangering the lives of millions of our citizens. Because of this hypocritical spectacle, he no longer wants mere equal treatment, he expects and apparently intends to bludgeon the majority of this country's citizens into giving him preferential treatment.

I am not talking about all the Negro citizens of Alabama and of the Nation, but I am talking about the minority group of them. . . .

The physical danger I outline is no problem in the South. You and your family can travel to any place in the South, walk the streets of every section of cities and towns alone, without fear of bodily harm. But I know, as you know, that you and your family cannot walk the streets of our Nation's Capital without fear of mugging, raping, killing or other physical assault. . . .

Does not the present situation in Washington, D. C., give you some idea of the result you would obtain with this legislation? The Nation's Capital is supposed to be the supreme example of what civil rights legislation can accomplish. It's an example all right, an example of a city practically deserted by white people. If you in the Congress are really sincere about this civil rights business, why don't you give home rule to the people of Washington? Let's see how the local residents can run this city.

I believe in local self-government. I challenge you to vote for home rule in Washington, D. C. I suspect that if you attempted to do this, the Secretary of State would have to testify behind closed doors that this would result in damage to our image before the rest of the world. . . .

I ask you to ignore political pressures which will destroy our entire free enterprise system — that you determine that this country will not have government by intimidation — that is all that is, a matter of taking a mob in the streets after they have broken windows and stuck knives in policemen and burned buildings down and shooting people, and then say we will sit down and discuss that which you want. . . .

I challenge the President and the Congress to submit this proposed legislation to the people as a national referendum.

I promise you that you will get the shock of your life because the people of this country will overwhelmingly reject this encroachment upon their right to own and enjoy private property.

I say that it is high time freedom-loving people of this Nation stand up and be counted and if the tree of liberty needs refreshing by the political blood of those who ignore the heritage established for us by the Founding Fathers, then so be it.[15]

Senator Thurmond. Do you believe in equal educational opportunities, in equal economic opportunities, and equal political opportunities for all people?

Governor Wallace. Of course I do. Yes.

Senator Thurmond. And simply because you think the people of each State ought to be allowed to handle their social problems, and determine what is best to preserve law and order, and prevent riots and dissension and tensions does not indicate that you in any way favor discrimination on the part of or against any people?

Governor Wallace. No, sir. I'm not against any people because of their color. Of course, this is repetition. I believe that God made everybody and I'm one of these fellows who, as I said yesterday, I'm not one of these intellectuals who think there is no God. I think there is one. In fact, I know there is one. And I believe that He made all of the human family and that He loves all of the human family, and that anybody who mistreats anybody because of color, knowingly, I feel sorry for him. . . .

Senator Hart [Michigan]. . . . It is your belief, you say that God made us and loves us all —

Governor Wallace. Yes, I believe that.

Senator Hart (continuing). And there is an eternal destiny for us?

Governor Wallace. Yes.

Senator Hart. What will heaven be like? Will it be segregated?

Governor Wallace. Of course I don't think that you or I, either one, know what heaven is going to be like, Senator. . . . But I do have faith that there is an eternal destiny for all of us.

But of course God made me white and you white and He made other people black. That is His handiwork. In effect, He segregated us. . . .[16]

Statement of E. L. Forrester, Member of Congress from Georgia:

Mr. Chairman, I do deplore the fact that this present civil rights bill carries a public accommodations section, which is admittedly unconstitutional under the *Civil Rights Cases* decision of 1883. . . .

---

[15] *Ibid.*, pp. 434–443.
[16] *Ibid.*, pp. 435–505.

16   Justices appointed by Lincoln and Grant, all active upon the Washington scene, all thoroughly familiar with the disputations of the day, the
legislation as it was enacted, and so forth, were far more capable of
knowing the intent inspiring the wartime constitutional amendments,
and far more capable of interpreting them. It is my considered judgment
that what this Nation needs more than any other thing now . . . is a U. S.
Supreme Court that will serve, as the Supreme Court during the Reconstruction era said:

> Our province is to decide what the law is, not to declare what it
> should be.

We need a Court to say that. Our liberties, privileges, rights, responsibilities, and freedoms set out in our Constitution cannot be eroded by
the times, held out of fashion, or of the "horse and buggy era." They are
as enduring as the marble and granite of our Nation's hills. . . .

I just wonder, Mr. Chairman, how a Supreme Court Justice would
feel standing in the presence of Franklin, Jefferson,[17] Madison, and other
stalwarts who drafted our Constitution, and declaring that the Constitution, like a chameleon, changes its character according to the times. . . .[18]

Statement of William M. Tuck, Member of Congress from Virginia:

Title V of the Civil Rights Act deals with the invidious organization
called the Civil Rights Commission. It would make this group a permanent agency of the Government and would authorize and encourage it to
turn loose on the people of our Nation a swarm of investigators, detec-
tives, Hawkshaws, and inspectors with unlimited authority to inaugurate
inquiries, to harass the people, to issue subpoenas, to bring miscreants
before Federal judges and to have them enjoined, fined, and imprisoned.
To me establishment of such an agency is repugnant to every concept of
liberty and it will flare back to haunt those who empower it to intimidate, bullyrag, and torment an already aggravated citizenry.

. . . let me remind those of you who so complacently support this
bill that in a few years you may find yourselves in the plight of Haman of
old who constructed a scaffold upon which to hang Mordecai. But it was
Haman himself, not Mordecai, who was hung on the scaffold. And
Mordecai was there to witness the hanging while he luxuriated in the

---

[17] Authors' note: Jefferson was not present at the Constitutional Convention.
[18] U. S. House of Representatives, Committee on Rules, 88th Cong., 2nd sess.,
Hearings on H.R. 7152, p. 407.

luscious arms of Haman's paramour. I might remind you, too, of the little
limerick:

> There was a young lady from Niger
> Who smiled as she rode on the tiger,
> But at the end of the ride the lady was inside
> And the smile was on the face of the tiger.

. . . These pious proponents of civil rights would feign righteousness. They masquerade in the habiliments of that universal force of
brotherhood and benevolence, but their very unctuosity and vigorous
protestations arouse our suspicions. . . .

By the actions of these impostors, I am reminded of the lady in the
play who protested too much. It also serves to bring to mind a vision of
the memorable episode which occurred on the field of Gideon in the time
of David, the King, when Joab met Amassa, whose face he caressed, but
whose body he despoiled. You no doubt remember the story. With the
customary salutation of affection and friendship, Joab approached and
with his right hand stroked the beard of Amassa and asked: "Is it well
with thee, my brother?" And Amassa noted not the sword that was in his
other hand, and Joab smote Amassa under the fifth rib, dropping his
bowels upon the ground, leaving them to mingle in the dust of that
faraway and ancient battlefield.

The length of our beard may not be as long as Amassa's but we have
eyes keen enough to perceive the situation and to understand the stealth
of this approach, even though the true intent may be concealed by the
language used.[19]

Five days after the assassination of President Kennedy, the new
president went before Congress and added his support to the Civil Rights
Bill. In President Johnson's words, no eulogy could "more eloquently
honor President Kennedy's memory than the civil rights bill for which he
fought so long."

Southern senators carried on a 57-day filibuster against the bill before
they were stopped by a cloture vote — the first in the nation's history on a
civil rights bill, and the sixth successful cloture attempt on any issue.

Malcolm X (leader of the Black Muslims) saw no help for Negroes in
the bill: "You can't legislate good will. . . . The passage of this bill will do
nothing but build up the Negro for a big letdown by promising that which
cannot be delivered."[20]

---

[19] *Ibid.*, pp. 391, 398.
[20] Quoted in Congressional Quarterly Service, *Revolution in Civil Rights* (1965), p.
68.

18   Senator Allen J. Ellender (Louisiana) agreed but for different reasons:

I hope that I am in error when I say that its passage . . . will bring on more strife than one can contemplate. For those who see progress in this civil rights bill they will be sadly disappointed. . . . The moral, intellectual and cultural standards of the white race perhaps leave a lot to be desired, but until the American Negro approaches this standard in large numbers, he will not be accepted. . . . Make no mistake about it, this is what we have been debating these past weeks—the social acceptance of the American Negro by his white countrymen. . . . It is not possible to force one, by law, to associate with another not of his own choosing. . . . What is not recognized is that in many parts of the nation, and especially in the South, integration is considered immoral.[21]

The Civil Rights Act of 1964 (P.L. 88–352) was the most comprehensive and far-reaching legislation on Negro rights since the days of Reconstruction. The main provisions of the long and complex law: Title I prohibited voting registrars from applying different standards to white and Negro voting applicants. Title II prohibited refusal of service on account of race in hotels, restaurants, gasoline stations, and places of amusement if their operations affected interstate commerce. Title III required that Negroes have equal access to, and treatment in, publicly owned or operated facilities. Title IV authorized the U. S. Office of Education to give technical and financial assistance to schools undergoing the desegregation process. Title V broadened the duties and extended the life of the Civil Rights Commission. Title VI prohibited racial discrimination in any program receiving federal aid. Title VII barred discrimination by employers or unions with 25 or more employees, or members. Title IX authorized the Attorney General to intervene in private suits where persons have alleged denial of equal protection of the laws under the 14th Amendment.

The constitutionality of the accommodations sections of the Civil Rights Act was promptly contested in the Heart of Atlanta Motel case.[22]

Mr. Justice Clark delivered the opinion of the Court:

The Factual Background and Contentions of the Parties. The case comes home on admissions and stipulated facts. Appellant owns and operates the Heart of Atlanta Motel which has 216 rooms available to transient guests. The motel is located on Courtland Street, two blocks from downtown Peachtree Street. It is readily accessible to interstate highways 75 and 85 and state highways 23 and 41. Appellant solicits patronage from

---

[21] *Ibid.*, p. 67.
[22] *Heart of Atlanta Motel, Inc.* v. *United States*, 379 U. S. 241 (1964).

outside the State of Georgia through various national advertising media, including magazines of national circulation; it maintains over 50 bill-boards and highway signs within the state, soliciting patronage for the motel; it accepts convention trade from outside Georgia and approxi-mately 75 per cent of its registered guests are from out of State. Prior to passage of the Act the motel had followed a practice of refusing to rent rooms to Negroes, and it alleged that it intended to continue to do so. In an effort to perpetuate that policy this suit was filed.

The appellant contends that Congress in passing this Act exceeded its power to regulate commerce under Art. I, S. 8, cl. 3, of the Constitu-tion of the United States; that the Act violates the Fifth Amendment because appellant is deprived of the right to choose its customers and operate its business as it wishes, resulting in a taking of its liberty and property without due process of law and a taking of its property without just compensation; and, finally, that by requiring appellant to rent avail-able rooms to Negroes against its will, Congress is subjecting it to involuntary servitude in contravention of the Thirteenth Amend-ment. . . .

It is said that the operation of the motel here is of a purely local character. But, assuming this to be true, "if it is interstate commerce that feels the pinch, it does not matter how local the operation that applies the squeeze." *United States* v. *Women's Sportswear Mfrs. Assn.,* 336 U. S. 460, 464 (1949). See *Labor Board* v. *Jones & Laughlin Steel Corp., supra.* As Chief Justice Stone put it in *United States* v. *Darby, supra:*

> The power of Congress over interstate commerce is not confined to the regulation of commerce among the states. It extends to those activities intrastate which so affect interstate commerce or the exercise of the power of Congress over it as to make regulation of them appropriate means to the attainment of a legitimate end, the exercise of the granted power of Congress to regulate inter-state commerce. See *McCulloch* v. *Maryland,* 4 Wheat. 316, 421.

Thus the power of Congress to promote interstate commerce also includes the power to regulate the local incidents therefor, including local activities in both the States of origin and destination, which might have a substantial and harmful effect upon that commerce. One need only examine the evidence which we have discussed above to see that Congress may — as it has — prohibit racial discrimination by motels serv-ing travelers, however "local" their operations may appear. . . .

There is nothing novel about such legislation. Thirty-two States now have it on their books either by statute or executive order and many cities provide such regulation. Some of these Acts go back four-score years. It has been repeatedly held by this Court that such laws do not

20   violate the Due Process Clause of the Fourteenth Amendment. Perhaps the first such holding was in the *Civil Rights Cases* themselves, where Mr. Justice Bradley for the Court inferentially found that innkeepers, "by the laws of all of the States, so far as we are aware, are bound, to the extent of their facilities, to furnish proper accommodation to all unobjectionable persons who in good faith apply for them." . . .

We, therefore, conclude that the action of the Congress in the adoption of the Act as applied here to a motel which concededly serves interstate travelers is within the power granted it by the Commerce Clause of the Constitution, as interpreted by this Court for 140 years.

Voting Rights

After the Reconstruction period following the Civil War, Negroes were first prevented from voting by intimidation and later by a variety of state laws which did not ordinarily contain the word "Negro" but which were obviously aimed at preventing Negroes from voting. Some of the common devices used were literacy tests, the white primary, and the poll tax. The wording of the 15th Amendment appears to be clear and unequivocal; but the Supreme Court, in *United States* v. *Reese* (1876)[23] and reiterated in *United States* v. *Harris* (1883),[24] declared that neither the 14th nor 15th Amendments was intended to take control of elections away from the states. The poll tax was finally struck down (in voting for president, vice president, and members of Congress) by the 24th Amendment in 1964.

The white primary laws were particularly effective because the South had traditionally been a one-party area. Victory in the Democratic primary therefore almost guaranteed victory in the general election. By preventing Negroes from voting in the primary under the concept that the political parties were private organizations (and hence could choose their own members), they were effectively barred from voting. The white primary was eventually declared to be contrary to the 15th Amendment by the Supreme Court in the case of *Smith* v. *Allright* in 1944.[25] The Court held that since the state regulated the primaries and accepted the names of the winners to place on the general election ballot, the parties were agents of the state (not private organizations) and hence came within the prohibitions of the 15th Amendment.

Notwithstanding these improvements in their political status, Negro organizations continued and, in fact, accelerated the tempo of their drive for equal voting rights. They alleged that they were still prevented from voting by discriminatory local practices.

---

[23] 92 U. S. 214.
[24] 106 U. S. 629.
[25] 321 U. S. 649.

We should notice that, with few exceptions, laws pertaining to the **21** conduct of elections are *state* laws. Not only are state and local officials elected according to state laws, but state laws also govern in the elections of president, vice-president, and members of Congress.

According to the U. S. Commission on Civil Rights:

The practices used by voter registrars today to prevent Negro enfranchisement are the same as those described in the 1961 *Voting Report.* . . .

Several methods were cited in 1961. One was the discriminatory application of legal qualifications, such as literacy tests, constitutional interpretation tests, calculation of age to the exact day, and requirements of good moral character. Others involved the use of plainly arbitrary procedures. These included requirement of vouchers or some other unduly technical method of identification, rejection for insignificant errors in filling out forms, failure to notify applicants of rejection, imposition of delaying tactics, and discrimination in giving assistance to applicants.[26]

Despite the voting provisions of the Civil Rights Act of 1957 and the Civil Rights Act of 1960, the Commission's voter registration data indicated that Negro registrations in some parts of the South were still very low (in some cases zero). Comparative Negro and white registration figures for selected counties in Mississippi follow in Table 1–1 as a case in point.

The Voting Rights Bill of 1965 was introduced by Representative Emanuel Celler in the House and by Majority Leader Mike Mansfield in the Senate. On May 25, 1965, cloture was again voted in the Senate to stop a filibuster — the second time in two years. On August 3, the House adopted a conference report on the bill and the Senate followed on August 4. The President added his signature on August 6.

The Voting Rights Act of 1965 (P.L. 89–110) empowered the Attorney General to appoint federal voting examiners to supervise voter registration and the conduct of elections in states or subdivisions thereof where literacy tests or other qualifying devices were used and where less than 50 percent of persons of voting age had registered or voted in 1964. This "triggering" clause included the states of Alabama, Alaska, Georgia, Louisiana, Mississippi, South Carolina, Virginia, and 34 counties in North Carolina.

The act suspended literacy or other qualifying tests in the areas included in the above formula and established completion of the sixth grade as evidence of "literacy."

The act also authorized federal examiners to apply a Federal Court order to impound the ballots in an election where qualified persons had

---

[26] *Report of the U. S. Commission on Civil Rights, 1963,* p. 22.

Table 1–1 Mississippi Registration Statistics,
by County, for January 1, 1964*
(29 of 82 counties)

County	White persons over 21	White persons registered	Percent	Negro persons over 21	Negro persons registered	Percent
1. Benton	2,514	2,226	92.0	1,419	55	3.0
2. Chickasaw	6,388	4,548	72.0	3,054	1	.003
3. Claiborne	1,688	1,528	90.5	3,969	26	.65
4. Clarke	6,072	4,829	80.0	3,998	64	2.2
5. Copiah	8,153	7,533	92.3	6,407	25	.39
6. Forrest	22,431	13,253	59.0	7,494	236	3.1
7. George	5,276	4,200	79.0	580	14	2.4
8. Hinds	67,836	62,410	92.1	36,138	5,616	15.5
9. Holmes	4,773	4,800	100.0+	8,757	20	.23
10. Humphreys	3,344	2,538	68.3	5,561	0	0
11. Issaquena	640	640	100.0	1,081	5	.46
12. Jasper	5,327	4,500	82.2	3,675	10	.23
13. Jefferson Davis	3,629	3,236	89.0	3,222	126	3.9
14. Lamar	6,489	5,752	88.6	1,071	0	0
15. Lauderdale	27,806	18,000	64.7	11,924	1,700	14.3
16. Leake	6,754	6,000	88.8	3,397	220	6.4
17. Leflore	10,274	7,348	71.5	13,567	281	1.6
18. Lowndes	16,460	8,687	52.7	8,362	99	1.1
19. Madison	5,622	6,256	100.0+	10,366	218	2.
20. Marion	8,997	10,123	100.0+	3,630	383	11.
21. Marshall	4,342	4,229	97.3	7,168	177	2.5
22. Oktibbeha	8,423	4,413	52.3	4,952	128	2.5
23. Panola	7,639	5,922	77.0	7,250	878	12.
24. Scott	7,742	5,400	69.7	3,752	16	.42
25. Sunflower	8,785	7,082	80.1	13,524	185	1.4
26. Tallahatchie	5,099	4,464	87.5	6,483	17	.26
27. Tunica	2,011	1,407	69.9	1,407	38	.6
28. Walthall	4,536	4,536	100.0	2,499	4	.124
29. Warren	13,530	11,654	86.1	10,726	2,433	22.6

* U. S. Commission on Civil Rights, *Voting in Mississippi* (Washington, D. C.: U. S. G.P.O., 1965), p. 71.

been prevented from voting, and to hold the ballots until such persons had been allowed to vote.

Penalties of up to $5,000 in fines and/or five years imprisonment were provided for voting fraud and for acts designed to intimidate or interfere with persons attempting to vote.

On signing the act, President Johnson said:

There were those who said this is an old injustice, and there is no need to hurry. But ninety-five years have passed since the Fifteenth Amendment gave all Negroes the right to vote. And the time for waiting is gone.

There were those who said smaller and more gradual measures should be tried. But they had been tried. For years and years they have been tried, and tried, and they had failed, and failed and failed. And the time for failure is gone.

There were those who said that this is a many-sided and very complex problem. But however viewed, the denial of the right to vote is still a deadly wrong. And the time for injustice has gone. . . .

The Issue of Equal Justice Under the Law

"Is it then true" Alexis de Tocqueville asked a Montgomery, Ala., lawyer in 1832, "that the ways of the people of Alabama are as violent as is said?"

"Yes," said the lawyer dolefully. "There is no one here but carries arms under his clothes. At the slightest quarrel, knife or pistol comes to hand. These things happen continually; it is a semi-barbarous state of society."

"But when a man is killed like that," de Tocqueville pressed, "is his assassin not punished?"

"He is always brought to trial," sighed the lawyer "and always acquitted by the jury. . . ."

There have been, by one solid count, no fewer than 58 race murders in the South in the past decade. Only six have ended in convictions, with penalties ranging from seven-month suspended sentences for second-degree manslaughter to a single life term for murder. The remaining 52 have gone unpunished — or unsolved.[27]

On March 25, 1965, a protest march from Selma to Montgomery, Alabama, ended at the state capitol. That evening a volunteer civil rights demonstrator from Detroit, Mrs. Viola Liuzzo, was shot and killed at the wheel of her car while returning from transporting marchers back to Selma. By the next morning, the FBI had arrested Collie Leroy Wilkins, who was accused of the murder by an eyewitness who was riding in the car with him at the time of the shooting.

The following is one reporter's account of the trial that followed:

How to Sway a Jury in Alabama[28]

Hayneville, Ala. — The Judge had a bottle of coke in his hand. He stood up and told the jury, "All right now, you go inside there and when you reach a verdict just knock on the door and the bailiff will let you come out."

On the fourth day of the trial of Collie Leroy Wilkins in the murder of Mrs. Viola Gregg Liuzzo, it now was up to the jury. They received the case in an atmosphere of country-store informality that was held here from the moment court opened. And they received a case which had been carefully constructed, mainly by the Federal Bureau of Investigation.

---

[27] Quoted in "Opening a Second Front," *Newsweek* (November 8, 1965), p. 33. Copyright by Newsweek, Inc., 1965.

[28] Jimmy Breslin, *Denver Post* (May 10, 1965). © 1965 by Jimmy Breslin. Reprinted by permission of the Sterling-Lord Agency.

24   Gary Rowe, an eye-witness, who gave one of the strongest eye-witness testimonies in a murder case that anybody can remember said that Wilkins had shot Mrs. Liuzzo. The ballistics and many small, but dangerous corroborating facts seemed to back him up.

The defense opened its case Thursday, and lawyer Matthew Murphy took exactly 21 minutes. He called a few witnesses who testified to absolutely nothing. The defendant, Wilkins, did not take the stand. Then, from nowhere, Murphy said he was resting his case.

So the jury heard nothing from him. But in the afternoon the jury listened to Matt Murphy. And in Lowndes County, Ala., the words that Murphy said in his summation seemed to have more meaning in them than all the facts and figures and testimony that the jurors had heard come down from the witness stand.

"I'm up here to throw you a straight ball," Murphy told the jurors. "Right down the line. One white man to another white man. What kind of a man is this Rowe? What kind of a man is this that comes into a fraternal organization by hook or by crook? What kind of a man is this who took an oath and joined the You-Nited Klans of America, took the oath with his hand raised to his almighty God? And then sold out like Judas Iscariot. And ah say, gentlemen, he betrayed himself, his God, and his oath. He is a liar, a perjurer. He'll do anything.

"He'll accept money from the Communist party.

"He'll accept money from the NAACP.

"He'll accept money from this Martin Luther King organization.

"Yes! He sold his soul for a little gold. Pouring himself out to be a white man. He's worse than a white nigger.

"And the FBI expert. A great man in the laboratory and the Federal government of the You-Nited States for 26 years. He lives in Washington. No, I'm sorry he doesn't. He moved to Virginia. He moved out of Washington because he got children and he didn't want them to go to school in Washington, D. C. He moved to Virginia, where they still fight the battle against integrating and mongrelizing the race.

"The white confederacy." Murphy was screaming.

"And this other FBI agent, the one who told you that Gary Rowe wasn't drunk when he informed the FBI of the murder. You heard me. I asked him his name. He said 'Shanahan.' And you heard what I asked him. I asked him, 'Are you Irish?' and he said, 'Yes.' And I said, 'Are you shanty Irish? Are you a Catholic?' You heard me ask him that. Well, I'm not Catholic. But I know how to deal with these shanty Irish.

"And this woman, this white woman who got killed. White woman? Wait a minute." He turned around. "Where's that NAACP card?" A Ku Klux Klansman at the defense table brought Mrs. Viola Gregg Liuzzo's NAACP membership card over to Murphy. He held it out in front of the jury and spoke softly.

"Ah never thought ah'd see the day," he said. "Ah never thought ah'd see the day when Communists and niggers and white niggers and Jews was flyin' around under the banner of the United Nations, not the American flag we fought for, not the flag of the country which we are in and I'm proud to be white and I stand here as a white man and I say we're never gonna mongrelize the race with nigger blood and the Martin Luther Kings, the white niggers, the Jews, the Zionists who run that bunch of niggers, the white people are not gonna run before them. I say 'never!' You know that she was in the car with three black niggers? One white woman and three niggers sittin' back there! Black nigger Communists takin' us over. White niggers! Some of 'em infiltrated this courtroom."

Murphy, arms waving, sweat pouring from his face, swung around and pointed to the press section.

"Never!" he yelled. "We shall die before we lay down. Niggers are against every law God ever wrote. Noah's son was Ham and he committed sin and was banished and his sons were Hamites and God damned them and they went to Africa and the only thing they ever built was grass huts. Black man in a straw hut covered with mud. No white lady ever can marry a descendant of Ham. If you do, you shall be destroyed. That's God's law. You cannot overcome God.

"Do what the people with God said. White woman, nigger man. You shall be destroyed!"

Murphy's arms were spread wide. The words bellowed out of him so loudly that they could barely be heard: "Rabbi with a nigger . . . white woman, nigger man, nigger woman, feet to feet. . . ."

This was the defense of Collie Leroy Wilkins for killing Mrs. Viola Gregg Liuzzo on the night of March 25 while she rode in a car on United States Highway 80 with a Negro who had taken part in a civil rights march that day from Selma to Montgomery.

And the jury looked at him, and they took his words, and the testimony of the tight case with them into a small room off the courtroom and sat down and decided to weigh the words and 200 years of narrow-mindedness against the facts. [Editor's Note: After deliberating for more than 24 hours the jury reported that it was hopelessly deadlocked and unable to reach a verdict.]

A report on the second trial of Collie Leroy Wilkins follows:

Trial by Jury

Some 700 miles south of Washington, in the muggy hamlet of Hayneville, Ala., Ku Klux Klansman Collie Leroy Wilkins went on trial

26   again last week for the murder of Mrs. Viola Gregg Liuzzo. The case was essentially a rerun of Wilkins' first trial, which ended with a hung jury — except this time Alabama justice stood in the dock with Wilkins and the Klan.

On precisely this pretext, state Attorney General Richmond Flowers — a politically lonesome moderate — took over prosecution of the case from local authorities. It was, he said, "the strongest criminal case I've ever had," complete with the eyewitness testimony of an FBI agent. . . .

Flowers did fight, opening with a gambit virtually unheard of in a small-town Dixie racial case — quizzing each prospective white juror about his racial views. "Do you believe a white person is superior to a nigra?" Most did. How about a white who, like Mrs. Liuzzo, "associates with nigras . . . people who come down here and try to help nigras integrate our churches and schools?" Again, a majority thought such a person inferior. Flowers lost a rush appeal to the Alabama Supreme Court to purge eleven of those veniremen. But he made his point: he was up against a jury dominated by white supremacists.

Once again, Flowers built the state's case around the testimony of paid FBI informant Gary Thomas Rowe, an impermeably cool witness who repeated his story as if by rote. The night the Selma-to-Montgomery march ended, Rowe said, he rode U. S. Highway 80 with Wilkins and two other Klansmen until they pulled up alongside the car Mrs. Liuzzo shared with a young Negro rights worker. "The woman turned to look at us, and as she looked, Wilkins fired . . . I said 'I don't think you hit them' . . . Wilkins slapped me on the right leg and said, 'Baby brother don't worry about it. That bitch and that bastard are dead and in hell. I don't miss'." . . .

The jury deliberated an hour and 45 minutes, then filed back to announce its verdict: not guilty. There was a burst of applause. A smile split Wilkins' pudgy face as he walked away free. And a morose Flowers contemplated the latest display of Alabama justice: "We prosecuted the best we could. The case was defended ably. We have no alternative but to abide by the decision of the jury."[29]

There is, however, an opposite point of view which holds that Negroes get preferential treatment in the courts and in law enforcement simply because they are Negroes. Radio and television commentator Dan Smoot comments on a Chicago case:

But in Chicago, as elsewhere, law enforcement is handicapped by racial agitators and by the courts. For example: two Chicago policemen

---

[29] *Newsweek* (November 1, 1965), p. 36. Copyright Newsweek, Inc., 1965.

noticed two men on a sidewalk, one menacing bystanders with a broken **27**
beer bottle. The men resisted arrest. One officer was jabbed in the face
with the broken bottle, knocked to the ground, and kicked. The police
drew their guns and subdued the thugs, but did not fire. The wounded
officer spent 23 days in a hospital. On March 5, 1965, Criminal Court
Judge George N. Leighton freed the two men, saying that, by drawing
their guns, the policemen used excessive force. Judge Leighton, a Negro,
was formerly president of the Chicago chapter of the NAACP.[30]

James Mills, a free lance writer, has protested against the influence of
Negro groups on law enforcement in New York in the following
statement:

Not sure what they can legally do, the police have frequently responded by doing nothing. And when a policeman does take action, he
may find himself subjected to great pressure and criticism, especially if
the person he acts against is a Negro. Reasonable police force often is
equated with brutality. Two recent and widely publicized killings, which
have had a profound effect on the New York police force, show how this
can happen.

In July 1964, an off-duty police lieutenant named Thomas Gilligan
was in a Manhattan radio repair shop when he heard shouts outside and
ran to the sidewalk to investigate. The superintendent of an apartment
building had sprayed some summer-school pupils with a hose, and they
had responded by throwing bottles and garbage can covers at him. One
of the pupils, a Negro teen-age boy, declared that he was going to "cut"
the superintendent. The super ran into a hallway, pursued by the boy.
Gilligan arrived, produced his badge and gun, announced that he was a
police lieutenant, and ordered the boy to come out of the hallway and
drop the knife. The boy lunged at Gilligan with the knife. Gilligan fired a
warning shot into the front of the building. The boy then swung with the
knife, cutting Gilligan's right arm. The boy attacked again, and Gilligan
fired a bullet through his arm into his chest. Still stabbing, the youth
once more went at the cop. Gilligan then fired into the boy's abdomen,
killing him.

The boy's death sparked six nights of rioting in Manhattan and
Brooklyn. Posters displaying Gilligan's picture said, "WANTED FOR
MURDER—GILLIGAN THE COP." CORE leader James Farmer accused Gilligan of having killed the boy in cold blood. The policeman's
home was picketed and finally he was forced into hiding.

A grand jury ultimately upheld Gilligan's account of the incident

---

[30] *Dan Smoot Report* (June 7, 1965), p. 181.

and cleared him of improper action. One of two Negroes on the jury revealed that the decision was unanimous and added, "I did the right thing, and so did the rest of the jury." But Gilligan's home continued to draw pickets, and he was secretly transferred to another precinct. Today harassment continues and placards still show up around New York with the words, "When Will Gilligan Kill Again?"

Last July, one year after the Gilligan affair, Patrolman Sheldon Liebowitz was on duty at a crowded corner in a Negro section of Brooklyn when he saw a Negro man acting in "a loud and boisterous manner." Liebowitz tried to quiet the man, an ex-convict named Nelson Erby who, it turned out later, had had two convictions for felonious assault, one against a policeman. Erby turned and tried to attack Liebowitz with a stiletto. The patrolman got the knife away from Erby and was trying to handcuff his hands behind his back when Erby charged forward, throwing the patrolman over his back onto the sidewalk. Erby grabbed the patrolman's gun and fired one bullet into his left arm, splintering the bone. Erby kept fighting with the wounded cop until a passing truck driver jumped to the cop's aid and struck Erby with a club. Liebowitz then regained his revolver and in the continuing battle shot Erby and killed him.

That night CORE sponsored a protest rally, and Black Nationalists harangued crowds at the site of the shooting. Threats and abusive phone calls flooded into Liebowitz's hospital room, and police put the hospital under special surveillance and placed a 24-hour-a-day guard outside the patrolman's room. A few days later he was secretly moved to another hospital. The day after the shooting, CORE demonstrators marched on police headquarters chanting, "Down with the killers in blue," and "The next cop's bullet may be yours."

The grand jury's report supported Patrolman Liebowitz, exonerated him completely. . . . Nevertheless, CORE continued to insist that Liebowitz had acted without justification, and the patrolman himself remained the object of harassment and abuse. . . .

By these cases, and by the continuing public badgering of the police department by pressure groups, both white and Negro, the cops have received a message. They have been told that what they don't see can't hurt them. Rather than be another Gilligan, many off-duty cops would stay in the radio repair shop and let the superintendent get knifed. Rather than be another Liebowitz, many patrolmen would walk quietly to the other end of their post. They have adopted the tactics of look-away waiters.[31]

---

[31] James Mills, "The Detective," *Life* (December 3, 1965), pp. 115–116. © 1965, Time Inc.

The Politics of Nonviolence

A Harlem proverb reads "Blessed is he who expects nothing for he shall not be disappointed." For most of the last century, Negroes expected nothing so they were not disappointed and for the most part remained docile and easily controlled. It is only when people have expectations which are frustrated or violated that they revolt. If a date could be chosen to mark the current upsurge in Negro expectations, possibly 1954 (the year of the *Brown* decision) is as good as any. The next year, Montgomery Negroes staged the first of a long series of organized nonviolent protests by boycotting the Montgomery bus lines. The bus boycott was successful, but it was after the Greensboro sit-in of 1960 that the idea of nonviolent resistance came to be adopted as the principal tactic of the burgeoning Negro revolt.

On February 1, 1960, four college students in Greensboro, North Carolina, entered a variety store, made several purchases, sat down at the lunch counter, ordered coffee, and were refused service because they were Negroes. They remained in their seats until the store closed. Thus began the sweeping protest movement against entrenched practices of segregation.[32]

During 1961, thousands of "Freedom Riders" rode public vehicles and used terminal facilities to protest segregation practices on common carriers. Hundreds were arrested — 300 in Jackson, Mississippi, alone. Ordinarily they were charged, not with violation of segregation laws, but with breach of the peace.

In September 1962, Negro James Meredith entered the University of Mississippi with the help of the U. S. Army at a cost of several million dollars. In the ensuing riot at "Ole Miss," two men were killed and 375 injured.

Civil rights demonstrations in 1961 and 1962 had aroused Negroes, but they had also aroused and alarmed Southern segregationists. In his inaugural address, Alabama's Governor George Wallace pledged "segregation now, segregation tomorrow, segregation forever." Southern police officers, harassed by demonstrators and irate segregationists alike, resorted to methods which shocked much of the rest of the nation. In the words of Paul Tillett, "In the land of the blueberry pie and the white picket fence, the symbols of law and order became the fire hose and snarling police dogs, the cattle prod and the truncheon."[33]

---

[32] *Report of the U. S. Commission on Civil Rights, 1963*, pp. 107–108.

[33] Paul Tillett, "The Negro 'Revolt' — 1963." *American Government Annual, 1964–65* (New York: Holt, Rinehart & Winston, 1964), p. 1.

30   During 1963, a series of planned demonstrations, sit-ins, and selective boycotts was carried out in Birmingham, Alabama. Several hundred people were arrested — among them the Reverend Martin Luther King. Four Negro girls were killed when a church was bombed; Negroes rioted; police used dogs and fire hoses against demonstrators and to control rioters.

The tumultuous events of the summer of 1963 were climaxed with a massive march on Washington in which over 200,000 persons participated. The gigantic demonstration was carried out with dignity and without violence.

The year 1964 was relatively quiet as compared with the previous three years, possibly because of the passage of the Civil Rights Act of 1964. But 1965 was to be different.

The Road from Selma

They started down U. S. 80 out of Selma on a Sunday clear as crystal, and they marched into Montgomery four days later in a warm spring rain. They arrived a nomad army, their feet blistered, their clothes mud-spattered, their faces sun-scorched, their ragtag column led by two flag-bearers and a one-legged man on crutches and a piper playing "Yankee Doodle" on a reedy fife. "Walk together, children, don't you get weary," Martin Luther King had told them as the trek began "and it will lead you to the promised land." And if the marchers halted considerably short of that goal last week, they did bring off a protest demonstration unmatched in the history of the Negro revolt — a symbolic triumph that could not be undone by the tragedy that struck immediately in its aftermath. . . .

In a growing stream, the marchers assembled in Selma. The men, women, and children who had followed King into the streets — and into jail — all through the campaign were ready to walk again. And outsiders flocked to his call: clerics and nuns, pert coeds and hot-eyed student rebels, VIP's like the U.N.'s Ralph Bunche and anonymous farmhands from the Southwest Alabama cattle, corn, and cotton country. A blind man came from Atlanta, a one-legged man from Saginaw, Mich. . . . And a little Selma Negro girl tagged along "for freedom and justice and so the troopers can't hit us no more."

The marchers were not to leave Alabama in peace. A few hours after they dispersed, a night-riding lynch party ambushed a Detroit volunteer rights worker, Mrs. Viola Gregg Liuzzo, 39, on U. S. 80 in swampy Lowndes County and shot her dead at the wheel of her car.[34]

---

[34] "The Road from Selma: Hope — and Death." *Newsweek* (April 5, 1965), pp. 23, 25, 27. Copyright Newsweek Inc., 1965.

Dan Smoot had a different version of the march and the marchers: **31**

> On March 17, 1965, Federal Judge Frank M. Johnson issued an order authorizing the Selma-to-Montgomery demonstration. It began on March 21, ended on March 25, under protection of U. S. armed forces all the way.
>
> Many of the marchers were human scum: beatniks, prostitutes, degenerates, drunks, bums, and communists — some of whom were paid to join the march.
>
> U. S. Representative William L. Dickinson (Alabama Republican) has made a careful investigation of the Selma-to-Montgomery demonstration. Here is a sample of his findings:
>
> "Drunkenness and sex orgies were the order of the day in Selma, on the road to Montgomery, and in Montgomery. There were many — not just a few — instances of sexual intercourse in public. . . .
>
> "The Communist Party . . . is the undergirding structure for all of the racial troubles in Alabama for the past 3 months. Look at the speakers on the platform in front of the capitol of Montgomery or participating prominently in the march and demonstration . . . Carl Braden . . . Abner Berry . . . James Peck . . . Bayard Rustin. . . .
>
> "And what about the king himself—King Martin Luther? . . . Martin Luther King himself has amassed the staggering total of more than 60 communist-front affiliations since 1955."[35]

The philosophy of nonviolent protest is probably best expressed by the acknowledged leader of the movement, Martin Luther King. During the Birmingham demonstrations of 1963, King was arrested and jailed. While in prison he wrote the now famous letter from Birmingham City Jail.

April 16, 1963

My Dear Fellow Clergymen, . . .

I think I should indicate why I am here in Birmingham, since you have been influenced by the view which argues against "outsiders coming in." I have the honor of serving as president of the Southern Christian Leadership Conference, an organization operating in every Southern state with headquarters in Atlanta, Georgia. . . .

Moreover, I am cognizant of the interrelatedness of all communities and states. I cannot sit idly by in Atlanta and not be concerned about

---

[35] "The March from Selma to Montgomery" in *The Dan Smoot Report* (May 10, 1965), p. 151.

32   what happens in Birmingham. Injustice anywhere is a threat to justice everywhere. We are caught in an inescapable network of mutuality tied in a single garment of destiny. . . . Never again can we afford to live with the narrow, provincial "outside agitator" idea. Anyone who lives inside the United States can never be considered an outsider anywhere within its bounds. . . .

In any nonviolent campaign there are four basic steps: collection of the facts to determine whether injustices exist; negotiation; self-purification; and direct action. We have gone through all these steps in Birmingham. There can be no gainsaying of the fact that racial injustice engulfs this community. Birmingham is probably the most thoroughly segregated city in the United States. Its ugly record of brutality is widely known. Negroes have experienced grossly unjust treatment in the courts. There have been more unsolved bombings of Negro homes and churches in Birmingham than in any other city in the nation. These are the hard, brutal facts of the case. On the basis of these conditions Negro leaders sought to negotiate with the city fathers. But the latter consistently refused to engage in good faith negotiation. . . .

You may well ask, "Why direct action? Why sit-ins, marches, and so forth? Isn't negotiation a better path?" You are quite right in calling for negotiation. Indeed, this is the very purpose of direct action. Nonviolent direct action seeks to create such a crisis and foster such a tension that a community which has constantly refused to negotiate is forced to confront the issue. It seeks so to dramatize the issue that it can no longer be ignored. . . .

The purpose of our direct action program is to create a situation so crisis-packed that it will inevitably open the door to negotiation. I therefore concur with you in your call for negotiation. Too long has our beloved Southland been bogged down in a tragic effort to live in monologue rather than dialogue.

One of the basic points in your statements is that our action is untimely. . . . We know through painful experience that freedom is never voluntarily given by the oppressor; it must be demanded by the oppressed. Frankly, I have yet to engage in a direct action campaign that was "well timed," in the view of those who have not suffered unduly from the disease of segregation. For years now I have heard the word "Wait!" It rings in the ear of every Negro with a piercing familiarity. This "Wait" has almost always meant "Never."[36] . . .

Two years later, the Reverend Dr. King wrote an article for the *Saturday Review* in which he reiterated some of the concepts expressed

---

[36] Martin Luther King, "Letter from Birmingham Jail," reprinted with permission of the Reverend Dr. King.

in "Letter from a Birmingham Jail" and generally set forth the tactics and
objectives of nonviolence. That article stimulated the following commentary from Frank S. Meyer, which carries the implicit endorsement for a *Policy of Status Quo.*

In the *Saturday Review* of April 3, the Rev. Dr. Martin Luther King presents for us the etiology of nonviolence in the ongoing Negro revolution. To achieve his aims . . . it is necessary, he writes, that four things take place:

"(1) Nonviolent demonstrators go into the streets to exercise their constitutional rights. (2) Racists resist by unleashing violence against them. (3) Americans of conscience in the name of decency demand federal intervention and legislation. (4) The Administration, under mass pressure, initiate measures of immediate intervention and remedial legislation." . . .

Most obviously (and clearly stated by Dr. King in the second point of his paradigm), the entire tactic of nonviolence depends upon its success in provoking violence on the part of the defenders of existing civil order. The corollary implied by this proposition, since on Dr. King's own witness such violence is an essential element of his program, is that if nonviolent provocations are not outrageous enough to provoke violence, they must be escalated until they do. . . .

But this blatant admission, that the aim of the nonviolent movement is to provoke violence, only exposes the surface. It is not merely in its commitment to the provocation of violence by others that this movement betrays the hypocrisy of its name; it is violent in its very essence, relying as it does upon the terror inspired by mobs to destroy the processes of constitutional government. . . .[37]

On the evening of April 3, 1968, Martin Luther King spoke to a crowd of his followers in Memphis, Tennessee. "It is no longer a question of violence or nonviolence in this day and age," he said. "It is nonviolence or nonexistence." Then he went on to say, "I've been to the mountaintop . . . and I've looked over, and I've seen the promised land." ". . . I may not get there with you, but I want you to know tonight that we as a people will get to the promised land." The next day Dr. King was killed.

CORE's Floyd McKissick, distraught and shaken, said, "Dr. Martin Luther King was the last prince of nonviolence. Nonviolence is a dead philosophy and it was not the black people that killed it." Regardless of who killed it, the philosophy of nonviolence was undoubtedly dead before Martin Luther King was killed. By April 1968, hardly anyone remembered "We Shall Overcome."

---

[37] Frank S. Meyer, "Principles and Heresies," *National Review* (April 20, 1965), p. 327.

The Politics of Violence

We often hear it said that, in the United States, we decide issues "through ballots rather than bullets." A democracy, we say, ultimately rests upon the ballot box. As a consequence, the writings of political scientists tend to concentrate on "ballots" and ignore "bullets." Nevertheless, there always exists, in the words of Norton Long, "the tacit assumption of violence."

Watts: "Burn, Baby, Burn"

In a speech to the International Association of Chiefs of Police in 1956, Los Angeles Police Chief William H. Parker said:

If organized violence occurred anywhere, it should by all socio-economic standards, have been Los Angeles. . . .

Its two million, two hundred-thousand people, the hub of a five-million person metropolitan area, is a melting pot of races, colors, creeds, and ideas. . . .

But its peoples of different background are learning to live together.

The story of that city's freedom from strife is largely the story of the professionalization of its police department.

Nine years after Chief Parker's speech, the most destructive racial riot in the nation's history exploded in Los Angeles. According to a *Newsweek* article:

The eruption came, by tragic irony, a bare day after the first Federal voting examiners began signing up the disfranchised black masses of the South. Their mission made plainer than ever the nation's commitment to equality for the Negro. Yet the promises of the present could not undo in a day the ugly legacy of the Negro past. . . .

Night upon howling night, Negro mobs swirled through the streets of the nation's third biggest city in a raging, blood-letting fury that paled the 1964 rioting by comparison. Cars and cops and passersby, black and white, were stoned and beaten. Whole blocks were put to the torch — and burned to the ground when rioters turned back firemen with bricks, rocks and chunks of asphalt ripped up out of the streets. Looters sacked stores in broad daylight — and snipers fired at 900 hopelessly outmanned cops at night. Before it ended, almost thirty persons lay dead, hundreds more were injured, more than 1,800 were jailed, property losses approached a staggering $100 million — and 10,000 National Guard troops marched into a major American city, heavily armed and under orders to put down the proclaimed "state of insurrection" with whatever force necessary. . . .

The riots began in the classic pattern of 1964 — with a police incident. A state trooper stopped a Negro youth for drunk driving; the boy's mother materialized, and behind her a crowd of onlookers, and behind them more cops. There were angry words — and suddenly, out of the clinging, muggy night, the rocks flew.

Through that first midweek night, throngs of Negroes milled in the streets — and a hard core of a few hundred young toughs pelted anyone who moved, white or Negro, with bottles and bricks. Windows shattered; street lights popped; a mobile TV unit's station wagon was set afire. Burglar alarms clanged unheeded like fire bells in the night. Police swarmed in, rushed the rioters, retreated when that seemed to inflame them still more — and charged again when the cooling-off spell failed.

Nor could peacemaking missions of civil rights and community leaders damp the fires next day. By nightfall Thursday, the mobs were bigger than ever, waging a hit-run guerrilla war up and down a twenty-block stretch of Avalon Boulevard. A lumberyard, a clinic, a restaurant, a liquor store went up in flames. A Molotov cocktail triggered a four-car pile-up; howling rioters dragged a white man from one of the autos and beat his face bloody. A white couple was pummeled by rioters yelling, "Kill! Kill!" — and another white man was mauled so badly that one eye dangled out of its socket. . . .

Gunfire and the crunch of billies punctuated the night; mobs clogged the streets roaring, "Get whitey . . . white devils, what are you doing here?"[38]

During the next three years the "Watts pattern," with some variations, occurred in Newark, Detroit, Washington, and other American cities. In the summer of 1967 alone, there were 55 racially related riots.

As violence increased, the attitudes of many white Americans changed from sympathy and a desire to help to indifference and fairly frequent hostility. Incidents of violent white backlash occurred, but even those whites who did not "lash back" were less sympathetic and more apprehensive and hostile. University students became interested in other issues and other causes.

A Louis Harris survey, taken in the fall of 1966, indicated that 75 percent of the whites thought Negroes were trying to move too fast. The number had been 50 percent in 1964.

President Johnson's Civil Rights Act of 1966 died in the Senate. In

---

[38] "Los Angeles: The Fire This Time," *Newsweek* (August 23, 1965), pp. 15, 16, and 17. Copyright by Newsweek, Inc., 1965.

36   1967, he submitted essentially the same package which was "broken up" by civil rights supporters in Congress into separate bills for each item of the President's proposal. Only the relatively minor and least controversial items were passed.

The Civil Rights Act of 1968 was passed six days after the assassination of Martin Luther King and was signed by the President the following day. Whether the bill would have passed if this tragedy had not occurred is, of course, a matter of conjecture. The open housing provision of the act had been before Congress in 1966 and 1967 but congressional leaders had been unable to bring the question to a vote.

Undoubtedly, the most important provision of the Civil Rights Act of 1968 was the section on open housing. Housing was probably the most sensitive issue among the many demands set forth by civil rights leaders over the years. In essence, the 1968 act prohibited discrimination in the sale or rental of housing. By 1970, when the law becomes fully effective, it will apply to about 80 percent of all housing in the United States.

The act also provided criminal penalties for persons who interfered with or injured others who were attempting to vote, serve on juries, work, attend school or enjoy public accommodations. At the same time, the act provided criminal penalties for those who used interstate facilities to incite or participate in riots, and for the manufacture or instruction in the use of firearms and explosives in civil disorders.

The Kerner Report

At the height of the 1967 riots, President Johnson appointed a National Advisory Commission on Civil Disorders, with Illinois Governor Otto Kerner as its chairman. The commission issued its report in early 1968. The report was lengthy; we shall include only the commission's summary of "why did it happen?"

We have seen what happened. Why did it happen?

In addressing this question we shift our focus from the local to the national scene, from the particular events of the summer of 1967 to the factors within the society at large which have brought about the sudden violent mood of so many urban Negroes.

The record before this Commission reveals that the causes of recent racial disorders are imbedded in a massive tangle of issues and circumstances — social, economic, political, and psychological — which arise out of the historical pattern of Negro-white relations in America.

These factors are both complex and interacting; they vary significantly in their effect from city to city and from year to year; and the consequences of one disorder, generating new grievances and new demands, become the causes of the next. It is this which creates the "thicket of tension, conflicting evidence and extreme opinions" cited by the President.

Despite these complexities, certain fundamental matters are clear. Of these, the most fundamental is the racial attitude and behavior of white Americans toward black Americans. Race prejudice has shaped our history decisively in the past; it now threatens to do so again. White racism is essentially responsible for the explosive mixture which has been accumulating in our cities since the end of World War II. At the base of this mixture are three of the most bitter fruits of white racial attitudes:

Pervasive discrimination and segregation. The first is surely the continuing exclusion of great numbers of Negroes from the benefits of economic progress through discrimination in employment and education, and their enforced confinement in segregated housing and schools. The corrosive and degrading effects of this condition and the attitudes that underlie it are the source of the deepest bitterness and at the center of the problem of racial disorder.

Black migration and white exodus. The second is the massive and growing concentration of impoverished Negroes in our major cities resulting from Negro migration from the rural South, rapid population growth and the continuing movement of the white middle-class to the suburbs. The consequence is a greatly increased burden on the already depleted resources of cities, creating a growing crisis of deteriorating facilities and services and unmet human needs.

Black ghettos. Third, in the teeming racial ghettos, segregation and poverty have intersected to destroy opportunity and hope and to enforce failure. The ghettos too often mean men and women without jobs, families without men, and schools where children are processed instead of educated, until they return to the street — to crime, to narcotics, to dependency on welfare, and to bitterness and resentment against society in general and white society in particular.

These three forces have converged on the inner city in recent years and on the people who inhabit it. At the same time, most whites and many Negroes outside the ghetto have prospered to a degree unparalleled in the history of civilization. Through television — the universal appliance in the ghetto — and the other media of mass communications, this affluence has been endlessly flaunted before the eyes of the Negro poor and the jobless ghetto youth.

As Americans, most Negro citizens carry within themselves two basic aspirations of our society. They seek to share in both the material resources of our system and its intangible benefits — dignity, respect and acceptance. Outside the ghetto many have succeeded in achieving a decent standard of life, and in developing the inner resources which give life meaning and direction. Within the ghetto, however, it is rare that either aspiration is achieved.

Yet these facts alone — fundamental as they are — cannot be said to

38 have caused the disorders. Other and more immediate factors help explain why these events happened now.

Recently, three powerful ingredients have begun to catalyze the mixture.

Frustrated hopes. The expectations aroused by the great judicial and legislative victories of the civil rights movement have led to frustration, hostility and cynicism in the face of the persistent gap between promise and fulfillment. The dramatic struggle for equal rights in the South has sensitized Northern Negroes to the economic inequalities reflected in the deprivations of ghetto life.

Legitimation of violence. A climate that tends toward the approval and encouragement of violence as a form of protest has been created by white terrorism directed against nonviolent protest, including instances of abuse and even murder of some civil rights workers in the South; by the open defiance of law and federal authority by state and local officials resisting desegregation; and by some protest groups engaging in civil disobedience who turn their backs on nonviolence, go beyond the Constitutionally protected rights of petition and free assembly, and resort to violence to attempt to compel alteration of laws and policies with which they disagree. This condition has been reinforced by a general erosion of respect for authority in American society and reduced effectiveness of social standards and community restraints on violence and crime. This in turn has largely resulted from rapid urbanization and the dramatic reduction in the average age of the total population.

Powerlessness. Finally, many Negroes have come to believe that they are being exploited politically and economically by the white "power structure." Negroes, like people in poverty everywhere, in fact lack the channels of communication, influence and appeal that traditionally have been available to ethnic minorities within the city and which enabled them — unburdened by color — to scale the walls of the white ghettos in an earlier era. The frustrations of powerlessness have led some to the conviction that there is no effective alternative to violence as a means of expression and redress, as a way of "moving the system." More generally, the result is alienation and hostility toward the institutions of law and government and the white society which controls them. This is reflected in the reach toward racial consciousness and solidarity reflected in the slogan "Black Power."

These facts have combined to inspire a new mood among Negroes, particularly among the young. Self-esteem and enhanced racial pride are replacing apathy and submission to "the system." Moreover, Negro youth, who make up over half of the ghetto population, share the growing sense of alienation felt by many white youth in our country. Thus, their role in recent civil disorders reflects not only a shared sense of deprivation and victimization by white society but also the rising **39** incidence of disruptive conduct by a segment of American youth throughout the society.

Incitement and encouragement of violence. These conditions have created a volatile mixture of attitudes and beliefs which needs only a spark to ignite mass violence. Strident appeals to violence, first heard from white racists, were echoed and reinforced last summer in the inflammatory rhetoric of black racists and militants. Throughout the year, extremists crisscrossed the country preaching a doctrine of black power and violence. Their rhetoric was widely reported in the mass media; it was echoed by local "militants" and organizations; it became the ugly background noise of the violent summer.

We cannot measure with any precision the influence of these organizations and individuals in the ghetto, but we think it clear that the intolerable and unconscionable encouragement of violence heightened tensions, created a mood of acceptance and an expectation of violence, and thus contributed to the eruption of the disorders last summer.

The police. It is the convergence of all these factors that makes the role of the police so difficult and so significant. Almost invariably the incident that ignites disorder arises from police action. Harlem, Watts, Newark and Detroit — all the major outbursts of recent years — were precipitated by routine arrests of Negroes for minor offenses by white police.

But the police are not merely the spark. In discharge of their obligation to maintain order and insure public safety in the disruptive conditions of ghetto life, they are inevitably involved in sharper and more frequent conflicts with ghetto residents than with the residents of other areas. Thus, to many Negroes police have come to symbolize white power, white racism and white repression. And the fact is that many police do reflect and express these white attitudes. The atmosphere of hostility and cynicism is reinforced by a widespread perception among Negroes of the existence of police brutality and corruption, and of a "double standard" of justice and protection — one for Negroes and one for whites. . . .

In the summer of 1967, we have seen in our cities a chain reaction of racial violence. If we are heedless, we shall none of us escape the consequences.[39]

Many Americans did not agree with the findings of the Kerner Report. One of them was Senator Robert C. Byrd of West Virginia. In his words:

---

[39] The National Advisory Commission on Civil Disorders, *Report of the National Advisory Commission on Civil Disorders,* (New York: Bantam Books, 1968) pp. 203–206.

40   Mr. President, the usual excuses are being made for violence in the streets. They are the same excuses that were trotted out in the wake of the Watts riot. We hear that slums constitute a basic cause. Yet, Plainfield, N.J., is not a slum, with its tree-lined streets and two-family apartments. Watts was not a slum.

No slum was ever deliberately planned to be a slum. No slum was ever deliberately built. Slums develop as a result of the carelessness of the inhabitants. Slums are developed by slummy people. The people may be taken out of the slums, but the slums cannot be taken out of some people. As long as people throw their trash into the hallways, and throw their beer cans and their whiskey bottles and their rotting garbage into the yards and onto the streets, there will continue to be slums. And wherever these same people go, the slums will follow after them. As long as they insist upon ripping up the steps and the bannisters, tearing off the wallpaper, punching holes in the walls, kicking the panels out of the doors, breaking the windows, and ripping loose the plumbing fixtures, there will be slums, and the landlord can scarcely be blamed for his reluctance to repair such destruction.

As to the ghetto, a ghetto need not be a slum. It depends upon the inhabitants thereof.

Many immigrants who have entered our country have been housed in ghettos, but, for the most part, they have taken a personal interest in their surroundings and have sought to keep the ghettos clean. They have not considered this to be an excuse or justification to riot, but rather they have sought to make their surroundings livable and they have sought to improve those surroundings.

There are those who blame the riots on poverty. Yet, poverty-stricken white Americans outnumber poverty-stricken Negroes, but white Americans have not resorted to violence in the streets. Moreover, there are millions of poor Negroes in America today who deplore the riots.

If poverty were an excuse for rioting, Abraham Lincoln would have been the Stokely Carmichael of his day and Booker T. Washington would have been the Floyd McKissick of his time.

I remember the depression of the early 1930's. Thousands of men and women and children in West Virginia were inadequately clothed, fed, and sheltered, but they did not attempt to take the law into their own hands. Negroes and whites saw hunger in the mining communities, but they did not find in this an excuse to burn and loot and destroy. The mining communities where I lived as a boy, and during my early adult years, were areas of grinding poverty.

I have seen men wearing hemp sacks around their feet in the wintertime because they lacked shoes. I have seen Christmases come and go without a stick of candy in many a home. I have seen children without shoes and tables without food. I have seen men without jobs, and I have seen rat-infested houses. As to plumbing fixtures, there were none. Air conditioning was unheard of. Few people could boast of owning a radio or a refrigerator, and fewer still possessed an automobile.

There were times when an owner of an old automobile could not afford the cost of a new license plate. Running water in the houses was but a dream. A washtub constituted the bathing facilities. Yet, these poor people, as a general rule, kept their floors scrubbed and their steps clean. Here and there they planted a flower or a piece of shrubbery. Their few bits of clothing were washed on a scrubboard in a No. 3 tub. They could not afford the luxury of a washing machine. Yet, these people, Negro and white, were law-abiding citizens and they taught their children to obey the law and to respect governmental authority.

Negroes and whites got along well together. I often visited in Negro churches and Negro homes when I was a young man. Whites and Negroes respected one another. They worked together, and they helped one another during difficult days.

As I indicated in a Senate speech recently, I formerly worked in a coal company store as a produce clerk and as a meat cutter. Many times I placed an empty flour barrel at the end of the meat counter and started off a "pounding" for a stricken Negro miner. Whites and Negroes lining up at the counter contributed lard and bacon, meal and flour, pinto beans and potatoes to the stricken family. People tried to help one another rather than to hurt one another. People sought to give, even when they had little to give, instead of taking that which was not rightfully theirs. And, believe it or not, people did not have to lock their doors at night and bar their windows. Nobody ever heard of homes being burglarized, of women being raped, of old men being knocked to the ground and robbed, and of pockets being picked in those communities.

So, Mr. President, I cannot have much sympathy with those who attempt to blame the riots upon poverty. Strangely enough, many of these so-called poverty-stricken rioters seem to be mainly interested in looting the liquor stores. According to the news reports, these are the establishments that are first looted. . . .

Discrimination, some say, is the cause of the riots. I referred earlier to millions of foreign immigrants who have come to this country, immigrants who could not even speak the English language and who were thus placed at great disadvantage as against people born here. They were Germans, they were Poles, they were Hungarians, they were Italians, Jews, Lebanese, Greeks, and other nationalities. They were discriminated against. Even the Irish were discriminated against in earlier years. But these people did not riot. They went to work and lifted themselves up by their own bootstraps, so to speak. If they could not find work, they peddled papers or fruits and vegetables, or opened their own shops.

42   Many of them walked the country roads in my State or the streets of big cities and peddled laces, liniments, and other wares, until they could get enough money to establish a shop. They contributed to the communities in which they lived, and they proved themselves to be responsible citizens and thereby earned the respect of other people. They did not resort to violence in the streets, to rioting and looting and burning.

The same can be said of many of our Negro citizens. They, too, have shown themselves to be worthy of respect. They have worked hard and saved a little here and there and bought themselves a home. They, too, have lifted themselves up through their own initiative. Many of these responsible Negro citizens have been the first to suffer in Detroit and other cities at the hands of rioters. Many of their homes have been burned by the raging fires.

So, Mr. President, many people, Negroes and whites, have been subjected to discrimination through the years, but they have not joined the mobs in the streets. No, discrimination is not an excuse. Moreover, there are more laws on the statute books today against discrimination than ever before in the history of our country, while at the same time there is more unrest, more crime, and more violence in the streets. The Federal Government is doing more today than it has ever done before to wipe out discrimination. . . .

The charge is often made that police brutality is at the root of the growing unrest in our cities. One is at a loss, however, to understand how this can be the case, when the vastly overwhelming majority of such charges have been proved untrue and utterly unfounded. Our Nation has come to a sad state of affairs when a police officer cannot make an arrest in the proper performance of his duty, and in properly enforcing the laws of the community, without being immediately surrounded by a jeering, threatening mob shouting "Police brutality." It has become virtually a pattern throughout the country, and the fuse to many of the recent riots has been ignited by an arrest properly executed. What is going to happen to law and order if the community is unable, through its properly constituted authorities, to enforce the law? Anarchy will result. Mob rule will prevail. Every man will be a law unto himself. And every man will arm for his own protection and for the protection of his own family.

> Society based on the rule that each one is a law unto himself would soon be confronted with disorder and anarchy. (Justice Harlan, U.S.S.C.)

No, Mr. President, police brutality is not the cause of the unrest sweeping over the Nation. I do not condone police brutality, and I do not believe that much of it can be found to exist. It is reasonable, however, to believe that the citizen who obeys the laws and who conducts himself properly will need have no fear of police brutality. All too often, the individual who charges police brutality has been guilty, first, of breaking the law, and then of resisting the officer who made the arrest. The policeman is more often abused and mistreated than is the person who cries "Police brutality." . . .

Mr. President, I do not maintain that poverty and slums and unemployment are to be ignored or that we should close our eyes to these things. Indeed, we should take feasible action to effectively deal with them. I do say, however, that they are not a justification for insurrection and riot. They are not an excuse for violence. Most people have had to work for what they own. Most people are willing to work for what they receive. Most people have demonstrated the patience, the initiative, and the effort to get where they are, and the obstacles they have had to overcome have often been great.

The issue here is whether any minority group in the country should be able to bring such pressure to bear on Government by the threat of violence that it can exact funds from the Public Treasury.

If democracy means anything at all, it means that the taxpayers' money — that the people's property which has been taken for public purposes — shall be spent only in accordance with laws and policies determined by the people's representatives. And if democracy means anything at all, it means that such laws and policies are formulated and adopted only through a process whereby the people's representatives are persuaded to support them by rational arguments presented in democratic debate.

To shortcut the process of debate by threatening violence is to attack democracy itself. Whoever takes up and uses — however indirectly — the threat of violence, is guilty of something like blackmail. And it may behoove us all to remember Mr. Justice Frankfurter's admonition: "Respect for law cannot be turned off and on as though it were a hot-water faucet."

Increasing numbers of public leaders are attempting to persuade Congress to vote more funds for various urban and antipoverty programs by warning Members of Congress of the violent consequences that will occur should Congress not fund such programs. It might be said that this is a most effective argument. In fact, it is not an argument at all.

An effective argument is made by reason. Violence is not reason — it is the very opposite of reason. To use the probability of consequent violence as a means of argument is to corrupt the democratic process of persuasion through debate.[40]

---

[40] Robert C. Byrd, U. S. Senator, in a speech delivered on the floor of the Senate, July 25, 1967.

44   In the 1968 presidential campaign, former Governor George Wallace of Alabama ran as a third party candidate and garnered about 14 percent of the votes. His campaign was centered around an appeal to return to "law and order." Presumably he would have received more votes if the candidates of the two major parties had not also come out strongly for orderly government and strengthened law enforcement.

The Politics of Social Status:
Dreams, Callouses, and Black Power

In the continuing Negro revolution, most attention has been given to unemployment, education, voting, and housing. These explicit issues are real and important, but the authors contend that the main thrust of the Negro revolution has been a drive for equal social status. Matters such as unemployment, education, housing, and the like are admittedly ingredients of social status; but regular employment, the acquisition of an education, and adequate housing do not, in themselves, bestow social status. The old concept of "separate but equal" was not acceptable to Negroes, even if the facilities had been approximately equal.

In this section we shall concentrate on what we consider to be the basic reason for the Negro revolution — the drive for equal social status.

John C. Calhoun: Liberty and Equality

The traditionally hard-fisted policy of the Southerner toward the question of Negro rights was succinctly stated as early as 1853 in a posthumously published volume of works by John C. Calhoun. This distinguished statesman addressed himself directly to the subject of the status and role of the Negro in society in a manner which can be, and still is, used by the active segregationists.

. . . it is a great and dangerous error to suppose that all people are equally entitled to liberty. It is a reward to be earned, not a blessing to be gratuitously lavished on all alike — a reward reserved for the intelligent, the patriotic, the virtuous and deserving, and not a boon to be bestowed on a people too ignorant, degraded, and vicious to be capable either of appreciating or of enjoying it.

. . . *This dispensation seems to be the result of some fixed law; and every effort to disturb or defeat it, by attempting to elevate a people in the scale of liberty above the point to which they are entitled to rise, must ever prove abortive and end in disappointment. The progress of a people rising from a lower to a higher point in the scale of liberty is necessarily slow; and by attempting to precipitate, we either retard or permanently defeat it.* (Italics ours)

There is another error, not less great and dangerous, usually associated with the one which has just been considered. I refer to the opinion that liberty and equality are so intimately united that liberty cannot be perfect without perfect equality.

That they are united to a certain extent, and that equality of citizens, in the eyes of the law, is essential to liberty in a popular government is conceded. But to go further and make equality of *condition* essential to liberty would be to destroy both liberty and progress. The reason is that inequality of condition, while it is a necessary consequence of liberty, is at the same time indispensable to progress. . . .

It is, indeed, this inequality of condition between the front and rear ranks, in the march of progress, which gives so strong an impulse to the former to maintain this position, and to the latter to press forward into their files. This gives to progress its greatest impulse. To force the front rank back to the rear or attempt to push forward the rear into line with the front, by the interposition of the government, would put an end to the impulse and effectually arrest the march of progress.[41]

More than a century later, in hearings on the Civil Rights Act, Congressman Thomas G. Abernethy of Mississippi echoed Calhoun's sentiments.

Individuals of any race or creed have but one route to social acceptance and economic abundance. (There is no such thing as social equality.) That route is the narrow trail of personal exertion, perseverance, study, work, and savings.

This hard road leads to self-respect and the respect of one's fellows. It leads to good will and understanding. It leads to economic abundance and security. And there is no other way.[42]

Senator Richard Russell of Georgia, floor leader of the opposition to the Civil Rights Bill, agreed:

Ours is not a perfect system; the American system of law and order and economy has many defects. But, Mr. President, with all its error and all its weaknesses, it is the finest system yet devised by man. It has brought more of the good things of life, more happiness, and a greater

---

[41] From John C. Calhoun, *A Disquisition on Government and Selections from the Discourse,* edited by C. Gordon Post, copyright © 1953, by The Liberal Arts Press, Inc., reprinted by permission of the Liberal Arts Press Division of The Bobbs-Merrill Company, Inc., p. 42–43.

[42] U. S. House of Representatives, Committee on Rules, 88th Cong., 2d sess., Hearings on H.R. 7152, p. 497.

46 degree of freedom to more people than have ever before been enjoyed by any other people, under any other governmental system. . . .

Mr. President, what does equality mean?

It does not mean that a child can stand on the street corner and cry for a car in which he sees another child of his own age riding. That is not equality. Equality does not mean that one person shall be admitted to a club merely because he desires to be, and because to be refused admission would cause him embarrassment or anguish. Our system never contemplated any such "equality" as that. . . .

No, Mr. President, equal rights in this land of ours means that each citizen has an equal opportunity to acquire property through honest means, that once that property has been acquired he has a right to exercise dominion over it. . . .

It is not equality to pass laws that give any group, whoever they may be, the right to violate the property rights of another that are guaranteed by the Constitution.[43]

LBJ: Freedom and Equality

In a commencement address at Howard University shortly after the passage of the Voting Rights Bill, President Johnson set forth his concepts of the meaning of freedom and equality as applied to Negroes:

Freedom is the right to share, fully and equally, in American society — to vote, to hold a job, to enter a public place, to go to school. It is the right to be treated, in every part of our national life, as a man equal in dignity and promise to all others.

But freedom is not enough. You do not wipe away the scars of centuries by saying: "Now, you are free to go where you want, do as you desire, and choose the leaders you please." You do not take a man who, for years, has been hobbled by chains, liberate him, bring him to the starting line of a race, saying "you are free to compete with all others," and still justly believe you have been completely fair. Thus it is not enough to open the gates of opportunity. All our citizens must have the ability to walk through those gates. . . .

Negroes are trapped — as many whites are trapped — in inherited gateless poverty. . . . But Negro poverty is not white poverty. Many of its causes and many of its cures are the same. But there are differences — deep, corrosive, obstinate differences — radiating painful roots into the community, the family, and the nature of the individual.

These differences are not racial differences, they are solely and simply the consequence of ancient brutality, past injustice, and present

---

[43] U. S. Senate, *Congressional Record*, 88th Cong., 2d sess., June 10, 1964, V. 110, Part 10, pp. 13308–9.

prejudice. And they cannot be understood as isolated infirmities. They **47** are a seamless web. They cause each other. They result from each other. They reinforce each other. Much of the Negro community is buried under a blanket of history and circumstance. It is not a lasting solution to lift just one corner. We must stand on all sides and raise the entire cover if we are to liberate our fellow citizens.[44]

Martin Luther King: "I Have a Dream"

To Martin Luther King, equality was a dream:

I have a dream that one day this nation will rise up and live out the true meaning of its creed: we hold these truths to be self-evident, that all men are created equal.

I have a dream that one day on the red hills of Georgia the sons of former slaves and the sons of former slave owners will be able to sit down together at the table of brotherhood.

I have a dream that one day the state of Mississippi, a state sweltering with the people's injustice, sweltering with the heat of oppression, will be transformed into an oasis of freedom and justice. ____.

I have a dream that my four little children will one day live in a nation where they will not be judged by the color of their skin, but by the content of their character.

This is our hope. This is the faith that I go back to the south with — with this faith we will be able to hew out of the mountain of despair, a stone of hope.[45]

Dick Gregory: Callouses on Our Souls

Perhaps Dick Gregory best expressed the Negro drive for equal status and opportunity:

The Negro has a callus growing on his soul and it's getting harder and harder to hurt him there. That's a simple law of nature. Like a callus on a foot in a shoe that's too tight. . . .

That shoe — the white man's system — has pinched and rubbed and squeezed his soul until it almost destroyed him. But it didn't. And now a callus has formed on his soul, and unless that system is adjusted to fit him, too, that callus is going to wear out that system.

---

[44] Lyndon B. Johnson, Howard University, Washington, D. C., June 5, 1965.
[45] Martin Luther King, excerpt from address of August 28, 1963, Washington, D. C.

. . . this isn't a revolution of black against white, this is a revolution of right against wrong. And right has never lost.

This is a revolution. It started long before I came into it, and I may die before it's over, but we'll bust this thing and cut out this cancer. America will be as strong and beautiful as it should be, for black folks and white folks. We'll all be free then, free from a system that makes a man less than a man, that teaches hate and fear and ignorance.

You didn't die a slave for nothing Momma. You brought us up. You and all those Negro mothers who gave their kids the strength to go on, to take that thimble to the well while the whites were taking buckets. Those of us who weren't destroyed got stronger, got calluses on our souls. And now we're ready to change a system, a system where a white man can destroy a black man with a single word. Nigger.

When we're through, Momma, there won't be any niggers any more.[46]

Black Power

Apparently Stokely Carmichael of SNCC (Student Nonviolent Coordinating Committee) first popularized the term "Black Power" in the summer of 1966. Along with the cry of black power went a poster picturing a snarling black panther and bearing the inscription, "Move on over or we'll move on over you."

Author Gordon Parks once asked Stokely Carmichael:

"What do you *really* mean by Black Power?"

"I've given up trying to explain it," he said. "The whites never really listen when I do, anyway."

"But I'm not white and I'm listening," I insisted.

"*For the last time,*" he said, "Black Power means black people coming together to form a political force and either electing representatives or forcing their representatives to speak their needs. It's an economic and physical bloc that can exercise its strength in the black community instead of letting the job go to the Democratic or Republican parties or a white-controlled black man set up as a puppet to represent black people. *We* pick the brother and make sure he fulfills *our* needs. Black Power doesn't mean anti-white, violence, separatism or any other racist things the press says it means. It's saying, 'Look, buddy, we're not laying a vote on you unless you lay so many schools, hospitals, playgrounds and jobs on us.' "[47]

---

[46] Dick Gregory, *Nigger* (New York: E. P. Dutton & Co., 1964), pp. 195, 224.
[47] Gordon Parks, "Whip of Black Power," *Life* (May 19, 1967), p. 82.

Whether or not Carmichael's definition adequately defined Black
Power, Roy Wilkins of the NAACP said,

No matter how endlessly they try to explain Black Power, the term
means anti-white. . . . It has to mean going it alone. It has to mean
separatism. . . . This offers a disadvantaged minority little except the
chance to shrivel and die.[48]

And President Johnson was reported to have explained the failure of
the Civil Rights Act of 1966 in four words: "Black Power" and "Stokely
Carmichael." According to one story, the President added, "He's a young
man who doesn't know his rear end from his elbow."

However Black Power was explained, it was principally a drive for
social status. It was a drive to eliminate whatever feelings of inferiority
Negroes may have had. African artifacts enjoyed a sudden burst of
popularity. Black dolls were sold. "Black is beautiful" became a catch-
phrase. Negroes who had formerly driven new cars and worn forty dollar
shoes now appeared in plain clothing and a "natural" hair style. College-
educated Negroes deliberately adopted the vernacular of the ghettos and
Southern plantations.

In January 1969, *Look* magazine devoted an entire issue to Negro
culture, with articles and pictures on "Black America's African Heritage,"
"Black Artist in a White World," "Black Brains for White Business" and
several pages of "Black Beauty."

But Black Power was not only concerned with improving the image of
the Negro; it also represented the most militant of Negro groups. There
have always been black militants, but Malcolm X can probably be regarded as the founder of the Black Power concept. Here are some
excerpts from a 1965 speech by Malcolm X called "Message to the Grass
Roots."

. . . You don't catch hell because you're a Baptist, and you don't
catch hell because you're a Methodist. You don't catch hell because
you're a Methodist or Baptist, you don't catch hell because you're a
Democrat or a Republican, you don't catch hell because you're a Mason
or an Elk, and you sure don't catch hell because you're an American;
because if you were an American, you wouldn't catch hell. You catch hell
because you're a black man. You catch hell, all of us catch hell, for the
same reason.

So we're all black people, so-called Negroes, second-class citizens,
ex-slaves. You're nothing but an ex-slave. You don't like to be told that.
But what else are you? You are ex-slaves. You didn't come here on the

---

[48] *Ibid.*, p. 80.

50   "Mayflower." You came here on a slave ship. In chains, like a horse, or a cow, or a chicken. And you were brought here by the people who came here on the "Mayflower," you were brought here by the so-called Pilgrims, or Founding Fathers. They were the ones who brought you here.

We have a common enemy. We have this in common: We have a common oppressor, a common exploiter, and a common discriminator. But once we all realize that we have a common enemy, then we unite — on the basis of what we have in common. And what we have foremost in common is that enemy — the white man. He's an enemy to all of us. I know some of you all think that some of them aren't enemies. Time will tell. . . .

And when you and I here in Detroit and in Michigan and in America who have been awakened today look around us, we too realize here in America we all have a common enemy, whether he's in Georgia or Michigan, whether he's in California or New York. He's the same man — blue eyes and blond hair and pale skin — the same man. . . .

Look at the American Revolution in 1776. That revolution was for what? For land. Why did they want land? Independence. How was it carried out? Bloodshed. Number one, it was based on land, the basis of independence. And the only way they could get it was bloodshed. The French Revolution — what was it based on? The landless against the landlord. What was it for? Land. How did they get it? Bloodshed. Was no love lost, was no compromise, was no negotiation. I'm telling you — you don't know what a revolution is. Because when you find out what it is, you'll get back in the alley, you'll get out of the way.

The Russian Revolution — what was it based on? Land; the landless against the landlord. How did they bring it about? Bloodshed. You haven't got a revolution that doesn't involve bloodshed. And you're afraid to bleed. I said, you're afraid to bleed.

As long as the white man sent you to Korea, you bled. He sent you to Germany, you bled. He sent you to the South Pacific to fight the Japanese, you bled. You bleed for white people, but when it comes to seeing your own churches being bombed and little black girls murdered, you haven't got any blood. You bleed when the white man says bleed; you bite when the white man says bite; and you bark when the white man says bark. I hate to say this about us, but it's true. How are you going to be nonviolent in Mississippi, as violent as you were in Korea? How can you justify being nonviolent in Mississippi and Alabama, when your churches are being bombed, and your little girls are being murdered, and at the same time you are going to get violent with Hitler, and Tojo, and somebody else you don't even know? . . .

Revolution is bloody, revolution is hostile, revolution knows no compromise, revolution overturns and destroys everything that gets in its way. And you, sitting around here like a knot on the wall, saying, "I'm going to love these folks no matter how much they hate me." No, you need a revolution. Whoever heard of a revolution where they lock arms, as Rev. Cleage was pointing out beautifully, singing "We Shall Overcome"? You don't do that in a revolution. You don't do any singing, you're too busy swinging. It's based on land. A revolutionary wants land so he can set up his own nation, an independent nation. These Negroes aren't asking for any nation — they're trying to crawl back on the plantation. . . .

To understand this, you have to go back to what the young brother here referred to as the house Negro and the field Negro back during slavery. . . . The house Negroes — they lived in the house with master, they dressed pretty good, they ate good because they ate his food — what he left. They lived in the attic or the basement, but still they lived near the master; and they loved the master more than the master loved himself. They would give their life to save the master's house — quicker than the master would. If the master said, "We got a good house here," the house Negro would say, "Yeah, we got a good house here." Whenever the master said "we," he said "we." That's how you can tell a house Negro. . . .

In those days he was called a "house nigger." And that's what we call them today, because we've still got some house niggers running around here.

This modern house Negro loves his master. He wants to live near him. He'll pay three times as much as the house is worth just to live near his master, and then brag about "I'm the only Negro out here." "I'm the only one on my job." "I'm the only one in this school." You're nothing but a house Negro. And if someone comes to you right now and says, "Let's separate," you say the same thing that the house Negro said on the plantation. "What you mean, separate? From America, this good white man? Where you going to get a better job than you get here?" I mean, this is what you say. "I ain't left nothing in Africa," that's what you say. Why, you left your mind in Africa.[49]

But all Negro militants did not agree with Malcolm X. According to James Farmer of CORE:

The danger in Malcolm's doctrine is that it may readily be subverted into an excuse for generalized and indiscriminate violence, generalized and indiscriminate revenge. A War: White vs. Black. I think Malcolm

---

[49] Malcolm X, "Message to the Grass Roots," *Malcolm X Speaks*, George Breitman, Ed. (New York: Merit Publishers, 1965), pp. 4–11.

52   often succumbed to this danger, at least verbally, and many young people under his spell openly advocate a kind of purgative violence. Mostly they just talk and talk. Actually, if these violence-mongers were serious about what they say, they wouldn't say it. They would plan their violence privately and execute it clandestinely, and then brave the consequences. But I suspect many of these men have no heart for that kind of anonymity. . . .

But I think Malcolm's philosophy of violence deserves a second comment. As mistaken and misguided as it may be doctrinally, it has a certain psychological validity. I have mentioned the resentment Negroes feel over the way whites swarm over them with criticism the moment they abandon pure love and merely consider the notion of self-defense. The hypocrisy of this criticism is galling. The Negro sees analogies everywhere. There was silence in the press during the years in which hundreds of thousands of Congolese were being slaughtered; but then there came huge headlines: FIFTY WHITES KILLED IN CONGO.[50]

Then Farmer went on to say:

But we must call injustice by its given name. America is racist and it is a man called Negro who is specially victimized beyond his class and beyond any other formal classifications one might coin. And he knows he is. He will not cease to be victimized nor will he cease to victimize himself until segregation of mind and spirit ends. And to end segregation this nation must turn directly to the Negro and undo what it has done. We are not so worried if we get to be known as Negroes in the process. We rather like the name these days. Again, we are desegregationists, not necessarily integrationists. . . .

I remember the comment of a red-necked young man from St. Augustine, Florida, the leader of a gang of whites who had attacked Negroes trying to swim in the Atlantic Ocean: "If I thought the niggers would be satisfied with just swimming, I'd let them in. But they won't be. First it's this, and then they'll want more, and before you know it they'll be laying hands on our women. We've got to take a stand now, because the more we let them have, the harder it'll be to draw the line."

Sometimes, I think that the racists have a deeper insight into things than the moderates. The gentleman is right. Nothing short of full equality will stop us. One cannot simply draw up a list of ten or twenty things whose fulfillment would spell equality. In countless details we are une-

---

[50] James Farmer, *Freedom — When?* (New York: Random House, 1965), pp. 99–100.

qual and elements in our society discover new ways each moment to keep us unequal. The moderate sincerely searches for the concession which will finally satisfy and silence us. He is willing to negotiate and temporarily sacrifice his security to get rid of the problem. The racist knows better how deep the problem is and how long he will need to resist our efforts. But we shall persist, that I promise.[51]

While James Farmer was conducting a campaign of nonviolent rebellion, Stokely Carmichael continued in the Malcolm X tradition. Here is an excerpt from one of his speeches:

Brothers and Sisters, we have been living with The Man too long. Brothers and Sisters, we have been *in a bag* too long. *We have got to move to a position where we will be proud, be proud of our blackness.* From here on in we've got to stick together, Brothers and Sisters, we've got to join together and move to a new spirit and make of our community a community of love . . . LOVE. There's no time for shuckin' and jivin'. We've got to move fast and we've got to come together and we've got . . . we've got to realize . . . that this country was conceived in racism and dedicated to racism. And understand that we've got to move . . . WE HAVE GOT TO MOVE. . . . We've got to build to a position so that when L.B.J. says, "Come, heah, boy, I'm gonna send you to Veetnam," we will say, "Hell, no." ("Preach, boy, preach. . . . Tell 'em, Stokely. . . .")

Brothers and Sisters, a hell of a lot of us are gonna be shot and it ain't just gonna be in South Vietnam. We've got to move to a position *in this country* where we're not afraid to say that any man who has been selling us rotten meat for high prices should have had his store bombed fifteen years ago. We have got to move to a position where we will control our *own* destiny. We have got to move to a position where we will have black people represent us to achieve *our* needs. This country don't run on love, Brothers, it's run on power and we ain't got none. Brothers and Sisters, don't let them separate you from other black people. Don't ever in your life apologize for your black brothers. Don't be ashamed of your culture because if you don't have culture that means you don't exist and, Brothers and Sisters, we do exist. Don't ever, don't ever, don't *ever* be ashamed of being black because you . . . you are black, little girl with your nappy hair and your broad lips, and *you are beautiful*. Brothers and Sisters, I know this theatre we're in — it used to be the Alhambra. Well I used to come here on Saturday afternoon when I was a little boy and we used to see Tarzan here and all of us would yell like crazy when Tarzan beat up our black brothers. Well, you know Tar-

---

[51] *Ibid.*, pp. 125, 49–50.

54 zan is on television now and from here on in I'm rooting for that black man to beat the hell out of Tarzan. . . .

There is a system in this country that locks black people in, but lets one or two get out every year. And they all say, "Well, look at that one or two. He's helping his race." Well, Ralph Bunche hasn't done a damn thing for me. If he's helping his race, then he should come *home.* Brothers and Sisters, there's nothing wrong about being all white or all black. It's only when you use one to exploit the other — and we have been exploited. You gotta understand what they do. They say, "Let's integrate." Well integration means going to a white school because that school is good and the black school is bad. It means moving from a black neighborhood to a white neighborhood because one neighborhood, they tell you, is bad and the other is good. Well, if integration means moving to something white, moving to something good, then integration is just a cover for white supremacy. . . .[52]

Eventually, whites were no longer welcome in the black militant organizations, including SNCC, no matter how helpful they might have been. John Lewis of SNCC maintained that "whites must consent to let Negroes run their own revolution without being alarmed at the sacrifices and difficulties involved." According to Julius Lester:

The reaction of the white liberal was sad to see:
. . . most white liberals simpered and moaned. SNCC had been their romantic darling, a kind of teddy bear that they could cuddle. The time had come, however, when blacks could no longer be the therapy for white society. White liberals had had a cause, something that would put meaning into their lives, something that their country and society had not given them. They had it in the Negro. So they came south and they loved us when we got our heads beat, our asses kicked, and our bodies thrown in jail. They loved us as we bled, loving loving loving all the while. How noble, how courageous, how wonderful it all was.[53]

Lester concluded that:

It is clear that America as it now exists must be destroyed. There is

---

[52] Bernard Weinraub, "The Brilliancy of Black," *Esquire* (January 1968), p. 132. Reprinted by permission of Bernard Weinraub c/o Marvin Josephson Associates, Inc. Copyright © 1968 by Esquire, Inc.

[53] Julius Lester, *Look Out, Whitey! Black Power's Gon' Get Your Mama!* (New York: The Dial Press, Inc., 1968), p. 103. Copyright © 1968 by Julius Lester and used by permission of the publisher, The Dial Press, Inc.

no other way. It is impossible to live within this country and not become a thief or a murderer. Young blacks and young whites are beginning to say NO to thievery and murder. Black Power confronts White Power openly, and as the SNCC poet Worth Long cried: "We have found you out, false-faced America. We have found you out!"

Having "found you out," we will destroy you or die in the act of destroying. That much seems inevitable. To those who fearfully wonder if America has come to the point of a race war, the answer is not certain. However, all signs would seem to say yes. Perhaps the only way that it might be avoided would be through the ability of young white radicals to convince blacks, through their actions, that they are ready to do whatever is necessary to change America.

The race war, if it comes, will come partly from the necessity for revenge. You can't do what has been done to blacks and not expect retribution. The very act of retribution is liberating, and perhaps it is no accident that the symbolism of Christianity speaks of being washed in Blood as an act of purification.[54]

Leaders of militant Negro organizations rose and fell rapidly during the decade of the 60s. In general, the trend was away from the "moderates" and toward the more militant leaders. Eldridge Cleaver, author of *Soul on Ice,* an ex-convict, and Minister of Information for the Black Panthers, was the hero of the extreme militants in the late 1960s. He was, he said, "a law unto myself — my own legislature, my own supreme court, my own executive." In the 1968 campaign, Cleaver was the presidential nominee of the Peace and Freedom Party. Here is an account of one of his campaign speeches.

"America is up against the wall," he declared. "This whole apparatus, this capitalistic system and its institutions and police . . . all need to be assigned to the garbage can of history and I don't give a —— who doesn't like it.

"If we can't have it, nobody's gonna have it," he continued. "We'd rather provoke a situation . . . that will disrupt cities and the economy so that the enemies of America could come in and pick the gold from the teeth of these Babylonian pigs" — this last, presumably, a reference to police officers, whom the Panthers regularly refer to as "pigs."

". . . The right to revolution can't be taken from the people," asserted Cleaver in the Panthers' defense. ". . . We can go nowhere unless we have the right to defend ourselves against the pig cop."

After some further strictures in this vein, Cleaver turned on his audience and observed with some vehemence:

---

[54] *Ibid.,* p. 137.

56   "Up against the wall, mother ——. You may think you're riding in luxury liners, that you can put a fool like Richard Nixon or an unconscionable man like George Wallace in the White House, but none of those pigs can solve the problem."

He dwelt next on his own candidacy on the Peace and Freedom ticket:

". . . I could go into the White House poor and come out fat —— rich, but I'm too young. [Cleaver, 33, is too young to hold the office.] So I have to say —— the White House, —— the electoral system, and —— all the pigs and —— the power structure.

"You're all chasing dollars, but there are other people who are chasing dollars to buy guns to kill judges, and police and corporation lawyers," said Cleaver to the attorneys. "We need lawyers today who have a lawbook in one hand and a gun in the other . . . so that if he goes to court and that ——doesn't come out right, he can pull out his gun and start shooting.

"If I could get two machine guns out of this crowd I wouldn't care if you applauded me or threw glasses at me, I'd get my black ass out of here."

Lest anyone mistake his meaning, Cleaver concluded with these remarks:

"I meant all my insults to those who won't choose my side — the right side. You people can take your wallets, credit cards and cut your mother —— necks.

"You people on the other side, I love you . . . I hope you'll take your guns and shoot judges and police."[55]

As the years wore on, many of the moderates became militants. Dick Gregory no longer spoke of taking "a thimble to the well." Instead, he said:

Black people have invested their money, their lives, their labor, their faith and their trust in America for 300 years. And we have received nothing for our investment. We took our problem to those who we thought would do something about it.

So in the form of Watts, Newark and Detroit we kicked the American machine, trying desperately to get the attention of the nation. And in the form of the police, the National Guard, and even federal troops, the

---

[55] Eldridge Cleaver, "A Word From the Peace and Freedom Candidate," *Newsweek* (September 16, 1968), p. 30. Copyright by Newsweek, Inc., 1968.

machine kicked back. Our desperation is now complete. We are saying to this country, "Cancel the flight." We are going to dismantle this American machine piece by piece.[56]

---

[56] Dick Gregory, *Write Me In* (New York: Bantam Books, 1968), pp. 95–96. Copyright © 1968 by Dick Gregory. By permission of Bantam Books, Inc.

The Poor: A War on Poverty

For the poor shall never cease out of the land.

Deuteronomy 15:11

The world is very different now. For man holds in his mortal hands the power to abolish all forms of human poverty. . . .

John F. Kennedy,
Inaugural Address

Most people in the world today are poor and most people throughout the history of mankind have been poor. But we have thought of the United States, especially since World War II, as being an "affluent society." We are told that Americans have the highest *average* living standard in the world. However, there still exists what Michael Harrington has called *The Other America,* peopled by individuals who are still poor and who are becoming increasingly invisible to the rest of society.

There is a familiar America. It is celebrated in speeches and advertised on television and in the magazines. It has the highest mass standard of living the world has ever known.

In the 1950's this America worried about itself, yet even its anxieties were products of abundance. The title of a brilliant book was widely misinterpreted, and the familiar America began to call itself "the affluent society." There was introspection about Madison Avenue and tail fins; there was discussion of the emotional suffering taking place in the suburbs. In all this, there was an implicit assumption that the basic grinding economic problems had been solved in the United States. In this theory the nation's problems were no longer a matter of basic human needs, of food, shelter, and clothing. Now they were seen as qualitative, a question of learning to live decently amid luxury.

While this discussion was carried on, there existed another America.

In it dwelt somewhere between 40,000,000 and 50,000,000 citizens of this land. They were poor. They still are.

To be sure, the other America is not impoverished in the same sense as those poor nations where millions cling to hunger as a defense against starvation. This country has escaped such extremes. That does not change the fact that tens of millions of Americans are, at this very moment, maimed in body and spirit, existing at levels beneath those necessary for human decency. If these people are not starving, they are hungry, and sometimes fat with hunger, for that is what cheap foods do. They are without adequate housing and education and medical care. . . .

The other America, the America of poverty, is hidden today in a way that it never was before. Its millions are socially invisible to the rest of us. . . .

Poverty is often off the beaten track. It always has been. The ordinary tourist never left the main highway, and today he rides inter-state turnpikes. He does not go into the valleys of Pennsylvania where the towns look like movie sets of Wales in the thirties. He does not see the company houses in rows, the rutted roads (the poor always have bad roads whether they live in the city, in towns, or on farms), and every-thing is black and dirty. And even if he were to pass through such a place by accident, the tourist would not meet the unemployed men in the bar or the women coming home from a runaway sweatshop. . . .

Clothes make the poor invisible too: America has the best-dressed poverty the world has ever known. For a variety of reasons, the benefits of mass production have been spread much more evenly in this area than in many others. It is much easier in the United States to be decently dressed than it is to be decently housed, fed, or doctored. Even people with terribly depressed incomes can look prosperous. . . .

Then, many of the poor are the wrong age to be seen. A good number of them (over 8,000,000) are sixty-five years of age or better; an even larger number are under eighteen. The aged members of the other America are often sick, and they cannot move. Another group of them live out their lives in loneliness and frustration: they sit in rented rooms, or else they stay close to a house in a neighborhood that has completely changed from the old days. Indeed, one of the worst aspects of poverty among the aged is that these people are out of sight and out of mind, and alone.

The young are somewhat more visible, yet they too stay close to their neighborhoods. Sometimes they advertise their poverty through a lurid tabloid story about a gang killing. But generally they do not disturb the quiet streets of the middle class.

And finally, the poor are politically invisible. It is one of the cruelest ironies of social life in advanced countries that the dispossessed at the bottom of society are unable to speak for themselves. The people of the other America do not, by far and large, belong to unions, to fraternal organizations, or to political parties. They are without lobbies of their own; they put forward no legislative program. As a group, they are atomized. They have no face; they have no voice.

Thus, there is not even a cynical political motive for caring about the poor, as in the old days. Because the slums are no longer centers of powerful political organizations, the politicians need not really care about their inhabitants. The slums are no longer visible to the middle class, so much of the idealistic urge to fight for those who need help is gone. . . .

Forty to 50,000,000 people are becoming increasingly invisible. That is a shocking fact. But there is a second basic irony of poverty that is equally important: if one is to make the mistake of being poor, he should choose a time when the majority of the people are miserable too.

J. K. Galbraith develops this idea in *The Affluent Society,* and in doing so defines the "newness" of the kind of poverty in contemporary America. The old poverty, Galbraith notes, was general. It was the condition of life of an entire society, or at least of that huge majority who were without special skills or the luck of birth. When the entire economy advanced, a good many of these people gained higher standards of living. . . .

Some of those who advanced in the thirties did so because they had unique and individual personal talents. But for the great mass, it was a question of being at the right point in the economy at the right time in history, and utilizing that position for common struggle. Some of those who failed did so because they did not have the will to take advantage of new opportunities. But for the most part the poor who were left behind had been at the wrong place in the economy at the wrong moment in history. . . .

Out of the thirties came the welfare state. Its creation had been stimulated by mass impoverishment and misery, yet it helped the poor least of all. Laws like unemployment compensation, the Wagner Act, the various farm programs, all these were designed for the middle third in the cities, for the organized workers, and for the upper third in the country, for the big market farmers. If a man works in an extremely low-paying job, he may not even be covered by social security or other welfare programs. If he receives unemployment compensation, the payment is scaled down according to his low earnings. . . .

Indeed, the paradox that the welfare state benefits those least who need help most is but a single instance of a persistent irony in the other America. Even when the money finally trickles down, even when a school is built in a poor neighborhood, for instance, the poor are still deprived. Their entire environment, their life, their values, do not prepare them to take advantage of the new opportunity. The parents are anxious for the children to go to work; the pupils are pent up, waiting for the moment when their education has complied with the law.

Today's poor, in short, missed the political and social gains of the thirties. They are, as Galbraith rightly points out, the first minority poor in history, the first poor not to be seen, the first poor whom the politicians could leave alone. . . .

Poverty in the United States is a culture, an institution, a way of life. . . .

There is, in short, a language of the poor, a psychology of the poor, a world view of the poor. To be impoverished is to be an internal alien, to grow up in a culture that is radically different from the one that dominates the society.[1]

Who Are the Poor?

Poverty can be defined in many ways. One way is to set a minimum dollar level for family incomes and assume that anything less constitutes a state of poverty. Any such figure must be somewhat arbitrary, but some "poverty line" must be designated if the extent and seriousness of poverty is to be measured. Disagreements over the level of the poverty line are not simply quibbles over statistics; the lower the level, the fewer the persons who will be included in the "poor" category and the less serious the problem will appear to be. Conversely, the higher the benchmark, the greater the number of persons who will be included and the more serious the problem. In its 1964 Annual Report, the Council of Economic Advisers proposed an income below $3,000 as a test of family poverty.

Using the $3,000 poverty line, about 9.3 million families, comprising 30 million persons, were classed as poor in 1962. In addition, 5 million "unrelated" persons had incomes under $1,500. These 35 million people constituted about one fifth of the total population.

By 1964 the percentage of poor people had dropped from 20.1 percent (in 1962) to 18 percent, but it still numbered 34.1 million people.[2] But these figures do not tell the whole story. Of all the families in the United States in 1964, one tenth had incomes below $2,000 and 3.2 percent had incomes under $1,000.[3] In the same year, 42 percent of the unrelated individuals (those not living in family households) had incomes under $1,500.[4]

---

[1] Michael Harrington, *The Other America* (Baltimore, Maryland: Penguin Books, 1962), pp. 9–24. By permission of the author.

[2] "The Annual Report of the Council of Economic Advisers" included in the *Economic Report of the President,* transmitted to the Congress, January 1966 (Washington, D. C.: U. S. G.P.O., 1966), p. 111.

[3] U. S. Bureau of the Census, *Statistical Abstract of the United States, 1966* (Washington, D. C.: U. S. G.P.O., 1966), p. 336.

[4] *Ibid.,* p. 337.

While the proportion of Americans living in poverty has declined over the years, their share of aggregate income has remained almost constant. Since 1947, the lowest 20 percent of the income strata has consistently received about 5 percent of aggregate income for families and about 3 percent for unrelated individuals.[5] Apparently very little redistribution of income has occurred in the last 20 years.

We recognize that the poor are individuals with differing personalities and problems. However, we may be better able to understand the problem of poverty if we first attempt to establish some general characteristics of poor people. Who are the poor? What kinds or categories of people have the highest concentrations of poverty?

Children. One fourth of all American children live in poverty.[6] Michael Harrington says: "The most shocking thing to emerge from this calibration of economic suffering in the United States is that the young are 'poorer' than the rest of the society."[7]

Young people. Not only is there a high concentration of poverty among children, but the same poverty carries over to young adults. The median money income for males 20–24 years of age in 1964 was $2,978 and for females in the same age bracket it was $1,951. Furthermore, 50 percent of the males and 69 percent of the females had incomes under $3,000.[8] Young people not only work for lower wages, but they are likely to be unemployed more frequently and for longer periods. They have become in Michael Harrington's words "The New Lost Generation."

Old people. Median money income for males 65 and over in 1965 was $2,116 and for females it was $984.[9] The Council of Economic Advisers estimated that 38 percent of the nonfarm households headed by a person 65 or over lived in poverty.[10]

The high incidence of poverty among elderly people is also a relatively new phenomenon. According to Charles Schottland:

Prior to the turn of the century, two-thirds of the men over 65 in the United States were gainfully employed; today the corresponding propor-

---

[5] *Ibid.*, p. 336.

[6] "The Annual Report of the Council of Economic Advisers," 1965, p. 163.

[7] Michael Harrington, "The World of Poverty," *The American Federationist*, Vol. 73 (April 1966), p. 3.

[8] *Statistical Abstract, 1966*, p. 343.

[9] U. S. Bureau of the Census, *Current Population Reports*, Series P-60, No. 50, August 26, 1966 (Washington D. C.: U. S. G.P.O., 1966).

[10] "The Annual Report of the Council of Economic Advisers," 1966, p. 113.

64   tion is less than one-third, and the relative number of employed men over 65 continues to decrease.[11]

Walter Reuther has said that, more than any other highly industrialized nation, we neglect "those who are too old to work and too young to die."[12]

The dropouts. The lower the education, the higher the probability of poverty. Thirty-seven percent of white families and 56 percent of Negro families had incomes of under $3,000 (in 1964) when the head of the household had less than eight years of school.[13]

It is this basic fact which has stimulated the campaign against school dropouts. The dropouts are not only likely to be unemployed but many of them are *unemployable* because of lack of education. The Department of Labor's report, "One Third of a Nation," pointed out that a quarter of the young men who were drafted were rejected because they were not up to the seventh grade level. Perhaps one might say that those who are too ignorant to fight are also too ignorant to work.

There is always the suspicion that the ignorant are also the stupid — that their IQ's are simply too low to make them employable. But, as Michael Harrington points out:

Every time there has been a shooting war in the twentieth century, with its concomitant full employment in the advanced nations, hundreds of thousands of "unemployables" have suddenly been discovered to have viable skills. From this point of view, the creation of a full-employment economy is a fundamental prerequisite for doing anything about this new lost generation.[14]

Widows with children. Poverty envelops 48 percent of all fatherless families. No other major category of Americans has such a large concentration of poor people. Women not only receive lower salaries than men but, when they must remain at home to care for children, their incomes are still further reduced.

Mrs. Willie Craig points up the problem in this letter to Congressman Adam Clayton Powell of New York:

---

[11] Charles I. Schottland, "Poverty and Income Maintenance for the Aged" in Margaret S. Gordon, ed., *Poverty in America* (San Francisco: Chandler Publishing Co., 1965), p. 228.

[12] Quoted by Leon Keyserling, *Progress or Poverty*, Conference on Economic Progress, 1964, p. 11.

[13] *Statistical Abstract, 1966*, p. 342.

[14] Michael Harrington, "The New Lost Generation: Jobless Youth," *New York Times Magazine* (May 24, 1964), p. 68. © 1964 by The New York Times Company. Reprinted by permission.

Dear Representative Powell: I hope with all my heart that you can understand me and my write. Also hold my name (P.S. I Civil Ser.) Reverend Stevenson is so right. I wish it was most like him, for one thing I'm on A.D.C. till my baby get 3 months old or 4 than I go back to work. Take my case for instance, I only ask for help till I go back to work. You know what they do to me. My husband give me $15 a week that they ask him to do. After he got out of work in March they send me $112 for March me and three children $80 rent out of $112 to live off, $125 for April and keep said that they owe me. But it never will see it. Now they know my husband is out of work and where he is: I also ask them to let me pay them back, but just give me and my four children some food to eat now.

And the President Johnson get on the TV, said feed the people: Mr. Powell Chicago is bad as Mississippi. My home is Florida.

So here is a working mother only ask for help till she return to work, and can get two meals a day from them.

Mrs. Willie Craig[15]

The problem of poverty stricken families with female heads is likely to increase in scope because of the increasing rate of divorces and separations. According to Leon Keyserling "there has been since 1900 a 50 percent increase in the ratio of manless households to total households."[16]

Low wage earners. A popular bumper sticker reads "I'm fighting poverty. I work." While it is obvious that the chronically unemployed are likely to live in poverty, the figures show that many of the poor *do* fight poverty (unsuccessfully) by working. Herman Miller sums it up this way:

About 2 million families (about a fourth of all the poor families) were headed by a person who worked full-time throughout the year. Increases in aggregate demand and a full-employment economy probably would not benefit these families, except perhaps by providing work for wives and children. Although the heads of this large segment of poor families were fully employed, their incomes were insufficient to raise their families above the poverty line.[17]

---

[15] U. S. House of Representatives, *Examination of the War on Poverty Program,* Committee on Education and Labor, Hearings before the Subcommittee on the War on Poverty Program, 88th Cong., 1st sess., April 1965, p. 781.

[16] Keyserling, *Progress or Poverty,* p. 39.

[17] Herman P. Miller, "Changes in the Number and Composition of the Poor" in Gordon, ed., *Poverty in America,* p. 87.

66   *The disabled.* Persons with mental and physical disabilities constitute the stubborn hard core of the poor. The effect of disability is hard to measure because it may be temporary or permanent. Furthermore, disability for one kind of job may not be a hindrance in another. Nevertheless, it is estimated that from 1¾ to 2 million persons are absent from work on an average day because of temporary disability and about 3.3 million persons suffer from long term disabilities.[18]

To John Fischer, a part of the explanation is "The Stupidity Problem." Fischer writes:

It is perfectly clear, to me at least, why . . . [we have not] been able to find jobs for our three or four million unemployed. . . .

We'll have to face up to the fact that all men are not created equal, except in the limited political sense which Jefferson had in mind when he drafted the Declaration of Independence. Until we do that, it will be impossible for our public officials to find useful work for the 20-plus per cent of the population with below-normal intelligence, or to train them for jobs they are capable of handling. And it will remain almost equally hard to make the best use of our limited supply of high IQ's.[19]

Low IQ's notwithstanding, there is a high correlation between physical disability and poverty. The poor do "get sicker and the sick get poorer." Leon Keyserling sums it up this way:

There are a wide variety of data which point up the close relationship between poverty and inadequate medical care. In the low-income States, infant mortality rates are 17 percent higher than the national average. . . .

Comparing men aged 45–64 who earn less than $2,000 a year with those earning $7,000 or more, the incidence of heart disease in the lower income group is almost three times as high; orthopedic impairments nearly four times as frequent; high blood pressure more than four times as common; arthritis and rheumatism nearly five times as prevalent; and the incidence of mental and nervous conditions and vision impairment more than six times as frequent.[20]

Low IQ's, physical and mental disabilities undoubtedly cause poverty but they are also caused by poverty. Like the chicken and the egg, it is difficult to tell which came first. Regardless of whether these conditions

---

[18] See Herman M. Somers, "Poverty and Income Maintenance for the Disabled" in Gordon, ed., *Poverty in America*, pp. 241–242.

[19] John Fischer, *The Stupidity Problem and Other Harassments* (New York: Harper & Row, 1962), pp. 72–76.

[20] Keyserling, *Progress or Poverty*, p. 67.

are causes or effects, the situation is not hopeless. In Galbraith's words:

Much can be done to treat those characteristics which cause people to reject or be rejected by the modern industrial society. Educational deficiencies can be overcome. Mental deficiencies can be treated. Physical handicaps can be remedied. The limiting factor is not knowledge of what can be done. Overwhelmingly it is our failure to invest in people.[21]

Farmers. More farmers live in poverty than do persons in any other major occupation or major industry group. The median income for male farmers and farm managers in 1965 was $2,988, while farm laborers and foremen had median incomes of $1,452.[22] Forty-three percent of all farm families fall below the poverty line.

Varden Fuller describes it this way:

Rural poverty is intensive, extensive, and intractable. As elsewhere, being poor in the country is correlated with well-known factors — youth, advanced age, color of skin, technological impacts, poor education. In rural areas, these attributes come together in a maximum likelihood combination. Whether portrayed in photography or in statistical magnitudes, percentages, and index numbers, rural poverty is shocking. Yet, it is remote and obscure. The rural population — widely dispersed, racially and culturally heterogeneous, socially and politically incohesive — does not compete well for attention. Unemployment is easier to observe than is underemployment, and it is the latter which dominates the rural scene. Moreover, there is the widespread and mistaken notion that billions of agricultural subsidy dollars alleviate rural poverty.[23]

Southerners. In 1964, one fourth of all Southern families had incomes below $3,000.[24] Per capita income for the five lowest-income states in 1965 is listed below.[25]

	Rank Order	Per Capita Income
Tennessee	46	$1,992.
Alabama	47	$1,910.
South Carolina	48	$1,838.
Arkansas	49	$1,781.
Mississippi	50	$1,566.

[21] John K. Galbraith, *The Affluent Society* (Boston: Houghton Mifflin Co., 1958), p. 333.

[22] Bureau of the Census, *Current Population Reports,* Series P-60, No. 50 (Aug. 26, 1966).

[23] Varden Fuller, "Rural Poverty and Rural Area Development" in Gordon, ed., *Poverty in America,* p. 390.

[24] *Statistical Abstract, 1966,* p. 337.

[25] *Ibid.,* p. 330.

68   Part of the reason for low income in the South is the high concentration of Negroes in that area. About one half of all nonwhite families live in the South and about 60 percent of the Southern nonwhite families live in poverty.[26]

Negroes. Roughly four Negro families out of ten (38.6 percent) had incomes below $3,000 in 1965 as compared with 15.3 percent for white families. Median income of Negro families in that year was $3,724, as compared with $6,858 for white families.[27]

The sons and daughters of the poor. Today's poor are likely to be the sons and daughters of the poor. In the language of the Council of Economic Advisers:

Poverty breeds poverty. A poor individual or family has a high probability of staying poor. Low incomes carry with them high risks of illness; limitations on mobility; limited access to education, information, and training. Poor parents cannot give their children the opportunities for better health and education needed to improve their lot. Lack of motivation, hope, and incentive is a more subtle but no less powerful barrier than lack of financial means. Thus the cruel legacy of poverty is passed from parents to children.[28]

The situations outlined above often do not occur singly. They tend to overlap and reinforce each other. The same individual may fit into two or more categories. Thus, it would not be unusual to find an uneducated Negro woman in ill-health as head of a family in the rural South. Such a family would almost certainly be poor.

Finally, we should reiterate that poverty is a state of mind — an attitude and a set of expectations. An old folk saying of optimistic middle-class Americans runs, "I've sometimes been broke but I've never been poor." Millions of the permanent poor could say the opposite: "I've sometimes had money but I've always been poor."

What Is the Responsibility of Society to the Poor?

It may be helpful for analytical purposes to oversimplify the problem of society's responsibility to the poor by postulating two extremes of a

---

[26] See Herman P. Miller, "Poverty and the Negro" in Leo Fishman, ed., *Poverty Amid Affluence* (New Haven: Yale University Press, 1966), p. 107.

[27] *Statistical Abstract, 1966,* p. 338.

[28] "Annual Report of the Council of Economic Advisers" included in *Economic Report of the President,* 1964.

spectrum: Those at one end think of poverty as an *individual* concern and tend to find the cause in individual deficiencies, weaknesses, or misfortunes. Those holding the opposite view hold that individual deficiencies or misfortunes are the results of failures in *society* as a whole. If Johnny Jones did not go beyond the fifth grade, one group would assume that it was because he was too lazy or stupid to go any farther, while the opposite group would assume that the school system or the economic system was to blame. Even if this latter group were forced to admit that he was stupid or lazy, they would contend that society produced the conditions.

The "individualists" tend to assume that the solution to unemployment is for the unemployed to go to work. This point of view received a severe jolt during the depression of the 1930s, but the notion still persists.

While the long-term trend seems to be away from individualism and toward collective responsibility, Americans are still a highly individualistic people. Labor unions represent one attempt to assume collective responsibility for wages and working conditions. While the unions have been successful in enrolling some 17–18 million members, they have not been particularly effective politically. If this large bloc of individuals voted as a unit, they could probably dominate every national election and many state and local elections. But they do not vote as a bloc and the basic reason is probably that they do not really believe they will stand or fall with the union. They tend to see success or failure as determined by individual ability (or lack of it) and luck.

The attitudes and values of a society do not just happen; they are partially the result of historical circumstances and of more or less systematic indoctrination campaigns. Individuals and groups make estimates (consciously or unconsciously) of the probable consequences to them of given sets of public values and attitudes. They then attempt to shape the values of the society in their own image. Consequently, some groups attempt to strengthen individualism and other groups attempt to weaken it. In varying degrees, we are all involved in this battle for the minds of men.

Poverty has been so common throughout history that, until recently, it was generally assumed to be an inevitable condition for most of mankind. Indeed, it was even believed to be desirable by some people. Thus Herbert Spencer wrote:

Pervading all nature we may see at work a stern discipline, which is a little cruel that it may be very kind. That state of universal warfare maintained throughout the lower creation, to the great perplexity of many worthy people, is at bottom the most merciful provision which the circumstances admit of. . . .

Blind to the fact, that under the natural order of things society is constantly excreting its unhealthy, imbecile, slow, vacillating, faithless members, these unthinking, though well-meaning, men advocate an interference which not only stops the purifying process, but even in-

70   creases the vitiation — absolutely encourages the multiplication of the reckless and incompetent by offering them an unfailing provision, and discourages the multiplication of the competent and provident by heightening the prospective difficulty of maintaining a family. And thus, in their eagerness to prevent the really salutary sufferings that surround us, these sigh-wise and groan-foolish people bequeath to posterity a continually increasing curse.[29]

An American clergyman, Russell H. Conwell (1843–1925), agreed. In his "Acres of Diamonds" lecture (which he delivered some 6,000 times), Conwell said:

. . . the number of poor who are to be sympathized with is very small. To sympathize with a man whom God has punished for his sins, thus to help him when God would still continue a just punishment, is to do wrong, no doubt about it, and we do that more than we help those who are deserving. While we should sympathize with God's poor — that is, those who cannot help themselves — let us remember there is not a poor person in the United States who was not made poor by his own shortcomings, or by the shortcomings of some one else. It is all wrong to be poor, anyhow.[30]

Andrew Carnegie spoke of the "competitive system" in somewhat the same vein:

The price which society pays for the law of competition, like the price it pays for cheap comforts and luxuries, is also great; but the advantages of this law are also greater still, for it is to this law that we owe our wonderful material development, which brings improved conditions in its train. But, whether the law be benign or not, we must say of it, as we say of the change in the conditions of men to which we have referred: It is here; we cannot evade it; no substitutes for it have been found; and while the law may be sometimes hard for the individual, it is best for the race, because it insures the survival of the fittest in every department.[31]

---

[29] Herbert Spencer, *Social Statics* (New York: D. Appleton and Co., 1881), pp. 352–355.

[30] Russell H. Conwell, "Acres of Diamonds," quoted by Alpheus Thomas Mason in *Free Government in the Making* (New York: Oxford University Press, 1965), p. 597.

[31] Andrew Carnegie, "Wealth," *North American Review*, Vol. 148 (1889), p. 655.

And William Graham Sumner (1840–1910), a Yale professor, wrote on the obligations of free men:

A free man in a free democracy has no duty whatever toward other men of the same rank and standing, except respect, courtesy, and good will. . . .

In a free state every man is held and expected to take care of himself and his family, to make no trouble for his neighbor, and to contribute his full share to public interests and common necessities. If he fails in this he throws burdens on others. He does not thereby acquire rights against the others. On the contrary, he only accumulates obligations toward them; and if allowed to make his deficiencies a ground of new claims, he passes over into the position of a privileged or petted person — emancipated from duties, endowed with claims.[32]

A more recent concern over the costs of social welfare was expressed by Senator Barry Goldwater of Arizona:

A candidate for the Democratic nomination for President recently startled the country by charging that "17 million Americans go to bed hungry every night." I say "startled" advisedly because while most of us are aware that some Americans, because of unemployment and other factors, do not enjoy a diet on par with those gainfully employed, the figure "17 million hungry Americans" does sound a bit padded. It is also, of course, a well-worked Soviet propaganda stereotype that most Americans suffer from malnutrition and that thousands drop dead in the streets of America every day of hunger.

I am inclined to be charitable and I attribute this particular exaggeration to youthful exuberance and perhaps a bit of over-striving for political effect. What does disturb me is that the claim of so many millions of Americans as being ill fed, ill housed, and ill clothed is not unique or recent. Ever since the early days of the unlamented New Deal, we have been fed a regular and overfull diet of statistics along the same general line. . . .

Since 1939, the Federal Government has spent a total of $52 billion in 22 fiscal years. The Social Security Bulletin for October 1955 had an extended table showing local and State expenditures on social welfare from fiscal 1934 to fiscal 1954 as totaling $170.344 billion. As State and local welfare payments since 1954 have jumped to well over $20 billion per year, we can add another $100 billion for the past 5 years, making a grand total of at least $322 billion.

---

[32] William Graham Sumner, *What Social Classes Owe to Each Other* (New York: Harper & Brothers, 1883), pp. 39–40.

72   If, as it is claimed, we still have 17 million hungry people after spending $322 billion in 25 years, then it is obvious we must do one of two things. One, raise taxes still higher a la the New Deal dictum "tax and tax; spend and spend," boost the national debt still higher, and give the spiral of inflation another whirl. Or, two, try something else. That is, spend less, tax less, give away less abroad, balance the budget, and let people keep more of their earned income to prime the economic pump by old and tried economic laws which seemed to have worked pretty well until we started monkeying with them. . . .

Time and again, I have tried to show that no one is opposed to human welfare *per se*. We conservatives are merely opposed to the establishment of a government bureaucratic monopoly to deal with basic human problems traditionally handled and best solved, first, through religious and private organizations and, second, through the lowest form of political organization closest to the individual or individuals concerned. . . .

It is now considered shameful for older people to be taken care of in their declining years by their children whom they nourished and spent small fortunes on bringing up. Sending one's parents to the poorhouse, so that one can buy a new house or a new and flashier auto, would, of course, be considered a bit raw; but the same individual sees nothing shameful in turning his parents adrift to shift for themselves on a meager social security pittance. They earned this social security themselves; and any deficits which have to be made up come out of the public treasury — that is, somebody else's pocket.

The impersonal arm of a vast bureaucracy centered in Washington can never transmit to the individual recipient the warmth and personal feeling provided by a family which shelters and protects its own. Even religious, charitable, or fraternal assistance at the local level, because it has been, and remains, in direct personal contact with the recipient, is bound to be a warmer and more sympathetic bond than that of a mere statistical figure in a bureaucratic budget. . . .

Nor has anyone pointed out the fundamental immorality of taxing those who already take care of their own aged relatives, in addition to helping support others, whose children pass their own obligations on to the State. Then there are many spinsters and bachelors who devoted their lives to caring for their parents until they died and, as a result of discharging such an obligation, never married. They are now taxed at the higher rates for single persons, to help pay the enormous annual cost of caring for those whose own children refuse to do so. One of the most shameful situations presently plaguing welfare agencies in this country is the subsidization by the State of wholesale bastardy practiced by women who have made illegitimacy a profession, or at least a source of easy and steady income. . . .

All of us — left, right, and center — make numerous speeches and declamations against the evils of communism. We affect great horror and deep moral indignation over the brutal methods used by the Chinese Reds in setting up the commune system and their calculated destruction of the ages-old Chinese family system. We lose sight of the fact that it is just as easy to slip unintentionally into a hole on a dark night as it is to jump down into it deliberately in the daytime.

The gradual and imperceptible erosion of the family, through ill-advised and misguided welfare schemes over a period of years, may bring us in the not too distant future to a commune system of social organization, with cradle-to-grave welfarism. Goldsmith's often quoted couplet might well be paraphrased and brought up to date:

> Ill fares the land to hastening ills a prey,
> Where welfarism is accelerated and the family is permitted to decay.[33]

Americans have inherited British values to a considerable degree and, along with them, British methods for dealing with problems. So it was with poverty. The British Poor Laws, first enacted in 1601, came to be the basis for treating poverty in the United States until the depression of the 1930s.

The Poor Laws were based on the belief that poverty generally is caused by character deficiencies. The poor were assumed to be sinful or they would not be in such a condition. Only extreme cases of hardship were given public assistance. Responsibility for the poor was assigned to local units of government (welfare operations and parts of the "War on Poverty" are still administered in considerable part by local units of government in the United States). Paupers had to take an oath (the pauper's oath) before they could receive assistance. Their names were published in the "Poor Rolls" of local newspapers. Only persons who had established residence were eligible. Public assistance was financed by a "poor tax" so that taxpayers knew how much they paid for the poor and who the recipients were.

With some modifications, these old British practices were continued in the United States until well into the 20th century. Actually, Americans did less for their poor than did the British. After all, America was the land of opportunity; and just enough people managed to go from "rags to riches" to keep alive the belief that, with luck and hard work, it could happen to anyone.

With increasing industrialization (and increasingly dependent people), and with the end of the Western frontier, Americans became more and more aware of the existence of poverty in their midst. By 1928, Herbert

---

[33] Barry Goldwater, "What Price Social Welfare?" *Congressional Record,* Vol. 106 (August 25, 1960), pp. 17,650–17,653.

74   Hoover could say, "One of the oldest and perhaps the noblest of human aspirations has been the abolition of poverty. . . . We shall soon, with the help of God, be in sight of the day when poverty will be banished from this nation."[34] But that day did not arrive. Instead, the worst depression in the nation's history caused Franklin D. Roosevelt to say "I see one-third of a nation ill-housed, ill-clad, ill-nourished."[35]

During the "New Deal" era, the concept of local responsibility was jettisoned in part, and the Social Security Act of 1935 was enacted. The Social Security Act was not the first government social insurance program (workmen's compensation laws date back to 1910), but it inaugurated a new trend in the relief of poverty. Before 1935, individuals received public charity in the form of some kind of *assistance.* Since that time the emphasis has been on social *insurance* to supplement and hopefully to replace public assistance.

Despite the increase in the number and coverage of social insurance plans, and despite continued prosperity since World War II, welfare costs remained high and Americans were startled to learn that one-fifth of the nation still lived in poverty. True, one-fifth was considerably better than Roosevelt's one-third, but it was not good enough. There was widespread poverty in the midst of unprecedented affluence. Something had gone wrong.

The War on Poverty

The origins and purposes of the "War on Poverty" were recalled last week by Walter Heller, chairman of the Council of Economic Advisers under Presidents Kennedy and Johnson, and a chief strategist of the opening assault. . . .

During his year-end economic review in December 1962, Mr. Kennedy asked his chief economist: "What about the poverty problem in the United States?" . . .

Heller and his Council of Economic Advisers first explored the possibility of reducing poverty with a tax cut: "We concluded that even though the tax cut would create between 2 and 3 million new jobs, even though it would open up exits from poverty, the difficulty is that there are millions of people who can't use those exits, who can't move into new jobs." For Heller, that was the key conclusion. "These millions are caught in the web of poverty through illiteracy, lack of skills, racial discrimination, broken homes, ill health. These are conditions that are hardly touched by prosperity and growth. These are conditions which call for a specially focused and specially designed program."

---

[34] Herbert Hoover, on accepting the Republican nomination for the presidency, 1928.

[35] Franklin D. Roosevelt, Second Inaugural Address, January 20, 1937.

At about 7:30 P.M. on the evening of November 19, 1963, Heller went to see Kennedy. "When I got there, John-John followed me into the President's office. After we shooed him out, I asked the President whether he wanted our work to go forward on the assumption that the antipoverty measure would be part of his 1964 legislative program. His answer was an unhesitating, 'Yes'."

President Kennedy was dead three days later. And the following day, recalled Heller, "the first matter I took up with President Johnson was the poverty program. His immediate response was, "That's my kind of program . . . I want to move full speed ahead."[36]

On March 16, 1964, President Johnson asked Congress to declare war on poverty by enacting a proposed Economic Opportunity Act. Excerpts from the President's message follow:

With the growth of our country has come opportunity for our people — opportunity to educate our children, to use our energies in productive work, to increase our leisure — opportunity for almost every American to hope that through work and talent he could create a better life for himself and his family.

The path forward has not been an easy one.

But we have never lost sight of our goal — an America in which every citizen shares all the opportunities of his society, in which every man has a chance to advance his welfare to the limit of his capacities.

We have come a long way toward this goal.

We still have a long way to go.

The distance which remains is the measure of the great unfinished work of our society.

To finish that work I have called for a national war on poverty. Our objective — total victory. . . .

Our fight against poverty will be an investment in the most valuable of our resources — the skills and strength of our people.

And in the future, as in the past, this investment will return its cost manyfold to our entire economy.

If we can raise the annual earnings of 10 million among the poor by only $1,000 we will have added $14 billion a year to our national output. In addition we can make important reductions in public assistance payments which now cost us $4 billion a year, and in the large costs of fighting crime and delinquency, disease and hunger.

This is only part of the story.

Our history has proved that each time we broaden the base of

---

[36] From "Shriver and the War on Poverty," *Newsweek* (September 13, 1965), p. 22. Copyright, Newsweek, Inc., September, 1965.

76   abundance, giving more people the chance to produce and consume, we create new industry, higher production, increased earnings, and better income for all.

Giving new opportunity to those who have little will enrich the lives of all the rest.

Because it is right, because it is wise, and because, for the first time in our history, it is possible to conquer poverty, I submit, for the consideration of the Congress and the country, the Economic Opportunity Act of 1964.

The act does not merely expand old programs or improve what is already being done. It charts a new course. It strikes at the causes, not just the consequences of poverty. It can be a mile-stone in our 180-year search for a better life for our people.

The Administration bill was introduced in the House of Representatives by Congressman Landrum of Georgia as H.R. 10440, "a bill to mobilize the human and financial resources of the Nation to combat poverty in the United States."

On opening the Hearings on H.R. 10440 in the House Committee on Education and Labor, Chairman Adam Clayton Powell said in part:

Today marks a historic day in the life of our American society. At last we are coming to grips with one of the most important and crucial issues of our time. Today we are recognizing that all American citizens must have equal access to freedom, justice, and the right to work and make a living. Today we are concerning ourselves about one-fifth of our Nation's population who have been left out of the flowing stream of prosperity. Today we are admitting that America cannot be the great Nation which it is possible of becoming unless we provide for all of its citizens. In our actions at this point, we are rededicating ourselves to the proposition that all men are created equal and reaffirming our belief in the Declaration of Independence and the inalienable rights which it guarantees. . . .

Poverty is costly, not only to the poor, but to the whole society. Its ugly byproducts include ignorance, disease, delinquency, crime, irresponsibility, immorality, and indifference. Poverty is not a purely private concern, nor is it local. It is a social and national problem. To deal with it, therefore, requires a national attack on poverty, with the recognition of the fact that such an attack must come from many angles simultaneously.[37]

---

[37] U. S. House of Representatives, Committee on Education and Labor, Subcommittee on War on Poverty Program, *Economic Opportunity Act of 1964,* Hearings on H.R. 10440, 88th Cong., 2d sess., Part 1, pp. 1–3.

The bill was generally supported by the AFL-CIO, the National Farm-   **77**
ers Union, and the National Grange. It was generally opposed by the
National Association of Manufacturers, the Chamber of Commerce of the
United States, and the American Farm Bureau Federation.

George Meany, president of the AFL-CIO, endorsed the bill as a "step
forward" but said that it was only a beginning. Walter Reuther, president
of the United Automobile Workers, agreed that the bill was "wholly
inadequate" and went on to say:

. . . The bill before your committee is a good beginning, but it is
only a beginning. I hope that when you enact that bill in Congress you
will recognize that, while it is an important, necessary, historic step, it is
one step in a long road that this country has to travel if we are to abolish
poverty. I believe that we need to understand that we can deal with this
problem realistically and effectively only as we commit resources that
equal the dimensions of the problem.

There was a time in human history when poverty was inescapable,
when there were more empty bellies to fill than could be filled by
available food supplies, more naked backs to cover and more families to
house than the tools of production could serve. But that is a part of
ancient history.

We now have the science and the technology and the economic
capability in this country of ours to abolish human poverty. I believe that
we will not be true to ourselves and to the values that we believe in,
which are built around the worth and dignity of each human being, until
we find a more effective way of mobilizing our economic potential and
relating that potential to the basic needs of all the people. We have
learned how to create economic abundance, and now the task before us,
as a free people, working within the framework of a free society, is to
learn how to achieve higher forms of cooperation between labor and
management, farm groups, and other groups, so we can share that
abundance.[38]

The War on Poverty bill also encountered strong opposition. Harry L.
Brown, speaking for the American Farm Bureau Federation, thought the
bill would create "stabilized, Government-directed and subsidized
poverty."[39]

The anti-poverty bill was introduced in the Senate as S. 2642 and was
referred to the Committee on Labor and Public Welfare. The National
Association of Manufacturers came before this committee to express its
doubts about the effectiveness of the bill's methods for combatting
poverty:

---

[38] *Ibid.*, April 9, 1964, p. 422.
[39] *Ibid.*, April 13, 1964, p. 555.

78   The Federal Government has, of course, a large role to play and the bill before you is an attempt to define that role. After careful study we have concluded that it assigns the wrong part of the overall task to the National Government. It would place in Washington responsibilities which States, communities, individuals, and voluntary associations are much better fitted to assume. Moreover, it would thereby impede the Federal Government in carrying out the functions which are proper to it. . . .

We believe that the Federal Government should concentrate on creating and maintaining a national economic climate which encourages expansion, new investment, and consequently jobmaking, in the private economy. This is the unique function of the Central Government in the war on poverty.[40]

The Chamber of Commerce was somewhat more vehement in making the same objections:

Careful analysis of the proposals in S. 2642 indicates that this bill is an ineffective piece of legislation.

It ignores, evades, or confuses fundamental issues basic to the solution of the poverty problem. It ignores the primary relationship of training for employability to the rapidly changing job opportunities of our technological age: it ignores the immobility of the illiterate poor, even though greater mobility is known to be a key to existing job opportunities. . . .

It ignores the experiences of Federal agencies in administering the Manpower Development and Training Act, the Vocational Education Act, and the Juvenile Delinquency Act; it ignores — in fact, it denies — the experience and research of State and local governments in handling social and educational problems.

It ignores the many efforts of business and industry and of the many voluntary private agencies to minimize poverty — but invites other agencies to duplicate such programs at public expense, with no State or local agency to have coordinative power over such programs.[41]

In spite of these arguments, the Senate committee approved the bill (with amendments) by a vote of 13–2. The two dissenting members of the

---

[40] U. S. Senate, Committee on Labor and Public Welfare, *Hearings before the Select Committee on Poverty on the Economic Opportunity Act of 1964*, 88th Cong., 2d sess., pp. 278–280.

[41] *Ibid.*, pp. 280–281.

committee, Senators Goldwater and Tower, submitted a minority report, **79**
portions of which are reproduced below.

We consider it an attempt to reap political rewards from the American people's natural and human desire to improve the lot of our less fortunate citizens. The poverty program and the claims and justification which have accompanied it constitute a curious combination of the techniques made famous by the phrases "Madison Avenue" and "The Wizard of Oz."

This bill, with its generous use of programs tried during the depression-ridden thirties, is illusory in leaving untouched the difficulties which prevent some Americans from sharing in our general prosperity. At best, the hodgepodge of programs which make up S. 2642, treat only the results, not the causes of poverty.

We fully agree with the criticism of the administration program set forth in the platform adopted by the Republican Party at its recent presidential convention in San Francisco.

"The administration has proposed a so-called war on poverty which characteristically overlaps and often contradicts, the 42 existing Federal poverty programs. It would dangerously centralize Federal controls and bypass effective State, local and private programs." . . .

This bill does not address itself to the primary cause of poverty. It does nothing to provide our poorer citizens with the skills necessary to gain regular employment in this modern age. Instead, it resurrects the tired slogans and applies the ineffectual poultices of a bygone era.[42]

Criticisms notwithstanding, the bill passed the House by a vote of 226–185 and the Senate by a vote of 61–34 and was signed by the President on August 20, 1964 (P.L. 88–452).

Key provisions of the act included:

(1) A Job Corps to provide education and work experience for persons 16–21.

(2) A Work-Training program to help finance work experience and training for young people.

(3) A Work-Study program to assist low-income college students.

(4) Community Action Programs which authorized payment of up to 90 percent of the costs of antipoverty programs planned and carried out at the local level.

---

[42] U. S. Congress, Senate, Committee on Labor and Public Welfare, Report 1218, 88th Cong., 2nd sess., pp. 69–84.

80   (5) Grants and loans to combat poverty in rural areas.

(6) Participation in or guarantees of loans to small business on terms more liberal than those available under the Small Business Administration.

(7) Stimulation and assistance in financing work experience for training for the unemployed.

(8) Establishment of a domestic "Peace Corps" (VISTA) to assist in carrying out various programs under the Act.

In July 1965 (when the War on Poverty had been in existence less than one year), *Life* magazine editorialized:

"Nobody would be yelling if nothing was happening," says Sargent Shriver, who is running a war — the War on Poverty — almost as confusing and expensive as the one in Vietnam. Dispensing federal funds at the rate of $1 billion a year, he has stirred up hundreds of state and municipal patronage feuds; he has precipitated major controversies on civil rights and welfare; he has suffered headlines about knifings, sodomy and drunkenness in his Job Corps camps. The war has also inspired Al Capp to supplant his lovable Li'l Abner image of the poor with a repulsive crowd of "deep misery" Dogpatchers whose misery is their own fault. But Shriver remains serene in the conviction that "no federal program in peace time has ever gone so far so fast."

What actually is going on in the War on Poverty? The Economic Opportunity Act, not quite a year old, expressed the widely shared desire to "eliminate the paradox of poverty in the midst of plenty" and set up a grab bag of new welfare programs for the purpose, mainly these:

The Job Corps is a showpiece program for dropouts and other disadvantaged 16 to 21 year olds. It has so far enrolled 13,000 youths and has received applications from 250,000 boys and 50,000 girls. Despite isolated scandals, the great majority of campers have been working hard at training, learning and conservation chores. They are all kids with serious problems, many rejected by the armed services as well as by their families. About 17% have been dropping (or getting kicked) out of the Corps, but some have already graduated into jobs or the Army or more advanced training centers. If the 83 percent who are sticking it out become self-supporting instead of the reliefers many of their parents are, the Job Corps will have brilliantly justified itself.

Community Action Programs are an umbrella for a variety of welfare programs involving state or local agencies, public and private. The most visible CAP this summer is Project Head Start, now under way in some 2400 communities. It aims to make 560,000 underprivileged children of 4, 5, and 6 better prepared for school next fall, if only by showing them how to hold a pencil and giving them some square meals. The individual attention and assurance these children get is something altogether new for most of them and can make all the difference between learning something and not.

Adding in other programs (such as VISTA, alias the Domestic Peace Corps; the Youth Corps; loans to small business and rural aid), the Office of Economic Opportunity says it has by now reached 1,735,000 poor people and expects to reach as many more by the end of this year. OEO is still a minor part of the American welfare state, accounting for only 19 of 174 different federal aid programs from farm supports to social security. But Shriver's statute also lets him "coordinate" other kinds of welfare, which he does at the local level through the CAPs.

The statute also requires CAPs to be run with "maximum feasible participation" of the poor themselves. That is something new in the welfare business. The poor have usually been treated as "clients" — i.e., patronized — by the professional social workers who run this huge industry. OEO at least gives the clients a chance at a voice in it. In Philadelphia the reliefers held elections to choose 12 members of the local poverty program's 30-man policy-making committee. OEO welcomed this step toward what it calls the "deprofessionalization" of welfare. It is Shriver's answer to the charge that OEO is just "an extension of white welfare paternalism." Said one N.A.A.C.P. director, "We have to rescue the anti-poverty program from the social workers' profession as well as from politicians."

If that should happen, the War on Poverty would turn the poor into a more self-conscious political force than they have been before. In Chicago, Mayor Daley expects to funnel $140 million of OEO money through channels friendly to city hall. The poor will be helped but so will the Democratic political structure. In places like Philadelphia, on the other hand, the poor may acquire a separate voice that could lead to profound social change.

OEO has not taken sides on the method of the poor's "participation." It is a nice question whether the poor are better guardians of their own interests than the politicians who are supposed to represent everybody. In any case OEO's war affects only the margins of the poverty problem. If, as OEO reckons, there are 35 million "poor," most of them have more to gain from a general increase in prosperity than from special treatment, which should be aimed at the tougher problem of some eight million who are on relief.

The "war" was oversold from the beginning when L.B.J. declared its objective was "total victory." Yet OEO is already changing many lives for the better and spreading hope into some chronically hopeless corners. It may even give a good shake to the bureaucratic inertia of the established welfare industry which spends 20 or 30 times as much as OEO.[43]

---

[43] "What Poverty 'War' Is About," *Life*, Vol. 59 (July 16, 1965), © Time, Inc., p. 6.

82   Sargent Shriver, optimistic and unperturbed, called the War on Poverty a giant stride forward:

The national war on poverty is now in its eighteenth month. And we are winning that war. Not as rapidly as we would like to but faster than we thought possible when the Office of Economic Opportunity was created by law and charged with attacking chronic poverty on a broad front. . . .

Considering the magnitude of poverty in our society, one might say we have "only scratched the surface." But we feel we have taken that first giant stride that is the most important step of the journey.

During 1965, 2.2 million people in the United States moved out of the poverty class. This reduced the number of people living in dire poverty to 32 million, which is still a shocking number of poor people. But we are making inroads. The next year should bring an even more marked decline. . . .

These first 18 months are indeed just the beginning. But it has been an encouraging start. Our accomplishments in this brief span have not been limited to psychological and spiritual results. The human impact on entrenched poverty has already brought lasting changes and benefits to poor people. Here are some of them:

It has reached more than 3 million poor people directly with jobs and other kinds of services they did not have before.

It has involved more than 5,000 residents of the areas served by the poverty programs on community action boards, fulfilling the congressional requirement for the maximum feasible participation of the poor in choosing the best means for the eradication of poverty in their own localities.

It has enrolled more than 600,000 pre-school children in Head Start classes in less than one year.

It has provided jobs for more than a half-million teenagers through the Neighborhood Youth Corps projects.

It has approved more than 5,000 separate money grants for Community Action Projects, covering every state in the Union and more than one-third of all the counties and more than one-half of the 182 poorest counties.

The Community Action Program has been and will continue to be the main attack in this war on poverty. It alone consumes more than half of all the funds allocated to the OEO. It has now clearly evolved from an experiment into an operational program. A new force working to shape the destiny of millions of the poor, bringing new vitality to community life in every state, Community Action is now a reality in more than 656 cities and towns and the number increases every day. . . .

Community Action can only succeed through the coordinated efforts of both private and public agencies. No one agency has the know-how to tackle all the problems that beset the poor. Effective local anti-poverty action needs the help of the churches, the established welfare agencies, employment offices, settlement houses, schools, youth groups, veterans organizations, labor unions — representatives of all the moving forces in the whole community and, of course, the poor themselves. For the poor should assist in determining what priorities are placed on their needs, which programs will work best and what techniques are most likely to bring the desired results.

I would like to emphasize here that the participation of the poor themselves is one thread that runs through the Community Action plans. Not only is this a requirement of the basic law authorizing the war on poverty, but this provides an important insight which comes most meaningfully to those who have experienced real poverty. . . .

There is a natural inclination to associate the war on poverty with the civil rights revolution. Poverty claims victims in all race groups. Indeed, the majority of the poor in America are white. But one-half of the non-white population is poor and the solutions to the overall problem of poverty are closely related to the lowering of the barriers to equal civil rights. Poverty cannot be substantially eliminated until the galling problems of discrimination are more nearly solved. . . .

What we have planned and the money we have asked for will not solve the poverty problem in 1967 but it will enable us to keep winning this war.

This war on poverty will go on. It will continue to be noisy, visible, often dirty, uncomfortable and sometimes politically unpopular. For grinding poverty itself is not a pretty, neat or nice affair to those afflicted by it. But this war will be won.[44]

The War on Poverty did go on and it was "sometimes politically unpopular." In 1967, Senator Joseph S. Clark (Pennsylvania) chaired a Subcommittee on Employment, Manpower, and Poverty which conducted extensive hearings and compiled voluminous testimony on the War on Poverty. Senator Clark set forth the objectives of the hearings in this opening statement.

The war on poverty program, designed to aid 35 million impoverished Americans and to encourage them to help themselves, is now 2½ years old.

---

[44] Sargent Shriver, "The War on Poverty, A Giant Stride Forward," *The Federationist,* Vol. 73 (April 1966), pp. 6–9.

84   This is an appropriate point, therefore, to review the program's past and assess its potential for the future. It is also an appropriate time to pause and inquire: What has been accomplished by this most comprehensive and potentially meaningful humanitarian crusade, one of the greatest in mankind's history? What are the prospects of victory in this war, and how soon? Or, on the other hand, are we losing this crucial struggle? Do we need to make a new appraisal of the durability of our enemy, poverty, and perhaps of the need for new strategies and tactics?

The war on poverty is officially only in its third year, but actually its origins go back 30 years and started with these words:

> I see millions of families trying to live on incomes so meager that the pall of family disaster hangs over them day by day.
> I see millions whose daily lives in city and on farm continue under conditions labeled indecent by a so-called polite society half a century ago.
> I see millions denied education, recreation, and the opportunity to better their lot and the lot of their children.

Even more important, the Nation's continued prosperity, its economic health, internal strength, and capacity for helping other nations in their struggles for freedom and independence — all these will be affected by the extent to which we succeed in wiping out poverty and unemployment permanently here in America. . . .

There is an urgency in these hearings. The entire poverty program has been in jeopardy in the recent past and it can find itself in jeopardy in the near future. Last year, for example, the war-on-poverty program squeaked through the House of Representatives by a margin of only 39 votes. Thus, if only 20 out of the 435 Congressmen had switched and voted against the program last year, Congress might have adjourned last October without authorizing 1 cent for the Economic Opportunity Act, and there is a new Congress — to a certain extent in the Senate, in the House to a very significant extent. We have to frame in the end legislation which a majority of the Congress will approve and we will be considering, as we move ahead on these hearings, the recommendations of the administration for the funding, the authorization of the program for fiscal 1968.

Those hearings will come later; we want to get a good start, first, on our overall evaluation of how the program is working now.

Even now, in fact, the war on poverty is handicapped by having to operate with far less money than it needs. I speak now only for myself. Congress last fall appropriated $137.5 million less than the $1.75 billion authorized by the 1966 amendments to the Economic Opportunity Act. This slash has crippled many community action programs.

The blighting of whole cities — and the blighting of millions of lives — by poverty can be halted and perhaps halted forever if we can somehow breathe new life into the poverty program and insure the success of the war on poverty, but we cannot breathe new life into a patient which is itself ill and failing. We have to give him some medicine first, fix his physical condition so that he will be able to spend wisely the money which is authorized and appropriated.

This is a war we cannot afford to lose. It is the only war we want to escalate; it's the only war that we must escalate, for our Nation's future and the victory of humanity.[45]

One of the most cogent and knowledgeable analyses of the poverty program in the Clark hearings was presented by Paul N. Ylvisaker, Commissioner of the Department of Community Affairs for the State of New Jersey. Portions of his testimony follow.

Given the complexity of the poverty problem and the absence still of any sure-fire methods for attacking it, the members of this committee may find it difficult to ask the right questions. Certainly we who come before you won't find it easy to give the right answers.

Perhaps it might be most useful to you if I were to start with the hard questions we who are in the business ask ourselves.

I want to make clear immediately, however, that there is one question we do not ask — or answer — with any uncertainty: Should the war against poverty be abandoned, and the Office of Economic Opportunity disbanded?

Clearly not. I would come to the same conclusion even if double the number of present criticisms of the program were proved in fact to be correct.

I think, as historians will some day document, both the program and the Office have already proved vital to this country's survival: To the survival of its ideals at a time when the growing impersonality of life and the sharpening competition for resources could easily replace the Golden Rule with the ethic of "I've got mine, now you get yours"; to the survival of its democratic form of government at a time when disparities threaten to break the ties that bind, and social change threatens to outstrip the capacity of public and private institutions to keep up with it.

In the thick of debate, it is sometimes hard to see through to this long perspective. But a look back — even over the short span of the

---

[45] U. S. Senate, Committee on Labor and Public Welfare, Subcommittee on Employment, Manpower, and Poverty, *Examination of the War on Poverty, Part 1, Hearings on the War on Poverty*, 90th Cong., 1st sess., March 13, 15–17, 1967 (Washington, D. C.: U. S. G.P.O., 1967), pp. 4–5.

86   program's life — may help fix that perspective and judge the program's long-range contribution:

(1) *As a carrier of the Nation's ideals:* The program has jarred the country with its insistent reminders that with one person in five living in disadvantage, America's most noble business remains unfinished. It has attracted the talents of tens of thousands of younger and older citizens, many of them serving at little or no pay, and posted notice that there is still another frontier of public service that remains open and exciting. It has taken the values of participation and self-help into hundreds of communities too isolated, too defeated to believe in them, and roused new chances of their being accepted.

This is a spark far too promising, far too critical for the spirit of our Nation, to be suddenly extinguished by the cold water of momentary impatience or skepticism.

(2) *As a support for the Nation's institutions:* The program has absorbed the punishing initial impact of social discontent that for the first time since the depression in this country has reached the point of mass resistance and violence, and raised the real threat of internal security. It has factored almost insoluble social problems into at least the beginnings of workable programs. It has scouted the no man's land between the public and private sector, and among the fixed jurisdictions of private and public agencies, and begun securing the ground for the kind of cooperative programs and coherent policies that had too long proved impossible in this country to achieve. It has moved the inventiveness of the private sector into the formation of public programs and policy, creating for the first time in many places a public capacity for research and development. It has experimented with new institutional forms at a point when experimentation was sorely needed and none else was in a position or a mood to try. It has prodded, stimulated, and cooperated with labor, business, church, neighborhood, civic, governmental, and professional groups and oriented all of them anew to the point of view of consumer groups and clienteles all too often forgotten.

And the program has done all of this where the need is greatest and the job the toughest: In the local communities of America, block by block, shack by shanty, one by one.

These essential accomplishments of the program, and its fundamental importance to the Nation, cannot be missed by anyone with an eye to see, an ear to hear, and some sense of history.

But it's still fair to ask questions about it, and those of us in the business do. Here are some of them — in every case asked with fervent hope that we can strengthen what has already proved its essential validity and vitality.

Question 1. Is the program being threatened by its successes?

Given the alleged and even some of the admitted shortcomings of the program, this may seem an ironic question to ask. But, at least in my view, it's the most important one, and the most troubling. Let me cite some illustrations.

The program, both nationally and as community action, was designed as a mechanism that could deal creatively with unfamiliar problems. Increasingly, however, the external pressures and the internal tendencies are to deal routinely with familiar solutions. The success with Headstart is a prime example: an experimental beginning that has been legislated into a foregone conclusion.

The pressures and the tendencies are easy to understand: the political risks of continuous trial with even a small margin of error are such that even the most enterprising of legislators and administrators are anxious to avoid them.

Yet anyone living with the problems of poverty knows how demanding they are of new solutions and unorthodox approaches — and now is not the time to freeze even yesterday's innovations into today's standard practice.

The danger becomes more acute when — as under the fiscal stringencies imposed by the war in Vietnam — the standardization of existing programs (such as Headstart) is financed at the expense of the more vital and progressively more limited discretionary funds available for breaking new ground. The importance of such discretionary funds cannot be overemphasized — and it outweighs, at least in my estimation, the political administrative hazards of occasional error and misuse. . . .

Equally disturbing, the pressure toward "success" slowly but surely forces the poverty program away from dealing with the very poor and the not-so-easily reached. As this pressure continues, the program begins "to cream" — to help those most nearly in a position to help themselves — and thus to repeat the history of too many other programs and agencies — a history which brought us to the problem the poverty program was created to face in the first instance, not avoid.

Question 2. Is the creative potential of the program being fully exploited?

Some of us who originally helped design the program may have expected too much of it. Certainly, we expected too much of the limited numbers of people who were available in the short run to staff a program of such complexity on a national scale.

While admitting that, it still is fair to ask whether the creative potential of the program is being fully realized. Again, let me cite an example or two:

88   A national awareness seems to be growing that some form of income maintenance may be necessary — and in fact, may be more effective in alleviating poverty than the service approach we are presently emphasizing. So far, however, we are closer to agreement about the desirability of income maintenance than we are to a feasible way of providing it. Some form of experimentation — carefully devised and geographically selected — seems essential.

Is the poverty program being considered as the vehicle for such experimentation? Shouldn't it be?

Similarly, national sentiment seems to be moving toward broader and more flexible grants and shares of revenues from Federal to State and local governments. Yet the poverty program is tending in the opposite direction: From the general to the categorical, from discretionary to earmarked funds. Should such be the case? . . .

Question 3. Can a national war on poverty be successful without a national strategy, without a larger commitment of resources, and without more powerful weapons?

It has become increasingly apparent that the poverty program is without a coherent set of goals and tactics, and it may well be that none is either possible or presently available.

If not, then experimentation and flexibility should all the more be the order of the day. Yet as indicated above, the legislative and administrative trends are in the opposite direction — seemingly to assume that there is an overall strategy, but not making it readily apparent. As a result, the program suffers the worst of both worlds.

If strategy is missing, so are the resources; we are not working at scale. That much can be said confidently from impressions, experience, and unavoidable fact. Still some facts are needed before judging the scale we would move toward and this would include, I think, a calculation of the dollars it would take if the citizens in poverty were to be raised to the level of income and services essential to a decent standard of living — with that standard also more precisely defined.

Even more important than the amounts of money to be made available, is the more secure commitment of funds over a longer period of time, and I would like to emphasize this: No industry I know of would venture the development of a new product on a sudden-death basis and with uncertain financing. Yet this is what the poverty program has had to do — attempting fundamental reforms and incredibly complex innovations on short-time budgets subject to change without notice. . . .

One wonders, too, whether without more powerful levers than it has to work with, the poverty program can more than slightly alter the conditions which cause poverty in the United States. Part of this question may be the dreams of a Walter Mitty for powers which will never be ours and solutions which have yet to be invented. But the question can't be dismissed that easily. Economic leverages which have contributed so much to the stabilization of the aggregate economy have still to be applied to the problems of urban growth and decline, to the rapid and uncontrolled shifts which produce dangerous unbalances between ghetto and growth areas, and which leave entire cohorts of the population unnoticed and unemployed even though the national indicators show overall prosperity.

In short, the poverty program cannot be effective unless major national policies are moving with rather than against it. . . .

Question 4. Is now the time to integrate the poverty program into the more traditional structure of government and community action?

The answer, I think, depends on whether one is ready to say yes to two other questions: First, is the purpose of integration to expand rather than contract the motivation and influence of the program? Second, does the alternative structure have the same or improved capacity to fulfill the essential purposes of the poverty program?

We in New Jersey have answered yes to these two questions. On March 1, the State's office of economic opportunity — which under the leadership of John Bullitt has won national acclaim for its concepts and performance — became an integral part of a new department of community affairs. It was the intent of Governor Hughes and the Legislature of New Jersey that the influence and effectiveness of the poverty program would grow rather than diminish, that it would gain by its association with the powers and perspective of physical planning, housing, urban renewal, and the variety of other agencies the new department includes — and that these other activities would gain as well.

To strengthen that intent, Governor Hughes has asked for substantial increase in the State's appropriation for the poverty program, doubling the State's support of local CAP discretionary funds — the delicate and difficult political funds we referred to earlier — and also asking for sizable additional sums for the development of employment and other specialized programs.

Our Department also has replicated its OEO pattern of activity by taking an active role in helping develop model city programs among communities of the State.

We are convinced that the model city approach not only is compatible with the poverty program but, when tied in with the poverty program, may represent the next stage in developing its essential purposes.

90   Beyond both these programs, hopefully stands the community with humane objectives, coherent policy, and the capacity to act with alacrity and foresight.

We believe this to be the strategy and purpose underlying Federal development of the model city program — but perhaps the question is one that ought to be explicitly and regularly asked. . . .

Question 5. To what extent should the poverty program become involved with advocacy and agitation?

I wish there were a simple answer to this question. There isn't. Unless it is President Truman's warning to the neophyte, that he'd better not come into the kitchen if he can't stand the heat.

There is no simple answer, but there are some outer boundaries by which one can at least struggle to find a defensible, if not a middle, position.

On the one hand, it is pragmatically clear that public moneys cannot long or exclusively be used to support protests or to fight city hall. . . .

On the other hand, it is equally clear that if one is to fight poverty and find new ways of doing so, he can't always or often be neutral to the status quo.

In short, warring on poverty — like warring in general — is a manly art. One learns by experience; one acquires experience only as one survives but one survives never forgetting and always ready to pay in blood for the cause that brought him into the battle.

And we all have different styles. It is perhaps this chance for diversity that was the poverty program's original, and I hope will be its continuing, contribution. . . .

Question 6. By what standards and criteria should the poverty program be evaluated?

This is another question I wish there were a single answer to. And there isn't. As director of the public affairs program of the Ford Foundation — which made the prototype grants preceding the poverty program — I helped commission a variety of evaluations ranging from one-man travel-look-and-reflect assignments to full-fledged and costly research operations.

All of them pointed up the need for better statistical data and better criteria — and, I would say, better recordkeeping — than has been the case so far.

But sooner or later every one of these evaluations reached the point where one's own feelings and reactions took over. The final judgment is bound to be subjective, and this is the greatest risk involved in the poverty program, for the taxpayer who foots the bill, for the boards and staff who take responsibility, and most of all for the citizen of poverty who dares hope once more that help will come.

Then it becomes a question of values and of motive. And here one has a right to ask, that a program fashioned by the noblest of American values be judged with a purpose that is equally constructive.[46]

---

[46] *Ibid.*, pp. 129–134, 136, 139–143.

Educators: Generators of Culture

The Athenians missed Socrates
when he was gone.

Robert M. Hutchins

3

Today, more than a quarter of all Americans spend most of their waking hours in school buildings, and another quarter spend some time there each day. This is indeed a unique phenomenon in world history. Nothing in any nation's history has won so much support and acclaim as education in America. As former Chancellor Hutchins of the University of Chicago noted three decades ago:

American education has, up to now, been the idol of our people. Ever since the days of the Northwest Ordinance we have thought of it as the foundation of our democracy and bulwark of our liberties. It was expensive, but it was worth it.[1]

We Americans have valued education so highly and have expressed so much faith in it that we tend to watch it very closely and criticize it harshly when we find something wrong with it or when it fails to live up to our expectations. Paradoxically, then, the great trust and faith we have in education often turns schools into centers of controversy.

Yet the sources of the arguments over education are not so easily

[1] Robert M. Hutchins, *No Friendly Voice* (Chicago: University of Chicago Press, 1936), p. 100.

94   spelled out. We are also a people who value experience and practicality over formal learning. The same man will defer to learning in one breath and condemn it in the next.

The common cultural framework consists, first of all, in the widespread "faith in education," noted by foreign observers as characteristic of the American scene for well over a century. Yet there is also a strong tendency to deprecate the value of formal education. Education in general receives tremendous acclaim; education in particular is the object of widespread disaffection, criticism, and low esteem. . . .

The observant traveler finds that in the small American town the public school building dominates the scene much as the cathedral dominates the towns of Latin America and much of Europe. On the other hand, a very large, although not exactly ascertainable, proportion of those Americans who profess enthusiasm for education are giving their support to a symbol or an ideal creed, not to the realities presented by schools. Organized education raises problems — about the pay of teachers, the degree of equality of opportunity for students, the freedom of the teacher to pursue inquiry. Education-in-practice is frequently attacked as "too impractical," or as too expensive, or as corrosive of established beliefs and values, or as an incitement to discontent, or as too much concerned with irrelevancies or frills. Faith in education is not universally shared, nor is it all of one piece. Its components deserve closer examination.[2]

Paradoxically, too, our faith in education and our demands for more of it have made it exceedingly costly; many persons who dislike the high costs will deprecate education, and others will lower the quality to avoid increasing the financial burdens. Most Americans, for example, are not exposed to learned or highly educated instructors. The typical teacher the majority of us face for most of our school lives is a young, unmarried, and unremarkable woman from a middle or lower middle class family. Even in the small colleges where a very large number of Americans still receive all or most of their higher education, the qualifications, training, and skills of many instructors are frequently very low. The educational labor market has recruited heavily from lower and lower middle income levels. This policy has enabled lower income persons to acquire higher incomes, education, and status rather quickly. Indeed, it has made the education system appear to be both democratic and essential to the maintenance of democracy.

Yet, despite our deep-seated belief that education and democracy go together and must be preserved, expansion of our educational plant has raised controversy over quantity, quality, costs, and value received from it.

[2] Robin M. Williams, *American Society: A Sociological Interpretation* (New York: Alfred A. Knopf, 1951), pp. 273–274.

Dr. Hutchins has said it was worth it. Was it? Most Americans agree that it **95** has been, but they do not necessarily agree on many major questions about it: (1) Who is to be taught, and how much? (2) What is to be taught? (3) Who is to teach at which levels and in what areas? (4) How is teaching to be accomplished? (5) Who is to control the system? (6) Who is to provide the services and pay the bills? All such questions are intertwined and cut across each other, but each stimulates issues. In the pages that follow, we shall use some of these questions to provide a focus for the current issues.

Who Is to Be Taught?

Two positions have dominated this issue. According to the program proposed by Thomas Jefferson, the race would be an open one which everyone could enter; but the contestants would be weeded out as the race progressed:

. . . This bill proposes to lay off every county into small districts of five or six miles square, called hundreds, and in each of them to establish a school for teaching reading, writing, and arithmetic. The tutor to be supported by the hundred, and every person in it entitled to send their children three years gratis, and as much longer as they please, paying for it. These schools to be under a visitor who is annually to choose the boy of best genius in the school, of those whose parents are too poor to give them further education, and to send him forward to one of the grammar schools, of which twenty are proposed to be erected in different parts of the country, for teaching Greek, Latin, geography, and the higher branches of numerical arithmetic. Of the boys thus sent in any one year, trial is to be made at the grammar schools one or two years, and the best genius of the whole selected, and continued six years, and the residue dismissed. By this means twenty of the best geniuses will be raked from the rubbish annually, and be instructed, at the public expense, so far as the grammar schools go. At the end of six years' instruction, one-half are to be discontinued (from among whom the grammar schools will probably be supplied with future masters); and the other half, who are to be chosen for the superiority of their parts and disposition, are to be sent and continued three years in the study of such sciences as they shall choose, at William and Mary College, the plan of which is proposed to be enlarged, as will be hereafter explained, and extended to all the useful sciences. The ultimate result of the whole scheme of education would be the teaching all the children of the State reading, writing, and common arithmetic; turning out ten annually, of superior genius, well taught in Greek, Latin, geography, and the higher branches of arithmetic; turning out ten others annually, of still superior parts, who, to those branches of learning, shall have added such of the sciences as their genius shall have

96   led them to; the furnishing to the wealthier part of the people convenient schools at which their children may be educated at their own expense. The general objects of this law are to provide an education adapted to the years, to the capacity, and the condition of every one, and directed to their freedom and happiness. Specific details were not proper for the law.[3]

This competitive selection process contrasts sharply with the policies of the Jacksonian position, which dominates today. In 1965, another president and former teacher, Lyndon B. Johnson, underlined the Jacksonian position in an effort to get his Administration's most important educational goals enacted into law:

I propose that the Eighty-ninth Congress join me in extending the commitment still further. I propose that we declare a national goal of *Full Educational Opportunity.*

Every child must be encouraged to get as much education as he has the ability to take.

We want this not only for his sake — but for the nation's sake.

Nothing matters more to the future of our country: not our military preparedness — for armed might is worthless if we lack the brain power to build a world of peace; not our productive economy — for we cannot sustain growth without trained manpower; not our democratic system of government — for freedom is fragile if citizens are ignorant.

We must demand that our schools increase not only the quantity but the quality of America's education. For we recognize that nuclear age problems cannot be solved with horse-and-buggy learning. The three *R's* of our school system must be supported by the three *T's* — *teachers* who are superior, *techniques* of instruction that are modern, and *thinking* about education which places it first in all our plans and hopes.

Specifically, four major tasks confront us:

to bring better education to millions of disadvantaged youth who need it most;

to put the best educational equipment and ideas and innovations within reach of all students;

to advance the technology of teaching and the training of teachers;

to provide incentives for those who wish to learn at every stage along the road to learning.[4]

---

[3] Thomas Jefferson, *Notes on Virginia* (Washington, D. C.: The Thomas Jefferson Memorial Association of the United States, 1904), pp. 203–204.

[4] U. S. Congress, House of Representatives, *Message from the President of the United States Transmitting the Education Program,* 89th Cong., 1st sess., Document 45 (January 12, 1965), pp. 1–3.

The Jacksonian School insists that everyone should have full opportunity to obtain as much education as he desires and can successfully master. It also insists that this is necessary if democracy is to work. It is necessary if America is to grow, to develop, and to keep pace with the rest of the world. And it is necessary, the Jacksonian School says, if we are to win the war on poverty and the consequences flowing from it. If the underprivileged are to cease being underprivileged and mired in the slough of despondency, they must be given an education. Above all, however, the Jacksonian School believes that to do other than educate everyone to the fullest possible extent — or at least to offer him wide educational opportunities — would foster the development of educational elites, which would defeat the goals of democracy.

Not everyone agrees. Many contend that the Jacksonian ideal is self-defeating.

Under the influence of vocationalism and the fetish-worship of size and numbers, they [the universities] have stuffed out the content of this popular instruction to an incredible volume. No institution could afford to be behind its neighbours in this; all alike had to have a hand in it, for such as did not would go to the wall. It is fair, I think, to say that our institutions have conducted among themselves a grand competition for numbers, on ruinous terms; first, by shifting the burden of education from the student to the instructor, and putting pressure on the instructor to let his students go through as lightly and quickly as possible; and second, by offering a choice among an immense number of subjects that are easily taught, and easily accessible to a very low order of mind.[5]

Nock's was not the first voice to be raised in protest, nor would his be the last. Early in the 1960s, Admiral Hyman Rickover uttered criticisms that brought the proponents of mass education to their feet.

We are plagued with serious deficiencies in virtually every class of occupation that makes demands upon a person's general and specialized education, whether it is at the level of the "learned" professional, the semiprofessional, the skilled craftsman, or the technician. Despite our enormous and costly educational establishment, this country has more functional illiterates than most other industrially advanced nations. . . .

Developing intellectual powers and developing youth with agreeable personalities are not interchangeable accomplishments.[6]

---

[5] A. J. Nock, *The Theory of Education in the United States* (New York: Harcourt, Brace, 1932), p. 81.

[6] Hyman G. Rickover, *American Education — A National Failure* (New York: E. P. Dutton, 1963), pp. 106–119.

98 This controversy stems from the Northwest Ordinance of 1787 and its two successors — the Morrill Act of 1862, which provided for the establishment of the land-grant college system, and the second Morrill Act of 1890, which broadened the role of the national government in education. These acts provided that government lands be set aside and that the proceeds from the lands be used to further the educational benefits offered the American people. Senator Justin Morrill, author of the Land-Grant Act, asserted:

The object of the [land-grant college] laws was not to injure any existing classical institutions, but to reinforce them and bring liberal culture within the reach of a much larger and unprovided for number of the industrial classes in every state. It was designed to largely benefit those at the bottom of the ladder who want to climb up, or those who have some ambition to rise in the world, but are without the means to seek far from home a higher standard of culture. This and more was sought to be accomplished by bringing forward at less cost of time and money, courses of study . . . of greater use in practical affairs . . . [for those] needing higher instruction for the world's business, for industrial pursuits and professions of life.[7]

Yet, as the historian Henry Steele Commager states, the new emphasis on mass education did change the orientation and character of the system.

. . . Even before World War I, the American university came to differ almost in kind, as well as in degree, from its Old World ancestor. I speak here of things that are familiar and hackneyed and need not enlarge upon them: the quantitative character and the vocational character of our colleges and universities. . . . Americans were the first to democratize college and university education. Where, in the Old World, those who go on to the university and those who do not were (and are) pretty sharply distinguished at an early age, Americans permitted no such distinctions. The university was not a thing apart — it was a continuation; it was, indeed, an almost imperceptible merging of one experience into another, not too different. Thus where, in the Old World, the university differed qualitatively from whatever secondary school prepared for it, in the New World the difference was — and is — largely quantitative. This was in part because American college students were (and are) younger than their European cousins; in part because they were intellectually and socially unprepared for scholarly or professional work; in part because Americans believe in the prolongation of youth; in

---

[7] From *Congressional Record*, 46th Cong., 3rd sess., December 15, 1880, p. 147.

part because, like the House of Lords, the American college was not supposed to do anything in particular, and did it very well. In any event the American college like the American secondary school was speedily confronted by the problem of numbers; perhaps inundated is a better verb for our own time. The college and university was called on to do what no British or Continental university was expected to do — to provide some kind of education for almost everybody who wanted it, or who was persuaded that he did, or, in our more affluent society, for almost everyone who could not otherwise be disposed of during the dangerous years from eighteen to twenty-two.

Along with the quantitative task went the vocational. In the early years of the Republic, when the economy was undifferentiated, it was enough for the colleges to prepare young men "for life" as the amiable phrase goes, or, if something more was required, for the ministry and for teaching. But as the American economy became more mature and American society more exacting, more and more tasks were laid upon the only institutions prepared to perform them: the college and the university. Universities were called on to provide not only for the professions, but for many of the other skills needed by a rapidly expanding society; they were called on to supply doctors and lawyers, surveyors and engineers, merchants and bankers, and, in time, farmers, journalists, artists, and athletes.[8]

Intended or not, the extension of educational opportunity to the lower reaches of society did change the character of the educational experience. Unquestionably it changed the content of education and broadened the fare that was placed in front of the prospective student. Thus, once the public policy became "education for the masses," the issues over who should be educated were soon blended or turned into issues over educational content (What is to be taught?).

What Should Be Taught?

Again, it was the two major schools of thought, Jeffersonians and Jacksonians, who took positions on the opposite sides of this question. Very early in our history, Benjamin Franklin clearly defined the philosophy that has underlain the Jeffersonian or traditionalist view.

As to their Studies, it would be well if they could be taught *every Thing* that is useful, and *every Thing* that is ornamental . . .

---

[8] Henry Steele Commager, *Education in a Free Society,* Vol. 2 (Pittsburgh: University of Pittsburgh Press, 1960), pp. 4–5.

100   All should be taught to write a *fair Hand,* and swift, as that is useful to All. And with it may be learnt something of *Drawing,* by Imitation of Prints, and some of the first Principles of Perspective.

Arithmetick, Accounts, and some of the first Principles of *Geometry* and *Astronomy.*

The *English* Language might be taught by Grammar; in which some of our best Writers, as *Tillotson, Addison, Pope, Algernoon Sidney, Cato's Letters,* &c., should be Classicks: the *Stiles* principally to be cultivated, being the *clear* and the *concise.* Reading should also be taught, and pronouncing, properly, distinctly, emphatically; not with an even Tone, which *under-does,* nor a theatrical, which *over-does* Nature.

To form their Stile they should be put on Writing Letters to each other, making Abstracts of what they read; or writing the same Things in their own Words; telling or writing Stories lately read, in their own Expressions. All to be revis'd and corrected by the Tutor, who should give his Reasons, and explain the Force and Import of Words, &c.[9]

Jefferson himself found education to be largely a matter of training and disciplining the mind, as well as a process for instilling morality.

. . . The first stage of this education being the schools of the hundreds, wherein the great mass of the people will receive their instruction, the principal foundations of future order will be laid here. Instead, therefore, of putting the Bible and Testament into the hands of the children at an age when their judgments are not sufficiently matured for religious inquiries, their memories may here be stored with the most useful facts from Grecian, Roman, European and American history. The first elements of morality too may be instilled into their minds; such as, when further developed as their judgments advance in strength, may teach them how to work out their own greatest happiness, by showing them that it does not depend on the condition of life in which chance has placed them, but is always the result of a good conscience, good health, occupation, and freedom in all just pursuits. Those whom either the wealth of their parents or the adoption of the State shall destine to higher degrees of learning, will go on to the grammar schools, which constitute the next stage, there to be instructed in the languages.

. . . The learning of languages being chiefly a work of memory, it seems precisely fitted to the powers of this period, which is long enough,

---

[9] Benjamin Franklin, "Proposals Relating to the Education of Youth in Pennsylvania," as cited in John Hardin Best, *Benjamin Franklin on Education* (New York: Bureau of Publications, Teachers College, Columbia University, 1962), pp. 133–134.

too, for acquiring the most useful languages, ancient and modern. I do not pretend that language is science. It is only an instrument for the attainment of science. But that time is not lost which is employed in providing tools for future operation; more especially as in this case the books put into the hands of the youth for this purpose may be such as will at the same time impress their minds with useful facts and good principles. If this period be suffered to pass in idleness, the mind becomes lethargic and impotent, as would the body it inhabits if unexercised during the same time. The sympathy between body and mind during their rise, progress and decline, is too strict and obvious to endanger our being misled while we reason from the one to the other. As soon as they are of sufficient age, it is supposed they will be sent on from the grammar schools to the university, which constitutes our third and last stage, there to study those sciences which may be adapted to their views. By that part of our plan which prescribes the selection of the youths of genius from among the classes of the poor, we hope to avail the State of those talents which nature has sown as liberally among the poor as the rich, but which perish without use, if not sought for and cultivated. . . .[10]

To this philosophy, Emerson added the proposition that education was to stimulate genius and inspire the imagination as well as to make men into critical thinkers.

Of course there is a portion of reading quite indispensable to a wise man. History and exact science he must learn by laborious reading. Colleges, in like manner, *have their indispensable office — to teach elements. But they can only highly serve us when they aim not to drill, but to create;* when they gather from far every ray of various genius to their hospitable halls, and by the concentrated fires, set the hearts of their youth on flame.[11] (Italics ours)

Following the Civil War, a countervailing philosophy, progressive education, soon overtook the classical and traditionalist view. Much of the leadership and stimulus was supplied by the eminent educational philosopher John Dewey. As he saw it, the obligations of the educational system extended far beyond training and disciplining of the mind. This is the way he put it:

---

[10] Jefferson, *Notes on Virginia*, pp. 204–206.
[11] Ralph Waldo Emerson, "The American Scholar," *Works*, Vol. 4 (New York: Hearst's International Library Company, 1914), pp. 67–68.

I Believe That

All education proceeds by the participation of the individual in the social consciousness of the race. . . .

The only true education comes through the stimulation of the child's powers by the demands of the social situations in which he finds himself. . . .

The school is primarily a social institution. . . .

Education, therefore, is a process of living and not a preparation for future living. . . .

The school must represent life, life as real and vital to the child as that which he carries on in the home, in the neighborhood, or on the playground. . . .

Much of the present education fails because it neglects this fundamental principle of the school as a form of community life. It conceives the school as a place where certain information is to be given, where certain lessons are to be learned, or where certain habits are to be formed. . . .

The true center of correlation on the school subjects is not science, nor literature, nor history, nor geography, but the child's own social activities. . . .

The only way to make the child conscious of his social heritage is to enable him to perform those fundamental types of activity which make civilization what it is. . . . This gives the standard for the place of cooking, sewing, manual training, etc., in the school. . . .

It is the business of everyone interested in education to insist upon the school as the primary and most effective instrument of social progress and reform. . . .[12]

Dewey's philosophy was a natural ally of the Jacksonian and land-grant educational outlook. Everyone should be given an opportunity to acquire an education; and this meant a broad educational curriculum, so that the needs of each student or child could be met. The child was seen as the center of the entire system. Indeed, it was the "whole child" that must be considered. Educators must direct their attention to the child's interests and needs, and they must also introduce him to the society in which he was to live. A school's curriculum should be centered around the child and his needs rather than formal subjects and disciplines. In determining whether a person need study algebra, for example, it was no longer merely a matter of training the mind and judgment. Nor was it a matter of a need to study trigonometry or calculus later. It was a matter of

---

[12] John Dewey, as cited in R. Ulrich, ed., *Three Thousand Years of Educational Wisdom* (Cambridge: Harvard University Press, 1954), pp. 629–638.

whether the child could understand it and use it later in life. Schools, **103**
accordingly, were to be miniatures of society.

The difference that appears when occupations are made the articu-
lating centers of school life is not easy to describe in words; it is a
difference in motive, of spirit and atmosphere. As one enters a busy
kitchen in which a group of children are actively engaged in the preparation of food, the psychological difference, the change from the more or
less passive and inert recipiency and restraint to one of buoyant outgoing
energy, is so obvious as fairly to strike one in the face. Indeed, to those
whose image of the school is rigidly set the change is sure to give a
shock. But the change in the social attitude is equally marked. The mere
absorption of facts and truths is so exclusively individual an affair that it
tends very naturally to pass into selfishness. There is no obvious social
motive for the acquirement of mere learning, there is no clear social gain
in success thereat. Indeed, almost the only measure for success is a competitive one, in the bad sense of that term — a comparison of results in
the recitation or in the examination to see which child has succeeded in
getting ahead of others in storing up, in accumulating the maximum of
information. So thoroughly is this the prevalent atmosphere that for one
child to help another in his task has become a school crime. Where the
school work consists in simply learning lessons, mutual assistance, instead of being the most natural form of cooperation and association,
becomes a clandestine effort to relieve one's neighbor of his proper
duties. Where active work is going on all this is changed. Helping others,
instead of being a form of charity which impoverishes the recipient, is
simply an aid in setting free the powers and furthering the impulse of the
one helped. A spirit of free communication, of interchange of ideas,
suggestions, results, both successes and failures of previous experiences,
becomes the dominating note of the recitation. So far as emulation enters
in, it is in the comparison of individuals, not with regard to the quantity
of information personally absorbed, but with reference to the quality of
work done — the genuine community standard of value. In an informal
but all the more pervasive way, the school life organizes itself on a social
basis.[13]

Across the nation, every elected school board, every school administrator, and every parent-teacher or other educational group faced in one
way or another the political questions and issues raised by Dewey. What
sort of education was to be provided? What would be its content?
Certainly traditionalism did not expire. In fact, it found new life once

---

[13] John Dewey, *The School and Society* (New York: McClure, Phillips, 1899), pp.
20–21.

104   Dewey had introduced the issue during the first quarter of the 20th century. About 1930, a leading spokesman for a "newer traditionalism" emerged at the University of Chicago. He was Chancellor Robert Maynard Hutchins, and his message was a departure from the older positions. He asked first, "What is a university?"

A university is a community of scholars. It is not a kindergarten; it is not a club; it is not a reform school; it is not a political party; it is not an agency of propaganda. A university is a community of scholars.

The scholars who compose that community have been chosen by their predecessors because they are especially competent to study and to teach some branch of knowledge. The greatest university is that in which the largest proportion of these scholars are most competent in their chosen fields.[14]

Hutchins and his supporters contended that by overemphasizing the needs of the learner and his capacity to adjust to society, we neglected equally important obligations of an educational system. Indeed, acquiring social and technical skills, learning how to make a living, and learning how to live a full life were important; but none of this enabled the student to grapple, or cope, with the larger questions he faced as a member of society and as a citizen of a mighty nation and the world. Students must be given a basis on which to meet the larger and ultimate questions; for example, what is the proper role of the United States in the international system of nations? Educational experience must broaden horizons and raise visibility.

Furthermore, as the new traditionalist saw it, educational institutions were obligated to assume leadership in the acquisition of new knowledge and the correction of the old, well-worn information. In fact, schools would cease to be schools if the search for new discoveries (research) were sacrificed for teaching. As Hutchins viewed it, the issue was not research or teaching, but how to reconcile research with teaching.

A university may be a university without doing any teaching. It cannot be one without doing any research. But there is an essential conflict between teaching and research. Education is synthetic and generalized. Research is analytical and detailed. Education is becoming more generalized. Research is becoming more specialized. The college teacher, after intensive training in a minute field of physics, is expected to teach a general course in the natural sciences. The teacher aims at comprehension. But in the natural sciences in this country alone, 20,000 research workers are digging up important new facts and announcing new discoveries, some of which are as yet incomprehensible to their sponsors, to say nothing of those who are compelled to fit them into an

---

[14] Hutchins, *No Friendly Voice*, p. 5.

intelligible scheme which may be communicated to the rising generation.

Nor is this all. American education confronts certain national peculiarities which present almost insoluble problems. A much larger proportion of our population gets into higher education than in any other country on earth. Enormous numbers of students have poured into the colleges and universities since the beginning of the century. Such numbers mean that you must have elaborate machinery; and before you know it, the machinery becomes an end in itself, cherishing its own special sanctity, and standing between you and education like a lattice-work screen, obscuring the vision and blocking the path.[15]

Progressive education, said Hutchins, defeated the most important educational objectives.

It seems likely that this age will be one either of innovation or of extinction. Without innovation the human race may not be extinguished, though the technical means of achieving this result are now available. . . .

The demands of this new world, like the demands of the political community, are first of all demands that we think, and learn. We face them ill-prepared. Our educational system is not unfairly characterized by reference to the course in Family Living in the high school of Lockport, New York. The last unit of this course is called, "How to be Livable, Lovable, and Datable." Or, as bearing more directly on our topic, you may prefer reference to the Resource Guide for English and Social Studies for the 10th Grade, published by the Pasadena schools. It reads as follows: "In the 10th Grade, study is concentrated on the growth of democracy, and especially on the form of government which developed. Such a study should be brief and to the point, in order to allow time for the unit on Driver Education."

. . . It sometimes seems as though we were trying to combine this ideal of no schools at all with the democratic ideal of schools for everybody by having schools without education.[16]

Who Is to Control?

If the student is to be the central focus of the system, according to the Jacksonians and Progressives, where does he stand on the above issues?

---

[15] *Ibid.*, p. 175.

[16] Robert M. Hutchins, "The American Character," *Bulletin* (Santa Barbara: Center for the Study of Democratic Institutions, October 1961), pp. 4–5. Quoted by permission of Dr. Hutchins.

106   One thing is certain — students in recent years have not stood silently on the sidelines.

Student Power

Recent strikes and riots at Berkeley, Columbia, Princeton, and many other educational institutions point up the issues relating to curriculum and control.

Protest has replaced dissent for college students across the country, in the view of many educators.

Not so long ago, thousands of undergraduates gave vent to their opposition to the war in Vietnam, the draft and the manufacture of munitions, napalm and other military articles.

In recent months, however, students have turned their attention to problems closer to home and are challenging the rules under which they study and live at universities, according to reports by correspondents for The New York Times.

They are asking for greater leeway in dormitory hours, a voice in determining course structure, a part in establishing administrative procedures and a role in scholarship selections.

One official of a Southern university, who asked that his name not be used, put it this way last week:

"The students, whether they know it or not, are asking more than a few rule changes. They are challenging an attitude and a system."

The differences between the students and the administrators can seem picayune to observers, but they become major issues once resistance develops. . . .

Their approach varies. At Columbia University, for example, it included blocking the use of some buildings. At the University of Georgia, a sit-in was held in administration offices and an auditorium. At the University of Oregon, there was a three-day sleep-in.

Why do students take these steps? A sophomore at Kentucky State College gave this answer: "We wanted to show the administration that we're tired of its paternalistic treatment."[17]

One of the focal points of student protest is what they call the lack of a "good substantive education." This seemingly implies that they cannot relate to the educational experience and that it lacks relevance for them personally.

---

[17] Martin Ginsberg, "Ferment on the Campus Challenges Rules," *New York Times* (May 6, 1968), p. 50. © 1968 by The New York Times Company. Reprinted by permission.

. . . The lack of "a really good education" is what's bothering college students today — not Viet Nam, sex or the bomb.

That is the central thesis of a recent report on a national conference on student stress, and the key word is "relevance."

"One criterion of a good education," the report said, "is relevance — relevance to the world of modern politics and social ferment, relevance to the human condition in mass society, relevance to the doubts, fears and hopes of thoughtful youth."

The report grew out of a conference held last fall in Warrenton, Va., by representatives of 33 colleges and universities, usually two students and one faculty member from each.[18]

Lack of relevance and inability to relate to the educational experience are serious charges, especially when they are being levelled by the central objects of the educational system — the students. Objections vary from protest about the dictatorial manner in which universities are managed to charges that teacher-student contact is lacking.

A student at Columbia University, who had taken part in the temporary capture of five academic buildings, said last week: "We won't accept punishment because the power of the administration is illegitimate."

Similar rebellion and denial of the legitimacy of the established order flared up in many places.

At Princeton the Students for a Democratic Society, who are in the vanguard of the revolt everywhere, demanded that university president Robert F. Goheen pledge the gradual elimination of the power of the trustees.

In Paris, bloody riots over student power on Friday closed the Sorbonne for the first time since 1253.

The issues varied. Some students, in the old college tradition, tried to get rid of restrictions against girls in dormitories or, as at the University of Georgia, tried to end discrimination against coeds who are not permitted to drink as much or stay out as late as the men.

But more often, the issues were substantial — getting more scholarships for Negroes (at Trinity College), ending discrimination in fraternities (at Colgate University), establishing a Martin Luther King professorship (at the University of Michigan).

Whatever the issues, militancy had grown. The occupation of buildings, along with turning presidents, deans and trustees into hostages, had become the pattern that made the earlier sit-ins seem tame.[19]

---

[18] Geoffrey Gould, "Education Lack Biggest Worry," *Fort Collins Coloradoan* (July 13, 1966), p. 1.

[19] "Crises in Education," *New York Times* (May 5, 1968), p. E3. © 1968 by The New York Times Company. Reprinted by permission.

108   Despite this variance in objectives from one protest to the next, there
is a single strand of discord that runs through them all. That common
strand is the inability of education to relate to what goes on in the outside
world. Harold Howe, the recent U. S. Commissioner of Education, put it
this way:

> . . . the professors are boldly reshaping the world outside the cam-
> pus gates while neglecting to make corresponding changes in the world
> within.[20]

Students themselves say that neither the Dewey nor the Hutchins goal
is being fulfilled. They claim that they are being denied on both counts.
On one hand, students at the University of California, Berkeley, complain
about a curriculum that provides them with nothing they can use in
society when they leave school (a Dewey-type complaint).

> Graduate students and faculty members in the Department of Politi-
> cal Science are squaring off in a bitter dispute over the educational
> objectives of that discipline. . . .
> Behaviorists have been charged with orthodoxy and a tendency to
> eschew change by their opponents, the traditional school of political
> philosophy known as theory.
> Behaviorists have in turn charged that theorists are "pipe dreamers"
> and should be in the philosophy rather than political science department.
> Political behavior has sought to adopt "scientific methods" of prob-
> lem solving, long used in the natural sciences, for the study of human
> behavior, and from this study arrive at an understanding of politics. . . .
> In an attempt to stem the trend toward behaviorism, the Graduate
> Association in Political Science (GAPS) Educational Policy Committee
> recently published its counter-recommendations for curriculum reform
> within the department.
> GAPS called for "not a given model, method, or paradigm, but rather
> a dialogue about the nature of politics and its place in human life."
> Condemning the inability of the various schools to converse, it
> maintained that the student should be acquainted "with the major posi-
> tions which exist within the profession, . . . to have the background and
> perspective to enable him to reflect critically about all such positions." [21]

On the other hand, students elsewhere complain about being left
unprepared to face the larger questions of life (a Hutchins-type
complaint).

---

[20] *New York Times* (May 5, 1968), p. E3.
[21] Dave Graber, "Major Crisis Develops in Political Science Department," *The
Daily Californian* (March 28, 1968), p. 1.

We need relationships with teachers who will help us face the big tough hang-ups. . . . Am I a moral pacifist or a coward? Is abortion a human answer to the problems of unwed motherhood, and what has the pill got to do with my answer? Who am I, where am I, where am I headed, and do I really want to go there? What are the things that make society really worth fighting for?[22]

What then do students propose? The activists propose "student power," or something akin to it, invariably involving a greater voice in educational decision making.

The adult fear comes from the recognition that this generation is light-years removed from the goldfish-swallowers and panty-raiders of the past. Last week's outbreaks were something more than that familiar old spring fever. Today, the advocates of student power want just that — power. "Student power," says Edward Schwartz, 24, the president of the National Student Association and a moderate, "means not simply the ability to influence decisions but the ability to make decisions." Students, he says, should help "co-decide" curriculum, admissions and even university investment policies. At Cornell University just two weekends ago, students decided to do something about the school's investment policies. They asked Cornell to sell nearly $5 million worth of stock in five banks that are members of a consortium that makes loans to South Africa — and the students threatened a lock-in of the university's board of trustees to enforce the demand. (Cornell president James Perkins rejected the plan on the ground that the action would harm Black Africans and close off the narrow channels of U. S. influence still open.)

To the more radical activists, the university administrations and the trustees are merely the on-campus representatives of the real target: The System, U. S. society. Tom Hayden, 28, one of the founders of the Students for a Democratic Society and a participant in the Columbia invasion last week, describes the enemy as the "corrupt and imperial" American hegemony. In the same spirit, a pamphlet supporting the student strike at the University of Minnesota last week declared: "It is time for us to attack the cancer that plagues our society. Too many martyrs are dying in the streets of our cities and in the jungles of Vietnam."[23]

Student power extends beyond the campus to the general social and political system. As one of the authors was told by a Northwestern University activist, "Social scientists keep warning us that we can't es-

---

[22] A student quoted by Geoffrey Gould, *Fort Collins Coloradoan* (July 13, 1966), p. 1.

[23] Copyright, 1968, by *Newsweek* (May 6, 1968), p. 48.

cape bureaucracy or 'beat the system.' If that is so, we had better stop now and get some changes. And if it is true that the few always control the rest of us, as social scientists say, then a few of us can do big things."[24]

What the numbers fail to reflect is the caliber of the students involved. Activists usually turn out to be the brightest and most articulate students — the top 5 or 10 per cent who provide much of the effervescence on campus. They often are the students with the "fire" and the originality — and the grades — that admissions officers so assiduously cultivate in their freshmen classes. . . .

The new student activists are generally restless, impatient with adult "hypocrisy," moralistic, secure economically but uncertain psychologically. Psychologist Keniston calls them "post-modern youth" — the first generation to grow up with "modern" parents. . . .

Part of the success game, it seems, is to jettison ideals, like ballast on a balloon, in order to climb higher. That so many of the young apparently believe they can hold onto their ideals explains a great deal about the activists. Rather than change themselves, they propose to change society. It is an optimistic, even evangelical faith; why bother with politics if no reform or reconstitution is possible?

The activist is also optimistic about the economic future. Affluent or hard-working parents, of course, often provide the logistical support — the tuition, room and board, the clothes, the money for the dentist, the air-travel card and the Pill — for the continued youthful assault on established institutions. The student is in no hurry to marry or to begin a career: technological society will always need his college-honed skills. Political scientist Hacker contrasts the present generation of parents — "people who knew scarcity and were cautious" — with the new generation that has nothing to fear. "They're not worried about keeping their records clean. This independence is startling — it leads to all sorts of actions."

Like all zealots, the activists can be — and often are — exasperating, arrogant and offensive to the conventional wisdom and standards of behavior. They believe in confrontations (sit-ins, teach-ins), in order to sway their opponents by the sheer moral force of their position. This is often accompanied by a certain naïveté. With police, outsiders, reporters, sympathizers and counterdemonstrators milling about Columbia one night last week, a sophomore could say: "This is the beginning of a real dialogue."

At Berkeley in 1964, the dissent was genuinely directed at campus grievances. The university had become so big and impersonal that mass instruction was taking the place of inquiry and the IBM card was

---

[24] From a private interview by Duane W. Hill, May 6, 1968.

becoming the symbol of alienation. Massive protests wracked the campus — the specific issues were university regulations on political activity — and Berkeley has never been quite the same since. Last year a faculty committee concluded that the multiversity was still failing its students.

No university is free of the hazards of bigness. As Harold Howe II, the U. S. Commissioner of Education, reminded the American Association of University Professors last week, many professors are so busy consulting and helping run the world outside the campus gates that they have no time for the student or his problems within the gates. The siege of Morningside Heights is one result of that neglect.[25]

The student, then, seeks greater control over educational policy. He seeks to extend that control to the society at large. Seemingly he would mold policy in a manner that would permit him to relate to the outer world, fulfill his ideals, and clean up the mess his forebears made of their history.

The core of the current student movement consists of youths who are searching for an alternative to established middle-class values. And those who are engaged in this search come from families who are skeptical of conventional values. This tradition of skepticism and humanism is growing, and the families which identify with it are likely to increase rapidly in number.[26]

Glenn Roberts, chairman of the National Student Association's Supervisory Board and an Oberlin student, had this to say:

We, as students, sit in a classroom for four years; we're on a campus, we know people from other campuses, we *know* things about schools. Good administrators seek out students' advice. But the problem is there are very few like that. What we've got to do is find some way of getting our say institutionalized. . . .

There's nothing new about the concept of an educated man. He is someone who knows how to handle problems, how to organize information and use resources and who can deal with situations. [All of this] is stated on the first three pages of every college catalog. But then the first thing they do is give you a rule book and say you can't make any decisions, that they're going to make them for you! If people are going to

[25] Copyright, 1968, by *Newsweek* (May 6, 1968), p. 53.
[26] Richard Flacks, "Student Activists: Result: Not Revolt," reprinted from *Psychology Today* (Copyright, October 1967, Communications/Research/Machines/Inc.), Vol. 1, No. 6 (October 1967), p. 61.

learn, they've got to learn by doing. And universities don't give people the opportunity to *do.*[27]

During 1968, it soon became evident that the forces of student power were forming an axis with the black power movement. The outcome of this coalition was an expansion of student demands beyond those mentioned earlier. During the 1968–69 school year, university students at a number of institutions began to riot, protest, or strike for new as well as old reforms. Especially prominent among these new demands were requests for Afro-American studies programs and courses, the hiring of more Negroes on faculties, and the enrollment of more Negroes in student bodies. Charles V. Hamilton, a black professor and the chairman of political science at Roosevelt University in Chicago, has spoken out bluntly in behalf of the black student-power movement.

Today they're understanding that they are black, and that as they go into these colleges — both black and white colleges — they are not going to be made into little middle-class black Sambos. . . .

But the students today are saying that they are going to be black and skilled at the same time. They're saying that they are going to develop and keep this sense of group responsibility. Somehow or other, whatever skills they acquire, they are going to make sure that these skills can be applied to the development of black America. . . .[28]

Dr. Nathan Hare, a black faculty leader at San Francisco State College, explains some of the reasoning behind the demands:

We blacks at white colleges remain associated with racists physically, although we seek social and psychological independence from their oppression. The Amos 'n' Andy administrators at Negro colleges, by contrast, are physically separated but accommodated to their dependence on white racism as well as the establishment's remote control of their black destiny.

Blacks who teach at white colleges have argued long and bitterly over course content and instructor assignments with white departmental chairmen of various shades of racist persuasions. They would rather have a white moderate professor with a Ph.D. teaching a history sequence starkly barren of blackness than a black man without a degree who has spent long hours in research on the subject. They hold up the white Ph.D.'s publications in learned journals, unmindful of the fact that a

---

[27] Glenn Roberts, as quoted in Jean Briggs, "Student Power," *Glamour* (August 1968), p. 174.

[28] Copyright, 1969, by *Newsweek* (February 10, 1969), pp. 53–54.

black man doing research, for example, on the slavery era in "learned journals" is obliged to footnote slave-master historians or historians acceptable to a society which then condoned black slavery. Second-rate colleges require black persons with functionally white minds, using the Ph.D. as one tested means of policing that policy, yet at the same time, first-class universities think nothing of hiring an unschooled Eric Hoffer, who now holds forth at Berkeley.[29]

Hare's own college president, S. I. Hayakawa, claims that funds are not used to advance the black community educationally or economically when the black students get control of the money. He accuses the leaders of using the moneys for patronage.

Now, the most militant of the black students, with help from white radicals, have taken control of the Associated Students and are turning a considerable portion of these funds to their own uses. Instead of spending the money on activities supported in the past, they devise programs going under labels such as "tutorial help for ghetto youngsters" which are actually a way to ladle out patronage and reward their followers. There has been no satisfactory accounting for expenditures, and the programs themselves are pretty thin and unsupervised.[30]

Black student aims are clear, as *Newsweek* points out:

. . . Black college students — like many white students on campus today — want to claim their own identity. They want a curriculum that will help them better serve their communities. They want institutions that let them control their own lives. But they also have a unique goal; they no longer want to be dark imitations of whites.[31]

There is a question, however, as to how successfully these aims can be fulfilled in the face of the many obstacles which must be overcome before blacks acquire enough of the necessary skills to do the job for their community that Dr. Hamilton foresees. Students may not be demanding the type of education they need to perform the tasks. There has been a dearth of highly educated blacks. Moreover, many of the materials necessary to the educational program that blacks desire have not been plentiful. No one really knows what education for self-identity means.

---

[29] *Ibid.*, p. 56.
[30] S. I. Hayakawa, as quoted in *U. S. News and World Report* (February 24, 1969), p. 38.
[31] Copyright, 1969, by *Newsweek* (February 10, 1969), p. 53.

114   Finally, students, because they have had little opportunity to express
themselves politically, are generally low in political skills.

On the issue of student power the establishment still stands firm. Here
is California Governor Ronald Reagan's rebuttal:

In all the sound and fury at Berkeley one voice is missing. And since
it is the voice of those who built the university and pay the entire cost of
its operation, it's time that the voice was heard.

The people of California provide free access to an education unmatched anywhere in the world. They have a right to lay down rules and
a code of conduct for those who accept that gift.

No one is compelled to attend the university. Those who do attend
school should accept and obey the prescribed rules or get out.[32]

Faculty Power vs. Administrative Power

It has long been a scholastic ideal that schools are communities of
scholars run by the scholars. In theory, this principle is extolled and
followed in form by American school administrators; in actual practice, it
is simply not the case, as the historian Max Savelle notes:

It is a curious anomaly that in the United States, which thinks of
itself as the most democratic country in the world, the universities, which
should be living laboratories of democracy, are probably the most undemocratic in the world.

The norm in their administrative organization is something like this:
State universities usually provide in their charter that the governor of the
state shall appoint the board of regents or trustees; this board appoints
the president, who is the administrative head of the institution. The
regents may or may not consult the faculty with regard to this appointment; legally, in most cases, they are not required to do so. Legally, their
power over the university and all its concerns is absolute. The president,
once appointed, is answerable only to them. A wise president will consult
with his faculty on the problems relative to his administration of the
university's affairs, but he is not required by law to do so, being responsible only to the regents. So far as the faculty is concerned, he has the
authority and the power, given the approval of the regents, to act with
complete *irresponsibility*.

Among privately endowed institutions, it is usual for a board of
trustees to be a self-perpetuating closed corporation; when one member
dies or resigns, the remaining members of the board elect someone to
take his place. Otherwise, however, the situation is much the same;

---

[32] Gov. Ronald Reagan, as quoted in the *Denver Post* (December 1, 1966), p. 1.

customarily the president of a privately endowed college or university has no legally established responsibility to the faculty; his responsibility is to the board of trustees.

This institutional arrangement may be said to rest upon a "businessman's concept" of what a university is and should be. The university is thought of as a sort of factory; the president is the manager of the factory, and his word is absolute, requiring only the approval of his board of directors (regents). According to this concept the members of the faculty are hired hands. The manager of the factory may hire or fire at will; the labor force (the faculty) is not organized as a union. The fate of the university is in the hands of one man. All he has to do is convince the regents that they should support him; and if the regents are businessmen, with the "businessman's concept" of the university, they usually will.[33]

Administrators exist primarily to manage, to maintain stability and order, and to determine and oversee financing. There is no issue about the basic functions, but there is a battery of issues about the consequences of the functions. It is frequently claimed that administrative controls distort and even destroy the primary functions of a university. Students themselves have been among the first to notice this.

We are distressed because in the multiversity a critical and creative understanding of culture and self becomes more and more difficult. The multiversity has improved the packaging and promotion of education; its content has become depersonalized and fragmented. Narrowly specialized courses and research projects multiply, but opportunities for examining questions that matter in the living of a human life are fewer and fewer. . . .

The industrialization of the university means that knowledge has become a commodity, something detached from those who produced it and something which can be sold in the market. Education is no longer a process whereby a student learns to use his intellect in a dialogue between his inner self and the outer world. . . .

Between 1959 and 1964 private foundations poured $100,000,000 into political science departments in this country ($12,000,000 to U. C.). Somit and Tanenhaus' account of the allocation of both these and federal funds indicates that the term "behavioralism" has become the key to the big money: "Widespread knowledge of this situation, it is safe to say, did not adversely affect conversions to the faith. Even those who had private reservations about behavioralism sometimes found it possible, when

---

[33] Max Savelle, "Democratic Government of the State University — A Proposal," *AAUP Bulletin,* Vol. 43 (June 1956), pp. 323–324.

research grants hung in the balance, to render at least lip service to the new creed."

The influx of the big money has brought about a production boom. . . .

As the industrial ideal spread, industrial values have been translated into academic language. Thus interchangeability, now called "intersubjective transmissibility," has become the test for the usefulness of a piece of knowledge. Routinization and depersonalization of skills has become the ideal. . . .[34]

Money is the telling difference. An administrator can be expected to place a high priority on money and reward the teacher who adds to the school's income. Andrew Hacker argues that this defeats the most important function of schools — teaching.

At this year's meeting of my professional association the corridors buzzed with loud boasts of new professorial privileges and perquisites. Some told of all-salaries-paid sabbaticals every three years instead of the traditional seven; others spoke of "summer money" that automatically raises their already not inconsiderable incomes. A favorite was the easy access to large research projects, with the fringe benefits of research assistants, streamlined equipment, and jet travel to exotic places. But the trump card in this one-upping game was invariably held by the man able to exclaim: "And I don't have to teach undergraduates anymore!"

What is surprising — and, to some, disturbing — is how many professors are looking forward to when they, too, will be able to restrict their teaching to graduate students. Some have already arrived at this exalted status and more are graduating to it every year. Considering the shortage of academic personnel and the competition among universities to stud their faculties with stars, what professors want, professors are increasingly getting.

Those most affected are, of course, the students. A majority of American undergraduates now attend universities rather than colleges. They are enrolled at institutions offering graduate as well as undergraduate degrees. The consequences of this relatively recent development are just beginning to be felt.[35]

Of greatest consequence, however, is the impact on the faculty's treasured academic freedom. Three decades ago, Chancellor Hutchins noted:

---

[34] *Political Science at Berkeley,* Student pamphlet, 1968, pp. 1–8.

[35] Andrew Hacker, "Who Wants to Teach Undergraduates?" *Saturday Review,* Vol. 49 (December 17, 1966), p. 80. Copyright Saturday Review, Inc., 1966.

To a certain extent the ability of a university to attract the best scholars depends on the salaries it can pay. To a certain extent it depends on the facilities, the libraries, and laboratories it can offer. But great scholars have been known to sacrifice both salaries and facilities for the sake of the one thing that is indispensable to their calling — and that is freedom.

Freedom of inquiry, freedom of discussion, and freedom of teaching — without these a university cannot exist. Without these a university becomes a political party or an agency of propaganda. It ceases to be a university. The university exists only to find and to communicate the truth. If it cannot do that, it is no longer a university.

Socrates used to say that the one thing he knew positively was that we were under a duty to inquire. Inquiry involves still, as it did with Socrates, the discussion of all important problems and of all points of view. You will even find Socrates discussing communism in the *Republic* of Plato. The charge upon which Socrates was executed was the same that is now often hurled at our own educators: he was accused of corrupting the youth. The scholars of America are attempting in their humble way to follow the profession of Socrates. *Some people talk as though they would like to visit upon these scholars the fate which Socrates suffered. Such people should be reminded that the Athenians missed Socrates when he was gone.*[36] (Italics ours)

Broadly speaking, American scholars have generally insisted that academic freedom include the following features: (1) the freedom to investigate any topic, subject, or phenomenon without infringement; (2) similar freedom of expression, especially with regard to matters within the person's specialty or range of competence; (3) freedom of speculation and thought. In 1966 Richard M. Nixon asserted at the University of California, Berkeley, that such freedoms are really not freedoms unless exercised with self-restraint.

This brings me to the paradox that confronts the academic community today and which presents all of us with real problems of choice. The power of the scholar in the United States has never been greater. Yet that enormous power of the academic community, which is the product of academic freedom, potentially threatens academic freedom.

Let us remember that we are considering here a freedom which derives its protection not from the law but from the respect and confidence the academic institution enjoys in the community in which it is located. Members of the academic community have a special status in our society for two reasons. One, a determination by society that the

---

[36] Robert M. Hutchins, *No Friendly Voice*, pp. 5–6.

118   recipient must enjoy a maximum freedom of expression to serve society effectively; and, two, a respect by society for the judgment of the particular group, a confidence on the part of society that the privilege will not be seriously abused.

I believe that academic freedom in the United States is now so strongly supported that it will never be destroyed by its enemies — but it may be endangered by those who claim to be its friends.

Teachers must of course be free to take positions on all issues. But the position they hold in our society requires them to act with self-restraint. . . .

I believe also that academic freedom should protect the right of a professor or student to advocate marxism, socialism, communism, or any other minority viewpoint provided he does so openly and is not in violation of the law of the land.

But there is a far more difficult question: Should academic freedom protect a professor when he uses the forum of a state university to welcome victory for the enemy in a war in which the United States is engaged? I know that in answering "no" to that question I am expressing disagreement with many of the faculty and graduating class of this institution. However, since academic freedom includes the right to espouse an unpopular cause, let me tell you how I reached this strongly held conviction.

To those who would welcome victory for the enemy I would respectfully suggest that they do not know the enemy.

I have seen what the enemy has done to freedom in the third of the world which communism now occupies.

I am convinced that victory for the enemy in South Vietnam will mean not only the blotting out of freedom for fifteen million South Vietnamese but an immense escalation of the danger of World War III. I am convinced that history will record that what many believe to be a "quicksand war" was the war that had to be fought to prevent World War III.

In the light of these convictions I could not take what would have been the much more expedient course of refusing to comment on an issue of such importance to the freedom and security of the nation. I believe that any teacher who uses the forum of a university to proclaim that he welcomes victory for the enemy in a shooting war crosses the line between liberty and license. If we are to defend academic freedom from encroachment we must also defend it from its own excesses.[37]

Even liberal academicians tend to view academic freedom as something that necessitates restraint.

---

[37] Richard M. Nixon, "Academic Freedom," *Vital Speeches,* Vol. 32 (June 15, 1966), p. 551.

Dr. Albert Lepawsky of the University of California, on whose main campus at Berkeley the students' protest movement really got started, attacks the pressure tactics being employed by many students and not a few professors and their increasing use of the university "as a sanctuary from which to project upon society their own political preferences" under the guise of academic freedom.

Academic freedom, says Lepawsky, means more than the guarantee of intellectual integrity or political liberty.

It also includes "the freedom of members of the academic community to carry on their work unhampered by colleagues and students who engage in political activity and exert pressures to the point of disturbing the teaching, research and other relevant functions of the university."

Unless colleges have the power to discipline themselves, he warns, to fire teachers and expel students who show by their intolerant behavior that they lack the qualities required for membership in the academic community, the result will be to "downgrade academic standards to the lowest common denominator of political conduct in our society."

Where does freedom end and anarchy begin? This is a question apparently facing not only the emerging nations of the world but the emerging university in America as well.[38]

Federal vs. State Control

The control issue has consumed a great deal of public and official attention; yet the student power advocates seemingly could not care less. It centers on the financial support that Congress gives state and local schools. The issue is an old one, extending back in history to the Northwest Ordinance of 1787 and the Morrill Acts of 1862 and 1890.

Generally those who oppose such support entertain the basic premise that "he who pays the piper calls the tune." This is apparent in the terse letter of opposition to the National Defense Education Act which Senators Barry Goldwater and John Tower (Texas) entered in the record.

When the National Defense Education Act was favorably reported in 1958 from the Committee on Labor and Public Welfare, Senator Goldwater in his minority views made the following comment:

> This bill and the foregoing remarks of the majority remind me of an old Arabian proverb: "If the camel once gets his nose in the tent, his body will soon follow."
> If adopted, the legislation will mark the inception of aid, supervision, and ultimately control of education in this country by Federal authorities.

---

[38] Don Oakley, "Academic Freedom or Political Enclave?" *Fort Collins Coloradoan* (February 2, 1966), p. 24.

120   This prediction was confirmed in 1961 when the National Defense Education Act was further extended and its substantive provisions expanded in important respects. At that time we submitted our minority views and the position we took then is unqualifiedly relevant to the present committee bill which carries this expansion process even further. We quote from the opening paragraphs of those minority views:

> We oppose the bill reported by the committee amending the National Defense Education Act primarily because it constitutes a giant step in the direction of Federal control of our educational system. . . .

In conclusion we would like to say that all forms of financial assistance for education by the Central Government would be rendered superfluous if the Congress were to adopt a program of tax credits, as recommended in the Republican platform of 1964, one form of which was narrowly rejected by the Senate in the last session. We are optimistic that the tax credit approach will ultimately prevail.[39]

Earlier, Senator Harry Byrd of Virginia spoke eloquently for the "stock and trade" conservative view.

. . . There is not a single federal subsidy today which is not controlled by the Federal Government so far as the manner and method of its expenditure are concerned. . . . It is impossible to give any guaranty to the states that the expenditure of these funds will not be controlled by the Federal Government. When such a guaranty is given, it is not worth the paper it is written on. No such guaranty can be given. . . . It is obviously true that control follows the purse. Everybody knows that to be so. Federal bureaus may not control it the first year or the second year; they may not control certain other appropriations to such a point that one would hear complaint about it, but regulations are established by these bureaus, they are legal, and if not obeyed, the intended recipients do not get the money. . . . When local education is assumed by the Federal Government as a federal responsibility, then the states, which have been doing so much to improve their school systems, will say, "Let the Federal Government do it."[40]

Interestingly, another strong conservative, Senator Robert A. Taft of Ohio, rejected the Goldwater-Tower position sixteen years before they collaborated in their resounding dissent.

---

[39] *Congressional Record,* Vol. 110 (August 1, 1964), pp. 17,699–17,700.
[40] Cited in *Federal Role in Education* (Washington, D. C.: Congressional Quarterly Service, 1965), p. 20.

. . . The balance of power is involved. I simply decided that the danger of federal control can be guarded against. We can stand on the principle of not permitting federal control. We have already established throughout the United States many avenues of federal aid to states, and there is no possibility of getting away from it in many fields. If we want to defend against federal control, the thing to do is to refuse federal control, to draft our law so there is no federal control, as the pending bill is drafted. I would rather stand on that ground than stand on the ground . . . that the Federal Government has no concern with education, has no concern with housing, has no concern with health; that those are matters solely for the states to take care of, and if there are poor states which are unable to give [their] citizens what they need, why that is too bad; those people cannot have equal opportunity. I do not think that is a defensible position. I think it is much easier and sounder to stand on the ground that we should provide federal aid, and we are interested in the people of the states, but that we will stand against any effort to extend federal control.[41]

At another juncture in the same year (1948), Taft also said:

. . . Four years ago, I opposed the bill on this subject; but in the course of that debate it became so apparent that many children in the United States were left without education, and then it became apparent upon further study, that that was not the fault, necessarily, of the states where they lived, but rather the financial abilities of the states, that I could see no way of meeting the condition which now exists regarding illiteracy in the United States and lack of education in the United States without some federal assistance, particularly for those states which are considerably below the average wealth of the United States. . . . I quite agree that the primary obligation to educating children is in the states and local communities. Under our constitutional form of government, they have the primary obligation. I think the federal obligation is a secondary one. It is one to back up the states, if I may use that expression, where it is necessary to back up the states. . . . I have not been able to find that the Congress of the United States, when appealed to on a major question, is prepared to refuse to act.[42]

Senator Eugene Milliken of Colorado, however, took a familiar position in opposition to Taft.

---

[41] *Ibid.*
[42] *Ibid.*, p. 21.

122   . . . I suggest that (the bill) which would put money into all these states regardless of their ability to educate their own children, tends toward a very dangerous precedent, for it can be applied in any number of fields and ultimately it will have the effect of making the states mere administrative agencies of the Federal Government. . . . I favor federal aid to those states which, out of their own resources are unable to provide themselves with minimum standards of education. . . . I cannot see any reason for putting federal aid in the states which have already met their burdens.[43]

Senator Harry Byrd stressed yet another point in his opposition to federal aid — the strain on the taxpayer.

. . . The pending bill, if enacted, will start a new federal subsidy to the states. . . . It opens up a Pandora's box of federal spending which will increase as the years go on and will, I predict, be greater in time than the grand total of all the present federal subsidies to the states. . . . Let us never forget that the strength of America is in a strong and virile system of free enterprise, which is not possible if the taxes are so burdensome as to destroy the initiative and the prospect of profit of those from whose business operations the Government must obtain its funds to pay its costs. . . . This is certainly not a time to expand federal expenditures in a new field, but it is a time to meet the financial strain of the days to come.[44]

A few statistics would not be out of place in all this argumentation. Of the total education bill, both private and public, in 1935 the national government paid for 5.3 percent. By 1950 that figure had risen to 10.2 percent, but by 1964 it had dropped to 7.3 percent. During all of the years, the major costs, around 70–75 percent, were borne by state governments. Even the private sector of the economy supports more education than the national government.[45]

John Fischer of Teachers College, Columbia University, points to the faulty reasoning of the opponents of school aid and the great need for financial support if educational opportunity is to be equalized.

We had better avoid . . . the error of oversimplifying either the merits of the grass roots or the evils of central control. Some of the most arbitrary and shortsighted practices to be found in American schools are

---

[43] *Ibid.*
[44] *Ibid.*
[45] *Ibid.*, p. 2.

the fruit of local action. And some of the best things that have ever happened to American students have come by Act of Congress and through the administrations of the Federal Government. G.I. educational benefits were not evil because they originated in Washington, and a child whose educational growth is stunted by a stupid teacher is no better off because the board who hired her to pay a political debt was elected by the townspeople. There are American cities with serious school problems whose difficulties are viewed more sympathetically in Washington than in their own city halls and state houses. The issue of local versus national control is no simple choice between good and evil. . . .

Three things at least are necessary if local control of schools is to be effective. The first two are: acceptance at the local level of responsibility for creating and maintaining good schools; and leadership from local board members, administrators, teachers, and citizens.

The third necessity is adequate financial support. Only in rare instances, however, can this support be produced entirely within the local district. The arguments in favor of local control are based mainly on the belief that those nearest to the schools will make the wisest decisions about them. We assume that the wisdom to make such decisions is widely distributed among the people. But we do not claim, because it is not true, that the financial strength to support good schools is equally available. Yet we repeatedly say that a child's access to education should not be limited by the poverty of the place in which he happens to be living. . . .

The implication is obvious. If those who hold authority over education at the state level actually believe in local control, they will, if they are honest and consistent, see that enough funds are allocated to local districts to place effective control in the hands of local boards. When they fail to do this, their neglect must signify either disagreement with the principle or ignorance of the only way it can be made to work.

At the national level, the logic is identical. That some of our states are unable to assure their children schools equal to the average of the nation is now so clear as to require no further proof. If we believe in equal opportunity for all American children, and we want to attain this equality within a system of state and local control, we must provide through federal means the propelling power — the money — when it is not sufficiently available within state lines.[46]

---

[46] John H. Fischer, "The Role of Education in National Goals," in Paul R. Hanna, ed., *Education: An Instrument of National Goals* (New York: McGraw-Hill, 1962), pp. 206–207.

Public vs. Private Control and
                                    Separation of Church and State

The American school system is only partially public. Private schools abound at all levels — primary, secondary, and college. But the proper relationship between public and private schools is an issue of formidable proportions. For example, the U. S. Constitution says, "Congress shall make no law respecting the establishment of religion, or prohibiting the free exercise thereof." Originally, this was interpreted by the Supreme Court of the United States as applying to Congress and national officials but not to state governments. In the 1930s, the Court adopted the view that the rule also applied to the states; and in 1943, the Court ruled that states could not compel a school child to salute the flag against his religious convictions.[47] If a child did not have to salute the flag, could he be compelled to participate in religious activities, even of his own or his parents' choice, at taxpayers' expense? Could parochial schools which provided religious instruction be supported by state funds?

Two fundamental questions have been at the center of the controversy. First, since private schools absorb many students and thereby reduce the tax load, should they not receive aid like public schools? Second, in view of the constitutional standard of separation of church and state, could religious instruction and prayer be made a standard item in the public schools?

In reply to the first question, the Court in 1947 upheld a New Jersey statute allowing local school districts to reimburse parents for bus transportation costs to Catholic schools.[48] But one year later, the Court said it was constitutionally improper for schools to provide students with released-time to attend religious classes on public property.[49] In 1952 the Court again said that released-time programs were improper, except when instruction was conducted outside school buildings and off state property.[50] The Court seemed to be developing one doctrine concerning religious instruction in public schools and another for tax support of parochial education. Controversies raged on both sides of the issues, and the dispute became even sharper when the Court invalidated a New York Board of Regents nondenominational prayer.[51]

State and federal support for parochial education was already an issue of great moment by the time the Court had ruled in the New York prayer case. Not all religious groups reacted favorably to the idea that tax support of parochial functions was proper, as is shown by the comments of Rabbi Richard Hirsh of the Union of American Hebrew Congregations in testimony before a Senate Education Subcommittee.

In 1960, the Central Conference of American Rabbis declared:

---

[47] *West Virginia* v. *Barnette,* 319 U. S. 624 (1943).
[48] *Everson* v. *Board of Education,* 330 U. S. 1 (1947).
[49] *McCollum* v. *Board of Education,* 333 U. S. 203 (1948).
[50] *Zorach* v. *Clauson,* 343 U. S. 306 (1952).
[51] *Engel* v. *Vitale,* 370 U. S. 421 (1962).

We believe that it is the obligation of the Federal Government, where the States are unable to do so, to provide the funds which will put our educational system on a sound basis. . . . It is our duty as teachers of spiritual values to help arouse public spirit in the citizens of our respective communities to vote the tax funds to meet the legitimate needs of the schools.

A resolution passed by the general assembly of the Union of American Hebrew Congregations in November 1963 states:

In keeping with our Jewish tradition, which declares study to be a divine command, we maintain that education is not only a personal or a local, but a national problem. . . . Because public education is essential to the preservation of democracy, we support the enactment of legislation offering more extensive Federal assistance. . . .

Our traditional Jewish love of learning has impelled us to create, as our own religious responsibility, a vast network of private educational institutions for the perpetuation of Jewish religious values. We believe that private education has a vital and necessary role in our society. At the same time, we are firmly committed to our public school system as the bulwark for preserving America's democratic heritage and advancing its civilization.

It has been most disturbing to hear proponents of this bill in its present form speak of the great partnership that it fosters between public and private schools. Public and sectarian schools can no more be considered partners than can church and state be partners. By tending to equate public and church schools in the eyes of the law as equally entitled to public support, this bill will greatly stimulate the creation of separate parochial school systems in every denomination. The temptation to sup at the trough is not one to which most religious denominations have shown any exceptional resistance. As a network of parochial schools mushroom, support for public schools would constantly be diluted.

Another factor largely overlooked in the consideration of this legislation is the relationship between segregation of a racial and economic character — and private education. America is now striving to achieve two great objectives — equal rights and opportunities for racial minorities, and higher quality of living for the economically and culturally deprived. It should be frankly stated that many of the parents who now send their children to private and parochial schools do so in order to remove the children from the neighborhood public schools which have heavy concentrations of nonwhite minority groups.

Since title VI of the Civil Rights Act of 1964 does not preclude religious discrimination, there would be a great temptation for parents in the South and in the major urban areas of the North to send their children to already existing or newly established sectarian schools — and thereby to avoid the integrated schools, or schools with large numbers of economically and culturally deprived children. Under present conditions, parents have the right, if they so desire, to provide a private education for their children at their own expense; but they should not have the right to a private education in a segregated school at public expense. How ironic it would be. . . .[52]

But U. S. Representative Lester Wolff of New York thought otherwise:

The first amendment to the Constitution of the United States declares in part:

> *Congress shall make no law respecting an establishment of religion, or prohibiting the free exercise thereof.*

This prohibition is not the outgrowth of an antireligious conviction on the part of our Founding Fathers nor a denial of the place of religion in the individual lives of our citizens or, in truth, in our national life. It represents, rather, a recognition of the necessity for Government neutrality in religious matters.

The Supreme Court has never been called upon to rule on the constitutionality of an act of Congress which establishes a program of assistance for the education of pupils in sectarian and public schools. There are, however, several opinions of the Supreme Court which have involved somewhat similar issues.

The case of *Cochran* v. *Board of Education* (281 U. S. 370), decided in 1930, involved a statute of the State of Louisiana under which money was appropriated for textbooks for schools of the State. The constitutionality of this law was challenged on the grounds that because schoolbooks were made available to private schools, including sectarian schools, property — tax money — had been taken by the State for private purposes in violation of the 14th amendment.

The Supreme Court upheld the Louisiana statute on the grounds that the schoolchildren and the State were the beneficiaries of the financial aid. The Supreme Court decision was premised on an important distinction. The distinction between the school as beneficiary and the child as beneficiary.

---

[52] U. S. Senate, Committee on Labor and Public Welfare, Subcommittee on Education, Hearings on the *Elementary and Secondary Education Act of 1965*, 89th Cong., 1st sess. (February 11, 1965), pp. 3120–312.

The appropriations were made for the specific purpose of pur- **127**
chasing schoolbooks for the use of the schoolchildren of the State,
free of cost to them. It was for their benefit and the resulting
benefit to the State that the appropriations were made. True, these
children attend some school, public or private, the latter, sectarian
or nonsectarian, and that the books are to be furnished them for
their use, free of cost, whichever they attend. The schools, how-
ever, are not the beneficiaries of these appropriations. They obtain
nothing from them nor are they relieved of a single obligation be-
cause of them.

Another relevant case is *Everson* v. *Board of Education* (330 U. S. 1)
decided in 1947 by the U. S. Supreme Court. This case involved a New
Jersey statute which authorized district boards of education to make
contracts for the transportation of children to and from all schools except
those operated for profit. Under this authority, a school board authorized
reimbursement to parents for fares which they paid for the transportation for their children to public or private schools.

Justice Hugo Black, speaking for the Court, referred to Thomas
Jefferson's remark that the first amendment creates a "wall of separation"
between church and state and declared that this wall must be kept high
and impregnable. Justice Black reasoned that the provision of funds for
school bus transportation for students in sectarian schools was not an aid
to religion. It is an aid to the students; the program was obviously
intended to benefit the child, not to aid or to establish a religion.

The first amendment was not intended to cut off church schools
"from those services so separated and so indisputably marked off from
the religious function." . . .

Under the GI bill a plan was provided whereby veterans received
Federal aid to continue their educations whether they attended a public
or private school. No Federal control over curriculum or infringement on
the separation of church-state postulate manifested itself. No one now
would question the utility and the worth to the Nation of this program.
Would anyone question the inuring benefits to the country secured by
Federal Government grants to universities for research even though two
of the largest grants went to Notre Dame and Yeshiva Universities? Here
we have two distinguished universities who certainly have not been
impeded by Federal regulation of their curriculum or other aspects of
school administration.

The Federal Government has also extended tax privileges to those
people who donate money to religious organizations by way of an
exemption. . . .[53]

---

[53] *Congressional Record* (March 24, 1965), pp. 5,600–5,602.

128   Professor Ernest Van Den Haag added the following supportive argument:

In one form or another, we all support public education with our taxes. If we have no offspring, we are supposed to benefit nonetheless: other people's children might be more of a nuisance if not kept in school; and there is always the chance that they might learn something useful to us there. (A tenuous justification, but let it go.) Those of us, however, who send our children to private schools pay for the public school they do not use and also for their private school. Is that fair?

Citizens often are taxed for services they spurn: pacifists must pay taxes to support armies they detest, criminals pay to support the police they would rather do without; we are taxed for a bridge even though we prefer to sail across in our own boat. Yet often we can avoid burdening those who do not use the service offered: some taxes are levied only on users or beneficiaries — for instance, amusement or sewer taxes, and various tolls and fees. It would be technically possible to reimburse, or not to tax for the support of public schools, those who prefer private ones; or, we could subsidize private schools at the rate public schools are subsidized — the effect would be almost the same as that of reimbursement.[54]

The second great set of issues, those concerning school prayer and religious instruction, stirred tempers to an even higher pitch. After the Court rejected the New York Regents prayer — "Almighty God, we acknowledge our dependence upon Thee, and we beg Thy blessings upon us, our parents, our teachers, and our country" — it declared invalid Biblical readings in the Pennsylvania public schools and recitation of the Lord's Prayer in the Maryland public school system.[55]

Responses were harsh and certain. August E. Johansen, a Republican Congressman from Michigan, said, "The upshot seems to be: Obscenity, yes; prayer, no." Democratic Senator James O. Eastland of Mississippi called it judicial tyranny; and Democratic Representative Robert L. F. Sikes of Florida said, "If the Supreme Court were openly in league with the cause of Communism, they could scarcely advance it more." Another Democratic Congressman, George Andrews of Alabama, stated, "They have put the Negroes in the schools, and now they've driven God out." A most interesting comment came from the famous evangelist, the Reverend Dr. Billy Graham, who said, ". . . The framers of the Constitution meant we were

---

[54] Ernest Van Den Haag, "Federal Aid to Parochial Schools," *Commentary* (June 1961), p. 58.

[55] *School District* v. *Schempp*, 374 U. S. 203 (1963).

to have freedom *of* religion — not freedom *from* religion." In Maryland, Madalyn Murray, who raised all the hackles by challenging the state laws providing for prayer, was asked by *Playboy* magazine why she did it.

I was shamed into it by my son, Bill, who came to me in 1960 — he was 14 then — and said: "Mother, you've been professing that you're an atheist for a long time now. Well, I don't believe in God either, but every day in school I'm forced to say prayers, and I feel like a hypocrite. Why should I be compelled to betray my beliefs?" I couldn't answer him. He quoted the old parable to me: "It is not by their words, but by their deeds that ye shall know them" — pointing out that if I was a true atheist, I would not permit the public schools of America to force him to read the Bible and say prayers against his will. He was right. Words divorced from action supporting them are meaningless and hypocritical. . . ."[56]

Mrs. Murray's action and her court victory brought a loud and clear response. Consider the following words from the Roman Catholic president of Gonzaga University:

We have Mrs. Murray, that truculent atheist from Maryland with her bawling child, effecting through her single stance a reversal of a whole long tradition of reverence, a sane and peaceful acceptance of the Christian environment of the country. Rudolph the Red Nosed Reindeer and Jingle Bells are constitutional. Silent Night and O Little Town of Bethlehem upset civil order. No longer may many public schools have baccalaureate services. Campaigns are being launched to take In God We Trust from our coins. So, in the name of what I call tenuous legalism, hallowed customs are declared wrong. And these are not customs like using a hanky to blow one's nose. They are so old and accepted that even primitives did them honor.

Let a public school bus, bought from common funds, stop on a country road on a cold day to pick up a child going to a Lutheran or a Catholic school and there is bloody hell to pay. That ubiquitous arm of secular righteousness, POAU, has mounted the parapets and guns are blazing. Yet *minorities* are engaged in this kind of ingenious manipulation. We have come to that humorous and frightening impasse where tails wag dogs.[57]

---

[56] "Playboy Interview: Madalyn Murray," *Playboy* (October 1965), p. 68.
[57] The Reverend John P. Leary, S. J., "Morality and the Public School," *Vital Speeches,* Vol. 31 (April 1965), p. 427.

130   Now to Senator Everett Dirksen, who took a similar stand:

There was a storm of protest over these decisions. For a time it subsided. But it is gathering again in all parts of the Nation.

The fears which these decisions have inspired, the implications which they contain, and the results which might accrue make it imperative that Congress take cognizance of this matter and begin to concern itself with a sustained course of action.

We might yet see school Christmas programs without the use of the word Christmas. Not even "Xmas" would do since it is but an abbreviation of Christmas. Santa Claus may become a memory and we may have to settle for Jolly Mr. Nick. Christmas carols might be excised from the school songbooks. The star which guided the Wisemen might have to recede into orbit. The Nativity scene may have to vanish from school programs, as evidenced by the advice tendered to the Gateway Union School in suburban Pittsburgh — incidentally, advice given, I think, by the district attorney — that if there were to be a Nativity scene, it might be proper and legal only if presented in "a cultural vein."

The Court crier who asks God to save this honorable Court every time he opens a session across the way does so in a magnificent marble building constructed with public funds. The Chaplains of the House and Senate offer their prayers in the people's own Capitol, built with public funds. In that Capitol is a prayer room where Members may go and it was designed and built from public funds appropriated by Congress. Every U. S. vessel, every Government-owned camp, cantonment, barracks, chapel, or other buildings where prayer is offered by service chaplains has been erected with public funds. The prayers pronounced over the caskets of the young dead coming back from Vietnam are said by chaplains who are paid from public funds. Any argument against providing a place for voluntary prayer because it takes place in a structure built with public funds would sound rather hollow in the face of reality.

The really alert hours — perhaps 6 or 7 — are spent in school. These are the formative years for 50 million youngsters. These are the hours when the habit of prayer can best be nurtured.

Prayer is the roadmap to God. It should become the greatest adventure for young minds. Each must find the way for himself. This takes some doing — the development of right habits, the building of spiritual muscle. This can come only from practice and rehearsal day after day when young minds are alert.

How strange that we spend hundreds of millions of public funds every year to develop physical fitness and harden the muscles of American youth, but when it comes to hardening the spiritual muscles through the practice and rehearsal of prayer, it becomes enshrouded in quaint legalism and the jargon of church and state.

Mr. President, I finish by saying: Give Caesar what he requires, but give God a little also.[58]

---

[58] The Honorable Everett Dirksen, U. S. Senator from Illinois, introducing S. J. Res. 148, proposing an amendment to the Constitution of the United States to permit voluntary participation in prayer in public schools. *Congressional Record,* 89th Cong., 2nd sess. (March 22, 1966), pp. 6,176–6,177.

People: The Silent Issue

Hell is a city much like London, a populous
and sooty city.

Percy B. Shelley

And the Poor Get Children.

L. Rainwater

4

"Population," quipped Morris Udall, the Arizona Congressman, "is something everybody does something about, but nobody talks about."[1] Those who do talk about it are arguing over the possible existence of a population crisis, the nature of that crisis, and what measures should be taken if such a crisis does exist. Moreover, there is considerable hesitancy and controversy about who should do something about the population explosion that is definitely occurring. What is the proper role of government? Should government play any role in matters as private as the limitation of family size or the relationships between the sexes in marriage?

These issues have been gathering momentum during recent years. More and more persons have begun to talk about them, and many leaders have finally taken a stand. In 1959, President Dwight Eisenhower said, "I cannot imagine more emphatically a subject that is not a proper political or governmental activity or function or responsibility. . . . That's not our business." Four years later, he wrote, "As I look back now, it may be that I was carrying that prediction too far."[2] While Eisenhower was changing his mind, the American population increased by 15 million — a growth that would have taken 50 years in the early 1800s.

---

[1] Morris Udall, *Congressman's Report*, August 10, 1964 (duplicated mailer).

[2] Dwight D. Eisenhower, as cited in *Intercom*, Vol. 6 (January-February 1964), p. 20.

134   This growing "floodtide of human beings," as Congressman Udall calls it, has emphasized the issues and caused many people to begin talking and changing their minds.

Population Growth: The Core of the Issues

Those who sound the alarm about a forthcoming crisis rely heavily upon a picture of the historical time schedule which shows the pace at which human beings have been added to our planet. It was not until about 1600 that the world had acquired half a billion people. In 230 years, this figure was doubled; and in another 100 years, about 1830, the population was again doubled. From 2 billion persons residing on the earth in 1930, the population will increase to 4 billion before 1980 (less than 50 years). At the present rate of growth, that figure will be doubled again to 8 billion in 25 years, or before the year 2005. That is well within the lifetime of most of us.

Turning to the U. S. population (see Table 4–1), present rates of growth will expand the numbers to some 340 million by the year 2000. Of these, 100 million will be school age. Our present population growth could fill at least five or six brand new cities the size of Denver, Colorado, each year. There is little wonder that some people are becoming alarmed.

Table 4–1   National Population Trends
(in thousands)

Census (year)	Total number (000)	Percent change from previous census
Continental United States Only		
1790	3,929	—
1800	5,308	+35.1
1810	7,240	+36.4
1820	9,638	+33.1
1830	12,866	+33.5
1840	17,069	+32.7
*1850	23,200	+35.9
*1860	31,450	+35.6
1870	39,818	+26.6
1880	50,156	+26.0
1890	62,948	+25.5
1900	75,995	+20.7
1910	91,972	+21.0
1920	105,711	+14.9
1930	122,775	+16.1
1940	131,669	+ 7.2
1950	150,697	+14.5
United States, Including Alaska and Hawaii		
1950	151,326	—
1960	179,323	+18.5

* These figures are estimates.
Source: U. S. Bureau of the Census.

Three factors are responsible for this growth rate: (1) *fertility,* which is measured by the number of births; (2) *mortality,* which is measured by the number of deaths; and (3) *migration and mobility,* which is measured by the way people move about. How do these three combine to set off a world-wide population explosion? One of the chief advisers to our national policymakers, Dr. Philip M. Hauser, comments:

Why has the rate of population growth increased so rapidly? Although some changes in birth rates were also involved, it is clear that the major factor in the great acceleration of population growth first evident in Europe and areas of European settlement was the decline in the death rate. Three factors contributed to this decline. The first was the general increase in living standards, resulting from technological advances, increased productivity and the achievement of long periods of peace and tranquility by reason of the emergence of relatively powerful and stable central governments. The second major factor was great progress in environmental sanitation and improved personal hygiene. During the 19th century great strides were made in purifying food and water and improving personal cleanliness, which contributed materially to the elimination of parasitic, infectious, and contagious diseases. The third major factor is, of course, to be found in the great and growing contribution of modern medicine, enhanced by the recent progress in chemotherapy and the insecticides.

During the Modern Era, these developments upset the equilibrium between the birth rate and the death rate that characterized most of the millennia of human existence. . . . As a result of the decrease in death rates, the 100 million Europeans of 1650 had, three centuries later, about 940 million descendants, including population in the areas colonized by Europeans.

The remarkable growth of population during the latter part of the Modern Era in the industrialized nations continued despite the onset of fertility declines. . . . population growth continued in the West because death rates continued to decline faster than birth rates. . . .

Prior to World War II, the spectacular decrease in the death rate of the economically advanced nations had not been shared by most of the population of the world. . . .

Since the end of World War II, declines in mortality among the economically underdeveloped areas of the world have been more dramatic than those which were experienced in the industrialized areas.

Longevity is increasing much more rapidly in the less developed areas than it did among Europeans and European stock because of the much more powerful means now available for eliminating causes of mortality. . . .

While death rates have fallen sharply in the underdeveloped areas, birth rates have remained at high levels. . . .

136   Thus, no issue will be resolved by mere attention to the birth rates. The death rate is equally significant, as is immigration and emigration.[3]

Nature of the Impact: The Basic Issue

Nearly every informed person acknowledges the existence of a population boom. Persons whose lives have spanned the past twenty years can hardly miss noticing that there are more and more people around each year. Indeed, when Edward R. Murrow of radio and TV fame asked Grandma Moses what she regarded as the greatest change in America during her lifetime, the famous artist replied quickly, "Why, people, so many more people." However, not everyone agrees about the effects of the boom. Dr. George Carter, an anthropologist at Johns Hopkins University, dissents:

The population alarmists are running wild and all too often only their side is heard.

. . . It is foolishness to project this curve and really believe that on June 1, 2001, at 1 P.M. the last square inch of the world will be occupied by humankind. Most of us learned in childhood that if each herring egg grew up to become a mother herring and lay eggs the sea would be solid herring eggs in three years. Such things don't happen in nature and they are most unlikely to happen in mankind either.[4]

Some see the population explosion as a boon for everyone. Colin Clark, an economist and commentator on church policies, cites the population pressure in 16th century Holland as the thing which spurred the Dutch on to a successful war against Spain and a long career of successful colonization.[5] Adolf Hitler viewed a high birth rate as an essential feature to the domination of the world. Both he and Benito Mussolini eulogized and rewarded parents who had a large number of children. For them it was a badge of national superiority, and therefore child-bearing was encouraged as a matter of national policy.

On the other hand, there are those who approach the population boom with foreboding and great concern. While Pope Paul VI and leading members of the hierarchy have taken a conservative stand, refusing to interfere with nature, many lay leaders of the Roman Catholic faith have expressed more liberal views. For example, former Governor Edmund G.

---

[3] Philip M. Hauser, *World Population Problems,* Headline Series, No. 174 (New York: Foreign Policy Association, December 1965), pp. 6–9.

[4] George F. Carter, *Are Population Experts Running Wild?* (Huntington, Indiana: Our Sunday Visitor, Inc., n.d.), p. 5.

[5] Cited in Lincoln H. Day and Alice Day, *Too Many Americans* (Boston: Houghton Mifflin, 1964), p. 135.

Brown of California told a medical symposium in 1966, "There is, in short, a growing realization in California that uncontrolled population growth is a serious public problem and that limiting births is an acceptable means — if not the only means — of dealing with it."[6] Likewise, at press conferences in 1963, President Kennedy, another Roman Catholic, vigorously endorsed research on reproduction and stressed the need to continue research and disseminate the information to everyone.[7]

The Malthusian Issue: The Food-People Balance

A focal issue is the balance between population and food supply. Dr. Earl Butz, a chairman of the U. S. delegation to the Food and Agriculture Organization of the U. N., has said that the world as a whole is on a "collision course and that the rapidly changing ratio between food and population threatens disaster."[8] This is not the first time such an ominous note has been sounded. Population tends to double in one half the time it took it to double previously. This means that population increases geometrically in a sequence represented as follows: 1, 2, 4, 8, 16, 32, 64, 128, and so on. In the *Republic,* Plato noted this geometrical progression, "which has control over the good and evil of births."[9]

It was Thomas Robert Malthus, an English clergyman, however, who gave this issue impetus, when he noted in 1798 that population increased geometrically, while food and fiber increased arithmetically:

Taking the whole earth . . . and supposing the present population equal to a thousand million, the human species would increase in the ratio of — 1, 2, 4, 8, 16, 32, 64, 128, 256, 512, and subsistence as — 1, 2, 3, 4, 5, 6, 7, 8, 9. In two centuries the population would be to the means of subsistence as 256 to 9; in three centuries as 4096 to 13; and in two thousand years the difference would be almost incalculable.

In this supposition no limits whatever are placed to the produce of the earth. It may increase for ever and be greater than any assignable quantity; yet still the power of population being in every period so much superior, the increase of the human species can only be kept down to the level of the means of subsistence by the constant operation of the strong law of necessity, acting as a check upon the greater power.

Impelled to the increase of his species by an equally powerful

---

[6] Governor Edmund G. Brown, *Address* at the University of California Medical Center, San Francisco, California, January 15, 1966.

[7] John F. Kennedy, as cited in *Intercom,* Vol. 6 (January-February 1964), p. 22.

[8] Earl L. Butz, "The World's Biggest Problem — How Experts See It," *U. S. News and World Report* (October 4, 1965), pp. 52–54.

[9] Plato, *The Republic,* Book VIII.

instinct, reason interrupts his career, and asks him whether he may not bring beings into the world, for whom he cannot provide the means of subsistence. . . . May he not see his offspring in rags and misery, and clamouring for bread that he cannot give them?[10]

These observations won Malthus a dubious title, "the gloomy prophet of a dismal science." His revelations were never quite forgotten, but they did recede in importance until the middle of the present century, when his name and theories were brought into the center of the population controversy. "Population growth has a grim arithmetic," said the philanthropist, business leader, and analyst of population problems John D. Rockefeller, III.[11] Rockefeller concurs with a typically Malthusian position: "Either the birth rate of the world must come down or the death rate must go back up."[12] And on the ratio of food supply to population, he stresses a need to determine not what it takes to survive, but what we need to maintain our levels of living.

From the days of Malthus, we have inherited a tendency to think that the successful solution lies in striking a healthy balance between numbers of people and quantities of food. To the difficult question of how much is enough, this allows a simple answer. But too often it is a wrong one, because it equates man with animal and food with fodder. The population is not one of two dimensions, but of three. The third dimension touches the very essence of human life — man's desire to live as well as to survive.

We may, in days to come, bring more acres under cultivation and vastly increase the yield of each acre. We may reap unimagined harvests from our oceans. We may at last free all mankind from hunger. But even this, I maintain, is not enough. . . .

Human needs such as these go far beyond the bare necessities, the creature comforts, mere material resources. They are the third dimension of which I speak. The opportunity to fulfill these needs for himself and for his children should be every man's birthright.[13]

However, one of America's important policymakers, former Secretary of Agriculture Orville Freeman, indicates that it may very well be a struggle for survival, to say nothing about the struggle to maintain and increase the levels of living:

---

[10] Thomas Malthus, *An Essay on Population* (1798), (London: J. M. Dent, 1914), p. 10 ff.

[11] John D. Rockefeller, III, "The Hidden Crisis," *Look* (February 9, 1965).

[12] *Ibid.*

[13] *Ibid.*

World food production in 1965 was exactly the same as in 1964 but we had to divide it among 63 million more people than the year before. Next year, barring widespread famine or some other unforeseeable catastrophe, the denominator will be even larger.

Each year we calculate in the Department the world index of food production per person. Over-all gains in food production in the less developed countries are not unimpressive. But each year we must divide total food production by the ever growing denominator of world population.

Even more significant than the actual increase in world population, most of the additions are coming in the less developed regions — those regions least prepared to feed them. High rates of population growth in the less developed countries and low rates in the developed countries are contributing more to the rapidly widening gap in living levels between the "haves" and "have nots" than any other single factor. Nowhere is this widening gap so noticeable as in the most basic of human needs — the need for food.

Two-thirds of the world's people live in countries where diets fail to meet the most basic nutritional needs. The number of people suffering from malnutrition is greater than it was a generation ago. Hunger today is commonplace throughout much of the world.

The food problem itself is not new; it has always existed. It is the magnitude of the problem that has changed. Two factors are responsible. First, . . . the *increase* in world population. . . . Secondly, this is occurring at a time when the amount of new land suitable for cultivation is rapidly diminishing.

Throughout most of history man has expanded the food supply along with population simply by expanding the area under cultivation. . . . This period in history is now drawing to a close. Bringing new land under cultivation cannot account for more than a small part of the projected increase in world food needs over the remaining one-third of this century. Lacking new land to bring under cultivation, we must look to greater output per acre. . . .

Today we know that concentrating our efforts on the food side alone will not be sufficient. . . .

The world must prepare for a billion people to be added over the next 15 years. This fact in itself is significant. But even more significant, fully four-fifths of this total will be added in the food-short, less developed regions.[14]

---

[14] U. S. Senate, Committee on Government Operations. Formal statement delivered by Orville S. Freeman at Hearings before the Subcommittee on Foreign Aid Expenditure. 89th Cong., 2nd sess., pp. 515–519.

Another agricultural expert and policymaker, industrialist David Lilienthal, re-enforces the Malthusian dilemma in agricultural production:

I have spent most of my adult life preoccupied with specific ways and means whereby men can so use land, and water, and advances of technology to increase food production and at the same time conserve the land and conserve the people who live on the land. . . .

So it was easy for me to believe that just such cases of increased yields in food production, multiples of 3 or 4 more per acre, could be duplicated throughout the less developed world and become in large part the answer to the need for more food for a greatly increased population. . . .

Great increases in food production — by factors of 3 or 4 . . . are feasible. They have been accomplished, in fact. . . . [But then Lilienthal goes on to point out:]

One must admit that half a generation of the efforts of international and national agencies and the expenditure of millions of dollars have thus far shown major increases in yields per acre in only a relatively few instances. In a significant number of nations since World War II, food production per person — largely because of rapid population growth — has actually gone down. . . .

The sad fact is that the less developed world is losing the ability to feed itself. Were it not for North American food shipments the greatest famine in history — with bloody uprisings in its wake — would scorch large areas of the world.[15]

Nevertheless quite a body of American and world opinion vigorously disputes the analysis of those who are alarmed. Norman St. John-Stevas argues that unequal distribution and failures to strike a balance on the scales of social justice may contribute just as heavily as population growth to a dismal picture of the future.

. . . in India, for example, the average daily diet is 1590 calories per person — less than half that of the United States — and two-thirds of the Indian population is underfed. In all, seventy to seventy-five per cent of the world's population does not have enough to eat, seventy per cent of these are concentrated in Asia and eighteen per cent in Africa and parts of South America.

A world in which material resources are so unequally divided, and where the poorest parts are those where the population is increasing most rapidly, raises an acute problem. . . . The goods created by God

---

[15] From *Address* delivered by David E. Lilienthal before the Annual Dinner of Planned Parenthood — World Population, New York City, October 19, 1965.

should be equitably shared, and wealthier countries are bound by principles of justice and charity to share their resources with countries which
are less well provided.[16]

On the other hand, a Jewish leader noted that advances in agricultural technology offered greater hope than many "gloomy" prophets
acknowledged.

In the many publications presented to the lay public, the basic
mathematics of the Malthusian nightmare goes unchallenged. Historically speaking, the projections of Malthus were totally inaccurate. He
failed to allow for the scientific and technological advances that have
kept food production increases ahead of population growth.[17]

St. John-Stevas also sees much promise in the intensification of
agricultural practices and in the demonstration Communist China has
given us of her capacity to feed more than three quarters of a billion
people.

To achieve this, a great technological effort would have to be made
by the richer nations. More scientists and agricultural experts would
have to be trained and made available, new methods of crop rotation and
soil management introduced, and more arable land developed by irriga-
tion, possibly using sea water. Genetic improvement of seed and stock
would also help to raise yields. Japan provides an encouraging example
of how food production can be raised. During the last sixty years, food
supplies have increased faster than the population, and Japan now
supports 3.6 times as many people per hectare of cropland than the rest
of the Far East, despite the lower fertility of her land.

Great areas of forest and scrub land could be cleared and brought
under cultivation. New sources of food supplies could be developed from
soil-less agriculture and synthetic manufacture, and the oceans themselves could be utilized for the vegetable substance and fungi that they
contain. All this would involve astronomic expenditure, one estimate of
the aid required to raise undeveloped countries to a subsistence level
being $18,000,000,000 per year. Huge as this figure is, it moves into the
range of the attainable, when one considers that the military expenditure
of the United States and the Soviet Union is already at least five times

---

[16] Norman St. John-Stevas, "A Roman Catholic View of Population Control," in M.
Shimm, ed., *Population Control: The Imminent World Crisis* (New York: Oceana,
1961), p. 87.

[17] Jacob Z. Lauterback, "Talmudic–Rabbinic View on Birth Control," *Yearbook of
the Central Conference of American Rabbis,* Vol. 37, pp. 369–384.

142   the amount. Utilization of solar and atomic energy could speed this revolution considerably. . . .

Sharing of resources, increase of food supplies, more emigration, are the solutions put forward by Roman Catholics. . . .[18]

There are also schools of thought that rest their faith primarily on a balance in nature which shields the species from extinction. If jackals overpopulate, they will reduce their numbers of prey and will die in sufficient numbers to decrease the pressure on their source of food (prey). This process will, in turn, allow the prey to replenish itself, thus providing more food for jackals. Permitting this law to function freely hardly accords with Western humanitarian and Christian values. Few propose to "let 'em die" in order to reestablish the balance. Doubleday's Law of Fertility (the balance in nature of fertility and sterility) argues that fertility increases and decreases to promote such a balance. Thus, there would be no moral problem to face on the issue, since the fertility rate would take care of a crisis. But experience in underdeveloped areas indicates that the fertility rate does not adjust automatically. Nor does biological science provide support for this automatic law of human fertility.[19]

The Neglected Issue: Population Growth and the Face of Our Environment

The crux of the issues flowing from the burgeoning numbers of human beings is, as John D. Rockefeller, III, says, not solely a matter of balancing food supply with numbers of people. Subsistence is not enough, says Rockefeller; there is the question of how we want to live — our level of living as well as the kind of world in which we live.[20] This issue of environmental quality engages the question of population growth only infrequently. Yet as former Secretary of the Interior Stewart Udall so picturesquely puts it, "each generation has its own rendezvous with the land."[21] And there is little question about the connection between population increases and the quality of our physical and cultural environment.

One week last fall two events came to my attention which seemed to sum up the plight of modern man: the first was a press report which indicated that T. S. Eliot, the poet, was a victim of London's latest "killer

---

[18] St. John-Stevas in *Population Control*, pp. 89–90.

[19] For an account of Doubleday's law, see T. Doubleday, *The True Law of Population Shewn To be Connected with the Food of the People* (London: Simpkin, Marshall, 1842), p. 3 ff.

[20] Rockefeller, "The Hidden Crisis."

[21] Stewart L. Udall, *The Quiet Crisis* (New York: Holt, Rinehart & Winston, 1963), p. vii.

fog" and lay gravely ill; the second was a call from a preservation-minded citizen of New Hampshire who informed me that Robert Frost's old farm — fixed for all time in memory by the poem "West-running Brook" — was now an auto junkyard.

The coincidence of these two events raised questions in my mind: Is a society a success if it creates conditions that impair its finest minds and make a wasteland of its finest landscapes? What does material abundance avail if we create an environment in which man's highest and most specifically human attributes cannot be fulfilled?[22]

Air and water pollution, traffic congestion, urban blight, and a host of other problems comprise great public issues in America; but they are seldom considered in terms of population growth. Yet it cannot be doubted that the multiplying masses have caused many new problems or have worsened the existing ones. Even alcoholism and drug addiction are partially consequences of the population boom.[23]

As David Lilienthal contends:

. . . Air pollution is the result of congestion, industrialization and the multiplication of automobiles — factors in direct relation to population density in urban areas. Los Angeles is not an industrial city, yet at times its air is hardly fit to breathe. And with the spread of industry in the sprawling cities of the nation, more and more places will be Los Angelized.[24]

According to Udall and many others, the addition of new live bodies to the planet not only means ultimately wider sharing of the physical and material resources and thus less of the material benefits for each, but it also means a lowering of the quality of the material resources available. Furthermore, it means reducing the quality of our cultural and social life and its benefits.

Again, those on another side of the issue say the threat is exaggerated. For example, Roman Catholic sociologist Thomas Burch retorts:

On balance, Mr. Lilienthal's conclusions do strike me as exaggerated, though I would not say "fantastic," for reasons to be seen later. There are some flaws in the argument, which bear examining. . . .

. . . questions have been too long neglected as meaningless or

---

[22] *Ibid.*

[23] Philip Hauser, "The Population Explosion — U. S. A.," *Population Bulletin* (August 1960), pp. 94–95.

[24] David E. Lilienthal, "300 Million Americans Would Be Wrong," *New York Times Magazine* (January 9, 1966, Reprint).

144   alarmist. We have long accepted the Chamber of Commerce approach to
population growth in the United States, whereby babies mean business,
and good business means a good society. Or we have accepted an
oversimplified Malthusianism, whereby food shortages are the only population problem, so that a well-fed population cannot by definition be
too large or too rapidly increasing. The inadequacies of either approach,
materialistic and oversimplified as they are, should be obvious to us, but
for some reason we remain largely blind to them.[25]

However, Burch does acknowledge the physical scientists' warning
that Mother Nature has only limited amounts on her tray.

. . . it is clear that the more of its space and resources the United
States must spend to support ever-increasing numbers, the less there will
be to share with others, at least in the long run.[26]

The Declining Issue: Population as a Power Base

One of the most fascinating of the population issues brings into
question the effects of population change on national power. Historically,
many observers have contended that a large population is essential to the
acquisition of international prestige, national "power," and success in
war. However, rapidly increasing technology and resource development
during this century have contributed to the obsolescence of these arguments. Still, it is recognized that population is a key factor in national
capabilities — technologically, industrially, militarily, and in other ways.
Even the noted international analyst Hans J. Morgenthau has asserted:

. . . it is still true that no country can remain or become a first-rate
power which does not belong to the more populous nations of the earth.
Without a large population it is impossible to establish and keep going
the industrial plant necessary for the successful conduct of modern war;
to put into the field the large number of combat groups to fight on land,
on the sea, and in the air; and, finally, to fill the cadres . . . which must
supply the latter with food, means of transportation and communication,
ammunition, and weapons. It is for this reason that imperialistic countries stimulate population growth with all kinds of incentives, as did Nazi
Germany and Fascist Italy. . . .

---

[25] Thomas Burch, "How Many Americans Will Be Too Many," *The Catholic World*, Vol. 203 (July 1966), p. 214.
[26] *Ibid.*, p. 218.

Since size of population is one of the factors upon which national power rests, and since the power of one nation is always relative to the power of others, the relative size of the population of countries competing for power and, especially, the relative rate of their growth deserve careful attention. A country inferior in size of population to its competitor will view with alarm a declining rate of growth if the population of its competitor tends to increase more rapidly. Such has been the situation of France with regard to Germany between 1870 and 1940. During that period, the population of France increased by four million, whereas Germany registered a gain of twenty-seven million. . . . In 1940, Germany had at its disposal about fifteen million men fit for military service, whereas France had only five million.[27]

Quincy Wright, another renowned international analyst, assumes an equally moderate position on the other side of the question:

A large area and population permit defense in depth, make possible industries capable of producing modern weapons, assure sufficient personnel for minimal industrial, transportation, and military services in time of war, and make unlikely total annihilation by sudden attack. Therefore, population is a military asset. But other factors are also important. A high level of education and professional skill; an extensive, efficient, and diversified industry; an advanced technology and inventiveness; easy access to essential minerals and other raw materials; immediate availability of a sufficient quantity of airplanes and atomic weapons. . . .

Manpower is undoubtedly important. . . . yet the United States is less dependent for military power on population than it once was, and it also needs to rely less on a large population for defense than many other countries. . . . For the last three centuries, wars between states of similar culture and technology have not usually been won by the country best prepared militarily when the war began, but by the country best able to get the world on its side before the war was over.[28]

The Moral Issue: A Hot One

"This is a hot one; fated to grow hotter," says Garry Wills.[29] What makes the moral issue so hot? Perhaps it is because few ideas get more

---

[27] Hans Morgenthau, *Politics Among Nations* (New York: Alfred Knopf, 1960), pp. 122–123.

[28] Quincy Wright, "Population and Power in the Free World," in Philip M. Hauser, ed., *Population and World Politics* (Glencoe, Ill.: The Free Press, 1958), pp. 266–267.

[29] Garry Wills in *National Review* (July 27, 1965).

146   support than the proposition that the human race must continue, despite
the many wars men have waged against each other and the bloody mess
they have made of much of their history. For thousands of years, procreation was guarded, protected, and promoted to insure the continuation of
human life. Customs, conventions, laws, religious beliefs and canons, and
other institutional supports were geared to fulfill the objectives of procreation. Suddenly it has appeared that this stress might actually threaten the
continuation of human life. It is not easy to change a traditional emphasis
that has endured for thousands of years. As demonstrated in the following
letter to Senator Ernest Greuning of Alaska, many ordinary citizens have
been thoroughly indoctrinated with traditional standards, and this indoctrination springs to the surface rather quickly when the question of
population control becomes a subject of political debate.

Dear Senator: The proposed bill (S. 1676) authorizing more federal
involvement in family planning coupled with President Johnson's State
of the Union Address advocating, among other things, new ways to deal
with the population explosion represents a dangerous, if not unconstitutional, attempt to encroach upon God's power and our civil liberties. This
bill, if passed, will be a serious threat to our individual freedoms and
bring disaster to our beloved country. Birth Control is intrinsically evil
and the Holy Bible will confirm that it is. In the book of Genesis, "God
slew Onan who prevented his wife from conceiving by spilling his seed
upon the ground." (Gen. 38: 9–10.) Man is usurping God's laws; he is
invading the province of God; the concepts of marriage and procreation
were created by God. Don't sell Christ down the river like Judas did!
You will be put to the test! Jesus Christ said: "No man can serve two
masters: either you are with me or against me." A vote for Bill S. 1676 is
a vote for Satan; a vote against is a vote for God. You know what
happened to the Roman Empire! Heed this warning: "A most severe
judgment shall be for them that bear rule." (Wis. 6: 6.)

Yours truly,[30]

Beliefs and expressions of this sort well up from the depths of our
past. They are not confined to Roman Catholics and Fundamentalists. Nor
are they exclusively the products of religious teaching and conviction.
Long before the birth of Christ, Plato said, ". . . teach persons in what
way they shall beget children, threatening them if they disobey, with the
terrors of law."[31] Historically, it was often believed that interference with
procreation defied Mother Nature herself. Even Jean J. Rousseau, who
fathered illegitimate children and unceremoniously carried them off to a

---

[30] Letter to The Honorable Ernest Gruening, U. S. Senator from Alaska, reported in
Hearings before the Subcommittee on Foreign Aid Expenditures (1966), p. 2884.
[31] Plato, *Laws* (many editions), Book VII.

foundling home, vigorously asserted, "What shameful methods are some-times practiced to prevent the birth of men, and cheat nature; either by brutal or depraved appetites which insult her most beautiful work — appetites unknown to savages or mere animals. . . ."[32]

Procreation has been elevated to a high perch on our ladder of beliefs and values. Many have deemed it nature's and/or God's highest art. It has been shrouded in mystery and presumably placed beyond the reach of political decision makers.

Many of the traditional goals and beliefs concerning procreation find strong support in the pronouncements of the Papacy. In 1951, Pope Pius XII said: "To spouses, who make use of the specific act of the marriage state, nature and the Creator enjoin the function of providing for the preservation of mankind. This is the 'gift of children.' . . ."[33] And in the words of Father Drummond, "Contraceptives frustrate nature."[34] That position is as old as written history, and it constitutes the bulwark of opposition to pleas that we choose between a lower birth rate and a higher death rate.

For the official Catholic doctrine, we should go to Pope Paul VI and his predecessors. The Papacy has shown concern about what John XXIII called the "ever-increasing multitude of men piling up." Pope Paul's concern was expressed in an address to a group of cardinals on June 23, 1964:

> The problem, everyone talks of it, is that of birth control, as it is called; and namely, of population increases on one hand, and family mo-rality on the other. . . . It is an extremely grave problem. It touches on the mainsprings of life. . . . The question is being subjected to study, as wide and profound as possible, as grave and honest as it must be on a subject of such importance.
>
> . . . we say frankly that up to now we do not have sufficient motive to consider out of date, and therefore not binding, the norms given by Pope Pius XII in this regard. . . . and it therefore seems opportune to recommend that no one, for the present, takes it on himself to make pronouncements in terms different from the prevailing norm.[35]

The norms established by Pius XII were based on the binding official church doctrine stated by Pius XI in 1930: "Any use whatsoever in Marriage, in the exercise of which the act of human effort is deprived of its natural power of procreating life, violates the law of God and nature. . . ."[36]

---

[32] Jean J. Rousseau, *On the Origin of Inequality* (many editions).

[33] Address to the Italian Union of Obstetrical Nurses (1951).

[34] See Drummond's article, "Contraceptives Frustrate Nature," *The Catholic World,* Vol. 203 (July 1966), pp. 202–206.

[35] *New York Times* (June 24, 1964).

[36] *Acta Apostical Sedes,* 22:560.

148   The world waited as the church's commission studied the problem. Several years elapsed; then in July of 1968, Pope Paul VI issued his famous encyclical. The words were soft and mild, but the edict was clear.

> Conjugal love reveals its true nature and nobility when it is considered in its supreme origin, God, who is love, "the Father, from whom every family in heaven and on earth is named."
>
> Marriage is not, then, the effect of chance or the product of evolution or unconscious natural forces; it is the wise institution of the Creator. . . .
>
> . . . This love is fecund, for it is not exhausted by the communion between husband and wife, but is destined to continue, raising up new lives. "Marriage and conjugal love are by their nature ordained toward the begetting and educating of children. Children are really the supreme gift of marriage and contribute very substantially to the welfare of their parents." . . .
>
> . . . We must once again declare that the direct interruption of the generative process already begun, and, above all, directly willed and procured abortion, even if for therapeutic reasons, are to be absolutely excluded as licit means of regulating birth.
>
> Equally to be excluded, as the teaching authority of the church has frequently declared, is direct sterilization, whether perpetual or temporary, whether of the man or of the woman.
>
> Similarly excluded is every action which, either in anticipation of the conjugal act or in its accomplishment, or in the development of its natural consequences, proposes, whether as an end or as a means, to render procreation impossible.[37]

The last item in the above quotation means that the church *expects* Catholics not to employ artificial means of contraception. The issuance of the encyclical prompted immediate responses, not just from the lay and Protestant worlds but from the Catholic clergy itself, both on the Continent and in the United States. In Europe, the Reverend Küng's reaction was representative.

> A noted Swiss Roman Catholic theologian, the Rev. Hans Küng, said today in West Germany that Pope Paul's renewed ban on contraception demonstrated not only that the Pontiff was not infallible but also that he was wrong.[38]

---

[37] From "Humanae Vitae," the seventh encyclical of Pope Paul VI.
[38] *New York Times* (August 2, 1968), p. 10.

The U. S. Catholic clergy also showed little hesitancy about speaking out.

"One hopeful sign is that educated Catholics are not going to pay any attention to this statement," said the Rev. Robert Johann, a prominent Jesuit philosopher. "If they did we'd be back in the Dark Ages."[39]

Catholic lay leaders also objected. Gerald L. Fitzgerald, an official of the Christian Family Movement, said:

"If Pope Paul had come out with it four, three, or even two years ago, it might have made a difference," Mr. Fitzgerald said. "But by now I think that most couples who have been struggling with the problem have made up their mind and settled their consciences."[40]

A large segment of the Catholic clerics, however, have accepted the encyclical and its consequences. In several instances, the hierarchy has taken steps to chastise priests who have refused to accept the letter of the teaching completely. Yet the average parish priest has many difficult problems in dealing with his parishioners, as is indicated by the remark of a devout Catholic woman: "The best time to be a Catholic is when you are very young or very old."

This does not mean that some forms of birth control cannot be practiced by Catholics. Abstinence is both approved and applauded. Another alternative is the "rhythm method," or taking advantage of the natural period of female sterility. Efforts to gain adoption of the method, especially in developing areas, have not been too successful, but neither have they failed completely, as St. John-Stevas reports.

. . . From 1952 to 1954, with the help of the United Nations, experiments were, in fact, carried out in India in the use of the rhythm method. Two locations were selected, Lodi colony, an urban middle-class center, and Ramangaram, a small rural town in Mysore. . . . only 13.6 per cent of the couples in Ramangaram and 28.3 per cent of those in Lodi colony proved capable of learning the method. By the end of March 1954, only five per cent and 7.5 per cent, respectively, were known to be following the method regularly. . . . on the other hand, Dr. Abraham Stone, who went to India to give instructions in rhythm methods under the auspices of the World Health Organization in 1951, reported a success rate of sixty-five per cent.[41]

---

[39] *New York Times* (July 30, 1968), p. 1.
[40] *Ibid.*
[41] St. John-Stevas in *Population Control,* p. 91.

150   The Catholic resolution to the problem is much like that given by Thomas Malthus — abstinence and use of natural periods of sterility. On the other side of the fence, of course, are those who advocate active "birth control" methods, ranging from complete sterilization to the use of special devices. Actually, the moral issue over limiting population boils down to some very sticky questions: What do we owe future generations? Do unborn children have rights? One of the more powerful arguments that Catholics advance is the "Right to Life." They feel that contraception, abortion, sterilization, and other means of birth control deprive the unborn child of his right to life. It is also often contended that God's intentions of having the person's soul united with him are frustrated. Says Norman St. John-Stevas, ". . . the only silent creature is the one most affected."[42] Russell B. Shaw punctuates this indictment of birth control by calling it a denial of status as a human being to the unborn.[43]

Other Catholic arguments contend that female health is endangered. Contraception may contribute to development of cancer. Cancer of the breast is more common among sterile married women. It is also said that the use of contraceptives induces sterility. Further, it is contended, that contraception corrupts the personality by reducing self-control and encouraging indulgence in sexual relations for selfish reasons. They contend that it turns marriage into legalized prostitution.[44]

What is the Protestant position? Some Protestants seek a basis of Christian unity while pushing in the direction of free and individual choice with respect to birth control practices.

The first thing that strikes anyone who looks at the position on family limitations of the Planned Parenthood Federation of America and other advocates of birth control on the one hand, and the position of the Catholic Church on the other, is not how different they are but rather how much they are alike.

Catholics and non-Catholics alike concur in the necessity for family limitation in the interests of life, health, individual, family and community welfare. Indeed, the Pope himself has mentioned inadequate housing as a reason for limiting a family's size.

There is, however, no consensus at the moment (maybe we in this group can develop one) as to the use of certain methods of birth control.[45]

This conciliatory view is not shared as broadly as Mrs. Pilpel infers. Roman Catholics are answered today rather directly by both the churched

---

[42] As cited in Jack Bacon, "Birth Control, Abortion Drives — How Closely Linked," *Denver Catholic Register* (December 22, 1966), p. 17.

[43] Russell B. Shaw, *Abortion and Public Policy,* pamphlet circulated by Family Life Bureau of the National Catholic Welfare Conference, 1965.

[44] St. John-Stevas in *Population Control*, pp. 72–74.

[45] Harriet Pilpel, "Remarks," *Birth Control and the Legislation of Morality* (National Conference of Christians and Jews, pamphlet, n.d.), p. 38.

and unchurched Protestant world. They argue that contraception prevents overpopulation, avoids the birth of unwanted children, reduces infant mortality and juvenile delinquency, safeguards the mother's health, and facilitates early marriage. They also argue that prevention of births is a right of the potential parents. The Anglican Church's Lambeth Conference of 1958 provided an illustration of official Protestant policy:

The Conference believes that the responsibility for deciding upon the number and frequency of children has been laid by God upon the conscience of parents everywhere; that this planning, in such ways as are mutually acceptable to husband and wife in Christian conscience, is a right and important factor in Christian family life and should be the result of positive choice before God. Such responsible parenthood built on obedience to all the duties of marriage, requires a wise stewardship of the resources and abilities of the family as well as a thoughtful consideration of the varying population needs and problems of society and the claims of future generations.[46]

This position is strongly supported by the population analyst Dr. Philip Hauser, who also argues for the rights of parents.

. . . Within the United States, as within the world as a whole, it is only the poor and the uneducated, who have not had the right, the privilege, the knowledge, and the access to the means of regulating family size. . . .

It is for this reason, Mr. Chairman, I would argue that we ought not to be swayed by what some people proclaim are bad morals — proclaim out of the context of American history. It is much more important to see that our poor and their children do have access to the same rights of family planning that our more affluent and educated people have, . . .[47]

And Dr. Shinn of the United Church of Christ testifies:

We hold that responsible family planning is today a clear moral duty. We believe that public law and public institutions should sanction the distribution through authorized channels of reliable information and contraceptive devices. . . .

I see three important moral values at stake in this proposal: the contributions to freedom, to peace, and to the dignity of man.

---

[46] Flann Campbell, "Birth Control and the Christian Churches," *Population Studies* (November 1960), p. 137.

[47] Testimony in Hearings before the Subcommittee on Foreign Aid Expenditure, (1966), p. 151.

1. *Freedom:* Man need not be the victim of his fertility. That fertility, important to the survival of the race in some periods of history, now threatens the race. But its threat does not make us helpless.

2. *Peace:* . . . A desperate people, suffering in poverty in a world where prosperity is a tantalizing possibility, are not likely to be patient. Those who feel they have nothing to lose by war are not likely to be impressed by the dangers of worldwide holocaust. But a people with moderate security, with hope, with a voice in their destiny, can see the importance of peace. . . .

3. *The dignity of man:* By extending the exercise of responsible freedom and reducing the mastery of fate and accident in human life, population planning increases the dignity of man. . . . There is plenty of evidence that most married couples and all societies want children. But couples and societies do not want an unlimited number.[48]

The Methodist Church policy is quite forthright.

We believe that planned parenthood, practiced with respect for human life, fulfills rather than violates the will of God. It is the duty of each married couple prayerfully and responsibly to seek parenthood, avert it, or defer it, in accordance with the best expression of their Christian love.

Thus, sheer common sense and a knowledge of the kind of world in which we live, as well as spiritual and moral considerations, determine the Protestant attitude. Immorality appears to lie in not making adequate preparation for the coming of children and in the failure to make responsible decisions.[49]

Judaism also veers sharply from the Roman Catholic position.

. . . Modern Orthodox Judaism does not fully endorse birth control, though it does support the logic of family planning. . . . we favor the wider dissemination of birth-control information and medical assistance, both by private groups such as the Planned Parenthood Federation of America, and health agencies of local, state, and the federal government as a vital service to be rendered in the field of public health.[50]

---

[48] Testimony in Hearings, *Ibid.*, pp. 171–174.

[49] Bishop John Wesley Lord, "The Morality of Birth Control: What the Major Faiths Say," *Together* (January 1965), pp. 23–24.

[50] Rabbi Balfour Brickner, "Judaism," *Together* (January 1965), p. 26.

It appears that the moral issue became more controversial when certain governments started moving into the business of birth control and its promotion. Until recently, governments had generally been involved in deterring birth control rather than promoting it.

"Hah! And the government thinks its gonna' tell me how many kids I can have? Nope! Not at all." The young Cheyenne, Wyoming, station attendant who said this had a point. But he missed a point, too. Many state governments and the national government have been telling him and his predecessors that there were a lot of ways in which they could *not* limit their families.

On the three major methods of population control — abortion, sterilization, and contraception — state and national laws have been generally more negative than positive. All fifty states have treated abortion as a crime except for those few states that have permitted abortion when the mother's health is endangered. Sterilization is the only method permitted in all states; and three states (Connecticut, Utah, and Kansas) permit sterilization only when the individual's health justifies it.

The most interesting policies historically are those regarding sale and use of contraceptives and the distribution of information about them. Beginning in 1873, the national government prohibited distribution of devices and information through the U. S. mails on the grounds of obscenity. This, the famous Comstock Act, had also been literally forced onto most state statute books.

The primary crusader against the Comstock Act was a feisty little Irish nurse, Margaret Sanger; and no doubt she was also a primary factor in getting the governments to face the issues and the problem over which the issues rage.

"Tell me the secret — tell me what rich women use," the women would cry out to Margaret Sanger. Sick at heart, the young nurse had to say that she knew no "secret." Most of the women suspected that she would disclose "the secret" for a price.

Less than 6 months after her [Margaret Sanger's] first visit to [a] Mrs. Sachs, another call came from Grand Street. This time Mrs. Sachs was beyond help. Victim of a five dollar abortionist, she died ten minutes after Margaret arrived.

That night Margaret put away her nurse's bag. She was never to open it again. Somewhere behind the curtain of silence there had to be some scientific equivalent of what the poor women called "the secret." She was determined to find it and give it to the world.[51]

Margaret Sanger went to jail for her efforts; but by 1923, the first planned parenthood clinic was open in New York State. In 1937, the

---

[51] Lois M. Miller, "Margaret Sanger: Mother of Planned Parenthood," *Reader's Digest* (July 1951), p. 28.

154   American Medical Association feted her. Today that association pursues the following policies:

We feel that after delivery all patients should be offered birth-control advice as their right, and physicians must be trained adequately if they are to supply the needed information. . . .

1. An intelligent recognition that the problems that relate to human reproduction, including the need for population control, are more than a matter of responsible parenthood; they are a matter of responsible medical practice.

2. The medical profession should accept a major responsibility in matters related to human reproduction as they affect the total population and the individual family.

3. In discharging this responsibility, physicians must be prepared to provide counsel and guidance when the needs of their patients require it, or refer the patients to appropriate persons.

4. The AMA shall take the responsibility for disseminating information to physicians on all phases of human reproduction, including sexual behavior, by whatever means are appropriate.[52]

By 1965 there was little question that policymakers had done an about-face. President Johnson said forthrightly in his State of the Union Message, "I will seek new ways to help deal with the explosion in world population." This policy is being implemented at a quickened pace in both foreign and domestic policy areas. The Gallup polls report that more than 70 percent of the American public supports voluntary "birth control" and also government support of some form of it. The Population Crisis Committee has outlined the major features of the policy:

It has backed U. S. participation in population conferences and has encouraged U. N. agencies to play a more active role. U. S. Ambassadors in all underdeveloped countries have been asked to appoint an officer to deal with population issues.

. . . AID announced that it would provide counsel, technical assistance, and other appropriate help to nations requesting help to deal with population problems. . . .

AID has provided $400,000 to the Chilean Center for Economic Development to establish a center for study of family planning. . . . the population center at North Carolina, Notre Dame, Michigan, and Johns

---

[52] Committee on Population, National Academy of Sciences, *The Growth of U. S. Population* (1965), pp. 18–19.

Hopkins have AID contracts for study of various population problems. . . .

Also, working with AID, the Census Bureau has provided technical assistance for population studies in some 30 countries. . . .

Census teams in the field are providing guidance now to the Governments of the Philippines, Taiwan, Thailand, Iran, Egypt, Pakistan, and Turkey. The Census Bureau depends on AID for the allocation of funds for these programs. . . .

In the United States . . . Federal funds have been used for birth control within community action programs.[53]

This outline of accomplishments illustrates congressional willingness to provide means for birth control but not leadership. According to Dr. Alan Guttmacher of the Planned Parenthood Federation:

"The light dewfall of tax funds invested in fertility — control research and services — less than $7 million Federal, State, and Local — seems hardly commensurate with the President's statement about the magnitude of the problem, especially when compared with the $9 billion now being spent on health programs."

In his introduction to the federation's 1965 annual report, Dr. Guttmacher said current efforts by the Federal Government and Planned Parenthood's clinics were able to reach only one of nine American women of child-bearing age who live in poverty.

"The stark fact is that at least five million impoverished U. S. women need effective birth-control help," Dr. Guttmacher said. He added that field research had shown that most poor women were eager to have only small families and were responsible about using birth-control devices when they were made available.[54]

The United States Supreme Court has joined the Congress in its policies to encourage the limitation of population growth. In 1965, the Court reversed its previous refusals to strike down state statutes that prohibited the dissemination of literature and devices. Speaking for the majority, Justice Douglas said:

The present case, then, concerns a relationship lying within the zone of privacy created by several fundamental constitutional guarantees. And it concerns a law which, in forbidding the *use* of contraceptives rather than regulating their manufacture or sale, seeks to achieve its

---

[53] Hearings before the Subcommittee on Foreign Aid Expenditures (1965), pp. 740–741.

[54] Quoted in *New York Times* (July 5, 1966), p. 39.

goals by means having a maximum destructive impact upon that relationship. . . . Would we allow the police to search the sacred precincts of marital bedrooms for telltale signs of the use of contraceptives? The very idea is repulsive to the notions of privacy surrounding the marriage relationship.

We deal with a right of privacy older than the Bill of Rights — older than our political parties, older than our school system. Marriage is a coming together for better or for worse, hopefully enduring, and intimate to the degree of being sacred. It is an association that promotes a way of life, not causes; a harmony in living, not political faiths; a bilateral loyalty, not commercial or social projects. Yet it is an association for as noble a purpose as any involved in our prior decisions.

Reversed.[55]

In a concurring opinion, Justice Goldberg was even more forceful:

"Adultery, homosexuality and the like are sexual intimacies which the State forbids . . . but the intimacy of husband and wife is necessarily an essential and accepted feature of the institution of marriage, an institution which the State not only must allow, but which always and in every age it has fostered and protected. It is one thing when the State exerts its power either to forbid extra-marital sexuality . . . or to say who may marry, but it is quite another when, having acknowledged a marriage and the intimacies inherent in it, it undertakes to regulate by means of the criminal law the details of that intimacy."

In sum, I believe that the right of privacy in the marital relation is fundamental and basic — a personal right "retained by the people" within the meaning of the Ninth Amendment. Connecticut cannot constitutionally abridge this fundamental right, which is protected by the Fourteenth Amendment from infringement by the States. I agree with the Court that petitioners' convictions must therefore be reversed.[56]

Everywhere the movement seems to be gaining momentum. By 1967, the Planned Parenthood Federation of America included 138 local organizations in 35 states. At least 20 states were dispensing family planning information and other services to the general public through the state welfare departments and bureaus. Thirty-three states, including Connecticut, supplied such services through welfare funds to families obtaining aid for dependent children. Nineteen of these states provided contraceptive supplies and services. There is little question that American governments,

---

[55] *Griswold* v. *Connecticut,* 381 U. S. 479 at 485 (1965).
[56] *Ibid.* at 499.

at both state and national levels, are becoming increasingly more committed to a policy that encourages population control. Still, there is caution and hesitancy at both levels.

The Pill: The Hottest Issue

The *pill* and the forthcoming immunization shot generate the most controversy at the present time. Both are means for avoiding pregnancy. The issue has two prongs — one concerns the physical and psychological effects of the pill or shot; the other concerns the impact on morals. In its July 1967 issue, the *Ladies' Home Journal* spoke of something it called the "chilling truth" about the pill. Dr. Selig Neubardt replied tersely to each of the charges.

A few months ago I did a question-and-answer radio show in Iowa. It was a joy. The women who called had questions about almost all the different techniques of contraception. The questions were sensible, the mood was happy, and I ended the program with the nice feeling that family planning had truly come of age in this country.

A return visit to the same show shortly afterward was quite another experience. The mood had changed from wedding to wake. The questions all centered around the oral contraceptives . . . and all were pervaded by fear.

A similar change had taken place in my private practice. . . .

Then, someone called my attention to the *Ladies' Home Journal* [July 1967]. There was the screaming headline: "THE TERRIBLE TROUBLE WITH THE BIRTH-CONTROL PILLS," and in large banner type, the promise of: "THE CHILLING TRUTH . . ."

What a relief! The threat came not from a lion but from a mouse. The Pill was as good as ever. Only the magazine needed correction. . . .

The *Journal* says: "What is known for sure about the pill? The truth is: practically nothing."

It would be a sad commentary on medicine today if that statement contained even an element of truth. Never in the history of medicine has any drug been so thoroughly studied and reported on as the oral contraceptives. Could all of this have taught us nothing? We have central agencies gathering information and electronic computers programed to digest this information. Scientific journals have become almost as topical as the morning newspaper. Almost every hospital in the country is geared to do research that only ten years ago was relegated to the large medical centers. We have millions of women taking the Pill and almost all of them returning for periodic checkup evaluation. And we know nothing?

We know that the Pill prevents pregnancy in the same way that nature prevents a pregnant woman from conceiving during the nine-month gestation period. The hormones of pregnancy put the ovary to rest and, therefore, a new egg is not formed each month. The Pill does the very same thing, but with only a small fraction of the amount of hormone secreted during pregnancy. It is quite accurate to say that the Pill produces the equivalent of a very mild state of pregnancy. A woman who has borne a child has been kept infertile by hormones for nine months, and, if she nurses that child, the period may stretch to eighteen, twenty-four, or as many months as she continues to nurse. . . .

The *Journal* says that the Pill was released in this country before adequate experimental trials were done, that these trials were run for only four years, and that the patients frequently did not return for periodic examination.

The fact is, although the conditions of the trials were far from ideal, the four-year experience was considered adequate for temporary approval by the Food and Drug Administration. This approval was given on a very limited basis. In 1960, it was primarily specialists who prescribed the Pill. We examined our patients frequently and observed them closely, for we, too, had some trepidation about this new technique. The Pill was approved for a two-year limit and only at the end of that period, when we [the specialists prescribing the Pill] had examined the results of our own experience, was the limit extended for another two years. Now the Pill may be used indefinitely, following full approval by the FDA.

The casual, reckless behavior that American doctors were accused of in the *Journal* article simply did not exist. Our approach was extremely cautious. . . .

The *Journal* says that all doctors don't agree on the safety of the Pill.

If we had to wait for all doctors to agree, we wouldn't even be using aspirin. All doctors won't agree on anything!

The *Journal* bemoans the fact that at a conference on the safety of the Pill, attended by thirty of the country's leading specialists, the Pill was approved for use, even though only twenty-eight of the thirty men voted for it. Twenty-eight out of thirty scientists agreeing on an issue? I believe that might be a world's record! . . .

The *Journal* says that the Pill may predispose to cancer. It is argued that cancer takes so long to develop that we are unable to tell in ten years what malignancy might be caused in another ten years.

But we can. . . .

While we cannot expect to see the effects of twenty years of oral contraception until 1980, we can draw some dramatic conclusions from the material we now have, in 1967, on premalignant cellular changes. These conclusions indicate that women on the Pill for twenty years will have a lower incidence of cancer than a comparable group of women not on the Pill. In the past ten years, we have found a lower incidence of cancer in women on the Pill than we would expect on the basis of statistical probability.

This is not surprising. There is good evidence that cancer in women is often preceded by long periods of hormonal imbalance. Women on the Pill all have perfect hormone balance. The estrogen-progesterone ratio arrived at by the drug companies is a very healthy one; and it can be maintained at a predictable, constant level for as long as the patient stays on the Pill. . . .

The *Journal* says that there might be a connection between the oral contraceptive and the incidence of a variety of diseases. To illustrate this point, the *Journal* article has bunched together a number of cases of illness with the implication that these occurrences are related to the Pill. Let us now set forth what these illnesses are, and what is known about their relation to the oral contraceptive.

Amenorrhea. "A small but unknown number of women" fail to resume menstruation when they stop the Pill. In fact, women occasionally fail to resume menstruation after childbirth, and a small but unknown number of women suddenly stop menstruating in the prime of life without ever having been near a contraceptive pill. This condition, called secondary amenorrhea, is a well-defined medical condition, has a host of causes, and is easily treated with medication. Most women after three or four years on the Pill will find their first spontaneous period arrives about two or even three weeks late. . . .

Liver disease and jaundice. People with existing liver disease should not take the contraceptive pill because it imposes an additional work load on the liver. To the normal liver it is insignificant.

There have been some cases of jaundice in women on the Pill who have no history of liver disease, but the condition clears up rapidly as soon as the Pill is stopped. This is a dose-related problem, and with the low-dose Pill now in use, it is extremely rare.

Diabetes. There is a minor variation in the glucose-tolerance curve of some women on the Pill, but this usually returns to normal even when the Pill is continued. Many women have similar changes during pregnancy. Most specialists in diabetes do not believe that the Pill will predispose women to the formation of true diabetes, although they continue to keep those women who demonstrate this variation under close observation. . . .

Emotional disturbances. There are a small number of women who become depressed or notice a loss of sexual desire with the oral contraceptive. This is a very *sneaky* kind of side effect, and I discuss it fully in

160

my book, *A Concept of Contraception.* Let me just say here that it is nothing to be feared, but very definitely a factor to be informed about. Women who note these symptoms should discontinue the Pill. . . .

Disturbance in blood flow. Problems of thrombophlebitis [blood clotting], migraine, stroke, and visual disturbance on a circulatory basis are the major causes of concern discussed in the *Journal* article; and these are the conditions that have given the medical profession the greatest pause in relation to the oral contraceptives.

Certainly, these diseases are not new. We saw them long before we had hormone pills, and we still see them today in women who have never taken a hormone pill. The question we must face is whether women on the Pill have a higher incidence of blood-clotting disease, which can cause stroke, than healthy women of the same age who are not on the Pill. It becomes a difficult question.

The difficulty stems from doctors never having been required to report cases of these diseases, and the natural incidence is therefore not known. Most of these cases were treated by the family doctor, with no permanent record of the cases having been written up.

When it was first suggested that the Pill may predispose patients to blood clots, a great deal of effort was made to establish the natural incidence of this disease. All efforts indicated that women on the Pill had the same incidence as women not on the Pill.[57]

Neubardt's opinion is stoutly defended by Dr. John Rock, one of the developers of the pill.

. . . there are always some undesirable side effects in every potent medication. And there are always scaremongers. What these critics don't realize or mention — some readily admit that they know little about ovulation — is that these disturbances occur only in women who are already susceptible to them during menstruation and pregnancy.

Oral contraceptives act by inhibiting ovulation in the same manner the body inhibits ovulation during pregnancy — to prevent multiple conceptions and miscarriage. Therefore, any of the common disturbances of pregnancy — nausea, headache, abdominal cramps, lethargy, nervousness, water retention, and so on — may be produced by the Pill.[58]

---

[57] Selig Neubardt, M.D., "A Doctor Blasts 'The Pill' Scare," *Cosmopolitan* (November 1967), p. 100 ff.

[58] John Rock, M.D., "The Hand That Rocked the Cradle," *Family Circle* (January 1968), pp. 78–79.

The impact on public morality, however, presents a totally different **161** question.

An era of vast change in sexual morality now is developing in America.

Fear is being expressed that the nation may be heading into a time of "sexual anarchy."

Just six years ago the birth-control pill came onto the market. To-day —

> College girls everywhere are talking about the pill, and many are using it. The pill is turning up in high schools, too.
>
> City after city is pushing distribution of the pill to welfare recipients, including unmarried women.
>
> Tens of thousands of Roman Catholic couples are turning to the pill as a means of practicing birth control.

These and other trends are expected to accelerate in times just ahead as laboratories perfect the long-term "contraceptive shot" and the "retro-active" pill which wards off pregnancy even if taken after sexual intercourse.

Result: Widespread concern is developing about the impact of the pill on morality.

Being asked are these questions: With birth control now so easy and effective, is the last vestige of sexual restraint to go out the window? Will mating become casual and random — as among animals?

Recently, John Alexander, general director of the Inter-Varsity Christian Fellowship, which has its headquarters in Chicago, said:

> I think it is certain that the pill will tear down the barriers for more than a few young people hitherto restrained by fear of pregnancy — and this will be even more true when the "retro-active" pill comes on the market. . . .

Disquiet is voiced even by an official of Planned Parenthood-World Population, which actively promotes birth control. Dr. Donald B. Strauss said:

> The two great supports of sexual morality in the past — fear of disease and fear of pregnancy — have now, happily, been largely removed. . . .
>
> This, I submit, leaves our generation of parents with a problem that largely remains unsolved.

162   *Early promiscuity.* The dimensions of that problem are being outlined daily by signs of growing sexual promiscuity among America's
young.

The Connecticut State department of health recently estimated that
one 13-year-old girl out of every 6 in that State will become pregnant,
out of wedlock, before she is 20.

Almost countless incidents have been reported, across the U. S., of
teen-age girls in high schools carrying birth-control pills. In some cases,
these have been supplied by their parents.

"Sex clubs" at high schools are reported from time to time.

On the East Coast, high-school girls of the middle and upper-income
classes join a steady traffic reported among college girls who fly to Puerto
Rico for legalized abortions. . . .

It is not just the young people who are causing worries about the
nation's sexual morality. Marital infidelity is becoming accepted by many
Americans as being of little importance. A "wife swapping" scandal
made headlines in California, while Long Island's suburbs were rocked
by police accounts of how housewives were earning money as
prostitutes — some with the knowledge and consent of their husbands.

"A whole new world." As many clergymen and educators see it, the
pill is becoming a major element in the crumbling of past standards of
sexual morality — especially among the young. A woman teacher at a
small college in upstate New York said:

> When you talk to the girls today, you're talking in a whole
> new world. They know how to get the pill. They think a girl is a
> fool not to use it if — and it's a big "if" — she is seriously in love.
> Promiscuity is still frowned upon, but it's not equated with morals.
> It's a matter of personal pride. . . .

At Brown University, it was disclosed last autumn that the campus
health director had prescribed the pill for two unmarried coeds at
Pembroke College, the undergraduate school for girls. The health director pointed out that both girls were over 21, and said applicants were
carefully questioned.

"I want to feel I'm contributing to a solid relationship and not
contributing to unmitigated promiscuity," he said.

The health director's action was defended by Brown University's
president and by the Pembroke student newspaper. The latter held that
"the social system is geared to safety and efficiency and not to the
ordering of the personal lives of its students, or to the legislating of
chastity."

From Brown's chaplain, the Rev. Julius S. Scott, Jr., came this comment: "This situation patently documents the moral ambiguity of the contemporary college campus, the collapse of tight ethical systems."

To obtain the pill, most women students must turn to private physicians — or to a "black market" said to exist on a number of campuses.

One news report from Austin, Tex., quoted a gynecologist there as saying he prescribed the pill "without qualms" for eight to ten coeds a month.

"I would rather be asked for the pills than for an abortion," this physician was quoted as saying.

In the medical profession, however, some uneasiness is beginning to be felt on the problem. It is being pointed out by some physicians that a doctor could be sued by a girl's parents — or charged with contributing to the delinquency of a minor — if he prescribes the pill without her parents' consent. . . .

Student action. Today, a movement appears to be developing among students to force colleges to make pills available to them at college health clinics.

At the University of Texas, a candidate for president of the student body proposed that the pill be dispensed at the student health center. He lost the election, but it was agreed that he had developed a "popular issue." . . .

The student senate at American University in Washington, D. C., recently called for dissemination of pills and other birth-control materials at the school's health center. The matter was dropped, and it was found that coeds at this Methodist-sponsored institution are having no trouble in getting the pill from private physicians. . . .

Changing attitudes. Until recently, church pressure was a curb on private, as well as public, clinics for birth control among the poor.

Today, however, welfare administrators everywhere are turning to the pill as a means of keeping women from producing large broods, many illegitimate, to be supported by the public treasury.

New York, Chicago and Washington, D. C., at first limited birth-control services among the poor to married women. Now unmarried women, too, are getting the pill in those cities. . . .

Still another moral dilemma is arising from use of the pill — this one involving Roman Catholic married couples.

Recently a Government-financed study showed that 21 per cent of Catholic wives under the age of 45 have used, or are using, birth-control pills despite the Church's ban on all unapproved means of family planning.

The comparable figure for Protestant wives was 29 per cent.

A number of Catholic clergymen have held the pill to be morally acceptable — not an "unnatural" process as the Church has held earlier contraceptives to be.

Dr. John Rock, a leading Catholic layman and one of the pioneers of the birth-control pill, said:

> There have been several statements made by authoritative theologians that the method by which the pill works is not clearly against nature, and that there is justification for use of the pill by those who, in all conscience, feel they should practice family planning by this means.
>
> Until such time as authoritative instruction comes from the Pope, these theologians believe that the question of "right or wrong" in regard to the pill is one to be decided by the parents.

Decision for the future. Dr. Rock and other Catholics make it clear, however, that all judgment must be reserved on the "retroactive pill" or the long-lasting "contraceptive shot" when these products appear on the market. Their view is that if either acts as an "abortive agent," it must be regarded as against the rule of nature, hence banned for use by Catholics.

These devices of the future, other clergymen are saying, are likely to multiply the moral dangers that are now arising as a result of the pill in its present form. . . .

What sociologists think. Sociologists point out that the pill, itself, is only one element in the danger of moral anarchy.

Dr. Mary S. Calderone, executive director of the Sex Information and Education Council of the U. S., said:

> Society provides young people with far too many examples of sex irresponsibly used. High-school kids see sex used as a commercial come-on, as an end in itself, presented to them. If the pill hadn't come along, we would be excited about whatever methods were being used.

Even so, the pill is becoming a major factor in the problem. Six million American women are using it.[59]

Again Dr. Rock asserts that the "scare" about moral decline may be a tempest in a teapot.

Several studies have been made on premarital sexual relations, and it was found that the permissiveness of the female is not dependent on

---

[59] "The Pill," *U. S. News and World Report* (July 11, 1966), pp. 62–65.

contraception; it's dependent on affection. And that female willingness to **165**
have intercourse is not increased by the Pill or decreased by the fear of
pregnancy.[60]

The issue is no longer a silent one; people are talking a great deal
more about it. What they do about population increase, however, may be
(indeed is) changing dramatically.

---

[60] John Rock, M.D., "The Hand That Rocked the Cradle," p. 86.

Consumers: Forgotten Citizens

There's a sucker born every minute.

Phineas T. Barnum

5

The Ignorant Society

American consumers constitute an ignorant society. They are ignorant of the goods and services they buy for three main reasons: the great variety of items available for sale; the complexity of many of these items; and the confusion caused by advertising and packaging, which are designed to sell products — not to inform.

The sheer number of items and services available makes it impossible for any person to be an intelligent judge of the safety or value of more than a very few products. A century ago the average family probably bought only a few dozen different items. Since the number of things purchased was small, the buyer could become knowledgeable about all of them without much effort. He need not have been an ignorant buyer. Today this same average family has access to thousands of different items. The family cannot possibly be an intelligent buyer of several thousand different commodities.

Perhaps even more significant than the rapid increase in quantity is the increasing complexity of the goods and services we commonly buy. Consider for example the differences in complexity between a wagon and an automobile or between an ice-box and a refrigerator. These comparisons become even more striking when we examine combinations of goods and services. Let us compare the situation of a cross-country traveler of a century ago with one today.

Our great-great grandfather probably traveled by stagecoach. Being reasonably intelligent and having the common experiences of his time, he could probably tell at a glance if the stagecoach was in good enough condition to make the trip; if the horses were capable of pulling it; and if the driver appeared competent. Furthermore, he would not be overly concerned about these matters because he could probably make temporary repairs himself if the stagecoach broke down, and he could drive the horses if the driver got drunk or had a heart attack.

Contrast this situation with that of the traveler who enters an airport today for a cross-country flight. Unless he makes a special effort, he may not even see the airplane until he is inside it. Not that it would help him to see it. Even if he should be an aeronautical engineer, he does not have the time or the opportunity to inspect the airplane. He ordinarily does not see the flight crew, but it would do him no good if he did see them. He is functioning altogether on faith and hope. He hopes the plane will fly. He hopes the traffic controllers know their business and are sane and alert. He hopes the pilot is competent, in good health, and not in his cups. He hopes and trusts — but he cannot know. He is almost totally ignorant of the purchase he has made.

Advertising, packaging, and labeling have the primary objective of *selling* the product. This is no news. However, the conflicting claims and sophisticated skullduggery common in advertising, packaging, and labeling are likely to make the prospective buyer less competent to decide in an intelligent manner. In this sense, these practices compound the inadequacies of the ignorant buyer.

The Dependent Society

Americans like to think of themselves as independent and self-reliant people. After all, who wants to admit that he is dependent? And when ours was a pioneer society, Americans could be largely independent of other people, although they were dependent upon the weather and other natural forces. The housewife grew and processed her own food and clothing; the farmer was also a carpenter, shoemaker, hunter, blacksmith, and so forth. Such a family made very few purchases in a lifetime, and the purchases they did make were simple items: salt and hand tools, for example. But the pioneer days are gone.

The family of today *must* buy almost everything it uses or consumes. There are very few items they can grow or manufacture themselves. They are dependent on others for all their needs.

This dependence is heightened by the fact that in most situations the amateur buyer is confronted by an expert and specialized seller. Business firms ordinarily employ expert purchasing agents to deal with these specialized sellers, so presumably there exists a rough "standoff" in expertise. But this is not the situation that confronts the individual consumer.

The Impersonal Society

We have characterized the American consumer as ignorant and dependent. In addition, the consumer moves in an impersonal world where buyers and sellers ordinarily do not know each other and are unlikely to have any personal interest in the welfare of the other. The person doing the selling has increasingly become a hired salesman who feels little responsibility for protecting the reputation of the manufacturer, processor, or distributor of the product. There is, of course, a wide range of product-knowledge among salesmen; but it seems reasonable to state that salesmen who sell to professional buyers are likely to be better informed on the products they sell and more responsible in attempting to maintain the reputation of their firm. Conversely, salesmen who sell to the ultimate consumer are least likely to know their product or to feel any responsibility for the product or the reputation of the selling organization.

When business firms are threatened with some form of government regulation or control, they will ordinarily maintain that the best and most effective control is competition among sellers — that this competition will keep down prices, maintain high quality, and minimize fraud and unethical or "shady" practices. There is no doubt that such statements are generally true. However, the "automatic" controls exercised through competition become less effective as the society becomes more impersonal and as business firms become larger. The automatic controls of the market place did not prevent the sale of automobiles that were "unsafe at any speed," the sale in Europe of thalidomide sleeping pills that caused 7,000 babies to be born without arms or legs, or the markup of 1,118 percent on a commonly used drug.

Let the Buyer Beware

Attempts to protect consumers have been slow in coming, have been hard fought when proposed, and have ordinarily been substantially "watered-down" if enacted. Probably the main reason why consumers have made little impact (through government) is that they have had no effective interest group organizations to speak for them. Since the interests of consumers are so diffused and varied, it is difficult for any of them to function effectively as a group. Furthermore, the regulation of any particular product is likely to be of minor interest to individual consumers,

170   whereas it is of vital, paramount interest to an association of producers.

An increase of one cent on a loaf of bread would be highly important to an association of bakers; but hardly any of us, as consumers, would be interested enough to organize for the purpose of opposing the one-cent increase. In most of these seller-buyer relationships we have a concentration of interests (benefits or costs) on the producer and a diffusion of interests on the consumer. In a contest between a small, concentrated, vitally interested, well-organized force against a large, amorphous, unorganized force, the latter will almost always lose.

Probably as important as the lack of organization is the lack of knowledge (although the two are related). A proposal to regulate the sale of certain drugs will not evoke much consumer support, because consumers will seldom be knowledgeable about the contents of the drugs and their effects. Also, many Americans (perhaps most of us) retain enough of the old "Yankee trader" orientation to be amused when some clever swindle is exposed. We secretly admire the "con man." Students are not insulted or indignant when they read that the Colgate-Palmolive Company, in a television commercial, had pretended to show that an application of its Rapid-Shave cream made it possible to shave sandpaper with a single stroke of the razor, when, in fact, the "sandpaper" was plexiglass sprinkled with sand. Students do not become indignant when they find that a large glass manufacturer's commercials were shot through an open window to reveal the "clarity" of the glass.

Americans are a highly individualistic people. We generally believe that we are personally responsible for our successes, our failures, and our misfortunes. This concept of individual (rather than collective) responsibility reinforces the old common law concept of "Let the Buyer Beware."

Ordinarily, Americans do not demand governmental regulatory action to protect consumers until a disaster occurs. The more spectacular the disaster, the more likely it is that corrective action will be undertaken. If two airliners collide in midair and several dozen people are killed, it is likely that the air traffic control measures will be overhauled (as has happened); but if several thousand people throughout the country are killed in auto accidents with highly predictable regularity, the chances of corrective action are considerably less.

None of us likes to be subjected to government controls. As Chief Justice Earl Warren once observed: "Most people consider the things which government does for them to be social progress, but they consider the things government does for others as socialism."

The documents which follow include details on three kinds of consumer problems. First, there is a summary of the development in the federal executive of instruments to protect the consumer. Second is a case study of the recent controversy over meat inspection. Finally, we have reproduced the bulk of a statement by General Quesada (first director of the Federal Aviation Agency) on his problems and frustrations in attempting to carry out regulations in air traffic safety.

Protecting the Consumer Interest

On March 15, 1962, President John F. Kennedy sent a special message to Congress entitled "Protecting the Consumer Interest." This was the first time that any president had devoted a message to this topic. President Kennedy's words laid the groundwork and set the pattern for much of the legislation since that time.

Consumers, by definition, include us all. They are the largest economic group in the economy, affecting and affected by almost every public and private economic decision. Two-thirds of all spending in the economy is by consumers. But they are the only important group in the economy who are not effectively organized, whose views are often not heard.

The Federal Government — by nature the highest spokesman for *all* the people — has a special obligation to be alert to the consumer's needs and to advance the consumer's interests. Ever since legislation was enacted in 1872 to protect the consumer from frauds involving use of the U. S. mail, the Congress and Executive Branch have been increasingly aware of their responsibility to make certain that our Nation's economy fairly and adequately serves consumers' interests.

In the main, it has served them extremely well. Each succeeding generation has enjoyed both higher income and a greater variety of goods and services. As a result our standard of living is the highest in the world — and, in less than 20 years, it should rise an additional 50 percent.

Fortunate as we are, we nevertheless cannot afford waste in consumption any more than we can afford inefficiency in business or Government. If consumers are offered inferior products, if prices are exorbitant, if drugs are unsafe or worthless, if the consumer is unable to choose on an informed basis, then his dollar is wasted, his health and safety may be threatened, and the national interest suffers. On the other hand, increased efforts to make the best possible use of their incomes can contribute more to the well-being of most families than equivalent efforts to raise their incomes.

The march of technology — affecting, for example, the foods we eat, the medicines we take, and the many appliances we use in our homes — has increased the difficulties of the consumer along with his opportunities; and it has outmoded many of the old laws and regulations and made new legislation necessary. The typical supermarket before World War II stocked about 1,500 separate food items — an impressive figure by any standard. But today it carries over 6,000. Ninety percent of the prescriptions written today are for drugs that were unknown 20 years ago. Many of the new products used every day in the home are highly complex. The

172   housewife is called upon to be an amateur electrician, mechanic, chemist, toxicologist, dietitian, and mathematician — but she is rarely furnished the information she needs to perform these tasks proficiently.

Marketing is increasingly impersonal. Consumer choice is influenced by mass advertising utilizing highly developed arts of persuasion. The consumer typically cannot know whether drug preparations meet minimum standards of safety, quality, and efficacy. He usually does not know how much he pays for consumer credit; whether one prepared food has more nutritional value than another; whether the performance of a product will in fact meet his needs; or whether the "large economy size" is really a bargain.

Nearly all of the programs offered by this Administration — e.g., the expansion of world trade, the improvement of medical care, the reduction of passenger taxes, the strengthening of mass transit, the development of conservation and recreation areas and low-cost power — are of direct or inherent importance to consumers. Additional legislative and administrative action is required, however, if the Federal Government is to meet its responsibility to consumers in the exercise of their rights. These rights include:

(1) The right to safety — to be protected against the marketing of goods which are hazardous to health or life.

(2) The right to be informed — to be protected against fraudulent, deceitful, or grossly misleading information, advertising, labeling, or other practices, and to be given the facts he needs to make an informed choice.

(3) The right to choose — to be assured, wherever possible, access to a variety of products and services at competitive prices; and in those industries in which competition is not workable and Government regulation is substituted, an assurance of satisfactory quality and service at fair prices.

(4) The right to be heard — to be assured that consumer interests will receive full and sympathetic consideration in the formulation of Government policy, and fair and expeditious treatment in its administrative tribunals.

To promote the fuller realization of these consumer rights, it is necessary that existing Government programs be strengthened, that Government organization be improved, and, in certain areas, that new legislation be enacted. . . .

Too little has been done to make available to consumers the results of pertinent government research. . . . With this in mind, I am directing:

First, that the Council of Economic Advisers create a Consumers' Advisory Council, to examine and provide advice to the government on issues of broad economic policy, on governmental programs protecting consumer needs, and on needed improvements in the flow of consumer research material to the public; this Consumers' Council will also give interested individuals and organizations a voice in these matters;

Second, that the head of each Federal agency whose activities bear significantly on consumer welfare designate a special assistant in his office to advise and assist him in assuring adequate and effective attention to consumer interests in the work of the agency, to act as liaison with consumer and related organizations, and to place increased emphasis on preparing and making available pertinent research findings for consumers in clear and useable form; and

Third, that the Postmaster General undertake a pilot program by displaying, in at least 100 selected post offices, samples of publications useful to consumers and by providing facilities for the easier purchase of such publications.

In addition to the foregoing measures, new legislative authority is also essential to advance and protect the consumer interest.

Strengthen regulatory authority over foods and drugs. The successful development of more than 9,000 new drugs in the last 25 years has saved countless lives and relieved millions of victims of acute and chronic illnesses. However, new drugs are being placed on the market with no requirement that there be either advance proof that they will be effective in treating the diseases and conditions for which they are recommended or the prompt reporting of adverse reactions. These new drugs present greater hazards as well as greater potential benefits than ever before — for they are widely used, they are often very potent, and they are promoted by aggressive sales campaigns that may tend to overstate their merits and fail to indicate the risks involved in their use. For example, over 20 percent of the new drugs listed since 1956 in the publication New and Non-Official Drugs were found, upon being tested, to be incapable of sustaining one or more of their sponsor's claims regarding their therapeutic effect. There is no way of measuring the needless suffering, the money innocently squandered, and the protraction of illnesses resulting from the use of such ineffective drugs. . . .

There are other problems to meet in this area:

An extensive underground traffic exists in habit-forming barbiturates (sedatives) and amphetamines (stimulants). Because of inadequate supervision over distribution, these drugs are contributing to accidents, to juvenile delinquency and to crime.

Two billion dollars worth of cosmetics are marketed yearly, many without adequate safety testing. Thousands of women have suffered burns and other injuries to the eyes, skin and hair by untested or inadequately tested beauty aids.

Factory inspections now authorized by the pure food and drug laws are seriously hampered by the fact that the law does not clearly require the manufacturer to allow inspection of certain records. An uncooperative small minority of manufacturers can engage in a game of hide-and-seek with the Government in order to avoid adequate inspection. But protection of the public health is not a game. It is of vital importance to each and every citizen.

A fifth of all the meat slaughtered in the United States is not now inspected by the Department of Agriculture, because the coverage of the Meat Inspection Act is restricted to meat products moving across state lines. This incomplete coverage contributes to the diversion of unhealthy animals to processing channels where the products are uninspected and can, therefore, be a threat to human health.

In short, existing laws in the food, drug, and cosmetic area are inadequate to assure the necessary protection the American consumer deserves. . . .

Require "truth in lending." Consumer debt outstanding, including mortgage credit, has almost tripled in the last decade and now totals well over $200 billion. Its widespread availability has given consumers more flexibility in the timing of their purchases. But, in many instances, serious abuses have occurred. Under the chairmanship of Senator Douglas, a subcommittee of the Senate Banking and Currency Committee has been conducting a detailed examination of such abuses. The testimony received shows a clear need for protection of consumers against charges of interest rates and fees far higher than apparent without any real knowledge on the part of the borrowers of the true amounts they are being charged. Purchasers of used cars in one study, for example, paid interest charges averaging 25 percent a year, and ranging well above this; yet very few were aware of how much they were actually paying for credit.

Excessive and untimely use of credit arising out of ignorance of its true cost is harmful both to the stability of the economy and to the welfare of the public. Legislation should therefore be enacted requiring lenders and vendors to disclose to borrowers in advance the actual amounts and rates which they will be paying for credit. . . .

"Truth in packaging." Just as consumers have the right to know what is in their credit contract, so also do they have the right to know what is in the package they buy. Senator Hart and his subcommittee are to be commended for the important investigation they are now conducting into packaging and labeling practices.

In our modern society good packaging meets many consumer needs, among them convenience, freshness, safety and attractive appearance.

But often in recent years, as the hearings have demonstrated, these **175** benefits have been accompanied by practices which frustrate the consumer's efforts to get the best value for his dollar. In many cases the label seems designed to conceal rather than to reveal the true contents of the package. Sometimes the consumer cannot readily ascertain the net amount of the product, or the ratio of solid contents to air. Frequently he cannot readily compute the comparative costs per unit of different brands packed in odd sizes, or of the same brand in large, giant, king size, or jumbo packages. And he may not realize that changes in the customary size or shape of the package may account for apparent bargains, or that "cents-off" promotions are often not real savings.

Misleading, fraudulent or unhelpful practices such as these are clearly incompatible with the efficient and equitable functioning of our free competitive economy. . . .

It is my hope that this Message, and the recommendations and requests it contains, can help alert every agency and branch of government to the needs of our consumers. Their voice is not always as loudly heard in Washington as the voices of smaller and better-organized groups — nor is their point of view always defined and presented. But under our economic as well as our political form of democracy, we share an obligation to protect the common interest in every decision we make. I ask the Congress, and every Department and Agency, to help in the fulfillment of that obligation.[1]

President Johnson carried on President Kennedy's efforts to protect the consumer by recommending additional legislation, by appointing a Special Assistant for Consumer Affairs, and by establishing a President's Committee on Consumer Interests.

Senator Estes Kefauver had introduced a bill to establish a separate Department of Consumers in 1959. A similar bill was introduced by Congressman Rosenthal of New York in 1965. Some of the testimony for and against the bill is reproduced below because many of the arguments, pro and con, have been and can be used to support or object to most consumer legislation. The bill's author, Congressman Rosenthal, said in part:

. . . Currently, through no fault of his own, the American consumer is the victim rather than the beneficiary of the distribution of economic and political power. As President Johnson said in his 1964 consumer message:

---

[1] John F. Kennedy, President, "Special Message to the Congress on Protecting the Consumer Interest" (March 15, 1962) *Public Papers of the Presidents of the U. S.: John F. Kennedy, 1962* (Washington, D. C.: U. S. G.P.O., 1963), pp. 235–243.

> For far too long, the consumer has had too little voice and too little weight in government. As a worker, as a lawyer or doctor, the citizen has been well represented. But as a consumer, he has had to take a back seat — we cannot rest content until he is in the front row, not displacing the interest of the producer, yet gaining equal rank and representation with that interest.

Mr. Chairman, that goal represents the principal reason for this legislation and, I hope, for these hearings.

The reduced influence of the American consumer has a complex origin. To begin with, we now have, in this country, a disproportionate influence exercised by producer groups over economic policy. It is, of course, natural that such groups should organize and finance powerful lobbies. Equally proper is their representation by Cabinet-level Departments — Agriculture, Commerce, Labor, and perhaps, Transportation. What troubles many of us, however, is the absence of any equivalent and countervailing political power for the consumer. It is no secret that the consumer interest and the producer interest are often in conflict. In the past 10 years, there has been considerable legislative study and documentation of that record. But where each group is assumed to pursue self-interest, and where there is an inequitable distribution of power among these groups, we have reason to start asking basic questions about our economic institutions. Such questions lie at the heart of this legislation.

What can we do for the American consumer? The Presidential messages of the last 4 years are an important start. Particular consumer-oriented legislation like "truth-in-packaging" and "truth-in-lending" help. So do legislative hearings such as those presently taking place on auto safety. The exciting and aggressive activities of Mrs. Esther Peterson and her organization have been particularly noteworthy.

But I believe two related goals must be served as the basis for strengthening the American consumer. We must seek to promote the consumer's self-awareness. And we must give that self-awareness distinct institutional representation and political power. These two goals are reciprocal. The consumer voice will best be heard if it can be expressed to and amplified by a Federal department. In turn, the existence of such a department itself is the foremost weapon we have to help mobilize the American consumer on his own behalf.

This process, then, represents what I take to be the central purpose of the bill. I believe it underlay the bill when it was initially introduced in 1959 by the late Senator Estes Kefauver. I think it addresses itself to certain realities in our economic life which all of us acknowledge and many of us fear. It was these realities, I believe, which then Senator Hubert Humphrey had in mind when he said, 6 years ago, in hearings similar to these:

I think we need a Department of Consumers. I am not at all sure that this bill has all the features in it that it ought to have, but I am convinced that somebody needs to speak up for the great multitude of the American people who are not organized into a consumers interest group.[2]

Dr. Ruby Turner Morris, an economics professor and former government employee, offered two examples of lack of consumer representation in governmental decisions.

Here I should like to cite a couple of instances in my own experience. I mentioned my little 2-hour stint before the Maritime Commission in Honolulu during the war. That was a hearing — a formal court procedure — at which appeared the board of directors of the Matson Steam Navigation Co., the representatives of the large banks, the "big five" of Honolulu's economic oligarchy, stockholders, even captains of vessels. It was a colorful occasion. And who was representing the consumer? Me. An instructor from Vassar.

The feeling of that meeting is unforgettable. I was the only one there who objected to the rate increase — who wanted prices of freight rates and passenger service to Honolulu to be kept as low as possible. The only one. I felt like a skunk at a picnic.

Again, when I was setting grocery prices for the OPA during the war, I could sense how it would be to be a regulatory commissioner. All day long coming, going, inquiring, demanding, complaining, I saw no one but grocers. Never once in 4 years of operations did I encounter the consumers I was being paid to protect. It was as though they did not exist. Pressure was entirely one sided.[3]

Senator Robert F. Kennedy argued that:

Of course, one original purpose of the regulatory agencies has been protection of consumer interests. Yet it increasingly occurs that the consumer's voice before these agencies is drowned out by the competition of some more particularized interests.

Why shouldn't young people who will be enticed to smoke by cigarette advertising be spoken for when the tobacco interests are heard so clearly?

Why shouldn't the users of electricity be heard when the giant utilities are spoken for so effectively?

---

[2] U. S. House of Representatives, Committee on Government Operations, Subcommittee on Executive and Legislative Reorganization, *Creating a Department of Consumers,* Hearings on H.R. 7179, 89th Cong., 1st sess., 1966, pp. 31–32.

[3] *Ibid.,* pp. 43–44.

Why shouldn't those who borrow from banks be heard as well as the financial institutions themselves?

Why shouldn't the purchasers and viewers of the television sets be heard as well as the spokesmen for the networks and the manufacturers?

Why shouldn't those who pay exorbitant prices for drugs be heard as well as the drug manufacturers?

And why shouldn't the airline passengers be heard as well as the airlines?

It is not easy to organize the consumers so that their point of view can be consistently and effectively set forth, but a Federal department specifically charged with that obligation could give the consumer the voice he needs in the regulatory process.

Both the White House and the Congress have reflected a growing concern of how to obtain better representation of consumer interests. The recent investigation of auto safety is an illustration of the growing legislative concern, as is the legislation that is emerging from that investigation.

Senator Douglas of Illinois has been a strong advocate of truth-in-lending legislation. And Senator Hart of Michigan has been an equally strong champion of truth-in-packaging legislation.

The Office of Economic Opportunity has funded programs for consumer education recognizing and trying to do something about the fact that the poor always pay more.

The common law concept of caveat emptor — let the buyer beware — is unfortunately, still with us in 1966. But better protection for buyers would mean better protection for sellers as well. The loss in sales to legitimate business because of counterfeit brand-name goods alone runs to more than $2 billion per year.

The individual consumer is hardly powerful enough to fight the deceit and misrepresentation of the unscrupulous merchant. The efforts of better business bureaus have been helpful. The programs and laws of several of the States have made a difference. But the fact remains that the cost of consumer fraud requires a national effort if it is to be overcome. . . .

I was interested to read about the reaction of one business executive to the recommendation of the National Commission on Food Marketing that a Department of Consumer Affairs be established. The executive commented that such a department would be "nothing more than a wailing wall, and modern America does not need one."

If a "wailing wall" means giving a voice to the consumers of this country, if it means giving a forum to those who have been deceived and defrauded, if it means protecting the poor, if it means permitting the American buyer to be informed and educated about his purchasing decisions, then I disagree with this executive's view that modern-day America does not need one.

We not only need one, it is long overdue.[4]

The National Association of Manufacturers presented some of the best arguments against the bill — arguments that might be effectively used against most legislation to protect consumers.

This statement is submitted on behalf of the National Association of Manufacturers, a voluntary association of companies — large, medium, and small in size — accounting for approximately 75 percent of the Nation's manufacturing production and employment. We would like to set forth and discuss the reasons why we believe the establishment of a Department of Consumers is neither necessary nor desirable.

We respectfully urge the subcommittee to reject the bill, H.R. 7179, to establish a Department of Consumers, for the following reasons:

1. Such a department is unnecessary.

   (*a*) Existing departments and agencies provide consumers with protection against the deceptive and fraudulent practices of a small fringe minority.

   (*b*) The freedom of choice of American consumers in an intensely competitive marketplace guarantees them an abundance of high-quality products at reasonable prices.

2. Such a department would have undesirable aspects.

   (*a*) It would institutionalize Government intervention in economic processes, and thus run contrary to experience everywhere in the world which has demonstrated that economic freedom, not centralized planning, is the key to a more abundant life.

   (*b*) It would be empowered to impose burdensome and harassing paperwork and redtape upon the American economy, thereby adding to the costs of consumers.

   (*c*) It would lead to inefficiency and waste in Government through overlaps, duplications, and administrative delays.

The first point we wish to make crystal clear is that manufacturers as producers and sellers are vitally interested in the welfare of consumers. It is an awesome power that today's consumers wield. They have the freedom and opportunity to choose one product over another. En masse, they hold the power of life or death over any firm or corporation, simply by refusing to buy its products if they find them unsatisfactory in any

---

[4] *Ibid.,* pp. 124–126.

180   way. First credit for this must go to the businessman who, back in the days when government had no way to check the occasional cheat and fly-by-night operator, pioneered in quality control, brand names, and integrity. As Secretary of Commerce John T. Connor stated at the recent annual meeting of the Brand Names Foundation, as reported by Advertising Age of April 18, 1966:

"'American brand names are the stamp of quality which has given our merchandise a preferred status in many markets around the world.

"'Because of the current discussion about consumer affairs,' he commented, 'it is important to remind ourselves that manufacturers pioneered the field of consumer protection long before Government even dreamed of such action.

"'You taught us the art of discrimination in the marketplace. Even more, you gave us faith in the marketplace. You told us we could rely on products with your names on them, that you staked your reputation on their quality, that they were reasonably priced and that you stood behind them as honorable business men.'"

Modern marketing concentrates on learning what it is that consumers want and providing it to them in the most satisfying form and manner. Therefore, it is without hesitation we state that the producers are the consumers' best friends, drawn and secured to their interests by a force far more powerful than any executive order or appointment of public office. This stronger force is the force of the marketplace — the power of consumers to buy or not to buy. Producers live by and because of the friendship of consumers, and producers reciprocate this friendship — or quit the marketplace.

For example, Business Week magazine of March 26, 1966, reported on a plant tour held in connection with a meeting sponsored by the Advertising Women of New York Foundation, Inc., and the New York State Department of Commerce women's program. The 40 housewives who toured 10 consumer-oriented companies returned with one message: "We didn't realize that business really does care." As the article states, "They were amazed at the amount of effort required to prepare a reputable product for the store shelves and they said so repeatedly, prefacing their remarks with 'I had no idea * * * .'"

Among their reactions were "It takes as long as 3 years to develop a bar of soap, and we never think about it," said one woman after her tour of a soap company. What impressed a visitor at a soup company was the amount of basic research the company does. "They work on the chemical nature of flavor. They study things like why does grapefruit taste sour. I had no idea how much they do." The group that went to a food products company learned that a cooking oil bottle was designed with an eye to the capabilities of a woman's hand.

As one company head has put it, "We believe, very strongly, that the principal reason we are in business is to earn the right to make a profit. We earn this right only by giving consumers the best values possible. [We are] very much aware that [we] can succeed as a company only to the degree that [we] can succeed in satisfying the needs and wants of American consumers.

"As a consumer goods company, we are acutely conscious of consumer needs and preferences. We work hard to learn them. We study them. We go to consumers for this information. We believe that in our business we must start with the housewife and then work back, gearing our selling, distribution, packaging, and production practices to those methods best fitted to meeting her requirements. We know of no other way to successfully conduct our affairs."

The result of this attitude has been that American consumers have a broad selection of fine products from which to choose, each in accordance with his or her own tastes and preferences. The abundance, quality, and reasonable price of these products are unmatched anywhere. They represent genuine values to U. S. consumers, who spend a smaller percentage of their incomes on these products than do the peoples of any other country. For example, Americans can buy their food for a smaller share of their income than ever before — only about 18½ cents out of every after-tax dollar. Just 15 years ago, this figure was 26 cents. In Russia today, the comparable figure is 53 cents. An average American factory worker can earn enough to buy a 1-pound loaf of bread in 5 minutes; in Paris or West Berlin, he would have to work 11 minutes; and in Moscow, he would have to work 36 minutes for the loaf of bread. He can earn enough to buy 1 pound of laundry soap in 3 minutes; in Paris, he would have to work 19 minutes; and in West Berlin, 22 minutes; and in Moscow, 28 minutes. It is certainly evident that, among the nations, the United States stands least in need of a Federal Department of Consumers.

The second major point is that millions of the American public play simultaneously or consecutively the roles of producers, marketers and consumers. Certainly, all members of the public are consumers all of their lives. It is for this reason that the establishment of a new department of the Federal Government purporting to represent "consumers" is such a strange and unnecessary phenomenon — because everybody is a consumer as well as a contributor to the national product. As a matter of fact, the proposed establishment of such a department appears to question the integrity of existing governmental departments and existing regulatory agencies, such as the Federal Trade Commission and others. It is not necessary to agree with all their actions to recognize that these established departments and agencies are fully representative of all members of the public and aware of their interest as consumers.

Perhaps it would be helpful to delineate a distinction which we feel

182   applies between the very proper role of government in protecting consumers from deceptive practices, and the inappropriateness of any government attempt to stand as an intermediary between buyers and sellers in their normal, free market relationships. Certainly, we do not contend that the great and complex marketplace is flawless. Nor do we assert that consumers require no protection in their shopping for goods and services. It is likewise not our view that the practices of every businessman are always legal or ethical, but it is only a very small minority that is responsible for abuses. As to these, we are convinced that such abuses can be disciplined quite adequately under the vast body of existing law, scores of enforcement agencies, and a host of voluntary programs and natural competitive economic forces.

As to statutory and regulatory protection for consumers, serious studies demonstrate that they are surrounded even now by a tremendous and fully adequate body of laws and agencies at all levels of government. At the Federal level alone, the Congress has reported that some 103 programs engage directly in consumer protection, at a cost of $272 million annually. Still another 150 forms of consumer interest activity were cited. In every community and in every State, there are additional officers and agencies dealing with weights, measures, standards, safety, purity, cleanliness, advertising, labeling trade practices, and with every other significant function of the marketing process. States spend more than $32 million annually in the regulation of food and related products alone, the Congress found. Our problem of the future, then, is not only to assure protection of the individual in his function as a consumer, but also to insure that the power of the Government regulation does not restrict innovation and efficiency to the long-range detriment of the consumer.

Within the marketplace, we find a host of natural forces and voluntary programs which we believe have made the American consumer the best served and best protected buyer in this or any other society. There are first the basic checks and balances provided by professional buyers and sellers of goods and services long before they are placed in retail stores within reach of the consumer. Each buyer and seller in the commercial world is an individual force demanding the best quantity and quality, at the best price, for his customers. Each stakes his fortune daily upon his ability to satisfy his customers and their willingness to buy from him again. It is in this sense that the consumer, contrary to many recent attempts to deprecate his role, is the ultimate chooser or "boss" of the character and price of the products and services we produce and sell.

In addition to these consumer-applied controls, the marketplace abounds with countless voluntary programs and mechanisms — motivated by enlightened self-interest which for years have been conducted by businessmen. These include such national programs as the business-sponsored and financed better business bureaus which serve consumers nationwide. They include self-policing codes and standards of **183** whole industries and literally hundreds of component trade groups. They include the ethical codes of the mass media — newspapers, magazines, radio, and television — rejecting annually millions of dollars in business which fails to conform to their standards. They include internal processes of inspection and quality control, and warranties protecting brand names. They include testing laboratories and formal complaint departments of large retail sellers. Also one must recognize that the personal integrity of the small merchant on Main Street, U. S. A., in the vast majority of his daily dealings with customers, is a part of these natural disciplining influences. None of these self-policing activities is perfect, but collectively they are a powerful influence in the marketplace. . . .

"Industry believes that any effort to superimpose upon Government new bureaus and departments seeking to represent its citizens solely as consumers is unnecessary and undesirable.

"It is fundamental that, in a free economy, the interest of the consumer is best protected by the market power inherent in the exercise of free choice. Industry believes that the established departments and agencies of Government are fully representative of all members of the public and are aware of their interests as consumers. The protection of the public interest is synonymous with the protection of the consumer interest."

This statement of policy was unanimously adopted by the board of directors and has been annually reviewed and reaffirmed by the marketing committee. . . .

Our economic system is already engulfed and clogged up by an ocean of paperwork, redtape, and administrative delay. Yet, the Department of Consumers would be authorized to require business firms to file annual and special reports and answers in writing to specific questions about their productive capacity; volume of production; selling prices; costs of production and distribution; volume of sales, assets, and earnings; and relations to other corporations. . . .

In conclusion, we would like to restate the reasons why we believe that a Department of Consumers should not be established. We believe that such a department is unnecessary because existing departments and agencies provide consumers with ample protection against the deceptive and fraudulent practices of a small fringe minority and because the freedom of choice of American consumers in our intensely competitive marketplace guarantees them an abundance of high quality products at reasonable prices. We further believe that such a department would have the undesirable aspects of institutionalizing government intervention in economic processes, and thus run contrary to experience everywhere in the world which has demonstrated that economic freedom, not central-

184   ized planning, is the key to a more abundant life; of empowering such a department to impose burdensome and harassing paperwork and redtape upon the American economy, thereby adding to the costs of consumers; and of leading to inefficiency and waste in Government through overlaps, duplications and administrative delays.

We appreciate this opportunity to submit our views.[5]

President Johnson continued his drive for consumer protection throughout his tenure as president, and in 1968 he summed up the progress made during his administration and made some additional recommendations:

Speaking for every American, I present to the Congress my fourth Message on the American Consumer.

President Truman once observed that while some Americans have their interests protected in Washington by special lobbying groups, most of the people depend on the President of the United States to represent their interests.

In the case of consumer protection, however, the President — and the Congress — speak for every citizen.

A hundred years ago, consumer protection was largely unnecessary. We were a rural nation then: a nation of farms and small towns. Even in the growing cities, neighborhoods were closely knit.

Most products were locally produced and there was a personal relationship between the seller and the buyer. If the buyer had a complaint, he went straight to the miller, the blacksmith, the tailor, the corner grocer. Products were less complicated. It was easy to tell the excellent from the inferior.

Today all this is changed. A manufacturer may be thousands of miles away from his customer — and even further removed by distributors, wholesalers and retailers. His products may be so complicated that only an expert can pass judgment on their quality.

We are able to sustain this vast and impersonal system of commerce because of the ingenuity of our technology and the honesty of our businessmen.

But this same vast network of commerce, this same complexity, also presents opportunities for the unscrupulous and the negligent.

It is the government's role to protect the consumer — and the honest businessman alike — against fraud and indifference. Our goal must be to assure every American consumer a fair and honest exchange for his hard-earned dollar.

---

[5] *Ibid.,* pp. 203–206.

Thanks to the work of the last two Congresses, we are now much closer to that goal than ever before. In three years, we have taken historic steps to protect the consumer against:

— Impure and unwholesome meat.
— Death and destruction on our highways.
— Misleading labels and packages.
— Clothing and blankets that are fire-prone, rather than fire-proof.
— Hazardous appliances and products around the house.
— Toys that endanger our children.
— Substandard clinical laboratories.
— Unsafe tires.

In addition to these, the first session of this Congress took important steps toward passage of other consumer proposals we recommended last year, including the Truth-in-Lending, Fire Safety and Pipeline Safety bills which passed the Senate, and the fraudulent land sales, mutual funds and electric power reliability measures.

This session of the Congress should complete action on these vitally needed proposals to protect the public. It has already begun to do so.

In passing the Truth-in-Lending Bill last week, the House of Representatives brought every American consumer another step closer to knowing the cost of money he borrows. I urge the House and Senate to resolve their differences promptly and to give the consumer a strong Truth-in-Lending law.

A New Program for 1968

But that record alone, as comprehensive as it is, will not complete our responsibility. The needs of the consumer change as our Society changes, and legislation must keep pace.

For 1968, I propose a new eight-point program to:

— Crack down on fraud and deception in sales.
— Launch a major study of automobile insurance.
— Protect Americans against hazardous radiation from television sets and other electronic equipment.
— Close the gaps in our system of poultry inspection.
— Guard the consumer's health against unwholesome fish.
— Move now to prevent death and accidents on our waterways.
— Add new meaning to warranties and guarantees, and seek ways to improve repair work and servicing.
— Appoint a government lawyer to represent the consumer.

. . . This is not a partisan program or a business program or a labor program. It is a program for *all* of us — all 200 million Americans.[6]

The Jungle

In 1906, Upton Sinclair published a book called *The Jungle* which described the degrading working conditions and the unsanitary methods used to process meat in Chicago packing plants. *The Jungle* created a nation-wide furor and was at least partially responsible for the Meat Inspection Act of March 4, 1907.

The Meat Inspection Act provided for the inspection of animals before they were slaughtered and for a post-mortem inspection of the carcasses that were being prepared for human consumption. The act applied only to meat that was to enter interstate commerce; it did not apply to meat that would be sold intrastate. This act continued as the federal meat inspection law, with only minor amendments, for the next 61 years. During this period, 29 states passed mandatory state meat inspection laws, but the rest of the states had either voluntary meat inspection laws or none at all. In some of the 29 mandatory inspection states, it has been alleged that inspectors were poorly qualified, insufficient in number, and had inadequate laboratory equipment to do a good job. Congressional hearings established that about 25 percent of commercially processed meat products was prepared without federal inspection and to a significant degree was not subject to adequate state or local inspection.

Eyeballs, lungs, hog's blood, and ground-up hides were used in processed ham. Detergents and chemicals of various sorts were used to make meat smell better and look fresher. Dyes were used to make meat products look more attractive. Antibiotics instead of sanitation were used to retard spoilage. Diseases such as trichinosis, cysticerosis, and salmonellosis were transmitted through contaminated meat.

Fast truck transportation and the use of various modern technologies made it possible for unscrupulous operators to evade the intent of the Federal Meat Inspection Act. The system worked something like this: Livestock buyers divided the animals they bought into three rough categories — the best animals would be sold to federally inspected packing plants; the second grade to state-inspected plants if they were known to have lower standards; and the diseased or crippled livestock would be trucked to packing plants that were not inspected at all. Once inside the noninspected or poorly inspected plants, the carcasses (plus other odds and ends) would be treated or "doctored up" as needed to make them salable. It was commonplace that the plants handling the diseased or defective animals were also the least sanitary, so the consumer was put

---

[6] U. S. House of Representatives, *The American Consumer,* Fourth Message on the subject from President Lyndon B. Johnson, Doc. 248, 90th Cong., 2nd sess., February 6, 1968.

in double jeopardy. Furthermore, the chemicals used to preserve meat or make it more attractive were sometimes injurious themselves. Finally, there appeared to be a kind of Gresham's Law of Meat Packing: the spoiled and adulterated meat drove the good meat off the market. The ethical packers with federally inspected plants found it difficult to compete with unscrupulous operators in nonfederally inspected plants.

Beginning in 1960, Congressman Neal Smith of Iowa began introducing bills to "tighten up" meat inspection. These bills all died a quiet death. In 1962 the Senate and House Appropriation Committees became worried about the rising cost of Federal meat inspection and asked the Department of Agriculture to determine if it could license state meat inspection services and thus reduce the cost of federal meat inspection. (We should note that the cost of meat inspection had increased not only because of increased volume but also because modern technologies of meat processing made inspection more difficult and hence more expensive.) The survey of state inspection services was conducted by the Agricultural Research Service, and the now famous "Clarkson Report" was submitted in January 1963. It has been alleged that the Clarkson Report was "hidden" or kept secret for the next four years. Whether such allegations were true or not, the report received little attention until 1967. In its introductory statement, the Clarkson Report said:

The Department's observations covered a cross-section of slaughtering and meat processing establishments. These varied in size from small operations, employing one or two persons, to large establishments employing many persons. USDA representatives visited these plants, sometimes in the company of State officials, sometimes alone. Visits were made to establishments in every State, except Alaska, whether or not the State provided for meat inspection.

The observations covered some very fine plants, with good construction, practicing modern principles of sanitation, and using trained inspectors who were doing a good job.

However, in other establishments the reverse was true — plants were poorly constructed for maintenance of adequate sanitation and operating without proper regard for sanitation and inspection. The observations revealed the presence of conditions and practices not acceptable under Federal meat inspection standards. Such conditions and practices were found in establishments operating in States with no inspectional controls of any kind; in some States where inspectional controls were weak; and in still others where inspection covered slaughtering operations but not the preparation of processed meats.

Some of the worst conditions observed included:

1. Allowing edible portions of carcasses to come in contact with manure, pus, and other sources of contamination during the dressing operations.

2. Allowing meat food products during preparation to become contaminated with filth from improperly cleaned equipment and facilities.

3. Use of chemical additives and preservatives that would not have been permitted under Federal meat inspection.

4. Failing to use procedures to detect or control parasites transmissible to man that would lead to diseases, such as trichinosis and cysticercosis.

5. Use of inspection and operating controls that were not sufficient to prevent possible adulteration of meat food products during their preparation, with substances such as water, gum, cereals, or sodium caseinate.

6. The use of false or deceptive labels and packaging materials.

7. Failing to supervise destruction of obviously diseased tissues and spoiled, putrid, or filthy materials.

8. Working without any inspector, or with unqualified and poorly trained inspectors, without adequate supervision.

Observers reported meat from sick or unfit animals set aside in some plants for use in preparing human food.[7]

The report went on to explain some "modern" methods of adulteration:

Every year, new chemicals are developed that will preserve, emulsify, soften, color, increase water-binding power or inhibit rancidity of meat, and in many other ways alter the natural properties of meat. These are being offered to the food industry in ever-increasing numbers. Some of these are good and represent progress in food technology. However, some are known to be unsafe and the safety of many others has not been established. . . .

Normally, the spoilage bacteria grow more abundantly and more rapidly than toxin or disease-producing bacteria. Usually, their products of growth delay or prevent normal development of toxin and disease formers. Therefore, whenever the normal growth of spoilage organisms is altered with chemical preservatives or antibiotics, the usual indications of spoilage may be absent. In this way, meat products may appear to have normal color, normal odor and flavor — yet these products, with preservatives but without evidence of spoilage, may contain toxins or disease-producing organisms.

Meat color can be improved by the use of dyes or the addition of

---

[7] Agricultural Research Service, United States Department of Agriculture, *A Review of Certain Aspects of State and Federal Meat Inspection Services and Procedures,* January 1963.

chemicals such as sodium sulfite. Other chemicals, such as benzoate **189**
compounds, would serve to act as preservatives. These and other harmful
practices deceive the consumer by making the product appear better
than it really is. The use of harmful or otherwise unacceptable additives
can be successfully prevented only by actions of trained inspectors
having at their disposal competent laboratory facilities, such as those
provided under the Federal system.

Antibiotics, such as aureomycin (chlortetracycline), can be used as a
substitute for good sanitation and to mask spoilage.[8]

The above quotations from the Clarkson Report were taken from the
summary which was submitted to the House Appropriations Committee.
Details of the "backup" reports which formed the basis for the summary
were not included. Some of these inspectors' reports were injected into
the record of the Hearings by Ralph Nader when he wrote Congressman
Graham Purcell on July 20, 1967:

Alabama (*no meat inspection laws, provision for voluntary municipal inspection*). There is no regulation on added moisture in pork products such as sausage, hams, picnics, etc. X Co. was pumping their hams
21%. Y Co. *said* they were pumping 12%, but I have reason to believe
the figure was closer to 20%.

The [voluntary] inspection legend is identical to [USDA] except
that the abbreviation Jefferson County Health Department is located
where the establishment number is on ours, i.e., at the top. Where the
initials U. S. appear on our legend, they have the establishment number.
It could easily be mistaken for a federal stamp.

Arizona (*voluntary laws*). It is my opinion that no plant conducting
slaughtering in Arizona or New Mexico could meet our minimum requirements of construction or facilities without a major remodeling
program of the plant and the purchase of a goodly amount of acceptable
equipment for the proper conduct of operations and inspections. . . .

Delaware (*no meat inspection laws*). In excess of 35,000 cattle,
swine, sheep and calves are reported by the producers as slaughtered
each year without ante-mortem or post-mortem inspection for local or
generalized disease conditions. Based on our knowledge of animal pa-
thology as seen on post-mortem inspection, this means that consumers in
Delaware are in grave danger of using as food meats and meat food
products prepared from animals which were afflicted with a large number of diseases ranging from localized abscesses and lesions of tuberculo-
sis to generalized septicemia and malignant growth . . . Unsound ani-

---

[8] *Ibid.,* Appendix II, pp. iv–v.

mals may be purchased at reduced prices. They present an opportunity for large financial gain to an unscrupulous, uninspected slaughterer. . . .

Florida (mandatory inspection laws). A view of the boning room and coolers showed beef dirty from lack of proper trimming and washing on the killing floor. Also, the grease and rust from the trolley hooks had been transfered to the hocks, rounds, and ribs of carcasses. Laminated boards on the boning table were cracked. Some solid boards were used supplemented by an old painted 2 inch board.

The tank room had maggots present on the floor, in empty barrels (condemned), in screw conveyors, and in the "pre-breaker." Flies were present everywhere in the room with doors and windows open. . . .

Oklahoma (voluntary inspection law). On September 20, I visited an establishment in Oklahoma City. The premises were very disorderly and numerous rats were seen. Holding pens for cattle and hogs had dirty, broken floors. . . . Livers, hearts and spleens were hung on what we call trees. When pushed to the coolers, they were dragged over containers of inedible feet and very dirty floor sweepings. No effort was made to eliminate this source of contamination. Beef tongues covered with sores and foreign matter, which no doubt entered food markets, were sent to the coolers.[9]

Grisly examples such as these could go on and on. Drew Pearson warned his readers in his July 17, 1967 column that "a lot of diseased intrastate meat, impregnated with chemicals to make it look fresh, has been palmed off on the housewife." Two days earlier, a Ralph Nader article entitled "We're Still in the Jungle" appeared in *The New Republic*.

Several meat inspection bills were introduced during 1967, and much time was devoted to Hearings on the various bills. On June 26, Congressman Neal Smith testified:

My interest in this kind of legislation really began before I came to Congress. I have attended a great many livestock sales and became curious as to why a certain few cattle buyers seem to be buying almost all of the diseased, sick, and maimed livestock. It is customary for the management of these sales to assign pens to livestock buyers who buy a substantial amount of livestock. When that individual is the successful bidder on cattle or hogs, they merely call out the pen number in which the livestock will be placed awaiting shipment. Whenever they would

---

[9] U. S. House of Representatives, Committee on Agriculture, Subcommittee on Livestock and Grains, *Amend the Meat Inspection Act,* Hearings on H.R. 1314, H.R. 1321, and H.R. 6168, 90th Cong., 1st sess., 1967, pp. 240–249.

sell a cancer-eyed cow or a diseased hog, I noticed it was the same pen number that was generally called out for the successful bidder.

The farmer may bring in 40 head of cattle. The veterinarian there may cut off one cow or one steer with a lump jaw or some evidence of infection or disease and say that it must go to market and that it is subject to inspection. That one steer will be run in the ring alone, and it will then sell separate from the other 39. There will be lively bidding on the 39, but on the one it will sell cheap and it is always the same few buyers who buy that kind of cattle.

A check as to who these buyers were buying for, and why they would want that kind of livestock brought forth evidence that those buyers were buying for slaughterhouses which were not federally inspected. . . .

This general situation of uninspected packers being able to use inferior meat has led to such unfair competition that federally inspected processors of meat have found it almost impossible to compete for the processed meat market in those areas where an uninspected slaughterer is selling processed meats, or customers are price conscious. And, some good processors who wanted to sell a good product have told me they have been run clear out of the market that you were talking about of prepared meats because these processors who are not inspected could simply sell so much cheaper and put almost anything into a can and get away with it. . . .

The renderer can pick up a dead cow and can cut it up into chunks to be sold to some manufacturer of dog food, but after it leaves his hands, and perhaps unbeknownst to him, it may be trucked to someone who processes it into sausage or even puts it into hamburger. There is no adequate provision in the meat inspection law to prevent a broker from selling or a processor of sausage from buying this meat. . . .

Mr. Mayne, you referred to the definition of adulteration and something about the container and that brought to my mind this example that I happened to have run into a few years ago where the retailer would wash out the pan or vat with a certain kind of preservative and he would always manage to leave enough in there so when he put the hamburger in it and mixed it around a little, the hamburger had a red color, even if it didn't have beforehand. This was mixed in and I would call it adulterated by the time the customer bought it, but this is a trick some of them also use. . . .

The detection of these additives and successfully preventing these practices can only be accomplished with the help of trained inspectors having at their disposal competent laboratory facilities, such as those furnished under the Federal meat inspection system. . . .

With the appearance of many new frozen food products and "ready to serve" products that are used following short periods of cooking at

192   relatively low temperatures, the danger of trichinosis, salmonella, and other diseases is increasing and it is even more important than ever that the protection offered by the Meat Inspection Service be extended to cover those meat products which now escape such inspection and proper labeling. . . .

I think we are sitting on a bomb that could go off at any time and I think the existing situation with millions of tons of adulterated, unwholesome and misbranded meat and meat products being sold to unsuspecting customers is not only bad for the consumer, but it also results in unfair competition for the legitimate meat packer, of which we have many in this country, and it is unfair to the farmer who finds some of the demand for his healthy livestock being replaced by unwholesome and adulterated products. I thank the committee for this opportunity to appear and I strongly urge action to strengthen the meat inspection service.[10]

Among the early bills that were introduced, Congressman Smith's H.R. 6168 received the most attention. H.R. 6168 provided for a cooperative meat inspection program between the states and the federal government. The federal government would provide up to 50 percent of total costs of state inspection programs, with the provision that the state have a meat inspection law imposing mandatory inspection and sanitation requirements for intrastate operators. This law would be consistent with federal meat inspection requirements.

H.R. 6168 was generally supported by the U. S. Department of Agriculture, the National Livestock Feeders Association, the American Veterinary Medical Association, the National Farmers Organization, the Amalgamated Meat Cutters and Butcher Workmen (AFL-CIO), the National Consumers League, the American Food Service Association, the AFL-CIO, and the National Grange. It was generally opposed by the National Association of State Departments of Agriculture, the American Meat Institute (representing about 365 of the biggest packers and processors), the Western States Meat Packers Association, the National Independent Meat Packers Association, the Illinois Independent Meat Packers and Processors Association, the Oklahoma Independent Meat Packers Association, the Independent Meat Packers Association of Utah, the American Farm Bureau Federation, the Greater New York Association of Meat and Poultry Dealers, the Kansas Independent Meat Packers, the American National Cattlemen's Association, the North Carolina Meat Packers Association, and the Virginia Meat Packers Association.[11]

As the summer of 1967 wore on, meat packing continued to receive much unfavorable publicity. Congressman Smith introduced a "tougher"

---

[10] *Ibid.*, pp. 36–41.
[11] *Amend the Meat Inspection Act,* Hearings on H.R. 1314, H.R. 1321, and H.R. 6168, 1967.

bill with Congressman Foley of Washington. Senator Mondale introduced **193** another "tough" bill in the Senate, and Congressman Purcell introduced still another bill in the House (H.R. 12144), which was almost identical to Smith's H.R. 6168.

Betty Furness, the President's Assistant for Consumer Affairs, came out strongly for the tough Mondale bill. Congressman Foley castigated the meat packing industry and the state departments of agriculture in these words.

I said on the House floor that if there was a Member from any State in the United States who believes that his own State met inspection standards that were equal to the standards of the Federal system of meat inspection, he should speak up. No one spoke up because no State has such a system.

Another hard fact is that for the industry there is only one advantage in a dual meat inspection system. Since the overwhelming bulk of meat today is federally inspected — 85 percent of the slaughtered and 75 percent of the processed meat — there is only one advantage to maintaining the State system. That is the opportunity for certain segments of the American meat industry to operate at less than Federal standards and thus less than adequate standards to protect the public.

The industry's desire to retain State jurisdiction reflects the desire to cut corners where the consumer's interests are concerned.

As far as the States are concerned the importance of retaining jurisdiction seems to me to be slim. The Federal balance is really not affected by whether the States do meat inspection or not.

Senator Montoya pointed out that this is in a sense a police power. So is the inspection of drugs and the pure food laws. And these functions have almost entirely passed over to the Federal Government because we have recognized this is the only way that the public can be protected.

I wish I did not have to say this, but the record of the State departments of agriculture — particularly through their national association — has been a record throughout the course of this legislation of opposing, delaying, and obstructing any adequate and timely protection for the consumer. It is a record that I think is shocking, because from the time of the first hearings in the House there was not the slightest indication that the State departments of agriculture, through their national organization, were even remotely concerned about the welfare of the consumers. They were concerned merely with retaining jurisdiction. They offered several proposed amendments to the Purcell bill. Then suddenly, when it appeared that perhaps the Smith-Foley bill might be offered, they quickly reversed themselves and in a telegram dropped all amendments and supported the Purcell bill without restriction.

The same is true of the American Meat Institute and other industry organizations. Their record has been one of cynicism and opportunism concerned only with avoiding more stringent bills. I think that is tragic. I would have hoped that the American Meat Institute and other meat processing and packing organizations would have been in the forefront of those insisting on stringent meat-inspection standards to protect the public. In my judgment, Mr. Chairman, the strongest possible safeguards for the American consumer are in the self-interest of every segment of the meat industry — the processor, the meatpacker, and of course, the cattlemen who raise the cattle. The record of the industry has been very disappointing in this regard.[12]

Ralph Nader testified:

The Need

. . . Eight billion pounds of processed meat escapes Federal inspection — and the absolute quantity of such nonfederally inspected meat has increased in the period since World War II and gives every indication of continuing to do so. Of this 8 billion pounds, about 5 billion pounds of slaughtered meat — 10 million head — receives no ante mortem, post mortem and processing inspections. The fact that Federal inspectors condemn an average of about 1 million pounds of meat a day as unfit for human consumption even under the more stringent Federal inspection is a clue to what the basis for concern is in the nonfederally inspected sector.

More ominous is the entrenchment of deep-rooted economic reasons for traffic in "4D" — dead, dying, disease, and disabled — animals. Ironically, bad meat is, and has been for a long time, good business. So much so that the animals are purchased by buyers who specialize in such trade. The traffic is drawn heavily to intrastate markets because of the nonexistence, laxity, or complicity of Government regulation.

The next step in the marketing process involves the conditions at slaughter and processing plants. Here, once again, the desire to cut costs stakes out sanitation as its priority victim. Even in more reputable plants, the search for cutting costs first alights on cutting the sanitation crews that clean up after hours. When unwholesome animals meet unsanitary plants, the challenge to successful merchandising is formidable. This challenge is met by the ingenuity of modern chemistry misapplied. Seasoning agents, preservatives, cover-up doses of antibiotics, and coloring agents are put to work as profound cosmetics that effectively mask

---

[12] U. S. Senate, Committee on Agriculture and Forestry, Subcommittee on Agricultural Research and General Legislation, *Meat Inspection,* Hearings on S. 2147, S. 2218 and H.R. 12144, 90th Cong., 1st sess., 1967, pp. 250–251.

the true condition of the products. The meanest deception of all is thereby achieved — that of rendering inoperable the natural detection processes of human beings — seeing, smelling, and tasting. Getting more money for less meat encourages the use of fillers — cereal, nonfat dry milk, water, and less savory ingredients. Deceptive labels and advertising put the finishing touches on the process. . . .

The health of the people — in the short and long run — is, of course, the more critical issue. The data leave a good deal to be desired, primarily because of deficient data-gathering programs to determine with greater precision the difficult connections between human diseases and debilitations, and diseased or spoiled meat. Where small "epidemics" occur, the facts are well known. This is the case when 43 workers came down with Bang's disease in a Virginia beef and pork processing plant during the past year. Or when 38 people developed trichinosis in Wisconsin not long ago. Documented is the sharp increase of salmonellosis — 20,000 cases reported last year, but many times that number believed to occur, in the judgment of the National Communicable Disease Center of the Department of Health, Education, and Welfare. Many of these cases come from consumption of contaminated meat. . . .

. . . By the very nature of the problem, the direct connection between unwholesome meat and human health is most difficult to establish under present knowledge. However, the burden of persuasion must not be on the victims but on the perpetrators. Public health authorities do know that diseased or otherwise contaminated meat has a deleterious effect on health that ranges from liver, kidney, and intestinal malfunctioning to fatalities. Pus-infected animals cannot be salutary influences on meat eaters. These are the more short-range effects with possible longer range consequences. It is also clear that the longer range risks of consuming federally banned additives to meat products should not be tolerated in intrastate meat markets.

A 1957 World Health Organization report estimates that trichinosis was more prevalent in the United States than in any other part of the world — about one in six inhabitants harbored trichinae with clinical symptoms displayed by 4.5 percent of the infected. Although this class of infection has been reduced considerably since 1957, the situation is a sober reminder against the complacency that is reflected in the monotonous litany that this country has the best meat inspection in the world.

In the animal disease area, brucellosis and hog cholera are two such animal diseases which have led some countries such as England and Sweden to ban the imports of pork products from the United States. The requirements which must be met under the House-passed bill by meat products imported into this country are much stricter than the requirements, if any, which must be met by intrastate meat products. This sounds like a paradox and, hopefully, one that will be eliminated. . . .

Aled P. Davies, of the American Meat Institute, in opposing most of the proposals before the House committee, tried to be comforting:

> We have had occasion to know something about some of these programs, and we believe that generally speaking they have provided the kind of consumer protection in the various states that the people living in those states have thought necessary and have been willing to pay for. . . . We wonder whether the benefits to be gained justify the kind of Federal expenditures that could develop.

L. Blaine Liljenquist, of the Western States Meat Packers Association, Inc., opposed entirely the legislation on the grounds that existing Federal law was ample for interstate plants and the States could take care of their intrastate plants.

John A. Killick of the National Independent Meat Packers Association also opposed the bill, which eventually passed the House of Representatives, for similar reasons.

To the delight and no surprise of the meat industry, the National Association of State Departments of Agriculture, took a similar stance by offering 10 amendments to the bill that would have eviscerated its substance.

None of these spokesmen gave any indication of the true conditions in intrastate plants. Nor did the U. S. Department of Agriculture give more than a broad brush indication of the distasteful conditions depicted by its veterinarians in the 1962 survey — a survey not even offered to the House committee until its contents reluctantly were made public a few days after the hearings by the Department in response to unyielding outside inquiries.

The House committee was seriously misled, in my judgment, a treatment which, upon subsequent exposure, some members, alas, did not find in the least dismaying. . . .

The Environment

The U. S. Department of Agriculture has been behaving in this meat controversy in a manner that suggests an untoward submission to powerful State agriculture departments and meat industry pressures. For a Department that has professed a long-standing desire for stronger meat inspection laws, its reluctance to support its cause with vigorous application of evidence in its own files staggers the imagination. Virtually every shred of information disclosed about unsavory meat practices by the Department has been in response to persistent inquiries and demands by the press, Members of Congress, and others. The process has been and continues to be agonizing and at times outrageous, given the deeply public interest nature of the information. The Department's lack of **197** responsiveness to its mandate to protect the public and to public information inquiries would make a cynic incredulous.[13]

Senator Mondale kept up the pressure.

This is based on some reports which I obtained from the Department of Agriculture — based on a laboratory analysis of nonfederally inspected meat products, 1967, and there were purchases made at national chain grocery stores of national branded meats of 162 samples, purchased by the Department's laboratory, and of those only 39 met all Federal standards, and a partial examination of this study revealed that nonfederally inspected meat products which do not meet Federal standards have been sold by such stores as Safeway, Piggly Wiggly, and A. & P., Kroger, and First National Stores. And products not meeting the standards have been manufactured by the Nation's two largest firms, Swift & Co. and Armour & Co., according to these same reports. There are many examples of this.

A purchase made at the Safeway store in Phoenix, Ariz., where the investigator bought skinless frankfurters which proved in laboratory analysis to contain 13 percent water and 7.6 percent fillers, that is, nonfat dried milk, soy flour, cereal, and the like, quite in excess of Federal standards, and in a Piggly Wiggly store in Mississippi, the investigator bought some bologna which proved to contain four times as much cereal fillers as would have been permitted under Federal regulations. And one purchase in Texas showed bologna with 20 percent water in it. And in Arizona, of skinless franks, with 13 percent water. And one in West Virginia with 14 percent water. And then there is another element that came out in these studies which, I think, is interesting and reveals the fact of the helplessness of the consumer in trying to deal for herself and her family in meat purchases. This was shown in terms of ascorbate. This is prohibited in processed meat, or nonprocessed meat by Federal plants that are federally inspected. If I understand it, this is a kind of a healthy formaldehyde. It makes meat that is starting to become stale look red and healthy, and in that the consumer would look at this meat and say, "Well, this is certainly fresh," but in fact it may be quite the opposite.

There was a purchase made at Rockville, Md., a purchase of pork sausage, which showed 445 parts per million of ascorbate which would never be permitted in a federally inspected plant. Another purchase made in Rockville[14] at a Safeway store of pork which contained 398 parts

---

[13] *Ibid.*, pp. 142–143, 147–148.

[14] In his original testimony, Senator Mondale said the two ascorbate purchases were made in Baltimore. He later corrected himself to say they were made in Rockville.

198   per million of ascorbate. I think that this further underscores the fact that the consumer, unless she will buy a meat with a Federal inspected stamp is taking her chances, and, of course, when we buy in a restaurant we do not know what we are getting. There is no way of knowing.

Thus, I agree with you that the time is long overdue when protection is needed in this field.

And then we arrive at the question as to whether the State, on its own, will now do a different job, a more effective job, than we have seen in the past 60 years.

We had testimony the other [day] from Mr. Liljenquist who represents, I think, some 12 or 14 States, and his testimony, despite all we have seen, is that there is nothing wrong, that these plants are really in good shape and that the consumer has nothing to worry about, that it is just the politicians and others who would like to be dramatic who are scaring the American public. . . .

I am a person who believes in States rights. I have spent more time in State government than I have in the Federal Government, but I believe in State responsibility, too, and I think that there can be no compromise on the objective of clean and wholesome meat, and the Federal Government and the State government have to assume total responsibility on this.

I agree with you that the worst thing that we could do here is to pass nominal legislation. We have got to deal with this problem fully and completely, so that the American consumer can be safe and secure in the purchase and consumption of meat.[15]

The press throughout the country was printing lurid stories of grim incidents — including such things as kangaroo meat in hamburger. By late fall of 1967, it became evident that the public would demand some kind of improved meat inspection law. At this point the meat packers' associations apparently decided that their only choice was between a weak or "tough" inspection bill. They consequently did an about-face and came out strongly for the weak bill H.R. 12144, which was almost identical to H.R. 6168 — the bill they had opposed only four months earlier.

Aled P. Davies, vice-president of the American Meat Institute (an association of the largest packing companies in the nation), was quite candid about his changed position. In response to a question by Senator Ellender, he said:

Senator, I know you served as a high official in the State legislature, and you know that State legislators, like everybody else, move when the people demand that you move. I think that the situation in this area, this

---

[15] *Ibid.*, pp. 162–163.

period, after all this discussion, much of it has been very painful to many people in the meat industry, that if we do not move forward honestly and firmly to correct the situation, well, then, we have nobody but ourselves to blame.[16]

Congressman Foley's appraisal of the packers' change of heart was not quite so charitable:

But it bothers me somewhat that these State departments of agriculture and the American Meat Institute can come before your subcommittee to say that they accept your bill now but could not say that in the House committee hearings. We could have had a bill — perhaps your bill — long since approved by the Congress if we had had some leadership from the industry.

Senator Montoya. They were not as close to the fire as they are now.

Mr. Foley. That is right — that is exactly the point. They have to have their feet held to the fire before they accept any responsibility. That is tragic.[17]

Along with the packers associations, the National Association of State Departments of Agriculture and the American National Cattlemen's Association changed their position and came out in support of H.R. 12144. With industry support, the bill whipped through Congress in record time. A press release from the House Committee on Agriculture, dated December 6, 1967, described the bill thus:

Basically, the bill provides that the federal government shall pay to a state up to half the cost of maintaining its own inspection system if that state system has standards at least equal to those of the U. S. meat inspection system. This was the crux of the original House bill.

The compromise further adopted Senate provisions to the effect that if a state fails within two years to have such a system in effect, the Secretary of Agriculture may step in and impose federal inspection, which heretofore has been applicable only at slaughtering and processing plants doing business in "interstate" commerce — across state lines. However, should the state show that it is progressing toward establishment of a system of its own which meets the required standards, the Secretary may give that state an additional year to put its program into operation.

The Secretary of Agriculture also is given authority to check on

---

[16] *Ibid.,* p. 131.
[17] *Ibid.,* pp. 252–253.

200   "intrastate" plants — those doing business solely within a state, and invoke federal regulations if he finds unsanitary conditions of a degree which he considers warrants such action to protect the health of the public.

The President signed the bill into law (P.L. 90–201) on December 15, 1967. At the bill-signing ceremony, Upton Sinclair, then 89, was present in a wheel chair and received the souvenir pen President Johnson used to sign the bill.

The passage of such a bill obviously is only a beginning. Persons and organizations who opposed the bill will continue to oppose the execution of the law. People with strong feelings do not give up easily.

Air Safety

In the selection below, E. R. Quesada describes the problems and frustrations of the head of the Federal Aviation Agency — an activity established to protect the safety of consumers of air travel.

In December 1958 I took on the job of eliminating "carelessness, neglect, and incompetence" from this nation's airways insofar as is humanly possible.

Aviation was at a dangerous crossroads. With the jet age dawning, civilian and military traffic were, for all practical purposes, conducted as separate operations without effective co-ordinated control. Tragedy dramatized the hazard early in 1958 — when sixty-one lives were lost in two mid-air collisions involving military and commercial aircraft.

I gave up my retired status as an Air Force officer to become the first civilian chief of the newborn Federal Aviation Agency which had been given authority far exceeding that of any previous regulatory body in this field. Our responsibility in fact embraces every aspect of civil aviation — from the construction of aircraft to the design of seats and ashtrays and the amount of whiskey consumed by passengers; from ground maintenance to pilot and crew competence. It embraces vital aspects of military flying as well.

When I took office, years of timid and indecisive regulation by the government had bred a dangerous spirit of complacency throughout the field of aviation. Someone, I knew, was going to have to meet this head-on. I did not shrink from this assignment, nor do I today.

The aviation industry on its own initiative devotes a vast amount of time, money, and effort to making flying safe. Yet, no one likes to be regulated — least of all the types of men whose adventuresome spirit has attracted them to flying.

And so I was prepared for resistance, arguments, and delays. But I was not prepared for the sustained, highly organized pressure campaigns that we soon encountered at every turn. I did not anticipate that my own motives — and those of the agency — would be constantly questioned, that the Congress and the public would be deliberately misled and misinformed, and that willful misrepresentations would be used to stir up grievances and foment resentment among the very men whose own lives were at stake in our safety rules.

From my first day in office, the irresponsible pressure asserted itself. The agency was still an embryo when Max Karant, vice president of the Aircraft Owners and Pilots Association (AOPA) — which purports to represent the fliers of private planes — bitterly warned his members of "increasing military domination of the FAA." (At that time, only two of the twenty top positions in the agency had even been filled. Today, of a complement of 38,000 only 130 are military men and only one of our major offices is headed by one.) Not long afterward, I was visited by the same organization's president, Joseph Hartranft. His purpose was to protest against our new medical requirements for pilots' licenses — a subject I will discuss in more detail later in this report. I listened to him attentively and then told him our decision would stand.

"This means war," he answered, his face flushed.

He has certainly fulfilled this threat. The AOPA has kept up a continuous drumfire of distortion and invective. Through its magazine and "confidential newsletter," it has even fought against rules that in no way affected private pilots. It has accused us of sinister plans and then taken credit for "defeating" proposals we never contemplated.

Equally hostile has been the Air Line Pilots Association (ALPA), spokesman for the commercial pilots. At times ALPA's tactics have embarrassed its own members and they have gone out of their way to tell us so.

One, for instance, sent us anonymously what we call the ALPA "Do-It-Yourself Kit." This is a collection of mimeographed material designed to teach pilots how to write to Congressmen in protest against FAA. It includes lists of key committee members, helpful hints on style, outlines, a collection of "suggested tidbits," and miscellaneous advice on how to give letters the ring of originality. Many of the communications from pilots which Congressmen refer to our agency have obviously been inspired in this way.

AOPA and ALPA have not been the only sources of pressure. More than forty such groups representing aviation interests have participated in our rule-making activities and — at one time or another — a number of them have managed to put stumbling blocks in our way. The new agency's devotion to duty — it appears — came as a great shock to many of them. They had grown used to a situation in which the regulator was

202   regulating with an eye more to the wishes of the regulated, than to the needs of the public. It was this situation which led to the creation of the FAA.

Crowding the Air

In the mid-1950s almost everyone concerned with aviation knew that the government's machinery for supervising our airways and supervising aviation safety was hopelessly out of date. Responsibility was split among three government bodies: the Civil Aeronautics Administration, the Civil Aeronautics Board, and the Defense establishment. The evils of lax administration, bureaucratic inertia, and red tape were all too apparent. A Presidential committee was appointed to look into the situation, and in the spring of 1957 it produced a blueprint of what needed to be done. After hearings in both houses of Congress, these recommendations were enacted into law with unprecedented speed, thanks very largely to the strong leadership of Senator Mike Monroney and Congressman Oren Harris. . . .

But the traffic problem in our skies continues to challenge our best efforts. For aviation has progressed faster than our methods of regulating it. In 1938 there were only some 29,000 planes aloft. Today there are more than 102,000, of which about 2,000 are commercial airliners (including 150 jets), 70,000 are private and business aircraft, and 30,000 are military planes.

The meteoric growth of air transport is not going to slow down — nor would we want it to. But the hazards inherent in our increasing air traffic and our ever faster planes are so great that the government's regulatory program is a matter of top public importance. For this reason attempts to discredit that program and to mire it down in delays and red tape cannot be viewed merely as an unpleasant — but natural — burden for a bureaucrat or agency. *They are a menace to public safety.* It is particularly dismaying to find that one of the leaders in the campaign of harassment has been the Air Line Pilots Association, whose members — in the main — are skilled and dedicated professional men.

Greek God in the Cockpit

The ALPA is a labor union — of a rather special order. Its more than 13,000 members earn from $11,000 to $32,000 a year. The union is said to have millions of dollars in its "war chest" and can pay strike benefits of $500 to $600 a month. Its president, Clarence N. Sayen, receives a salary of $36,000 a year. He recently described his membership as "highly individualistic."

This is a description few would dispute. Unfortunately, at the time FAA was created, individualism — in some instances — had assumed the form of complacency and open contempt for government regulations. In his new book, *The Probable Cause*, Robert J. Serling, the well-known and able aviation reporter, observed:

"The CAA almost seemed to be afraid of pilots. A few years ago a CAA inspector was asked why he didn't crack down on more flight crews.

" 'How do you spank a Greek god?' the inspector plaintively replied."

Perhaps because I am a pilot myself I do not regard fliers as godlike or infallible. In our first year we filed 235 violation reports against airline pilots. This represented an increase of almost 100 per cent over the average number filed in any one of the previous five years.

Among the actions which particularly roused the ALPA was my early announcement that I intended to keep pilots in the cockpit during flights. It was then a widespread practice — encouraged by some companies — for pilots to socialize with the passengers. I believe that a pilot's place is at the controls and I set about strictly enforcing our requirements for continuous cockpit vigilance.

Despite all the automated controls that we have developed, we must still rely very heavily on the human eye as an essential defense against collisions. For this reason the "see-and-be-seen" principle remains a cardinal rule of air safety. To illustrate — we fined the pilot of a DC-7 carrying thirty-five passengers because of a near miss involving an Air Force tanker engaged in refueling two fighter craft. The pilot of the tanker saw the DC-7 at a distance of more than a mile. But the pilot of the DC-7 gave no evidence of ever having seen the tanker because — as our investigation disclosed — he was back in the passenger cabin.

This is only one instance among many of the demonstrated need for cockpit vigilance. Yet when we undertook a program of strict enforcement, the ALPA attacked our efforts as those of a "childish Gestapo" and engaged in a public campaign of abuse and vilification against our agency.

It has taken a similar attitude toward the presence of our inspectors who go aboard about one of every 500 airline flights to make a first-hand check of safety practices. Calling these inspections "harassment" and a "hazard," ALPA objected strenuously to our inspectors being seated where they needed to be to observe what was going on. Underlying this absurd position was a battle the union was waging with the companies for an additional "pilot-qualified" crew member on jets. . . .

One of the most vicious attacks we have experienced occurred after a National airliner broke up in mid-air over the North Carolina coast last January. The next day Captain R. J. Rohan of ALPA's National Airlines Council made a public charge to the effect that the plane's structure had been fatally weakened by maneuvers required by FAA inspectors while checking pilots' performance. As it turned out, the wreckage yielded sufficient evidence to prove that a bomb carried aboard by a passenger

204　　had caused the crash. If, however, the plane had fallen into the sea instead of on land Captain Rohan's irresponsible charge might never have been disproved.

The Age-sixty Question

One very bitter clash with ALPA was over our ruling making sixty the age limit for pilots in air-carrier operations. The decision was prompted by medical considerations: with advancing years, men deteriorate psychologically and physically. Heart attacks and strokes are much more likely to occur after the age of sixty — and such physical accidents are unpredictable.

In aviation certain decisions must be reached largely through judgment. We cannot always back them up by comprehensive and proven statistics — as in the case of highway transport — for aviation is a young industry. We did not have enough old pilots in service to provide any meaningful comparison of the accident records of young and old pilots. But we could and did look to the common-sense example of the airlines of other nations. (BOAC, KLM have made fifty-five the compulsory retirement age for pilots; and SAS, sixty.)

In 1959 approximately forty airline pilots had reached the age of sixty. By 1967 there will be 250. Because of the seniority system, older pilots have first choice of the newer aircraft, which generally carry higher pay and greater prestige. As a consequence the average age of jet pilots today is considerably above the general average. (A year ago well over half of one airline's jet pilots were sixty or over.) In bygone years ALPA has readily conceded that flying is a young man's game. (This does not mean that a skilled pilot will be out of work after sixty — if he wants to stay in aviation there are plenty of jobs, on the ground or even in flight training and checking, in which his experience can be well used.) The union went to bat for its senior citizens and was joined in the ensuing pressure campaign by the private pilots organization, AOPA, which was not affected by the age limit and was — in many other ways — a strange bedfellow for the airline pilots. . . .

Their Day in Court

FAA has, naturally, concerned itself with the safety of private pilots. We have, for example, required them to have some instrument training — for when weather is so bad that you cannot see the horizon, only instruments can enable a pilot to fly straight and level and thus avoid disaster. We have also refused to issue certificates to persons suffering from such diseases as epilepsy, insanity, diabetes, and serious heart ailments. (Heart attacks have been a significant cause of private plane accidents and one recently is believed to have figured in the crash of one of our newest commercial jets during a training flight.) Unlike our predecessor agencies, we will not accept medical certificates signed merely by the applicant's personal physician. We require examination by one of several thousand doctors designated by FAA who are kept fully informed of our standards.

This was the practice followed by the government from 1926 to 1945. Then in 1945, against medical advice, the CAA relaxed the rule and agreed to let any doctor perform these examinations. When we at the FAA looked into the situation we found that of the airmen originally given a clean bill of health by an examiner and later rejected by FAA for failure to meet our physical standards, 84 per cent had been cleared by non-designated examiners.

Accordingly, last June — after a public hearing and with the approval of the American Medical Association — we issued a rule requiring certification by designated aviation medical examiners. This action evoked a storm of protest from AOPA. We were accused of — among other things — planning to "outlaw the family physician." In fact, any family doctor or any other physician can become a designated examiner by demonstrating an interest in aviation medicine and keeping informed of our standards and examining procedures.

We regard these rules as safeguards of the pilot's right to stay alive, but it was at this time that AOPA flashed the word to its members that *"Your right to fly is in jeopardy."*

Protesting both our "unreasonable medical regulations" and our "unreasonable age restrictions," AOPA, in a joint statement with ALPA, announced that the issue of "FAA dictatorship" and our "arbitrary and militaristic empire" would be taken directly to Congress. Both associations mounted an assault on Capitol Hill.

It is interesting to note that while the two organizations joined together, their motives were different. The AOPA's purpose was an increase in membership while ALPA — whose members have grown complacent through the previous years of government indecision — was objecting to FAA determination that it, not the regulated, shall do the regulating.

Meanwhile ALPA took the age-sixty question to court for a legal test. The courts in due course upheld the rule as "reasonable in relation to the standards prescribed in the statute and the facts before the Administrator." But ALPA continues its fight, going so far as to claim, at a Senate hearing, that our courts do not provide an adequate system of review. They have since said that they lost out legally only because they had been "outsmarted" by the government's lawyers.

In fairness to ALPA I must say it is not alone. Others in the aviation community share this attitude, and insist that the FAA Administrator's rules should be curbed by some additional layer of review above and beyond the courts — that, in other words, when a court agrees with the Administrator there must be something wrong with the court.

Over the years the airline industry and the Air Transport Association developed the idea that regulation should be some sort of co-operative effort between the airlines and the government, with the ultimate decision to be reached by mutual agreement. I recall at one meeting jolting a group of airline presidents by telling them that we had no notion whatever that the industry had to agree with an FAA regulation before it would be adopted. Inevitably there have been a number of occasions when they did not agree — but I believe the public has reason to be grateful for our strength of purpose.

Dollars versus Lives

From the management and industry side we have been under fire in the main because safety is expensive. For example, it costs as much as $25,000 per plane to install all-weather radar. None the less we have insisted that all commercial planes be so equipped and the program is scheduled for completion by next year.

Likewise we insist that all turbine-powered planes carry flight recorders connected to the instrument panel and that all recorded information be kept for sixty days. This data provides a detailed report on speed, altitude, direction, and time of day. This information is not only invaluable in accident investigations but provides a useful check on everyday plane performance. Flight recorders cost from $5,000 to $7,000. Even worse — from the business-office point of view — each one weighs about twenty-five pounds, which means twenty-five pounds less payload every trip. As expected, the airlines found many reasons why flight recorders were not needed.

Similarly they were displeased when we insisted that the copilots of jets must attain a standard of proficiency almost as high as pilots. This could be accomplished only by ten or fifteen hours of additional training. In the case of a new jet, rental for this purpose can run as high as $4,000 an hour. The airlines have estimated that this additional training is saddling them with an added cost in the millions. And they are not happy about it.

Generally speaking, the pressure from the management end has been more sophisticated though no less obstructive than the AOPA and ALPA campaigns. For instance, the companies complained at a Senate hearing this year that FAA did not seek the industry's views early enough to provide opportunity for full discussion.

When I looked into the matter I found — to my own consternation — that our Bureau of Flight Standards had conducted 506 meetings at which 5,158 people were present. The Bureau of Air Traffic Management had dealt with 2,077 people at 363 formal gatherings. The Bureau of Aviation Medicine had held 175 meetings attended by 2,038. In addition there had been too many informal and regional meetings to tabulate. I am inclined to doubt that this much discussion is necessary or even helpful.

I question too whether any amount of discussion can satisfy people who attend meetings only for the purpose of opposing. For example, in response to a demand to "take part in the early thinking" at a time when FAA's attitude was "still flexible," last August we called an exploratory meeting of 200 people to discuss airline maintenance problems. Yet William B. Becker, Director of Operating and Engineering for the Air Transport Association (the airlines' Washington lobby) walked out because, he said, we had not provided a sufficiently detailed agenda. He departed for the announced purpose of "developing a common industry position" — which, to no one's surprise, turned out to be an inflexible opposition to any change in regulations.

There is a point when conferences and committees serve no purpose beyond delaying necessary action. It seems to me, also, if we yield to false and insincere appeals for more "due process" and protection of the rights of the individual, going beyond what is legitimate and traditional in this regard, we can easily lose sight of the larger good.

The balance between legitimate concern for individual rights and the public good is well illustrated by the crash of an Arctic Pacific airliner near Toledo this past October, with a loss of twenty-two lives. The pilot, who was among those killed, was Donald F. J. Chesher. Several months earlier FAA had revoked his airline pilot rating after a hearing in which it was determined that he had violated the regulations and demonstrated a lack of care, responsibility, and judgment. However, our order was automatically stayed by his appeal to the CAB and he was able to continue flying pending the appeal. Legally this proceeding was quite proper. But one may well ask whether the correct rights were adequately safeguarded in this instance.

Now I do not question that there can be honest and valid differences of opinion on matters of air safety. Difficult questions of judgment are involved and few decisions are immune to plausible counter-argument. Criticism based on facts and documented by the record should always be welcomed by any public official. But opposition that is mere obstructionism is a different matter. Even more reprehensible is a calculated effort to attribute questionable motives to a government agency and to use intemperate attack to undermine confidence in its decisions.

Fortunately, through exposure to these tactics, we are onto their game. Two years of experience have lent us sophistication. We know what to expect. We know the pattern. It generally goes like this: The first

208   attack is to charge the agency itself with being "arbitrary and capricious." The second target is the procedure by which action was taken. This is inevitably discredited as being "unfair," "unjust." The third attack charges the agency with being a "dictatorship." The fourth target is myself, the Administrator. My resignation is demanded and letters are sent to the President calling for my dismissal.

I have refused to be intimidated by such attacks. But it is high time, I think, that the public became aware of the calculated campaigns of deliberate subversion to which regulatory agencies are exposed. In the field of aviation these pressures may well be considered the most serious menace to effective regulation and enforcement — and hence to air safety — that faces us.

FAA's Mandate

Air safety is the keystone of aeronautical progress. This is — or should be — well understood by everyone who earns his living in aviation, including the pilot, the union leader, and the profit-conscious airline executive.

My role is a different one though the goal is the same. As Administrator of the Federal Aviation Agency my most important job is to do for the American public, in the field of air safety, what the public cannot do for itself. My mandate was spelled out by Congressman Oren Harris, Chairman of the House Committee on Interstate and Foreign Commerce, in a 1957 report that helped lay the groundwork for the creation of our agency the following year:

> Any tendency by government agencies to proceed with caution in promulgating or enforcing regulations to promote safety must be avoided at all costs, even at the risk of being charged with undue harshness. . . . In achieving the maximum safety standards possible in the public interest, all segments of aviation have a responsibility to give and take for the common good. Those affected should gladly accept and co-operate in making effective needed controls in the interest of safety, disregarding the burdens involved.

Intemperate pressure campaigns clearly violate this concept. It is my belief that groups representing special interests — which are in fact segments of the public interest — have responsibilities beyond the mere pursuit of their selfish aims. . . .

We have come to think of exposure to irresponsible criticism as a normal hazard of public service. In time, a public servant can learn to shrug off such attacks. The danger, however, is that he may not have the firmness of purpose and that these attacks will ultimately erode his determination and courage. This is a problem that pervades our public **209** life. I regard the pressure-group activities in aviation as particularly ominous — not because I am personally involved, but because in this field we are dealing daily with decisions of life and death importance.[18]

A few days after the above article was published General Quesada resigned as director of the Federal Aviation Agency.

---

[18] E. R. Quesada, "The Pressures Against Air Safety," Copyright © 1960, by *Harper's Magazine,* Inc. Reprinted from the January 1961 issue of *Harper's Magazine* by permission of the author.

Laborers: Automation and the Right to Work

Women and children shouldn't have to go into the fields. . . . A farm worker should be able to make enough so that his wife can stay in her home and the children go to school.

Jim Drake

One day a minister came out here and called me a slave driver because people were working so hard. I said, "They want to work hard and make more money," and what in the world is wrong with that?

Jack Pandol

6

Trends, Ideologies, and Images

A century ago, most Americans were farmers, proprietors, or independent craftsmen, or they were employed on a small farm or business. Relationships between employers and employees were usually personal, and the employee was often considered to be part of the family.

Farmers and other self-employed persons were somewhat self-sufficient and were at least partially immune from changes in prices both for what they bought and for what they sold. Employees generally aspired to become proprietors, and with luck and skill their chances were good.

Within the last hundred years, a dramatic shift in employment has taken place. By 1900 the percentage of people employed in agriculture had declined to 37.5 percent; in 1940 it was 17.1 percent; and by 1960 it had dropped to 6 percent.[1] The percentage of other self-employed persons also dropped sharply.

One result of this change was that millions of Americans ceased to be independent. They no longer grew their own food or made their own

---

[1] U. S. Bureau of the Census, *Statistical Abstract of the United States: 1966* (Washington, D. C.: Government Printing Office, 1966), p. 219.

212 clothing and shelter, and they lost the necessary skills to do so — even if it should become necessary. They became dependent on wages and continued employment. Most of them no longer even owned their own tools — they used the ones provided by their employer. The old agrarian frontier values of independence, individuality, and self-reliance remained strong; but these values were increasingly inappropriate in an industrial society composed mainly of wage earners.

As workers came to realize that they would not go back to the farm and that their chances for self-employment were increasingly limited, they began to develop a group self-consciousness as workers (or employees). At the same time, they realized that the bargaining power of one person against a large company was extremely weak, especially when the supply of labor often exceeded the demand. These realizations gave impetus to a labor union movement.

Notwithstanding changed conditions and realizations, the potential strength of labor unions over the years has been diminished by a continuing influx of farm workers, who carried with them the old agrarian values. The failure of unions in the recently industrialized South stems partly from the high proportion of workers newly removed from farms and rural areas.

In recent years, two other major shifts have occurred: the percentage of working women has increased, and the proportion of blue-collar workers has decreased while the proportion of white-collar workers has increased. Both these trends have worked against increasing union memberships. Women are apparently less interested than men are in unions. They constitute about 30 percent of the labor force, but only one in six employed women is a union member. White-collar workers have traditionally been difficult to unionize presumably because they ordinarily enjoy some of the benefits sought by unions (more stable employment) and because they apparently are more likely to adopt managerial views and values. Increased automation (to be discussed later) is likely to further reduce the proportion of blue-collar workers and increase the percentage of people in white-collar jobs.

Union membership is mainly restricted to mining, manufacturing, transportation, and construction — over 80 percent of union workers are in these four general industries. Conversely, the number of union workers is small in wholesale and retail trade, finance, insurance, and the service industries. Very few farm workers are unionized.

Union membership is not only concentrated in certain industries — it is also concentrated geographically in the Middle Atlantic, North Central, and Pacific Coast areas. It is lowest in the South and in the Great Plains and Rocky Mountain states.

Historical Background of the Labor Movement

Some small craft unions existed as far back as colonial times, but the first large and general labor union was the Knights of Labor; it had a membership of 700,000 and enjoyed spectacular success in the 1880s. However, because of lack of support by the craft unions, diversified membership, and uncertain objectives, the Knights of Labor lost ground and, by 1917, had disappeared altogether.

In the meantime (1881), six prominent craft unions met in Pittsburgh and formed a Federation of Organized Trades and Labor Unions under the leadership of a cigar-maker — Samuel Gompers. From this nucleus the American Federation of Labor (AFL) was formed in 1886.

The AFL was, and still is, an association of craft or trade unions, organized on the basis of a particular skill rather than by industry. Each of the separate unions has considerable independence, so the AFL resembles a confederacy more than a federation as is implied by its name. The AFL membership grew rapidly — from 138,000 in 1886 to two million at the beginning of World War I. By 1920, the total was four million.

Although AFL membership continued to increase during the 30s, some union leaders came to the conclusion that craft unions were inadequate for dealing with some of the major industries. Large manufacturing industries (steel, automobiles, rubber) employed both unskilled and semi-skilled workers who ordinarily were not eligible for membership in a craft union. Furthermore, the individual craft unions were at a disadvantage in dealing with a large manufacturing company. A carpenters' union strike against General Motors, for instance, would be annoying to the company but certainly not disabling. In recognition of this situation, John L. Lewis formed the Congress of Industrial Organizations (CIO) in 1938. The CIO was organized on an industry basis rather than a skill basis.

In December 1955, the AFL and CIO merged. This combination did not create a single, monolithic labor union; rather, it was a merger of two federations of somewhat autonomous individual unions.

The early unions were considered to be "combinations in restraint of trade" and thus illegal under the Sherman Anti-Trust Act (1890). Later the *legality* of unions was admitted, but the courts disallowed most of their *activities.* Strikes were frequently broken by court injunctions and picketing strikers were often dispersed by state troops. A long series of state laws on child labor, minimum wages, maximum hours, and safety measures were struck down by the courts.

The first real breakthrough for labor on a national scale occurred with the passage of the Norris-LaGuardia Act in 1932. This law recognized the right of workers to form unions, made "yellow dog" contracts (agreements prohibiting workers from joining unions) unenforceable, and limited the use of labor injunctions.

Next came the National Labor Relations Act (Wagner Act) of 1935 which prohibited employers from engaging in four types of unfair labor practices: (1) interfering with collective bargaining, (2) refusing to bargain with employees' representatives, (3) attempting to dominate or interfere with labor unions, and (4) discriminating against union members in hiring or firing or in other ways. The Wagner Act also established a National Labor Relations Board to administer the other provisions of the Act.

The Fair Labor Standards Act (1938) was the next major advance for

American labor, both organized and unorganized. The act established minimum wage and maximum hour standards and prohibited the employment of children under 16 in industries engaged in interstate commerce. Probably this act was of greatest benefit to laborers outside of labor unions.

During World War II, there were some instances of mismanagement of union funds by labor leaders. By the war's end, widespread resentment existed against the "excesses" of labor. At the same time, the Republican party elected a majority to both houses of Congress for the first time since the Hoover administration. The result of this combination of factors was the passage, over Truman's veto, of the Taft-Hartley (Labor-Management Relations) Act of 1947.

While the Wagner Act had been concerned with unfair *management* practices, the Taft-Hartley Act prohibited unfair *union* practices. The most controversial provision of this complex act made the closed shop illegal. The Taft-Hartley Act was denounced by union leaders as "the slave labor act," but it is significant that it has not been repealed and that for most of its 20-year life the Democratic party has had a majority in both houses of Congress.

The Taft-Hartley Act was not the end of labor's troubles; in 1959, Congress passed the Landrum-Griffin Act, which, in prohibiting certain malpractices, reached considerably beyond the provisions of Taft-Hartley. In addition, some 19 states passed so-called "right-to-work" laws which had the effect of outlawing the union shop as well as the closed shop. (There are three general categories of "shops" in labor union parlance. A *closed shop* is one in which prospective employees must join the union *before* they are hired. A *union shop* is one in which a nonunion member may be hired but he must join the union within a specified time period. In an *open shop,* there are no requirements on union membership; it is "open" to both union and nonunion employees.)

The Political Effectiveness of Organized Labor

There were some 17 million persons in organized labor unions in 1964. If these 17 million people voted as a unit, they could probably "swing" every election in those areas where they have high concentrations of membership. That they have not been able to do so is obvious. The AFL-CIO endorsed presidential candidate Adlai Stevenson, who lost by resounding margins. George Meany, president of the AFL, was a staunch supporter of losing presidential candidate Hubert H. Humphrey. Even in such highly industrialized (and unionized) states as Michigan, Illinois, and Pennsylvania, the recent record of labor effectiveness in winning elections has not been impressive. We have seen that both federal and state legislation since 1947 has, on balance, been generally antilabor. Organized labor helped elect Presidents Truman, Kennedy, and

Johnson, but union members did not "swing" these elections any more than did the votes of the millions of nonunion persons who voted for these candidates.

Why is organized labor less effective politically than its large membership would suggest?

1. The unions "fight among themselves." As we have noted, the AFL-CIO is a confederacy of quasi-autonomous unions. On some policy questions there may be general agreement; on others there may be dispute. Proposals to give railroads more discretion in rate-making were supported by the railway brotherhoods and opposed by the Teamsters because of a fear that trucking might suffer from the more effective competition of railroads. At the same time, the railway brotherhoods opposed proposals for the development of coal slurry pipelines while the United Mineworkers supported them. In the 1962 senatorial race in California, the CIO generally supported the Democratic candidate Richard Richards while some AFL unions supported Republican Thomas Kuchel. Labor is often divided on issues and candidates; there is no single set of policies to which all adhere.

2. Unions have concentrated most of their resources in attempting to obtain jobs, increase wages, and improve working conditions through traditional "non-political" activities, such as collective bargaining, strikes, and so forth. Politics has been an important but secondary activity.

3. Since organized labor has accomplished many of its basic objectives, much of the old crusading missionary zeal is gone. Compared with an earlier era, labor has become relatively fat, prosperous, and satisfied.

4. Allied to item 3 above is the fact that the nonunion public no longer thinks of labor as the underdog. The successes of labor in acquiring higher wage rates has caused resentment, not only from employers but also from millions of people, many of whom work for lower wages than are paid union members. While the nonunion public may be generally sympathetic to the objectives of labor, it is no longer sympathetic to the unions themselves.

5. It is probable that the oligarchic tendencies that seem to be inherent in labor unions and the consequent long tenure of labor leaders[2] produces a rigidity or inability to adapt to changing political situations.

6. The structure and practices of Congress, the state legislatures, and city councils tend to frustrate the accomplishment of labor objectives. The committee system and the traditional practice of awarding congressional committee chairmanships to the senior member have not generally supported the interests of labor. Congressmen with seniority are most likely to come from the "safe" one-party states or districts, regardless of which party has a majority. These "safe" districts are also likely to be the most conservative and generally tend to be antilabor.

---

[2] Samuel Gompers was president of the AFL for 38 years. After his death in 1924, William Green held the presidency for almost three decades. Dan Tobin was the leader of the Teamsters for about half a century; Hutcheson led the Carpenters for 35 years and was succeeded by his son. John L. Lewis was president of the United Mine Workers for over 40 years.

216   Most state legislatures have been even less sympathetic to labor than has Congress. When the shift of power from rural to urban influences has been completed (as a result of Supreme Court decisions on apportionment), the various legislatures may become more receptive to labor than have been the rural-dominated legislatures of the past. However, this hypothesis remains to be tested.

Labor probably has least influence in city councils (even though unions are concentrated in urban areas). City councils are ordinarily controlled by "Main Street" or "downtown," so labor ordinarily has little impact.

7. Regardless of our insistence that the United States is a classless society, the social status of union members and union leaders has been, and still remains, very low. Harmon Zeigler sums it up this way:

Labor began as a protest movement. Of necessity its leaders were predominantly deviants — those whose aspirations were regarded with suspicion. America experienced the sudden rise to considerable power of men whose background was foreign to the customary career pattern of success, that of the business and professional people. As a result of their deviance, labor leaders past and present can attain wealth and varying degrees of influence but not necessarily the social acceptance that usually accompanies such attributes: "The labor leader's social status is equivalent to that of a street car conductor." The businessman can work his way up from the bottom and find not only financial but social rewards awaiting him. The labor union leader can follow a similar path and find only ostracism.[3]

The low social status of labor leaders is reflected in the low percentage of union members who are elected to public office. Donald Matthews' study of United States senators from 1954 to 1957 indicates that although 6 percent of them started as industrial wage earners, none of them stayed in this occupational category long enough to have it designated as his principal occupation.[4] Belle Zeller found that laborers and craftsmen constituted 5.6 percent of lower house members and 2.6 percent of all state senate members in 1949 — when labor was near its peak strength.[5] Very rarely is a union member, who makes his living in his union occupation, elected to a city council.

8. Probably the most important reason for the relative political ineffectiveness of labor has been the continued adherence of union members

---

[3] Harmon Zeigler, *Interest Groups in American Society* (Englewood Cliffs, New Jersey: Prentice-Hall, 1964), pp. 130–131.

[4] Donald R. Matthews, *United States Senators and Their World* (New York: Vintage Books, 1960), p. 32.

[5] Belle Zeller, ed., *American State Legislatures* (New York: Crowell, 1954), p. 71.

to individualistic ideologies. Most union members believe they will succeed or fail because of individual ability (or lack of it) and luck. They do not really believe that their individual lives or fortunes will rise or fall with that of the union. Ironically, it seems that the more successful the unions are, the weaker will be their hold upon their own members. As union workers become more prosperous, they are likely to lose whatever class consciousness they may have had; and they are less likely to identify ideologically with the unions.

We should notice in passing that many union members (possibly a majority) are not members by reason of any strong ideological conviction. Many of them belong to the union because it is necessary to keep their job (union shop) or because it is customary to be a member in certain industries or because of various social and other pressures exerted upon them by fellow workers and union organizers. The percentage of union workers who have a real ideological commitment to the principles of unionism is probably fairly small.

Notwithstanding the difficulties cited above, labor leaders have developed a variety of techniques and devices that have been remarkably effective in controlling their members and in mustering a solid and disciplined force in labor negotiations. This discipline has not carried over, however, into the political arena. Union workers, as much as any other Americans, resent having anyone tell them how to vote. Their wives are likely to be even more politically independent.[6] E. E. Schattschneider has estimated that the net gain to the Democratic party in presidential elections, attributable to unionization, could be as low as 960,000.[7]

This section has concentrated on the disadvantages of labor in the political struggle. Does this mean that labor will fail to achieve its objectives? Not at all. Monsen and Cannon sum it up this way:

History appears to favor many of labor's desires. This is so, not because the membership of unions continues to grow, but because in a democracy there is a continuous trend toward developing programs which will attract the votes of the majority of citizens. In this sense, despite the curtailing of some of labor's power in the past decade or so, the liberal coalition, which normally controls the Presidency of the United States, is likely to win further welfare measures over the opposition of the conservative coalition, which often controls Congress. Labor, therefore, will benefit from acquisitive mass psychology even if the strength of unions as a single power bloc should decrease.[8]

---

[6] George Meany, president of the AFL-CIO, ordered voter surveys after the 1952 and 1956 presidential elections. One of the findings of these surveys was that, while union members had generally voted for Stevenson, their wives had voted for Eisenhower.

[7] E. E. Schattschneider, *The Semi-Sovereign People* (New York: Holt, Rinehart and Winston, 1960), p. 51.

[8] R. Joseph Monsen, Jr., and Mark W. Cannon, *The Makers of Public Policy* (New York: McGraw-Hill Book Co., 1965), p. 65.

After this brief survey of labor in the political process, let us turn to three specific issues that have occupied the attention of both labor leaders and politicians for many years and which promise to remain continuing issues for many years to come: the effects of automation on labor, the perennial issue of "right-to-work" laws as permitted by Section 14(b) of the Taft-Hartley Act, and the right of farm workers to organize labor unions.

Automation

The term "automation" means "to make automatic," but this kind of dictionary definition does not tell us what automation really is and what its effects are likely to be on society in general and on labor in particular. Ted Silvey of the AFL-CIO attempts both to define the term realistically and to assess its impact on American society in the speech that follows.

Automation and the Changing Job Mix[9]

On the basis of the study I've been able to do during the last decade, my strongly held opinion is that the new industrial technology being called automation is the most powerful single force in American society today. I think it is a force more powerful than the family, or religion, or business, or political parties, or the labor movement, or the patriotic societies, or any other thing that one can say is a force or pressure in our society. . . .

Horse to auto gradual. When the automobile came (I grew up in the period when it was coming) we had about three decades to adapt to the changes. . . . During these three decades the changes brought automobile dealers, filling stations, automobile repair shops, roadside stands, insurance claims adjusters, and the whole gamut of things that followed the automobile.

In this present decade, the changes aren't coming over so many years to allow people to make gradual adjustments; they are coming with a force that sometimes brings changes literally within days and weeks. The people who prefer to hold to the idea "As it was in the beginning, now is, and ever shall be, world without end, Amen!" are most uncomfortable about the pressures for change which they do not want to make.

What is automation? I would like now to describe what automation is, and then talk about work and employment and some of the patterns I think are significant for the future as a result of the technology, things we in the labor movement are often talking about.

[9] Remarks delivered at the Marshall-Wythe Symposium, The College of William and Mary in Virginia, 1964. Reproduced with permission of the author.

When a human being works or engages in any of the activities of living he uses this marvelous mechanism which is his body and his brain in three rather separate and distinct ways which are coordinate to accomplish a job. . . . The first thing we use is physical strength and manual dexterity, which we call skill. We've got strength in our legs and thighs, our backs and shoulders, our arms and hands, which we can apply to work. Our fingers are trained to do things which range from crude to delicate; according to the amount of skill we have we can apply the strength of our body into movement of our fingers to do work.

The second thing we have is sensory perception and personal control. The five physical senses are the windows of the human being on his environment or the world about him. The input, the things we see, hear, smell, taste and feel enter into our consciousness. According to our training and our education we respond to the input with an output which is our personal control of the situation, as circumstances permit.

In addition, we utilize the third competence — the human brain. I will speak only of two of a number of functions of the brain — memory and decision-making. Memory is the stored-up newsreel of life. From the moment of birth we begin to accumulate information, received through sensory input. Each bit of information is stored in one of the neurons of the brain, of which we have something like thirteen thousand million.

Human brain miracles. The miracle of the brain is not only that every sensory perception we have ever experienced is recorded and stored there. The real miracle of the brain is in the inter-circuitry of the neurons, by which every thing we have received from any one of the senses can be related, interrelated, to everything we have received from every one of the other senses. So there is a continual cross circuitry, by which information in the brain is related and compared. I suppose this is the thinking process and imagination.

In addition to memory — this newsreel of life — we have decision-making. We say Yes! or No! and we do it two ways. One is by the cerebellum, a baseball-size section of the brain in the back of our cranium at the top of the spinal cord. The cerebellum operates automatically or, as the neurologists say, autonomically. The body has to function continuously about a lot of processes, to make an awful lot of decisions. If one consciously had to make decisions with respect to all the normal activities of life, we would never have time to do anything else. . . .

In addition to the autonomic nervous system with its Yes! or No! decision-making, we have the cerebral functions of the brain in the top of the head. Here we make conscious and deliberate decisions, saying Yes! or No!, thoughtfully considering out of information and experience, with advice and counsel. We use the cerebral area of the brain to consider more important things than how to feed ourselves, how to tie shoelaces, how to fulfill the other repetitive, less complex matters. We have thus delegated the processes of routine life and activity to the cerebellum so that we have time for the better use of our cerebral area.

Giant and clever machines. I go over these three points of physical strength and manual dexterity, the perceptive senses and personal control, and two functions of the brain — memory and decision-making — because I now want to assert that in the last dozen and a half years, for the first time in human history in the United States and in several of the other highly industrialized nations of the world, we have designed, built, installed and are operating inanimate apparatus which do these three things faster, cheaper, more continuously, better than human beings can do them. This is automation. This accomplishment has come quite quickly in the last fifteen to eighteen years, based on centuries of earlier and very much slower development.

To match these three traditional human ways of work, we have three systems of inanimate apparatus. . . . First, we have highly engineered mechanization. Mechanization, of course means machinery. Mechanization means parts moving in relationship to each other. Machinery is not new.

When we talk about the extension of a man's arm and hand with a tool, we also talk about the extension of the hand tool into an apparatus — such as my mother's early sewing machine, which she peddled by foot and leg power . . . such as an early household washing machine with a push-and-pull handle or hand-turned wheel . . . such as simple machines in early factories. During the last few years we have developed machinery that is very sophisticated, that can literally do work that human beings cannot do. . . .

Even more clever instruments. The second thing that is part of automation is instrumentation and automatic control. Instruments also are not new. The thermometer has been around quite a long time. The camera has been with us many decades, as well as a few other instruments. But the proliferation of instruments in recent decades, particularly during and since World War II, is such that we now have instruments capable of perceiving in the environment everything that a human being can perceive, and can perceive it in places where human beings cannot be, such as inside a hot furnace, or in a place so dark a man cannot see, and many other similar situations. . . .

But instruments do more than perceive a situation in a process. An instrument can record the information it perceives and transmit it by electrical signals to an automatic control device, so an action can be followed through to continue or to check and change. If an error is being made, if something is off quality control or out of dimension, then the instrument perceives the variation; and very rapidly sends a signal to correct it and the change is accomplished. . . .

The third unit of automation is the electronic computer. The electronic computer is new, very new. In fact, it is not even old enough to vote. The first one was made at the Moore School of Electrical Engineering at the University of Pennsylvania, in 1944. It was called ENIAC. At the same time this contract by the Army's Aberdeen Proving Ground was being carried out, the Naval Ordnance Laboratory was providing Harvard University with funds for the development of another computer which became the MARK series. The first computer evolved into UNIVAC of the Remington-Rand Corporation, the second evolved into the IBM complex. They both picked up and carried on from this original government-paid development and a big new industry was born.

The electronic computer has two abilities — it has a memory and it can make decisions. To be more precise, it has information storage capacity, and it can be instructed by human beings what decisions to make. . . .

Several thousand computers have been already set up to accomplish real work; marvelous things are being accomplished. The electronic computer with its memory and decision-making abilities, programmed by informed and competent human beings, is able to extend and replace the simple, repetitive, time-consuming functions of human beings at work. Checking accounts in large banks no longer are handled by people sorting checks and making individual entries; the electronic computer looks at the checks with figures printed with magnetic ink — as you see them on your own checkbook. Work is done without human beings having to handle such masses of paper.

Deliverance from drudgery. The electronic computer thus becomes an outside-of-the-head cerebellum for man, new environmental apparatus which takes over to relieve him of onerous, dull, repetitive, time-consuming tasks, freeing him — even more than does the inside-of-the cranium cerebellum — for time and ability to use his cerebral brain, the thinking, higher functioning of the human being. . . .

Take note that I emphasize that the three things together are expanding more rapidly than any one of them alone. Tools and machines have been developed for factory production over a couple of centuries from the Industrial Revolution in England in the early 18th Century. Instruments have some history, a few are in existence for upwards of a century (the thermometer actually being first made even before the early 18th Century Industrial Revolution) but industrial application of instruments is only some 50 years ago from about the time of catalytic cracking of petroleum. Rapid acceleration came out of World War II.

The impact of the electronic computer with all its sophistication has been much more sudden. The electronic computer added to mechanization and instrumentation makes the increase of technology a geometrical progression — with the resultant rapid changes I have stated.

Moral . . . immoral . . . amoral. The problem is that we have to adapt the slow-moving, economic, social and political institutions in our society to these changes. Here is where we get into trouble.

The question can be asked, is automation a good thing or bad thing? Well, people will have varying points of view. No good comes merely from denouncing it. Automation is here, we have it. The problem is to go down the road and meet it and take it by the hand and help it grow in the direction that will be good for human beings. But when I am faced with the question: Is it good or bad? I have to reply that it is neither good nor bad.

We use the words moral and immoral, but we often forget there is also the word amoral. Amoral is neutral. It is neither good nor bad. Amoral is what the apparatus is. The psychologist would say it is without motivation. It, by itself, will do nothing. But it can be used for moral or immoral things — for good or evil. It can be used for great far-reaching good, or it can be used for terribly destructive evil. . . .

Beyond collective bargaining. . . . So, as we cannot repeal the 20th Century, so we cannot order the electronic computer to please dissolve and disappear. These things we have built. We have to live with them and grow with them and we have to adapt them to our needs. Intelligently adapting them to our needs can be the growth of a great new civilization.

What actually happens in an industry that undergoes widespread automation? Perhaps the coal industry is a good example of an industry that has been extensively automated. Michael F. Widman, Jr., vividly describes the experience of the United Mine Workers of America.

A Labor Leader Looks at Automation[10]

. . . Automation of the coal mines resulted in a tremendous decrease in the work force in the coal mining industry. In 1948, there were 441,631 men employed in the mines. By 1964, this total had dropped to 143,300 men.

Again, these statistics do not tell the full story. For the real tragedy of automation lies hidden in the hills and valleys of Appalachia, in the shacks of unemployed coal miners and in the want and misery that comes with prolonged unemployment. It is shown in the eyes of desperate men and in the dull hopelessness in the hearts of little boys and girls who are deprived of the joys of childhood. . . .

[10] Presentation of Michael F. Widman, Jr., Director, Research & Marketing Department, United Mine Workers of America, before the American Society of Mechanical Engineers and the Institute of Electrical and Electronics Engineers, Materials Handling Conference, in Pittsburgh, Pa., on October 18, 1965.

From our own experience in the field of automation, we have come **223** to certain general conclusions.

First, we believe automation to be inevitable. It will come just as surely as men will always seek the better way. It cannot be stopped for long by those who would obstruct progress, or hinder the development of better technologies.

Second, the present economic environment in this nation will speed the introduction of automation. We are in a highly competitive economic atmosphere. This competition is not limited to our own nation, but extends to practically every nation in the world. Under these conditions, it is evident that our own industry will constantly strive to improve its efficiency and to use whatever means that it can to do so.

Third, the impact of automation will not be limited to the production workers of the nation. The use of computers can and has eliminated jobs in offices and even in some of the managerial positions of our industry. This trend will also continue.

Fourth, because of the pace of automation and the fundamental change that it entails, automation must be regarded as a very distinct break with the past. In this respect, it is our opinion that we have entered into an age of industrial revolution, an age when the people will have to make major adjustments in their living and working habits.

Fifth, we must guard against the surrender of our human values in the face of technical change, just as we must insure that technical progress is not impeded by unreasonable human obstruction.

In summary, we feel that automation can be of great benefit to mankind. Further, it is our opinion that the progress that is made in the technical field will enable all of the peoples of the world to live better and enhance their human dignity.

However, this is in the long run. For the short term, we must adjust to the rigors of automation and teach our people to adapt to them and make the transition with the least possible dislocation. During this transitory period we must preserve the individual worth of every human being. . . .

The Burroughs Corporation had a somewhat different point of view. In a statement prepared for the National Commission on Technology, Automation, and Economic Progress, the Burroughs Corporation said:

. . . The real danger facing our economy today is not automation. Rather, it is the possibility that we might fail to take complete advantage of every opportunity for technological progress which is economically feasible.

In the United States approximately 800,000 scientists and engineers

224   are working to advance our technological position on all fronts. This does not consider the many thousands of technicians and support personnel also involved in these efforts. We cannot afford to reject, out of hand, the accomplishments of these skilled people. Nor can we act as though the $100 billion spent since 1955 on research and development, currently at an annual rate of $20 billion, has been a waste of money.

To do this would be equivalent to saying, "We've progressed as far as we want to go. We're afraid to go down the road any farther, because what lies around the bend might startle us too severely, challenge us too boldly, and threaten the cocoon of security which we've made our primary goal." The writer doesn't believe for a minute that the American people intend to accept such a philosophy. . . .

To the extent that automation as we know it today is an extension of man's power and dominion over the world around him, it is nothing totally or radically new. It shares this same characteristic with the earliest and most primitive tools of man. Obviously, modern developments in electronics have helped us move quickly into more sophisticated kinds of automation than was possible 20 years ago, and to that extent automation is "new." Some say automation is dangerous because it extends the power of the central nervous system rather than mere muscle power. We could argue about that and point out that the first adding machine built in 1886 was an extension of man's mental powers — or for that matter, we could go back to the abacus.

Instead of debating the precise definition of automation — whether it is new or old — we should take a positive approach. We should consider the creative power which automation puts at our disposal as a means to provide a more fruitful and abundant life for all of our people. And we ought to be moving toward a better education for all of our citizens so that they can reap these benefits.

Before the climate necessary to do these things effectively can be created, we must dispel some of the popular fictions which surround the subject of automation. Let's examine a few of them.

Fiction number one: Automation is destroying anywhere from 2,000 to 40,000 jobs per week in this country. Which number you choose depends on how pessimistic you want to be.

The fact is that no reliable evidence exists for the Nation as a whole concerning the net number of jobs being eliminated by automation. There is little likelihood of our getting such information in the near future because jobs are seldom eliminated or created because of any one factor.

Job displacement or creation can be and often is the result of mergers and consolidations, changes in plant locations, or shifts in product demand. This last point — changing product demand — is one of the most characteristic features of our economy. Look, for example, at the changing demand for fuel over the last two decades. Production of anthracite coal has declined from 56 million tons in 1951 to 17 million tons in 1961. During the same period, production of natural gas doubled and there was a substantial increase in production of crude petroleum. The same can be said for electric power capacity. Automation in the coal industry was certainly not responsible for the change in consumer demand.

Not only do these widely circulated fictions concerning job displacement fail to take into account the whole network of factors affecting jobs, they also create an unwarranted climate of fear. In many cases this fear of job loss due to automation, rather than of automation itself, has generated bitter labor-management disputes. The harmful economic effects of such disputes can often be more damaging to job security than the automation feared by labor. . . .

A second fiction worth noting is the common belief that automation is a single, once-and-for-all kind of thing. But when we discover that literally hundreds of definitions are used to describe automation, we realize that it is not a single entity. Automation might be the application of a computer to an inventory control problem. It might be the use of very complex machine tools which perform dozens of separate operations automatically. It might be a multi-million dollar process control system which permits economical production of synthetic fiber. It is not one technique or one piece of gear. Automation will never be "here" in the sense that no further progress in technology of production, control, or computation is possible.

A great deal has been written implying that many industrial plants throughout the country are now great, empty caverns. Empty, that is, of human beings — filled only with the whirring and buzzing of automatic machinery, controlled electronically, monitored by a few white-coated scientists. The truth is that virtually no major industrial complexes in this country have been completely automated. Even though, in a few instances, such automation may be technologically possible, it is not economically feasible. In the final analysis, it will be the economics of each particular situation that will determine how far and how fast automation will proceed. . . .

The urgent reason for automating any given activity in business or industry goes beyond any desire to reduce labor overhead. The competitive forces at work both at home and abroad demand the continuous creation of new and better products and services — at prices people can afford to pay. In many instances computers and other automation devices are not performing tasks which had previously been done by men; they are performing tasks which hadn't been done at all. The extra checks in a system of quality control or the up-to-the-minute reports on inventory status facilitated by computers are activities which simply could not have been handled economically in the past.

The alternative to automation and other forms of scientific and technological progress is a downgrading of our industry, our economy, and our society in general. It would be planned obsolescence on a grand and tragic scale. . . .

It should be borne in mind that the social problems which many people attribute to automation will be quickly compounded if we do not maintain an acceptable productivity and competitive posture. There is no way that we can avoid all social problems. The question is whether we minimize these problems by maintaining the maximum competitive effectiveness in the world market, or suffer the even greater social negatives which would accrue from competitive failure.

A national policy which endorses and promotes increased productivity and utilization of the more efficient tools and methods stemming from technological progress is absolutely essential.

There is no acceptable alternative because failure to achieve the necessary success in productivity could, over a period of time, relegate the United States to the position of a second-class economic power.[11]

Howard R. Bowen summed up the problems and prospects of automation and advancing technology in these words:

Technology is not a vessel into which people are to be poured and to which they must be molded. It is something to be adapted to the needs of man and to the furtherance of human ends, including the enrichment of personality and environment.

Technology has, on balance, surely been a great blessing to mankind — despite the fact that some of the benefits have been offset by costs. There should be no thought of deliberately slowing down the rate of technological advancement or hampering the freedom of discovery. The task for the decades ahead is to direct technology to the fulfillment of important human purposes. Much of this technology will be derived from the social sciences and the humanities as well as the physical and biological sciences. It will be concerned with such values as individuality, diversity, and decentralization rather than conformity, massive organization, and concentration. It will be directed toward human, environmental, and resource development rather than the proliferation of

---

[11] "Statement by the Burroughs Corporation," *Statements Relating to the Impact of Technological Change,* The Report of the National Commission on Technology, Automation and Economic Progress, Appendix Volume VI, *Technology and the American Economy* (Washington, D. C.: U. S. G.P.O., 1966), pp. 63–65.

conventional consumer goods. It will seek to make work more meaning-**227**
ful rather than merely more productive.[12]

Section 14(b) and the Right to Work

The most controversial provision of the Taft-Hartley Act of 1947 was
Section 14(b), which allowed states to pass legislation outlawing the union
shop. Such laws were ordinarily called "right-to-work" laws, but they did
not grant the right to work or the right to a job. Presumably the phrase
"right-to-work" had strong emotional appeal, so the slogan alone may
have caused some people to support what union leaders called an attempt
at "union busting."

The exact wording of Section 14(b) follows:

Nothing in this Act shall be construed as authorizing the execution
or application of agreements requiring membership in a labor organization as a condition of employment in any State or Territory in which
such execution or application is prohibited by State or Territorial law.

Some 25 states passed right-to-work laws under this provision, but six
states later repealed them. The states which have retained right-to-work
laws are generally in the South, Rocky Mountain, or Great Plains regions.[13]

Labor unions made repeal of 14(b) a primary objective in successive
congresses. The 1960 Democratic platform pledged: "We will repeal the
authorization for 'right-to-work' laws. . . ." Again in 1964, the Democratic
platform said: "The industrial democracy . . . must be strengthened by
repealing Section 14(b) of the Taft-Hartley Act." President Johnson asked
for repeal in his State of the Union message in January 1965 and again in
1966.

On January 4, 1965, Representative Frank Thompson, Jr., introduced
H.R. 77 to repeal Section 14(b). The bill was generally opposed by the
National Right to Work Committee (supposedly made up of small busi-
nessmen and private individuals), the Associated General Contractors of
America, the Chamber of Commerce of the United States, the Farm
Bureau Federation, and the National Association of Manufacturers.

Most of the arguments in favor of retaining 14(b) are included in the
following statement by the Industrial Relations Department of the National
Association of Manufacturers.

---

[12] Report of the National Commission on Technology, Automation and Economic
Progress, Howard R. Bowen, Chairman, *Technology and the American Economy*,
Volume I (Washington, D. C.: U. S. G.P.O., 1966), p. xiii.

[13] Ala., Ariz., Ark., Fla., Ga., Iowa, Kans., Miss., Neb., Nev., N. C., N. Dak., S. C.,
S. Dak., Tenn., Tex., Utah, Va., Wyo.

Freedom to Choose

No subject is more basic to an understanding of labor-management relations today than the issue of compulsory versus voluntary unionism. And there is no issue on which emotions run so high — and none more currently alive. . . .

The basic issue is freedom — a man's freedom to hold a job without being compelled to become a union member.

One would think that in America there could be no argument against a man's right to work without having to join a union or any other organization because here particularly we have a deeply-imbedded tradition of relying on voluntary methods and organizations:

The 5th, 9th, and 14th Amendments of the Constitution of the United States implicitly protect the right to work. They prohibit the deprivation of "life, liberty, or property without due process of law" and forbid abridgement of "the privileges and immunities of citizens." As affirmed in a memorable case by Justice Charles Evans Hughes,

"It requires no argument to show that the right to work for a living in the common occupations of the community is of the very essence of the personal freedom and opportunity that it was the purpose of the [Fourteenth] Amendment to secure. . . ."

A closer look at the grounds on which right-to-work laws have been attacked reveals first of all that none of the well-worn phrases in the union "line" come to grips with the issue of compulsory versus voluntary unionism. . . .

1. The Union Charge That Right-to-Work Laws Destroy Unions

There is a very real question about the wisdom of maintaining any organization if it can be held together only when members are forced to join.

That unionism does not need the crutch of compulsion is amply demonstrated by the fact that during the years when the Railway Labor Act prohibited any form of compulsory union membership (1934–51), the non-operating unions trebled their membership, greatly strengthened their financial position and extended their jurisdiction to cover practically the entire railroad mileage of the country. It would seem that union professionals do not have enough faith in the benefits of unions offered freely to workers! Furthermore, many companies which have bargained collectively for years have consistently refused to sign a "union shop" contract which would deliver their employees to union rolls, without recourse. . . .

Trade unions today are not small, oppressed groups, struggling for survival. Instead, unions today

> exercise vast powers over people
> give or take away jobs

control the economic destiny of a business   **229**
have bulging treasuries from tax-free sources
enjoy extra-legal privileges denied to other organizations
are some 17,000,000 strong

Unions are obviously not in danger of liquidation — and nothing in right-to-work laws attempts to destroy them. "Right-to-Work" simply means that a worker must be given the opportunity to choose for himself whether union representation is good and is something he needs. To label these laws "right-to-wreck," "union-busting" laws is a typical attempt to slur with no more basis in fact than the branding of the Taft-Hartley Act as a "slave labor" law. Defamation is no substitute for truth.

2. The Union Charge That Right-to-Work Laws Permit "Free Riders"

A "free rider" is defined as one who gets the benefit of union representation without paying union dues. The "free rider" argument assumes that the only reason an employee may want to stay out or withdraw from a union is to avoid payment of dues. Many people desire to stay out of a union for religious reasons, or because they oppose the union leadership, or because they don't want their money spent for causes to which they object.

Moreover, since only a portion of the dues and assessments paid by members is spent for collective bargaining as such, many employees rightfully object to the additional purposes for which union funds are spent.

Unions spend the monies they collect from union members on many other activities — such as political campaigns, organizing campaigns, social and economic propaganda, strike benefits to other unions, private benefits to officers and legal fees. Rather than benefit the individual, in some cases these expenditures may actually be detrimental to his interests or in opposition to his beliefs.

Indeed, rather than being a "free rider," under compulsory unionism the employee becomes, in fact, a "captive passenger.". . .

3. The Union Argument That If a Majority of Employees Want to Organize, Then All Employees Should Be Forced to Join and Support the Union

Majority rule is a fine American tradition, but Americans are not forced to join the majority. If the union-advocated rule that the minority must support the majority were extended to other segments of our society an individual could, for example, be forced to join and support the majority political party in his election district or the church attended by the majority of people in his community.

Such compulsions clearly would be intolerable invasions of our basic rights and the situation is not changed because labor leaders are the invaders. The rights of the majority are always tempered by the rights of the minority. . . .

4. The Union Argument Regarding Freedom of Contract

Unions claim that any law which prohibits or interferes with the negotiation of compulsory-unionism clauses interferes with "freedom of contract," and therefore it impedes collective bargaining.

This line of reasoning fails when it is realized that the argument

a. Appears to Be a One-way Street

. . . There is little freedom of contract when coercion dominates the negotiating atmosphere. Notwithstanding the employer's strong personal convictions favoring freedom of choice for his employees, he many times has no alternative but to accede to the principle of compulsion lest his business be destroyed.

b. Ignores the Moral Issue

To use the "freedom of contract" argument to destroy the freedom of the individuals who make up the union is totally inconsistent with the basic moral right of an American citizen to pursue life, liberty and happiness. Destruction of the human right of freedom to choose, to preserve without limitation the union freedom to contract is an obvious contradiction, particularly when equated in the true purpose of the contract itself, to benefit the individual.

5. The Union Argument That Unions Need the Security of Compulsory Unionism

Union leaders say that they need the security of compulsory unionism to strengthen their position with employers, to protect themselves against rival unions, and to enable them to perform their mission of organizing the unorganized.

If the security argument ever had any validity, it has long since ceased to exist. The plain fact is that unions are the single most powerful, most dominating economic and political force in the country today. With their complete control over the individual through compulsory membership, unions acquire a monopoly power. Clearly legal restraints are needed. . . .

6. The Union Argument That Employees Want Compulsory Unionism

. . . After 30 years of legislation which fully protects the unions' right to organize and, in fact, encourages union organization, more than 39 million of the almost 56 million workers in non-agricultural establishments have not joined unions. In other words, only three out of every ten

workers have been persuaded of the virtues of union membership even in   **231**
non-agricultural establishments where most union members are found
and where organizing is concentrated. Should they be compelled to join?

Furthermore, unions have failed to organize large numbers of white
collar workers, notwithstanding the fortunes spent from union treasuries
in highly specialized organization campaigns. The 2.3 million estimate of
white-collar workers in all unions for 1962 must be viewed against an
organizable potential of about 22 million such workers in various occupational groups. The evidence points to a near-standstill in union organization in the white collar field. Should the wills of these people be bent to
compulsion? . . .

7. The Union Argument That Clergymen Are Opposed to Right-to-Work
Laws

This deception is perhaps the most dangerous of all because people
tend to regard the statements of clergymen as sacrosanct. An extra heavy
burden of responsibility therefore rests on every minister, priest or rabbi
who may, willfully or unwittingly, permit his high office to be used to
propagate unsound doctrines.

In the colonial days of America a "church tax" was levied to support
the church which happened, at that time, to be the accepted "state
church." Jefferson vigorously opposed this tax. The end result was the
now famous "Statute of Virginia for Religious Freedom," which contained in its preamble the following passage:

> To compel a man to furnish contributions of money for the
> propagation of opinions which he disbelieves and abhors is sinful
> and tyrannical. . . .

Compulsory unionism takes away a man's ability freely to decide a
moral question and in some instances forces him to act in a manner
contrary to the dictates of his conscience. Compulsory unionism is thus
immoral because it violates the basic moral tenet of freedom of will. . . .

Our society, dedicated as it is to freedom and the sanctity of the
individual, must decide whether unionism is to be voluntary or compulsory. The outcome of this stuggle could conceivably determine both the
socio-economic and the political future of our nation.

What course should we take? The answer to this question may be
evaluated by historians as the action pivotal to the shaping of America's
destiny.[14]

---

[14] *Freedom to Choose,* Industrial Relations Department, National Association of
Manufacturers, New York, *n.d.*

232   The position of the AFL-CIO on 14(b) is summarized in a pamphlet called

The Truth about "Right-to-Work" Laws

In Samuel Gompers' words:

> We sometimes still hear the demagogic claim put forth by organized labor's opponents that the union shop, with its agreement with employers, is improper and unjust. Our opponents pretend that they stand for the liberty and the rights of workmen.
>
> Is it not a novel position for the worst antagonists to labor's interests to assume that they are advocates and defenders of the rights and the liberties of workmen? The mere statement of such a position demonstrates its hypocrisy and absurdity.[15]

What are "right-to-work" laws? It is a tribute to the good sense of the American people that those who set out to destroy unions and do away with collective bargaining find it necessary to hide their true purpose.

There is not a single state in which a majority of the people would vote to take away the right of workers to organize and bargain with their employers on wages and working conditions.

There are not more than a handful of congressmen who would vote for such a law.

But there are 19 states where dishonest slogans have been used to enact laws which do weaken unions and do make it more difficult for workers to improve their conditions.

In the dishonest language of its sponsors, such laws have been labeled "right-to-work." Sometimes the term used is the equally misleading "voluntary unionism.". . .

What is important, of course, is not the label but the contents. Americans are entitled to know what these laws do, what they don't do, and, above all, whether or not they are good for the country.

The why of union security. Propaganda on behalf of "right-to-work" laws concentrates on the "right" of the average worker not to join a union. Yet that propaganda overlooks the fact that without a union, the individual worker would have little or no bargaining power in negotiations with his employer. . . .

Under the law of the United States, the union that wins certification as the bargaining agent of the majority of workers must represent *all* the workers in the bargaining unit.

As the bargaining representative of all the workers, the union can be

---

[15] Annual Report to Convention of American Federation of Labor, November 1905.

most effective — and it can best represent all the attitudes of the workers — when all the workers are members. . . .

Union security and democracy. Union security contracts are clearly in line with our great American democratic tradition.

But some people, although they may think that unions are "fine," feel that it is somehow undemocratic to compel anybody to belong to a union. So, these people are apt to oppose union security and give support to the so-called "right-to-work" laws on the mistaken basis that an individual is deprived of some essential liberty.

This line of argument looks reasonable — but let's examine the arguments, one by one:

1. These people say: "Union security deprives the individual of his 'right-to-work.'"

Under the union shop it is the employer rather than the union who decides what person shall be hired for a job. An applicant is hired only if he has the qualifications for the job. Then, and only then, is he required to join the union that holds the contract with the employer. . . .

For instance, the worker may be required to have a certain level of education; he may be required to have had certain work experience; he may have to be willing to wear certain types of uniform or work clothes; he may have to travel in connection with his job; he most certainly will have to work specified hours, perhaps not those of his own free choice; he may have to observe certain plant regulations or safety rules.

All of these are qualifications for getting or holding a job. The union security requirement that he join a union is only one of many qualifications.

2. The people who oppose union security are apt to say that union security is "undemocratic."

In fact, union security is simply an expression of our democratic concept of majority rule. Majority rule is the very basis of our society and civilization.

A union is a part of the industrial government which has evolved over the years to distinguish workers in a free society from workers in a totalitarian slave society. . . .

To argue against union security is, in effect, to argue that the minority has even more rights than the majority — and that goes counter to all the common sense rules for our democratic society.

The union shop operates where a majority of the workers have decided in its favor and where the employer has agreed with the union to a union security contract.

Minority rights must always be protected, but minority rights can't be allowed to take precedence over majority rights.

Obviously, an individual can't decide not to pay taxes because he doesn't like the policies of the government. A citizen can't drive his car down the left-hand lane because he disagrees with the local traffic rules. An individual can't yell "fire" in a crowded theatre just because he believes in free speech or because he likes to watch crowd reactions.

In other words, we Americans believe in the principle of majority rule, with protection for minority rights — and that's exactly what our system of union security is based upon. . . .

Workers want union security. The overwhelming majority of wage and salary earners in union-organized firms have shown they want union security. The proof is in the official records.

For four years — from 1947 to 1951 — the government conducted secret-ballot elections to find out if working people approved union security provisions in labor-management agreements.

A majority — almost always a tremendous majority — of the workers voted for union security in 97% of those 46,119 elections.

There were 6,542,564 workers eligible to vote in these elections, and 5,547,478 valid ballots were cast. Of those valid ballots, 91% were cast for union security. . . .

Union rights and obligations. Under the federal law, the union which is selected by a majority of the workers represents *all* the workers in the factory in collective bargaining relations with the employer.

The union has no choice: even if it wanted to, it could not refuse to represent any individual worker or group of workers. It must represent them all. . . .

If the union, under the law, must represent all the workers — then, it seems fair that all the workers should support the union by belonging to it. . . .

Unions build our economy. . . . In communities where unions are strong, wage and salary incomes improve — and so, the volume of sales improves, too. Where unions are weak, wages are low — and the sales of milk, meat, eggs, clothing, television sets and electrical appliances are also low.

So-called "right-to-work" laws, which tend to weaken unions, also tend to weaken their ability to improve the economic status of their members. That's why "right-to-work" laws weaken the economy of each community. . . .

Most of the states where industry and commerce have grown fastest, and prospered most, have no "right-to-work" law. There is no "right-to-work" law, for instance, in such big industrial states as New York, California, Michigan, Ohio, Illinois, Pennsylvania or Massachusetts — to name only a few. . . .

Exploding the myths. The deceptive "right-to-work" slogan is designed to conceal the union-destroying objectives of its sponsors. This is a serious charge, but the evidence backs it up. For example:

A fund-solicitation letter from the National Right to Work Committee carried the committee's slogan: "Americans must have the right, but not be compelled, to join labor unions."

The letter was signed by Roger Milliken, owner of a big textile chain.

Employees of one of Mr. Milliken's textile mills, at Darlington, S. C., voted for union representation. Mr. Milliken promptly responded by shutting down the mill. When, in desperation at losing their jobs, 83 percent of his employees signed a petition pledging to renounce the union if only he would keep the mill in operation, Milliken replied coldly that this indicated there were still 17 percent "hard-core" union supporters in Darlington. The workers were thrown on the streets shortly before Christmas and the textile equipment sold at auction. So much for the "right to work." . . .

The moral issue. Thus far, we have discussed the impact of "right-to-work" laws on the economy and on employee-management relations. But for many citizens the heart of the debate is the moral question.

Here, the overwhelming verdict of the nation's leading theologians of all major faiths is that the union shop is morally and ethically sound and the so-called "right-to-work" law is morally dishonest.[16]

In the summer of 1965, the House of Representatives considered a bill (HR 77) to repeal Section 14(b). On a roll call vote July 28, 1965, the House passed the repeal bill by a vote of 221–203. Senate debate on a similar bill started on October 4, 1965. At that time, Senate Republican leader Dirksen started a filibuster which continued until a try at a cloture motion failed on October 11.

The bill was again brought before the Senate on January 24, 1966, and again a filibuster was started to prevent the question from coming to a vote. The filibuster continued for two weeks. On February 10, 1966, another attempt was made to invoke cloture. The vote on the cloture motion was 50–49 — a majority but considerably below the two-thirds necessary to shut off debate. After the February 10 cloture vote, there was no further action on legislation to repeal 14(b) in the 89th Congress.

The Grapes of Wrath

Farm workers, led by Cesar Chavez, went on strike in the vineyards around Delano, California, in 1965, and the strike continued for years. California produces about 90 percent of the table grapes grown in the United States, and about one third of the California total comes from some

---

[16] "The Truth about 'Right to Work' Laws: Facts vs. Propaganda," Publication No. 46 (Washington, D. C.: American Federation of Labor and Congress of Industrial Organizations), revised April 1966.

70 ranches in the Delano area. Delano is located on Highway 99 in the lush San Joaquin Valley about 135 miles north of Los Angeles. It is in the Delano vineyards that "the grapes of wrath are stored."

The grape workers' strike had been in progress for about three years (but grapes were still being picked) when Cesar Chavez decided to organize a nation-wide boycott on grapes in an attempt to secure better wages and working conditions for his people. Jack V. Fox told the story this way:

A shabby one-story pink adobe house, with huge photographs of Mahatma Gandhi, Robert F. Kennedy and the Rev. Dr. Martin Luther King on the walls, is the nerve center of a national drive to persuade the American people to stop eating grapes.

The mastermind of this operation is a 41-year-old Mexican-American, Cesar Chavez, a small, soft-spoken man with a will of steel and a passion of fire beneath a gentle exterior.

It is no coincidence that those three pictures hang in the Chavez headquarters. To his followers he is cast in the same molds — apostle of nonviolence, liberal and champion of civil rights for the "brown" people of the United States.

To his opponents he is an opportunist, a demagogue and a liar. They say he embraces all the extremist and leftwing support he can get and stop just short of calling him a Communist.

They say his goal is to control agriculture across the nation. Chavez would, to an extent, agree. He says the organization and unionization of farm workers is coming in one way or another and that nothing can stop it. . . .

For three years his United Farm Workers Organizing Committee has sought to organize about 5000 workers who harvest the vineyards of those 70 ranches and to change what Chavez says are miserable wages, intolerable housing and a degradation of the dignity of the workers.

The growers say that picture is grossly exaggerated. They point to figures showing California farm wages are above the national average and conditions also are above averages. Over all, they say, the grape pickers have demonstrated they do not want to be under Chavez.

The UFWOC has been on "strike" since 1965 but the crop has been fully picked every year and is being picked this year, with the current harvest almost complete.

Picketing the fields did not work.

Early this summer Chavez sent his members fanning out across the nation. They are now operating in 34 cities and towns and working by telephone into 200 others.

Their goal is to persuade or pressure grocery stores not to put California grapes on their counters. The boycott has caught nationwide attention and has intensified the bitter feud here.

Whether the boycott is "succeeding" is a question almost impossible to answer. Emotions run so high on the matter that it is difficult to get rational assessments.

The UFWOC says government figures show shipments for the first two months of the season are down an average of 16.1 per cent to 12 major cities — St. Louis, Baltimore, Boston, Chicago, Cincinnati, Cleveland, Detroit, Kansas City, Minneapolis, New York, Philadelphia and Pittsburgh.

Growers contend that other government figures show that through Oct. 9, California shipped 14,944 carloads of table grapes compared with 15,331 in 1966, the last previous year blessed with ideal growing conditions.

The over-all California table grape crop is 13 per cent bigger than last year's poor weather crop and the growers say that could account for a drop of 25 to 35 cents on the price of a "lug" or 26-pound box of grapes.

The union says grapes are down more than $1 a lug and that in places like New York they are being dumped because they cannot be sold at all.

The boycott has brought an angry conflict reaching to the highest levels.

Richard M. Nixon criticized it as an unfair attack on one of California's basic industries and said he would "eat California grapes whenever I can." He was picketed, booed and heckled when he appeared at Fresno — the most hostile incident of his campaign.

Vice President Hubert Humphrey wrote Chavez: "I want to make it clear that I indorse your boycott efforts and I hope you will feel free to use this indorsement in any way you feel will best serve 'la causa' (the cause)."

California Gov. Ronald Reagan has branded the boycott "illegal and immoral" and said those conducting it are "falsifying information about agricultural labor conditions in California and are ignoring the desires of most grape pickers."

State Attorney General Thomas C. Lynch, a Democrat, said the boycott is legal, that it does not fall under the ban against secondary boycott under the National Labor Relations Act because the act does not cover agriculture.

The controversy has led in the San Joaquin Valley to a plastering of automobiles with stickers such as "Boycott California grapes" for the UFWOC supporters and "Eat California grapes — the forbidden fruit" by the growers. Now signs have appeared urging "Boycott New York and Detroit products" in retaliation against grape boycotts in those cities.

Chavez went East to lead a "Boston grape party" in which grapes rejected by a supermarket chain were dumped in the harbor. Then he addressed a rally on Boston Common which drew a large crowd including hippies, AFL-CIO union members, ministers, a number of Negroes and the curious.

The late Robert Kennedy came to Delano and drew a crowd of 12,000 at the "40 Acres" — a plot outside Delano which Chavez set aside for a national headquarters of farm workers but which today has only two small permanent buildings.

The AFL-CIO sent its No. 3 man to Delano, so great an importance does it place on this attempt to organize farm workers. It puts $10,000 a month into the UFWOC. The United Auto Workers, whose Walter Reuther also came here, donated $50,000.

The town of Delano is divided by railroad tracks almost 50-50 between Mexican-Americans and "Anglos" and therein lies the element that brings the greatest bitterness to the struggle — the argument of racism.

But this autumn the controversy has reached the point where not only the rights and wrongs but the basic facts have become obscured in the arguments from both sides.

Cesar Estrada Chavez got his first taste of working as a Mexican-American migrant in the fields of Arizona and California when he was 10. He recalled that he attended 67 schools as his mother, father and the four other children moved constantly with the crops and the seasons. He finally quit school after the seventh grade.

Now, at 41, he has become a national figure. He is idolized by some as the almost saintly leader of "la causa" and he is addressed by his followers as "Cesar."

He is scorned by others as a man using any tactic or power play to gratify an ambition to gain union control of agriculture.

He looks upon himself as a man whom fate has chosen to bring dignity and economic independence to those who — like him as a child — toil in the fields for their living.

Late last month Chavez was able to leave the hospital after a month of treatment for a spinal condition which made it almost impossible for him to make a slight movement, so great was the pain.

The illness was diagnosed as a degeneration of the tissues between the disks of the spine brought about by a lack of protein in his diet. It apparently was caused by a 25-day fast which ended March 10.

Chavez says he decided on the fast because he felt advocates of violence among his followers might get out of hand and he feared bloodshed in the struggle.

Still flat on his back, with his legs propped up by pillows in his small frame home where his wife and eight children live, Cesar talked for two hours with a reporter about events of the last three years and what lies ahead.

Chavez was in good spirits, buoyed by reports on the grape boycott across the nation. He can recall every incident, every setback, every small victory, in a drive that began in 1962.

It started as a fraternal type organization, mainly for Mexican-Americans but for all farm workers, to help them with problems concerning schools, hospital care, police problems, nonpayment of wages, life insurance, small co-operatives and a tiny newspaper. There was no talk then of boycotts or strikes.

"You can't organize a union and strike at the same time," Chavez says.

Then another small farm workers union forced Chavez to make his move. In September 1965, an AFL-CIO affiliated group made up mostly of Filipino farm workers struck Di Giorgio Corp. and Schenley Corp. — two of the largest corporate farming operations in California.

After insisting upon and getting a pledge of nonviolence from his members, Chavez called for a strike vote and the membership voted overwhelmingly for a walkout.

Chavez scored his first victory six months later when his followers staged a 300-mile march from Delano to the State Capitol in Sacramento, ending on Easter Sunday. Within days Schenley announced it would sign an agreement with the Chavez workers, who had also been boycotting Schenley products.

The Union later beat back another challenge from the Teamsters Union and signed a contract with Di Giorgio. Chavez then picked up contracts with 10 other growers, most of them producers of grapes for making wine.

But the Delano growers of table grapes, almost all of them family-run businesses, refused to recognize the union and they still do today.

Chavez recalls attempts to picket the fields and says bitterly his people were harassed by the police and subjected to violence and indignities. He says the growers have harvested their crops by bringing in from Mexico men and women willing to endure conditions to which no one should be subjected.

"If they only would have sat down and talked with us," he said, "that was all we asked. That is really all we are asking today."

Chavez dismisses grower arguments that the base pay for a grape picker is now $1.40 to $1.50 an hour. He says:

"You know what it was when we started? It was $1.10 an hour. And do you know what we were asking? It was $1.40 to $1.50 an hour and that is what it is today and we brought it there.

"But it's going to be a hell of a lot more than $1.40 now. For one thing they owe us an apology. An apology for what they have said to our women. For trying to put the Communist label on us. For beatings and for indignities.

"You know I spend half my time keeping my people from resorting to violence. They have incurred the wrath of a great many people. If it breaks loose it will make the ghetto riots look mild."

Chavez snapped back when asked what size he estimated his membership to be. "It's no estimate," he said. "We have 17,000 members."

Chavez concedes the boycott may do long-lasting harm to the table grape industry.

"It's a lot harder to turn off a boycott than to turn one on," he said. "But we are ready to talk any time."

Racism and prejudice are involved just as much or more than economics, Chavez contends.

"They'll just never accept us, they'll never see it," he said, shaking his head.

Chavez has drawn around him in addition to his Mexican-American supporters a small corps of "Anglos," women and men, who bear a marked resemblance to the enthusiastic young volunteers of the presidential campaign of Senator Eugene J. McCarthy.

His executive assistant is Jim Drake, a young man who joined Chavez in 1962 shortly after leaving a seminary and who has worked closely with him ever since.

Drake minces no words. He has no patience with the argument that agriculture by its nature cannot be unionized or that a piecework, incentive system is necessary to farm economics.

"Women and children shouldn't have to go into the fields," he said. "It's a matter of a job with dignity. A farm worker should be able to make enough so that his wife can stay in her home and the children go to school."

William Kircher, director of organization for AFL-CIO, is helping the UFWOC drive and says Chavez may in time become head of an over-all national farm union.

Chavez makes no personal claim to such leadership but he does say, "The organization and unionization of farm workers is coming in this country. I don't know how or in what form but it is coming and nothing can stop it."

Jack Pandol moved to Delano in 1941 when he was 18 and his father, an immigrant from Yugoslavia, that year put down the first grape vines that now spread over 1000 acres.

Pandol and his two brothers at the peak of the season employ 300 to 325 workers to harvest the grapes. The Pandols would be ranked near the top in production among the grape ranches in the San Joaquin Valley — which range from 40 acres upwards.

Now 45, Pandol is an outgoing and articulate man who thinks he and other growers have been getting a one-sided deal in the public's knowledge of the facts behind the attempted national boycott of California grapes.

Here are points he makes:

Grape pickers in the Delano area are paid more than other California farm workers, who in turn are above the national average. A man can make $150 to $200 in a week.

The image of squalid housing and intolerable field conditions for workers is false.

Agriculture — and particularly grapes — is an area that cannot be unionized like industry. "Grapes spoil, steel doesn't."

Chavez and his union have been repudiated by the majority of the workers in the Delano area and Pandol is not going to force his workers to join the union.

The UFWOC doesn't care if it ruins — and eliminates jobs in — the table grape industry which has seen per capita consumption drop from 11 pounds in the 1940s to four pounds in the 1960s.

Chavez has welcomed every extremist group — the Black Panthers, Du Bois clubs, Stokely Carmichael and Yippies. . . .

There has been no difficulty getting sufficient workers in any of the three years since the strike was called in 1965. A large percentage of those now working for him are residents of the area while those here from Mexico are "green card" workers who have a legitimate right to work any place in the United States for five years under federal immigration laws.

Pandol's base pay is $1.40 an hour and $1.50 an hour. The lower figure is paid to men who live in camps furnished by the Pandols, get transportation to work and receive three meals a day for $1.80. The $1.50 goes to persons living away from the camps. . . .

Says Pandol:

"This isn't a business where you can work 8 to 5. When grapes are ripe they have to be harvested and you can't skip Saturdays and Sundays and holidays. And I can't afford to be paying overtime and double time.

"If the grocers and housewives want to pay us more we don't care what we pay the workers but the fact is that prices naturally go down when the harvest season is on.

"I have found workers are natural capitalists. If they can get more by working harder, they will work harder. If they don't want to work, I can't afford to pay them. I'll be the first to admit I can't conduct a social reform program. I'm a farmer in a hard business.

"One day a minister came out here and called me a slave driver because people were working so hard. I said, 'They want to work hard and make more money,' and what in the world is wrong with that?"

Pandol, while acknowledging that he has property and equipment worth a vast amount in investment, says he has paid taxes on personal income of less than $10,000 the past years.

"And how do I come out? Jack Pandol, greedy grower."[17]

---

[17] Jack V. Fox, *St. Louis Post-Dispatch,* November 3, 1968, pp. 3-I, 11-I. By permission of United Press International.

Farmers: Problems without Solutions

. . . chosen people of God.

Thomas Jefferson

. . . the outstanding form of individual economic enterprise.

A. Whitney Griswold

Not all is well down on the farm, and it hasn't been for nearly a century, except for very brief periods. If we but let our minds drift back to the era of the Great Depression it is difficult to understand how sturdy conservatives who voted straight Republican tickets could engage in violence, participate in milk strikes, threaten to hang judges, and beat up sheriffs. Yet the record shows that many a conservative and kindly family man did just that. Just within the past decade we have witnessed these same sorts of people organizing, striking, and engaging in violence from Madison, Wisconsin, to Denver, Colorado. "Why?" we may ask:

Here's a good question for city folks who think they know a lot about farming or who think their farm neighbors have it easy.

How can you plant more acres, harvest less acres, get more bushels per acre and higher production and yet still lose money?

Wheat farmers have a ready answer. All you need is a dry winter that keeps your winter wheat from germinating well, followed by hail and a wet cold spring. Then add on good fall harvest weather and lower prices and you have the answer.

Yes, the city dweller might counter, but production was up. The acres finally harvested yielded 21 bushels to the acre compared with only 16 bushels to the acre in 1966. What's more, the total production subsequently jumped from 625,500 bushels to 699,200 for the county. Surely over 73,000 more bushels would result in a net profit, says the city cousin.

Not so says Ken Thayer, a wheat producer east of Fort Collins and a member of the Colorado Wheat Advisory Committee representing Larimer County. "During 1966 wheat prices got up as high as $1.74 per bushel," he says, "but the highest it got last year was $1.50 a bushel and now it's down to about $1.20 locally."[1]

> The problem is an old one. Income from what the farmer produces goes down, while the prices of what he must buy goes up. Hence, the argument is that the farmer's economic position worsens each year.

The economic position of the American farmer continued to decline throughout 1967 according to statistics released this week by the government.

A U. S. Department of Agriculture bulletin, "The Farm Income Situation," shows that realized net farm income last year declined from $16.4 billion to $14.5 billion. At the same time farm production expenses increased $1.1 billion further worsening the price-cost squeeze.

The plight of the rural segment of the economy has begun to draw Republican criticism of administration farm policies. "It's deplorable when realized farm income drops 11.5 per cent in one year," said Odin Langen, a Minnesota representative and chairman of the Republican Task Force on Agriculture.

"When you couple this loss of income with a 90 per cent increase in debt and a 31 per cent increase in the cost of production for the period 1960–1967, we have just about broken the back of this mightiest sector of our economy."

Agriculture is the largest of the 12 biggest U. S. industries according to figures compiled by the magazine "U. S. News and World Report." Although agriculture leads in total assets, spending for equipment and in number of workers, the magazine points out that farm sales are less than 17 per cent of assets while the next 11 largest industries have sales which average 108 per cent of their assets per year.

"As a result, 14 million Americans are living in poverty." . . .[2]

> There is an issue, of course, as to whether a problem exists at all; and among those who admit the existence of a problem, issues arise over its extent and severity. However, the biggest issues have arisen over pro-

[1] "A Question and Answer Series Spells Out the Farmer's Plight," *Fort Collins Coloradoan* (March 28, 1968), p. 17.

[2] "Farm Costs Rose in 1967 as Income Dropped Again," *Fort Collins Coloradoan* (March 28, 1968), p. 17.

posed and attempted solutions. Hardly any other policy area in American political life has had so many solutions suggested or tried. What underlies a problem that generates so many issues and solutions?

The Cost-Price Squeeze

In 1963, the Congressional Quarterly Service diagnosed the problem as follows:

Among the major issues of public policy during the postwar era, none proved more difficult to solve than the farm problem. Its essential characteristic was this: the tendency of production, despite a steady decline in farm population, to increase faster than effective demand, creating heavy agricultural surpluses. In Congressional debate, this problem produced some of the sharpest sectional and party clashes repeatedly throughout the postwar period. But it was little closer to solution in 1963 than it had been in 1945.

At the root of the difficulty lay a 20th-century revolution in agricultural technology which, after slacking off during the depression years of the 1930s, was accelerated by special military needs during World War II and continued apace throughout the postwar period. Mechanization, heavy increases in the use of fertilizers, lime and insecticides, and the spread of specialization and scientific farming were the chief features of the agricultural revolution. Its chief results were sharp increases in productivity and a trend toward concentration of farming in fewer, larger units capable of using the technical advances to best advantage.[3]

The problem is a very complex one which, in turn, confounds and confuses the issues. It is not quite so simple as "the gap between farm income and rising costs." A host of complicated circumstances and factors are involved in the creation of this gap. The consequences of the gap are even more unclear; and the picture of how the consequences themselves affect the gap is exceedingly muddy. As a result, Americans have never reached a consensus on a comprehensive and permanent policy for agriculture.

Generally speaking, policies and policy advocates can be divided into two camps — those who advocate a free market system and those who support a controlled market. To a considerable extent these two camps divide rather sharply; first, over the consequences of given policies which they perceive in the agricultural economy, and secondly, over the conditions which they would prefer to see there.

---

[3] "Review of the Postwar Period," *U. S. Agricultural Policy in the Postwar Years* (Washington, D. C.: Congressional Quarterly Service, 1963), p. 1. Copyright by Congressional Quarterly, Inc.

First of all we should look at what has happened in the farm economy. Since 1920 the farm population has dropped from 30 percent of the total population to 7.7 percent (in 1962). Between 1936 and 1959, the number of farm units decreased from 6.8 million to 3.9 million. Productivity increased phenomenally over the same period; in some cases it doubled, and in others even trebled. As the number of farmers decreased, the size of the farm units increased from 174 acres in 1940 to 320 acres in 1962. This rise reflected a phenomenal degree of mechanization, more extensive use of fertilizers, increased assets (land, buildings, machinery, stock, and the like), greater specialization, and higher costs generally. Such increases and changes only pressed the farmer, especially the small farmer, more firmly into the vise between costs and prices or the gap between income from production and costs for nonagricultural commodities. The major consequence was bigger farms and fewer farmers.[4]

Most major farm organizations, such as the National Farmers Union, the American Farm Bureau Federation, the National Grange, and the National Farm Organization, have been united in an effort to overcome the cost-price squeeze; but they have differed sharply on what should be done and which of the consequences are desirable.

The cost-price squeeze became a national issue shortly after the Civil War. Until World War I, however, farm organizations (for example, the Farmers' Alliance) and farmers themselves pictured the problem in terms of two types of unfair practices that were presumably draining their resources and profits. A major target was the so-called unfair practices and excessive charges imposed by the railroads, warehouse and storage firms, and selected marketing groups. A second target was the competition from foreign markets. Time and again, farmers turned to their state legislatures and courts to impose regulations and fix maximum fair rates for transportation, storage, and marketing of their products. As time progressed they also sought higher tariffs on agricultural products which competed with their own.

None of the measures were too successful, however. Many state statutes were successfully challenged in the courts, and others could be only half-heartedly enforced. Even federal legislation to regulate transport industries and carriers under the Interstate Commerce Commission (established in 1887) provided only a partial remedy. Federal regulation of the grain and stock exchanges did not get off the ground until after World War I, and the tariffs frequently created more problems than they solved. They frequently did more to aid the farmers' domestic competitors (manufacturers and speculators) than they did in behalf of the farmer.

The Surplus Issue

After World War I, it was apparent that the problem would not be solved so simply as it had once been anticipated. Furthermore, it was

---

[4] *Ibid.,* pp. 3–5.

apparent that the agricultural industry was producing large surpluses of farm products which served only to depress prices and place farmers in a cost-price squeeze.

The farmer took this issue straight to the U. S. Congress. The membership of that body came forth with the famous McNary-Haugen Bill, which it passed three times only to have it vetoed all three times by a president who stood on the other side of the issue. Let us allow the American Farm Bureau Federation, one of its strongest backers, to speak for the measure which was sponsored by two leading Republican legislators:

Go back to the McNary-Haugen days, and you will find that all we asked for was a law to permit farmers to segregate surpluses for which there was no demand in this country, and keep them off the domestic markets, to the end that the American farmer could receive an American price for products sold in this country.

The purpose of the bill, as stated at that time, was: To restore and maintain approximately the pre-war normal relationship between the prices of certain farm products, of which we have an exportable surplus, and the general price level by purchasing the surplus over and above what will sell at a fair price in the domestic market and disposing of the surplus abroad at the highest price obtainable, assessing the losses from foreign sales and the costs of operations in the case of each commodity to the producers of the said commodity.[5]

An emerging principle — parity — can be seen quite clearly in Representative Gilbert Haugen's argument for passage.

No great nation can safely reduce its production of foods to a point that may threaten shortage for actual consumptive needs. Unfavorable weather conditions, plant diseases, and insect depredations may, in spite of reasonable acreage, decrease supply to the danger point unless farm practice is regularly adjusted to the production of reasonable surpluses. Variation in annual yields and enforced abandonment of acreage must be allowed for.

The clear recognition of the fact that domestic price depends upon export price is one of the fundamental principles that must be faced in any attempt to give farm relief. The conclusion is unescapable that only a device such as the agricultural export corporation, based upon the converse of the protective tariff principle, that will separate the export surplus from the total domestic crop and sell it in the world market at the world price while disposing of the domestic part at a domestic price on a

---

[5] Edward A. O'Neal, President of AFBF, "The Farmer's Fight for Fair Prices," *The Nation's Agriculture*, Vol. 12 (November 1937), pp. 3–5.

parity with other commodities, can possibly afford agriculture the necessary relief.

This bill proposes to equalize domestic supply of export farm products to domestic demand at a fair exchange value in terms of all commodities; in other words, in terms of the general price level. This end is to be attained by diverting the surplus, which is small in relation to the whole annual production, to the world market at the world price. Existing private agencies and existing facilities of processing and distribution are to be used to the fullest possible extent according to their adequacy and availability for this purpose. Import duties on particular products in distress are to be raised to keep out foreign competition, or, if necessary, such products may even be excluded. The loss sustained in selling at the world price the fraction of the crop exported after buying it on a higher domestic level and the expenses of operation are to be borne by the farmer through the operation of a so-called equalization fund.

The bill proceeds on the fundamental fact that the price of agricultural commodities should bear a proper relation to the prices of other commodities. In other words, farm products are to have a fair exchange value in terms of all commodities.

This bill proposes that if, at any time, any basic commodity is actually bringing a price in the markets which is below what it would be if that particular commodity price had advanced since pre-war times as much as have wholesale prices in general, an emergency concerning that commodity is to be declared and, therefore, that the price at which that particular basic commodity is to sell will be determined by comparing its pre-war price with the advance of the all-commodities index number on a pre-war basis, that is, the 10 years 1905–1914.[6]

Haugen's Republican colleague, Edward Voight from Wisconsin, did not agree:

We are convinced that the McNary-Haugen bill is an unworkable measure; that it will not do what its sponsors claim; that if it were put into effect respecting the products mentioned in it, it would heap a great calamity not only on the farmer, but the Nation as well. In our judgment no greater blow could be struck at agriculture than to put this bill in operation.

The majority report pictures very fully the distressed condition of millions of our farming population. We agree that a very serious situation exists and has existed for several years, and that Congress should apply every remedy . . . those producers of agricultural commodities are

---

[6] The Honorable Gilbert N. Haugen, Chairman, House Committee on Agriculture, *The Congressional Digest* (May 1924), p. 267.

most severely affected whose products in a large degree have to meet world competition. The chief sufferers among the farmers are those whose principal business it is to produce wheat and hogs.

A price-fixing measure. It is proposed to create a practically nonfluctuating price. The only factor which can change the price is a rise or fall of the general index number, which is moving very slowly now. The fluctuation on wheat from January to March, 1924, would have been 2 cents on $1.50 wheat, and on lower grades correspondingly less. . . .

A colossal gift to nonproducers. When this bill takes effect, as to wheat, the price of dollar wheat will instantly rise to over $1.50. The elevator man, merchants, millers, and speculators who have wheat on hand will suddenly be made richer by operation of law. If an emergency is declared on cattle, hogs, and sheep, every head will instantly rise in value, whether in the hands of farmers or others. The hundreds of millions of dollars worth of pork, beef, and mutton in the hands of the Big Five and about 200 smaller packers would instantly rise in value. On this item alone there would be a sheer gift to the meat packers of this country of from $150,000,000 to $200,000,000 to be paid for by the consumers of the country.[7]

Processors were opposed on other grounds:

We protest against the passage of the McNary-Haugen bill for the following reasons:

We contend that the application of public funds for the benefit of any particular industry is wrong in principle.

We believe the proposed bill to be un-American in its conception and in principle, in that it proposes to place our Government in business for an unlimited time, giving it through the commission which it creates practically unlimited control over the agricultural products of the United States.

It proposes that a determined surplus of wheat, for example, shall be exported at the world basis of price, thus exercising a domestic market influence that it is hoped will advance the price of wheat in the United States. The direct result of such action would be to penalize the consumers in the United States in favor of foreign consumers.

It is economically unsound to export raw material from a country where facilities exist for converting such raw material into finished product.

The exportation of any amount of American wheat under such a plan would immediately destroy the foreign market for a corresponding

---

[7] *Ibid.* (a reply by Edward Voight, Member, House Committee on Agriculture).

250   amount of American flour, resulting in reduced operation of American mills, with the consequent loss of mill feeds to the farmers of the United States and loss in wages to American workmen employed in flour mills, as well as a reduced demand by mills for supplies, such as fuel, oil, cotton, and jute sacks, etc.[8]

Farm groups like the American Wheat Growers Associated replied vigorously, laying the foundation for many arguments that would be raised in years to come:

Is this government price fixing? Not in any respect. It is merely a reverse application of the tariff principle, making that principle apply to what the farmer has to sell as well as to what he must buy. His export business would be handled exactly as is that of the organized manufacturing interest which disposes of its surplus production on export markets at prices below those obtaining in this country in order to maintain production and protect domestic markets from a surplus.

Is this class legislation? It is not, but rather a method to remove the stigma of class legislation from the present tariff structure. It makes the tariff apply to all classes of American products instead of eliminating the agriculturists — a very large group.

Is this government entry into business? Not in any sense of the word. This proposed legislation contemplates merely an establishment to assist the farmer in collecting an excise tax on the total marketed wheat and applying it as a premium upon the exported portion. Financially the whole thing will be done by the farmers themselves. The only place in which the Government enters is in the provision of machinery to do the work, the cost being borne by the wheat growers.

Is this a government subsidy? Not at all. The money appropriated for use by the commission is merely a revolving fund to be returned intact when the emergency has passed and the operations of the export body cease. Financially the farmer stands on his own feet throughout.

Will this plan injure cooperative marketing associations? It will assist the operation of cooperative marketing associations. These organizations have made wonderful progress, but have been unable to sign up sufficient memberships as yet to control a percentage of the national wheat production sufficient in volume to protect domestic markets from the depressed conditions of world markets. This proposed plan will adequately dispose of the problem of the national surplus. It will leave to the cooperative marketing associations the problem of controlling orderly distribution of the domestic consumption.

Will it increase production? It will not increase production because

---

[8] *Ibid.,* p. 269 (statement from the Millers' National Federation).

the tax will be an ever-present argument to all farmers of the evil of growing an excessive surplus. And it is obvious that the greater the exportable surplus the higher the tax and the less the net result.

Is this plan economically sound? "Economic soundness" is an empirical term, determined by relative conditions. This plan is nothing more nor less than united action on the part of the producers of a certain commodity, assisted by Government action, to protect themselves from foreign competition. In other words, the tariff principle. If that principle, recognized by the Government for many years, is sound, then so is this plan. If steel bars may be, with economic stability, manufactured for sale in this country at a price above world prices under tariff protection and any surplus sold to foreign markets at lower prices, then so may wheat be grown and sold.[9]

The National Grange was extremely guarded and conservative in its statements. For example:

. . . as an emergency measure the executive committee of the National Grange regards the McNary-Haugen bill as the least objectionable, the most defensible, and the most likely to secure results which in a large measure will bring agricultural prices up to something near an equal plane with the prices of other commodities of the country. . . .[10]

In 1929, after the McNary-Haugen Bill had met with three vetoes, Congress established the Federal Farm Board under the Agricultural Marketing Act. President O'Neal of the Farm Bureau had the following to say about this new legislation:

Later, the objective of the Farm Board and the Agricultural Marketing Act of 1929 was similar. In its declaration of policy, it was declared: "That it is hereby declared to be the policy of Congress to promote the effective merchandising of agricultural commodities in interstate and foreign commerce, so that the industry of agriculture will be placed on a basis of economic equality with other industries, and to that end to protect, control, and stabilize the currents of interstate and foreign commerce in the marketing of agricultural commodities and their food products."

The Farm Board failed because buying the surplus and holding it proved too expensive. In its first annual report in 1930, the board said:

---

[9] *Ibid.* (prepared statement of the American Wheat Growers Associated, delivered January 22, 1924).

[10] *Ibid.*, p. 271 (statement by President Thomas C. Atkeson of the National Grange).

"Finally, the board regards measures for prevention of surpluses, through control of excessive production, as absolutely essential to stabilizing farm prices and farm incomes. Co-operative associations and stabilization corporations, supplemented by other devices, may prove able to deal with temporary or occasional surpluses. But none of these, nor all together, nor any government agency can protect farmers from the consequences of repeated or continuous production in excess of market requirements. Adjustments of production to market requirements are indispensable, in agriculture as in industry, to the solution of surplus problems."[11]

Hoover's Farm Board could hardly have found a worse time to begin operations, and its efforts were almost certainly doomed to failure.

The Issue of Market and Production Control

With the onset of the Great Depression, agriculturists began to experiment with new ideas and approaches. In some areas, sedate and conservative farmers were engaging in violence or were flirting with it. Again, President O'Neal of the Farm Bureau outlines the philosophy and attitude. Indeed, he sounds a bit like a civil rights leader of the 1960s.

The farm problem is truly a national problem. Farming is the basic industry. From the soil comes all of our new wealth. The farmers are the greatest producing class and also the greatest consuming class in the country. Upon the prosperity of the farmer depends the prosperity of countless citizens whose income depends, directly or indirectly, on the buying power of the basic industry. . . .

It is high time other groups were made to realize that the American farmer is also an American citizen, entitled to all the rights and privileges that other citizens are accorded as a matter of course and as a matter of national policy. If the American laborer is entitled to an American wage, and if the American manufacturer is entitled to an American price for what he produces, then the farmer is entitled to an American price for his commodities.

Farmers are getting tired of being treated as stepchildren of Uncle Sam. They are demanding that they be brought in under the same protective tent that is sheltering other groups.

Knowing the farmers as I do, I am convinced that they have made

---

[11] Edward A. O'Neal, in *Nation's Agriculture*, p. 13.

up their minds, as I indicated at the beginning of this talk, that they are going to have their fair share of the national income.[12]

At the time, even the Farm Bureau and the Grange began to entertain ideas about the needs for market controls. President Franklin D. Roosevelt, a Democrat, had just appointed Henry A. Wallace, a Republican and Farm Bureau leader, as Secretary of Agriculture. His policies, which a willing Congress enacted into law (Agricultural Adjustment Act of 1933), were designed not only to reduce surpluses through acreage controls but also to stop market manipulation that placed the farmer at a disadvantage. It was charged that speculators were running the market down at harvest time, when farmers were forced to sell to pay debts, and driving it up later by holding commodities off the market until processors were forced to pay high prices for them. Thus, middle men and speculators were presented as villains. Wallace's program sought to take the incentive out of manipulation by taxing the processors and using the money gained from taxes to pay farmers for their cooperation in the farm program (planting fewer acres and thereby reducing surpluses).

When the Supreme Court of the United States found the processing tax to be unreasonable seizure of property without due process of law, Wallace pressed the Congress to enact the second Agricultural Adjustment Act in 1938, which allowed farmers to "seal" their crop production in return for growing less acres. "Sealing" meant that farmers were paid a "fair" price for their crops, which were then held on the farm or in some facility provided by the government until the farmer could get his price on the open market and repay the money lent him by the government, or until his crop was claimed by the government for the price it paid him at the time it was sealed. Such a program would (and in many instances did) keep the crop out of the hands of speculators until the farmer could receive a "just" or "fair" price — that is, *parity,* or something approximating it. This policy enabled the Secretary of Agriculture to acquire the commodities from farmers in exchange for a "support" price that was paid to the farmer if the market prices of the commodity fell below a "fair" profit level. This policy remained in effect until the 1960s, and thus parity became a permanent basis for price supports, or subsidies.

Issues of Parity and Supports

The Wallace program combined production and market controls with the principle of parity. Again, the cost-price squeeze was the target, because its elimination is what parity is all about. According to the parity principle, the balance between income from farm production and costs of nonfarm products purchased by the farmer should be equivalent or

---

[12] *Ibid.,* pp. 3–5.

roughly on a par with the cost-price balance in other segments of the economy (for example, the auto or steel industry). However, a steel-producer or auto-maker index has never been employed. What has been used is a principle of "fair return" in relation to the purchasing power and something called a "decent level of living." The index or standard of fairness has been based on the cost-price balance during years that experts and members of Congress deemed to be adequate and fair (for example, the cost-price balance for farmers between 1909 and 1914 or 1919 and 1929). Using such a period as a base then, if the costs of things a farmer must purchase are higher today by a certain percentage, the things he sells should be higher by an equivalent percentage.

How to achieve this balance had long been the major question to which programs were directed. As we pointed out earlier, organizations such as the American Farm Bureau Federation sought to do it through a free market mechanism; others, like the National Farmers Union, sought more controls. Even the Farm Bureau toyed occasionally with the controlled market concept — but not always, as can be seen in the following remarks of President Charles Shuman:

Thirty-five years' experience has demonstrated that government control schemes do not work — that price supports and payments stimulate excessive production even though the acreage is reduced. Therefore, farmers were not surprised when President Lyndon B. Johnson in his State of the Union message admitted that "parity for our farmers who produce our food is still just a hope — not an achievement."

The unfavorable experiences with government control programs have caused farmers to be seriously and increasingly interested in finding ways to develop greater market power.

However, they do not want the government as a partner in their bargaining efforts.

In transferring their attention to marketing they will undoubtedly remember that any political program, whether designed to manage production or to support bargaining, must please the most voters — and consumers outnumber producers 94 to 6.

Midwest farmers will never forget the ruthless way in which the feed grain and wheat programs have been used to hold farm prices at low levels in unsuccessful attempts to halt the rise in food prices. They suspect that the present scramble by politicians to get on the bargaining bandwagon is intended to calm farmers down until after the election.[13]

The president of the National Farmers Union, Tony Dechant, takes a position squarely opposed to Shuman.

---

[13] Charles Shuman, a prepared statement for the *Salina* (Kansas) *Journal* (April 16, 1968), p. A-1.

We are for 100 percent of parity. Webster defines it as "equality." I like to explain it in terms of my experience as an accountant. When a tank is built by an industrial firm for Viet Nam, all of the costs are prorated on a cost-accounting basis into the price. This means every bolt, every nut, all of the labor and a share of the overhead, including management salaries, etc. go into the price.

When the tank is finally painted and ready for shipment with all costs figured, you then have 100 percent of parity. Industry then adds a profit. This is the way our free enterprise system works. I am for it. I believe it to be a good system.

I want to make sure, however, that the farmer participates in it and I want to serve notice that once we achieve 100 percent of parity for the American farmer, we, too, are going to start talking about profits.[14]

The National Grange has had a slightly different approach and viewpoint over the years, as indicated by its Master in 1943, Albert Goss:

. . . Our organization has never supported a program for curtailing production as a means of increasing farm commodity prices through scarcity. We have always believed that the most effective way of obtaining a well-balanced production, and still assuring an abundant supply, would be found in an adequate marketing system, one element of which would be a two-price system on crops of which we produce a surplus. It is not our purpose to enter a discussion of this phase of the problem, except to point out that in commenting upon the A. A. A. set-up, we do not want to leave the impression that the Grange approves all the principles and practices which have been followed. We recognize, however, that until a more practical plan is developed, the A. A. A. organization is the most effective means readily at hand for meeting a difficult situation. . . .[15]

Under the New Deal programs the federal government became heavily involved in the agricultural industry in five basic ways: (1) it was the largest farm mortgage holder for a short time, thus rescuing farmers from loss of their farms and also rescuing many lenders from heavy losses; (2) it advanced credit on farm production and began a crop insurance program; (3) it installed stringent restrictions on production, through acreage limitations and marketing restraints; (4) it was a large scale

---

[14] Tony Dechant, from an *Address* presented at the St. Louis Agribusiness Club Luncheon, St. Louis, Missouri (February 28, 1968).

[15] Testimony before the U. S. House of Representatives, Select Committee of the Committee of Agriculture, *Hearings on House Resolution No. 119* (June 7, 1943), p. 768.

purchaser of commodities, through loans and other means; (5) it distributed benefit payments or subsidies to farmers.

During World War II, the farmers' economic condition improved. Between 1943 and 1952, the agricultural industry as a whole had an income between 100 percent and 115 percent of parity. Since 1953, when income dropped to 92 percent, the farmer's income has failed to reach 90 percent of parity.[16] In response to the good agricultural times during the mid-forties, a Republican Congress ended price controls and began debates on the possibility of ending or phasing out farm price supports by legislating a flexible or sliding-scale type of support. In 1948, President Truman asked for a flexible support program which would allow the government to reduce supports to as low as 60 percent or 75 percent of parity for commodities that were in oversupply.[17]

Three basic arguments were made in favor of flexible supports: they would permit reduced production but still protect farmer income while not providing incentives to overproduction; they would avoid the tremendous wastes of a high-support system as exemplified by the potato situation; and they would return agriculture to a more normal market situation after the abnormal wartime conditions. The price-support system, it was argued, was never meant to guarantee all farmers a high income, merely to protect them against price collapses and ruinous losses.

The major arguments in favor of a higher support level were that transition to flexible supports would mean sharp immediate drops in prices and ruin many small farmers, who were not profiting but just making a living under the existing system; that the farmer was not the only producer being aided by the Government (tariffs for manufactures, import restrictions, federal procurements were cited); and that a sharp reduction in farm income would lead to a farm depression, which would drag the whole economy into a major collapse.[18]

After much debate and many votes, Congress enacted a flexible program for supports between 60 percent and 90 percent of parity for the basic crops (cotton, corn, wheat, wool, rice, peanuts, and tobacco). Tobacco would be supported at 90 percent whenever quotas were in effect. All other so-called nonbasic crops would be supported at the Secretary of Agriculture's discretion on a sliding scale between 0.0 percent and 90 percent of parity. However, sliding-scale parity was not to go into effect until 1950;[19] and price supports remained fixed at 90 percent of

---

[16] *U. S. Agricultural Policy in the Postwar Years*, p. 3.
[17] *Ibid.*, pp. 22–23.
[18] *Ibid.*, pp. 23–24.
[19] *Ibid.*, p. 24.

parity until 1955, since each Congress continued them by annual enactment.

Conservation as a Means of Control

Between 1953 and 1957, government stockpiles of farm commodities
increased at an alarming rate, production increased, and farm income
tended to follow a downward trend. One of Wallace's justifications for the
two Agricultural Adjustment Acts had been conservation of the soil and
restoration to fertility of depleted and overcropped acres. Senator Hubert
H. Humphrey, a Democrat from Minnesota, and the Republican President
Dwight D. Eisenhower picked up the theme in the mid-1950s.

Eisenhower's Secretary of Agriculture, Ezra Taft Benson, established
a "soil bank," which paid farmers in cash or in commodities from government stockpiles in return for retiring land from production. There was
hope that this system would reduce government expenditure for purchase
and storage of oversupplies. Others saw it as encouragement to marginal
farmers to place their entire farm in the "bank" and find other employment. A countermove by Congress to restore supports to 90 percent of
parity was vetoed by Eisenhower. The upshot was the compromise that
installed the soil bank and directed the Department of Agriculture to sell
stockpiles at a loss on the world market in order to reduce surpluses. In
return, the Administration consented to a freeze on transitional or flexible
parity as well as special concessions to certain growers like those raising
corn and rice.

This program was strongly supported by the Farm Bureau Federation.
Its legislative director, John Lynn, said:

Farm Bureau members are convinced that national policies affecting
farm production and marketing should promote a realistic balance between markets and productive capacity. We now have a greatly expanded productive plant. It is urgent that policies be adopted which will
regain and expand agricultural markets to a point where they balance
production. Any program which has the result of expanding agricultural
output in the absence of a comparable increase in effective market
demand is contrary to the interests of farmers. Likewise, programs which
induce producers to continue inefficient production render a disservice to
agriculture by contributing to the accumulation of surpluses, raising the
average cost of production and limiting production per man, all of which
tend to limit the opportunity of farm people to earn a good income.

This conviction that we must balance production with effective
market demand in order to increase farm income is basic to all of our
recommendations on agricultural programs. We state it here because we
believe that it is an essential element in our recommendations for a

surplus reduction and soil-bank plan. In the remainder of our statement, we are confining our testimony to surplus reduction and soil-bank legislation.

Farm Bureau's proposal for a surplus-reduction and soil-bank program was presented to this committee last year by the president of our organization, Mr. Charles B. Shuman, on February 29.

At that time, we stated that —

> the basic purpose of the surplus-reduction and soil-bank plan, as we conceive it, is to bring about at the earliest feasible date a balance between annual supply and effective demand and to make more rapid progress toward the liquidation of current surplus stocks.

We emphasized that —

> the present policy of piling up surpluses must be reversed and existing surpluses must be reduced if we are to improve the farm-income situation on anything more than a temporary basis. We must dispose of the present price-destroying surpluses; also we must adopt governmental policies designed to prevent an immediate rebuilding of such surplus stockpiles. . . .

We emphasized two underlying principles: (1) That maximum effort should be made to effectively utilize existing surpluses to carry out all phases of the surplus-reduction and soil-bank plan, and (2) that participants only be rewarded for their effective contribution toward balancing supplies with demand.[20]

The National Farmers' Union representative, Mr. Baker, was not so gracious in his assessment of the soil bank. He accused Secretary Benson of giving no more than half-hearted support to the major goal of the bank — soil conservation; and he found that the program was killing the small farmer and creating larger farms that were conducive to large corporate type farm enterprises which spelled disaster for family farming.

As you will remember, then we recommended adoption of a comprehensive combined conservation acreage reserve, not the wheezing two-valve model now in existence. We still feel that a comprehensive consolidated program rather than the existing two-way operation would be most effective for farmers and more understandable to the general public.

---

[20] U. S. House of Representatives, Committee on Agriculture, Hearings on the Soil Bank Program (January 7–10, 1957), pp. 107–108.

However, we recognize that the division into two parts of the conservation acreage reserve is now established under existing law as an operating program.

The acreage reserve, while it provides relatively adequate supply adjustment, applies to only the six basic commodities and one of them, peanuts, has been omitted by the Department. So for 1957 the acreage reserve is available to only 5 out of nearly 300 crops, and almost completely disregards conservation values.

The conservation reserve, while it covers all crops except grazing land, and includes conservation values, does not adequately provide for supply adjustment for any crop.[21]

What was needed, as Baker saw it, was a conservation program securely tied to high price supports.

Lowering the support levels for farm commodities is the bankruptcy way to reduce farm production. It is the way that will destroy family farms and the soil and water resources upon which fulfillment of future food and fiber needs depends.[22]

The soil bank was disappointing. In his 1959 veto message of a bill providing high price supports in exchange for acreage cutbacks, President Eisenhower told Congress that farmers merely retired their most unproductive acres and increased their yields on the remaining land.[23] Government stockpiles kept growing and farm income kept shrinking. The failures of the government program drove many farmers, primarily small ones, from their farms and into the rapidly increasing urban centers, where many of them faced severe personal hardships and economic difficulties because they lacked the skills and outlook necessary for adapting to city life. The upshot of all this was a search for fresh approaches, all of which are at issue today.

One approach was the imposition of sterner controls, which was proposed by the Kennedy administration. A second was the "farmers strike," which was initiated by the National Farm Organization. A third was an attempt to have the government sanction "collective bargaining" for farmers. Two pleas emerged from these approaches. The first asked that the decline in the rural population be halted and that a program be initiated to preserve the family farm operator. The second called for a countervailing force to speak for consumers who faced inflated food prices.

---

[21] *Ibid.*, p. 144.
[22] *Ibid.*, p. 166.
[23] *U. S. Agricultural Policy in the Postwar Years*, p. 44.

The Issue of Greater Controls

The fear of federal control is basic to American ideology. It has served throughout our national existence as a major fortress for those opposed to enlarging the scope of government activity. Agricultural programs have not been excepted, as we saw earlier when the McNary-Haugen Act was attacked as being un-American. Indeed, similar charges were heaped upon Wallace's Agricultural Adjustment Acts. Such charges were even brought against the federal government's Commodity Credit Corporation, which was set up to buy farm surpluses, store them, and dispose of them to aid farmers.

I conceive the greatest issue that has faced this country domestically since the Civil War to be the question as to whether or not we are going to have a government of law or a government operated on the theory that all the laws written will simply be blank checks on power and individuals may use arbitrary judgment. If we do not have dictatorship in the form and in the sense they have it in Europe . . . [we have bureaucrats who] are in themselves an arbitrary judge with unguided and unrestrained judgment, and can exercise capricious and whimsical action on matters of this kind.[24]

The same objections were soon to appear after President John F. Kennedy outlined his proposed farm program in 1961. Kennedy's program sought to raise farm income and keep small farmers from quitting. To do this he asked that stringent restrictions be placed on supply and production quotas, which would be tailored in terms of each farmer's production history. The "new wrinkle" in the program was Kennedy's request that limits be placed on the quantities supported in the markets. These restrictions were to replace the old limitations on acres planted. Secondly, he asked for broader controls that would apply not only to the six staples (cotton, corn, rice, wheat, tobacco, and peanuts) but to a host of other crops, including perishables like fruits and vegetables. Opposition to such a proposal was not slow in coming. Ezra Taft Benson, Eisenhower's controversial Secretary of Agriculture, pointed up the differences between his program and that of Kennedy's Secretary, Orville Freeman. Benson concluded that the program was socialistic and dominated by the federal government. *U. S. News and World Report* described the conflict as follows:

Farming today remains this country's biggest business — bigger by far than automobiles, or steel, or the railroads, or any of the other giants among industries.

Dairying and the raising of livestock account for close to half of

---

[24] Statement by the Honorable Lyle H. Boren, U. S. Representative from Oklahoma, before the U. S. House of Representatives, Committee on Banking and Currency, *Hearings* (September 29–October 12, 1943), pp. 377–378.

farmers' gross income, year in and year out. The key to control of these two farm enterprises lies in the so-called feed grains — corn, barley, oats and grain sorghum.

Whoever can control feed grains can control the livestock and dairy end of farming. The Kennedy Administration from the beginning had set its heart on this control. It also wanted to get tighter controls on wheat.

The White House hoped that, by getting power to control output of feed grains and wheat, the cost of farm programs, now counted in billions each year, could be cut sharply.

Early in 1962, Agriculture Secretary Orville L. Freeman laid the controversial farm bill before Congress. The heart of this bill was a "supply management" plan that would have placed tight controls on wheat and feed grains.

Republicans charged the plan was a "power grab." They said if it was enacted, control of the vast feed-grain, livestock and dairy segments of the farming industry would gravitate toward Washington.

Control from Washington, it was explained, would be applied through the network of county agricultural committees that blankets the country. Under the "supply management" plan, these county committees would parcel out to each farmer his share of the county's quota of grain that could be grown in any one year.

Though members of the county committees are elected by their fellow farmers, they operate under State committees that are appointed by the Secretary of Agriculture. Thus, in the view of many of those who opposed the bill, the Secretary would have a hand in the business of every farmer growing grain and feeding it to livestock.

Secretary Freeman, for his part, said that some way had to be found to control grain production, which, in turn, would stabilize production of livestock and dairy products.

If "supply management" were adopted, held Mr. Freeman, farmers could get their price in the market place and taxpayers could be saved 5 billion dollars in price-support costs over the period of 1963 through 1967. This argument, said many city Congressmen, won their support for the Kennedy-Freeman plan.

Secretary Freeman stated further that farmers would have a chance to vote on the plan in a referendum, and, unless two thirds voted for it, it would not go into effect. In that case, there would be no production controls, and price supports would be sharply lower.[25]

Here are former Secretary Benson's views of the program, including several features other than the supply-management, feed-grain aspects of it.

---

[25] *U. S. News & World Report* (July 9, 1962), pp. 46–47. Copyright 1962 by U. S. News & World Report, Inc.

When the Eisenhower Administration left office nine months ago, we bequeathed to our successors, along with our sincere good wishes, a five-point program of recommendations for future farm policy.

You may be interested in these five points and in what has happened to them.

First, we urged that the Food for Peace program should be expanded. This has been, and is being, done. One of the very important forward steps in this area is a recently completed survey of the world food budget. It shows food balances and food needs, country by country. It should be helpful in making the best possible use of agricultural abundance in the interests of world peace and economic development.

Second, we urged that the Rural Development program which we started in 1955 to help expand economic opportunity in low-income rural areas should be emphasized and expanded as rapidly as is feasible. Such a program can help small farmers make adjustments which they want and need to make to improve their standard of living. This operation has been greatly expanded. Unfortunately, the emphasis is now on federal action rather than on local voluntary effort where it belongs.

Third, we urged vigorous efforts to push forward programs of research to develop new foreign and domestic markets, including new industrial uses, for our farm products. Research is being continued along these lines.

Fourth, we urged that the use of farm land should be further adjusted in accordance with needs by such a program as an expanded conservation reserve. This has not been done.

Instead, the Kennedy Administration embarked on an ill-advised and ill-fated feed-grain program. This program, which was ballyhooed as one that would simultaneously raise the income of producers of corn and grain sorghums, cut down feed-grain stocks by hundreds of millions of bushels, and save taxpayers anywhere from half a billion to a billion dollars, is proving to be a monumental failure. Corn production, according to the October crop report, is down only 9 per cent instead of the 20 to 25 per cent predicted a few months ago — and, when the final returns come in, this reduction of 9 per cent may dwindle even more.

The hoped-for savings to taxpayers have vanished in the cold light of reality. . . .

Finally, we recommended legislation to improve the price-support mechanism by providing levels of price support that will allow farm commodities to move into regular marketing channels, and, at the same time, afford adequate price protection. We recommended that price be permitted to perform its traditional role of influencing production and consumption. The new Administration not only ignored this recommendation, it actually increased price support on 12 agricultural commodities. . . .

The unfortunate thing is that, when the bill for these unwise actions is finally presented, it will be paid many times over by farmers and consumers alike and by all the taxpayers of the nation.

But I do not believe our farm people and our nation as a whole will be fooled indefinitely. Farm people, above all other economic groups, understand that "As ye sow, so shall ye reap." They understand that the road to socialism, the road to a completely planned and subsidized economy, is a highway that leads to a loss of initiative, the discouragement of industry, the destruction of character, and the demoralization of a people.[26]

Secretary Freeman answered his critics in a curt and lucid manner:

The emergency feed-grain program is the first successful plan in the history of modern agriculture to bring production of farm commodities in line with demand while maintaining farm income. Its success can now be measured with the projections of the Department's November crop report.

Unfortunately, it is being subjected to more falsehoods and distortion than factual study.

From its inception at the beginning of 1961, when the nation found it owned more feed grains than any nation in history, the emergency feed-grain program has had strong, almost hysterical opposition. When it was proposed, opponents said it was unworkable.

When it was passed by the Congress, opponents said that farmers wouldn't participate. When farmers signed up to participate, opponents shifted ground again and said it wouldn't cut back production.

The program has proved them wrong on every count, and now the opponents are reduced to saying that it costs too much — while calling for programs which would spend millions more and which have failed in the past to do what the feed-grain program has accomplished.

When I testified before Congress on the feed-grain program, I said it would do four things — and it has done each as predicted. I said it would increase income for participating farmers. Net farm income is estimated to be up a billion dollars this year over 1960, . . . I said the program would reduce Government stocks. Feed-grain production is about 450 million bushels below 1960 levels, and more than 800 million bushels below what farmers would have produced under the kind of program in effect in 1960.

Government stocks will be reduced by 280 million bushels this year — instead of a 500-million-bushel increase expected under a wide-open production program.

---

[26] From an address by Mr. Benson at the University of Alberta, Edmonton, Canada, October 25, 1961. As cited in *U. S. News & World Report* (November 20, 1961), p. 87.

264   I said the program would lower costs to the taxpayer. Savings of over 500 million dollars will result during the next few years from storage, handling and transportation fees which will not have to be paid out because current Government stocks are going down instead of up. Expenditures this fiscal year are estimated to be less than they would have been under the Benson program. I said that fair and stable prices for consumers of meat, poultry and dairy products would flow from the program. Retail prices have remained fairly steady and have actually shown a modest decline.

These facts and figures have not been challenged. The opponents of the program have ignored them. In doing this, they simply are saying that the program has not been as successful as it might have been.

There is no argument on that count. At the time the signup for the 1961 program ended, the Department was surprised and pleased that farmers had agreed to divert to soil-conserving purposes about 19 per cent of all corn acreage and about 26 per cent of the feed-grain acreage.[27]

President Kennedy backed Secretary Freeman in his presidential message to Congress. He pointed out that during 1961 "net farm income rose $1 billion, and income per farm increased almost $350. Government stocks of farm products were reduced for the first time in nine years." He then asked Congress to enact a "broad new farm program" which would make maximum use of productive abundance, seek a balance between production and demand, and avoid waste of public and private resources. His two major goals were to improve farm income and reduce costs. These, he said, could be achieved "only if farm output can be reduced below needs for several years and then allowed to increase at a rate equal to the growth of demand. To do this, he first asked to retire some 50 millions of acres from production — as much land as that contained in the state of Nebraska. He further asked for presidential powers to negotiate and carry out multi-national programs and agreements for food assistance; and he asked for production allotments to cope with growing surpluses of particular products, especially poultry and dairy products.[28]

Before the end of the year, 1962, change was definitely in the air. Congress had refused to impose the tough controls. Secretary Freeman continued to call for stiffer controls, and one liberal Republican senator began to fear the probable effects of the disappearing surpluses:

Says Senator George D. Aiken (Rep.), of Vermont: "Our farm surpluses are disappearing. We have less than a year's supply of wheat

[27] *U. S. News & World Report* (December 4, 1961), pp. 101–102. Copyright 1961 by U. S. News & World Report, Inc.

[28] President John F. Kennedy, "Message on the Proposed Agricultural Program," House Document No. 323, *Congressional Record* (January 31, 1962), pp. 1177–1180.

on hand and only a four-month reserve of corn and feed grains. In **265**
today's world, it would be dangerous to reduce grain supplies further."

For his part, Agriculture Secretary Freeman points to studies that
show prices for many farm products would drop sharply — some by as
much as 50 per cent — if Government controls and price supports were
removed.

And yet a surprising number of American farmers appear to be willing to take that chance.[29]

Strikes and Threats of Violence

While Congress put the finishing touches on another farm bill, many
farmers out in the Midwest had other plans in mind.

There's a growing feeling that Government can't solve farm problems. Striking livestock producers attempted to take things into their own
hands. Wheat farmers nearly voted out controls.

All across Midwestern prairies, change is in the air.

A deep current of opinion running through the Midwest farming
country suggests that time may be running out on efforts to control
agriculture from Washington.

Ever since 1933, the Federal Government has been trying to devise
ways to limit farm production and to support prices of farm products.

Now it is 29 years later and the problems are the same as they were
in the beginning — many products of the farm are in oversupply, and
prices continue to be far from high enough to satisfy farmers. Evidence is
seen that the farmers themselves are increasingly disillusioned with
Washington's efforts to bail them out with price supports and production
controls.

There's just been a strike by thousands of livestock producers
throughout the Midwest. This strike took the form of holding livestock
from markets by members of the National Farm Organization.

The NFO says it is time for farmers to take matters in their own
hands and do for themselves what Government has been unable to do.

Wheat farmers, in a referendum on August 30, very nearly knocked
out the program of acreage controls and price supports that has been in
effect since 1938.

Earlier, turkey growers had turned down production and marketing
controls in a nationwide referendum. . . .

Early in September, attention centered on the strike against livestock

---

[29] *U. S. News & World Report* (September 24, 1962), p. 58. Copyright 1962 by
U. S. News & World Report, Inc.

markets organized by the National Farm Organization. The NFO called it a "holding action."

It was an effort to apply the techniques of labor unions to the farming industry.

The NFO aim was to force processors of livestock products to bargain with them for prices and set up long-term contracts to supply their needs. NFO officials also urged members to extend their holding action to corn and soybeans, soon to be harvested.

Marketing experts predicted that such techniques would never work in an industry as diverse and widespread as the production of grain and livestock. But the impact of the NFO strike, in the first few days of September, was surprising to many people.

Raised was the question of whether overproduction of some farm products is really as serious as pictured. A relatively small number of farmers had been able to reduce livestock sales enough to force prices up for a time.

Consumers were affected, too. Meat production in the first week of September dropped 8 per cent below the same period of 1961. Wholesale meat prices rose, forcing retailers to raise prices to housewives, or absorb the higher costs themselves.

Another measure of the ferment now at work in farm areas is seen in the reaction to the farm plan recently proposed by the Committee for Economic Development.

The idea of using Government power and subsidy to move 2 million workers off farms over the next five years jolted small-town businessmen as well as farmers. That would bring a reduction of one third in the present farm labor force.

Said Robert Iske, president of a bank in Springfield, Nebr.: "If this CED idea went into effect, it wouldn't be just 2 million farmers leaving the land. It would be the end of me and thousands and thousands of small businessmen."[30]

Collective Bargaining for Farmers?

The farm revolt of the 1960s was neither so determined nor so violent as the one in the 1930s, despite the continued pressure from the cost-price squeeze. Surpluses declined but they continued to depress the market. This, together with growing unrest among farmers, generally prompted policymakers to suggest new approaches. One approach that has gained considerable support and attention is a proposal to legislate

---

[30] *Ibid.*, pp. 57–58.

collective bargaining for farmers. John Schmiedeler of the *Salina* (Kansas) *Journal* explains it this way:

> Secretary of Agriculture Freeman calls it "muscle in the marketplace."
>
> Others have other descriptions, some of them not complimentary.
>
> What all are talking about is the hottest topic on the farm front — farm bargaining.
>
> The theory is that farmers should somehow achieve greater control over the capricious market for their products. Farmers should, farm leaders say, be able to set prices for what they sell just as others set prices on what farmers buy.
>
> Nearly all farmers agree the power to bargain for prices is an attractive idea. Labor unions, many say, have made collective bargaining work. Producers of the nation's food and fiber should do no less.
>
> But there agreement ends. . . .
>
> Sen. Walter Mondale, a Minnesota Democrat, has introduced a farm bargaining bill in the Senate. Called the National Agricultural Bargaining act, it would set up a national agricultural relations board which would act as sort of a referee in farmer-processor bargaining.
>
> Under the bill, producers of any commodity, through a referendum, would decide if they wanted to be represented in price negotiations by an elected farm marketing committee. If producers approved the idea, processors would form a committee and the two groups would negotiate prices for the individual commodity.
>
> Any agreement reached would be binding on all purchasers.
>
> Introduction of the bill, of course, is a long way from actual farmer–processor bargaining. Senator Mondale said he wanted to get "discussions started in Congress." . . .
>
> Farmers are attending meetings in greater numbers than in recent years. . . .
>
> Critics of the program, however, insist the 35-year history of federal farm programs is a history of failure.
>
> Farm bargaining is not without pitfalls. Some of these were examined at the National Farm Institute in Des Moines, Ia., earlier this year.
>
> G. E. Brandow, professor of agricultural economics, Pennsylvania State University, asked the question, what do farmers really hope to accomplish with bargaining power?
>
> Answering the question himself, he said:

>> (1) They want to remain the managers of agriculture and not turn farming over to the processing and supply firms.
>>
>> (2) They want to maintain or widen markets. Farmers don't want to lose the milk market to substitutes or the wheat export market to Canada.

(3) They want better prices and more stable prices.
(4) They want better terms of sale on certain products.

"It so often happens," Brandow said, "that these things cannot all be gained at the same time. Sharply higher prices for dairy products, for example, might cause substantial loss of markets to imitation milk and butterfat substitutes.

"High prices for wheat undoubtedly would force U. S. wheat out of the commercial export market.

"Something always to be watched is the possibility that pushing up prices will encourage food and farm supply firms to integrate into farm production, leaving farmers with a subordinate role if any.

"On the other hand, farmers scarcely can afford to be so eager to expand markets or to keep out integrators that they practically give products away.

"When farmers have no market power whatever, it makes little difference if they understand this matter of choice, among limited alternatives. . . .

"But if they do get market power then they have choices and can make mistakes. If they are going to use market power to advantage, they must realistically appraise the alternatives open to them and be good strategists in deciding what use to make of power.

"In short," Brandow continued, " 'muscle in the marketplace to raise prices is too narrow a way to look at bargaining power. . . .'

"With higher prices in effect (presumably from farm bargaining power), consumers and the export market will purchase less, so buyers will buy less from producers.

"But producers will want to produce more, not less.

"Buyers will decide whose production they will take. They are likely to favor the large producers and to welcome expansion by them, so numerous small producers will have no market."[31]

The National Farm Organization, which initiated the "farm strike" of 1962, is, of course, a strong backer — if not the primary stimulus — for collective bargaining for farmers. Organized in the mid-1950s by Oren Lee Staley and two Republican ex-governors (Andrew Mullen of Nebraska and Dan Turner of Iowa), it is the newest major farm group. Its president is committed to the principle of collective bargaining.

The need for collective bargaining for agriculture is obvious. Everyone else in the economy is organized except farmers. And when you have

---

[31] John Schmiedeler, "Farm Bargaining Raises Questions and Some Hackles," *Salina* (Kansas) *Journal* (April 16, 1968), p. A-1 *ff*.

an organized economy, those who remain unorganized get in a weaker and weaker position.

The reason that farmers' prices are so low in comparison with every other segment of the economy, is because farmers have remained unorganized. Large companies in all business sectors of our economy have organized themselves into strong, economic units. The strongest of these large companies sets the pace and are termed leaders in price in their particular economic field.

The working people have successfully organized. Therefore, the prices of the products farmers have had to buy have continued to go up. But farmers have continued to go to the market place as individuals and ask, "What will you give me?", with the results that could have been expected — lower and lower prices.

The law of supply and demand can operate successfully only when there is equal strength on the side of the buyer and the seller. This has not been true as far as agriculture is concerned, because farmers, as individuals or groups within areas, cannot have sufficient strength to meet the economic strength of those who buy their products.

The only answer to the farmers' low price problems is collective bargaining for agriculture. Collective bargaining for agriculture must differ in its structure from the other segments of the economy.

Farmers have the broadest anti-trust exemptions of any segment of the economy. When the Capper-Volstead Act was passed giving farmers broad anti-trust exemptions, it was noted in the discussions that the purpose of the Act was to give farmers the same legal right to bargain collectively as already enjoyed by the corporations where capital could be brought together by individuals to build the corporate structure. The second section of the Capper-Volstead Act protects the rest of the economy from unfair use of the legal rights for farmers.

Experience has taught NFO that there are six basic points necessary for successful collective bargaining for agriculture:

1. Farmers must organize to solve their problems — they do not solve their problems and then organize.

2. Collective bargaining for agriculture requires industry-wide bargaining. Farmers can not bargain successfully with companies that may have 40 plants in 30 states, unless their bargaining efforts are coordinated so their bargaining can be effective industry-wide.

3. Collective bargaining efforts for agriculture must include all major commodities as well as any minor commodities. . . .

4. The building of economic strength for farmers is not enough to gain success. That economic strength must be demonstrated and must be used to prove to large companies that they must have the production put together under a collective bargaining structure.

This means that a holding action must be used when necessary, in order to achieve success in collective bargaining for agriculture.

A holding action is nothing more than the use of the business principle that industry has used for such a long time. And that business principle is putting a price tag on the product and refusing to sell the product until the price on the price tag is paid.

No company will ever give a collective bargaining effort for agriculture anything. It is only human nature to buy products as cheaply as they can be bought. Therefore, without the use of a holding action or the willingness to use a holding action, there is no real bargaining. . . .

5. The ultimate goal in collective bargaining for agriculture must be contract. . . . contracts must protect the farmers' gains and the farmers must realize that they can and must meet the business needs of large processors. . . .

6. Collective bargaining for agriculture means farmers bargaining together and selling together. This means that as processor acceptance grows it is possible for farmers to use their production to build their bargaining power by moving production into new marketing channels.

At this stage of bargaining where the production can be used in this manner, new and keen competition can be brought about within old marketing systems and marketing channels and the general price level will be increased.[32]

President Charles Shuman of the American Farm Bureau Federation is opposed.

There are two ways to organize farmers to obtain greater bargaining power — voluntary and involuntary. Farm Bureau members have decided to use the voluntary method of organization because they believe it offers a greater opportunity for success.

The American Agricultural Marketing association is a cooperative affiliate of the AFBF that was organized in 1960 and has accumulated seven years of successful experience in voluntary organization to increase bargaining power. . . .

Each year these associations have gained in their ability to negotiate successfully with buyers for better prices and other terms of sale.

Farm Bureau marketing associations are now a most important factor in price determination for several commodities and, unless interrupted by some new government scheme, this marketing know-how and success will be extended to all commodities within a relatively few years.

---

[32] *Ibid.* (Oren Lee Staley's personal statement in the Schmiedeler column).

Our greatest present challenge is to protect the right of farmers to organize and to bargain on a voluntary basis and to keep the government bureaucracy in its proper role of administering rules of fair play.

The major objectives of Farm Bureau's voluntary marketing program are to get for farmers the full market value of their products and to earn a better price by supplying products that are worth more to consumers.

The source of power in any voluntary organization is the membership while the power source of an involuntary group comes from the outside — from the enforcing authority.

Legislation has been proposed to authorize compulsory bargaining for all producers when approved by a referendum. With Farm Bureau's head start of successful experience, substantial financial resources and 1¾ million members, we could be expected to win most of the elections. However, Farm Bureau is interested in success — not in monopoly power.

Those farmers who would be forced by referendum to join the Farm Bureau bargaining group would weaken the organization because they would probably work to undercut or disrupt the bargaining activity. Truly effective power comes through the willing cooperation of informed, conscious, loyal and active members and this kind of power far exceeds that which flows from a compulsory grouping.

There is an even more fundamental reason why Farm Bureau members reject compulsory bargaining. The only source of power that can be used to compel farmers to bargain together is the federal government and this authority must come from an act of the Congress.

The Congress, as well as the executive branch of our government, must be concerned with justice and equity for all citizens — not farmers alone. The Constitution spells this out and, furthermore, since 94 percent of the voters are consumers, not farmers, the politicians in Congress and the Administration will necessarily be more interested in low food prices to please voters than in high farm income.

Any federal government encouragement or enforcement of farmer bargaining would most certainly include rules or devices to "protect consumers" or the authority to issue cease-and-desist orders any time prices threaten to go higher than the Washington bureaucracy thinks they should.[33]

The National Association of Wheat Growers is somewhat more reserved but far more supportive than the Farm Bureau. Here is what George Meeker, their president, had to say on the matter:

The committee on National Farm Programs produced a resolution, which was approved by the board of directors, as follows:

---

[33] *Ibid.* (Charles Shuman's personal statement in the Schmiedeler column).

> With a view to improving farm income, the National Association of Wheat Growers directs its executive board to study means of obtaining effective bargaining power for wheat producers.

Until further study and action is taken by the National Association of Wheat Growers on this statement, the stand of the association appears to be favorable toward what it calls "effective bargaining power," for agriculture. . . .

First of all, I believe that the National Association of Wheat Growers is dedicated to the proposition that commodity problems in agriculture are best solved commodity–by–commodity, and not by an over-all rule.

Problems vary widely. Some commodities, for instance, are highly perishable, while others are storable.

In fact, the problems vary from section to section of the United States for the same commodity. . . .

Secondly, it appears to me that agricultural producers are realizing more and more that there must be more unity in agriculture. Not only must that unity be stronger, but it must extend over wide reaches of our vast nation. . . .

I do not believe that a unified program for effective bargaining power for agriculture can be achieved in any other way until the man on the farm and ranch recognizes the threats to his success in agriculture, and is willing to make common cause with other farmers and ranchers to meet these threats head-on.

During a time of uneasiness about the stability of currencies, there is a tendency to protect savings or to speculate by buying gold or by buying land. At the present time there also is the movement of big corporations into the field of agriculture production. Combined, these two situations are a real threat to the American family farm.

One of our members cautioned an audience, "You can get together and do something about it now, or you can work for the corporations and strike for higher wages!"

. . . There has been a great deal of talk about setting up a bargaining system for agriculture like that which is in operation for labor.

We feel this is a question that will require considerable study before we can approve or disapprove it.

A farmer cannot withhold his labor at a critical time and survive as a farmer. He must milk the cows when it is time, he must harvest when his wheat is ready — with or without a fair hourly wage.

The farmer also is a capitalist. He owns land and animals (agricultural factory) and carries on practices very much like those of management in industry. Again, however, the factory in agriculture cannot be shut down as easily as the factory in industry. Herds of feeding cattle and fields of growing crops cannot be laid off until they are needed again.

Farming today is in such a state of stress and crisis. We must band together for the very survival of the family farm system, a system which has made this country the greatest in history.[34]

Tony Dechant, President of the American Farmers Union is also highly supportive of collective bargaining. Like Meeker, he sees it as one possible means for preserving the family farm. He, too, supports Meeker's commodity–by–commodity bargaining principle. But he also warns against possible violation of the antitrust laws.

It seems clear, as Secretary Orville Freeman said last summer, that bargaining power for farmers is an idea whose time has come. . . .

We insist, as we have for years, that farmers need legal machinery to make commodity–by–commodity bargaining with processors and other buyers possible. We feel producers themselves should do this bargaining. And we want government involvement held to an absolute minimum. . . .

Most thoughtful people recognize that farmers occupy a weak and disorganized position in the market. Producers of farm commodities are one of the few economic groups, if not the only one, that must sell in markets largely controlled by buyers, brokers, commission agents, and other buyer representatives.

Agriculture has been, and still is, the only segment of American business still forced to sell its products at wholesale prices set by somebody else, and to buy its production supplies at retail prices, also set by somebody else. . . .

How can they achieve real bargaining strength without being subjected to boycotts and blacklisting and threats from processors and other commodity buyers who gang up on them?

How can farmers further strengthen the important part that farm cooperatives play in marketing — and must continue to play in the future?

And, most important, how can they achieve strength needed to set fair farm prices without running up against antitrust laws? In other words, how can they do this job without being hit by time-consuming and costly legal challenges?[35]

After commenting on several U. S. Supreme Court decisions, Dechant sees a very real threat to efforts involving group action in the marketplace.

The decision written on appeal conceded farmers may act together in cooperative associations and that legitimate objects of mutual help may be carried out with immunity. But otherwise, it said, the farmer

---

[34] *Ibid.* (George Meeker's personal statement in the Schmiedeler column).
[35] *Ibid.* (Tony Dechant's personal statement for the Schmiedeler column).

274 associations act as an entity with the same responsibilities under Section 2 of the Sherman Act as if they were private business corporations.

These cases are not all the decisions dealing with the problem of when, and under what circumstances, farmers are exempt from restrictions of the Sherman and Clayton Acts. But this review points up the dangers to farmers in this area and the need for dependable corrective legislation.

The challenge, then, is to do this bargaining job by law. The clear choice, put very simply, is between legislation and litigation.[36]

Then speaking directly to the Mondale Bill itself, Dechant makes the position of the Farmers Union perfectly clear.

Title I of the bill is pure bargaining, an approach that would provide the legal authority for commodity–by–commodity negotiating for price with buyers, handlers and processors.

Title II of the bill provides for improving the 1937 Agricultural Marketing Agreement Act and for expanding it to make any farm commodity eligible for a marketing order if a majority of the producers approve.

We favor both approaches and feel farmers should have an opportunity to decide which would work best in a given situation. The producers should decide which title works best and have the option to bring it into force.

The Mondale bill by itself, however, is not enough. I want to make it abundantly clear that we do not consider a bargaining act, no matter how good it is, a substitute or replacement for farm programs. . . .

There can be no effective bargaining for farm prices without effective and consistent supply control.[37]

As some of the above spokesmen indicate, particularly Mr. Shuman, it is not just a matter of farm income but also of costs to the consumer. Farmers could price themselves out of many markets. Farm leaders generally recognize this. Moreover, even housewives will revolt when the prices cut too far into their budgets.

Consumer Revolts: The Food Price Issue

Outside the Big Apple chain store in Atlanta's suburban Toco Hills Shopping Center, the group of housewives with their picket signs were joined by husbands, children and dogs — and all of them marched gaily in a circle for an hour or more. In San Francisco, a well-dressed matron

---

[36] *Ibid.*
[37] *Ibid.*

asked: "What should I wear to go picketing? A hat and high heels?" And in Houston, Mrs. Marie Mitchell, an attorney's wife and head of the Texas Housewives Association, was beaming. "Picketing," she exclaimed, "is so much fun!"

Indeed, to some housewives, picketing a food store was suddenly the "in" thing to do. But to most of the women marching, it was deadly serious business. And to the American food chain industry, there was nothing funny about it at all. For the boycotts of major chain stores that began in Denver in mid-October had spread last week across the nation. Some were slacking off — notably in Denver, where five chains cut prices soon after the boycott began. . . .

. . . housewives themselves had shifted their tactics — from simple demands for lower prices to concentration of their fire on promotional devices such as trading stamps and bingo-like games, along with such extra services as bag boys and late night hours. Here they were on firmer ground; this was an area in which cost savings could be made, though probably not to the extent that many housewives seemed to think. . . .

At the farm level, prices have suddenly turned upward after an eight-year slide. By 1964, farm products were worth only 94.3 per cent of the 1957–59 average; many farmers, in fact, were literally going out of business. But their departure reduced the supply of farm products, and the new shortages started driving prices up. By the middle of last month, the farm-price index was a full 7 per cent higher than it had been in October 1965. What's more, the farmer was keeping some of his gains; the prices he paid were up only 5 per cent in the same year.

But the farmer's share of the consumer's food dollar is less than 40 cents. Processors and wholesalers account for about 38 cents of the food dollar, and their prices have also risen — by 6.8 per cent in the past year. The processors, too, are prospering; according to a Standard & Poor's survey, their average profit margin rose to 2.8 per cent of sales last year from 2.6 per cent in 1964.

Last in the progression from farm to consumer are the chain stores, which mark up prices an average 22 per cent from the wholesale level. In the past year, they have raised retail prices by 5.4 per cent. But according to a Cornell University study, their profit margin for the year ending last June had actually fallen from the 1965 level of 1.4 per cent of sales to 1.3 per cent.

On the face of it, the store chains that are the prime targets of the housewives' ire have benefited least from rising prices. . . .[38]

The U. S. Department of Agriculture said farmers were not to blame:

. . . Agricultural Secretary Orville L. Freeman maintained that U. S. subsidies paid by his department could not be blamed [for increased

---

[38] Copyright (1966) by *Newsweek* (November 14, 1966), pp. 78–79.

276   food costs] because "only a small portion of the increased cost of food at the retail level can be traced to increased farm prices." Moreover, he added, "recent modest farm price increases are badly needed and have been earned."[39]

However, some farm groups, such as the New Jersey Farm Bureau Federation, blamed the federal government for rising food costs and called on housewives to march on Washington and state capitals where high taxes and big spending policies had produced inflation. A news analyst, Henry C. Wallich, described this position on farm policy in the following manner:

For many years, the American farm-support program has been designed to help farmers to help themselves — to Federal aid. But the farm program does not stop there by any means. It goes on to whipsaw the city dweller by using the taxes he pays to raise the price of farm products against him.[40]

Congressman Albert H. Quie, a Midwestern Republican, differed sharply with Henry Wallich as to whether the rise in farm prices was responsible for mounting food costs. He blamed heavy government expenditure generally and especially the Great Society programs.

We should set up guidelines to prevent the Secretary of Agriculture from controlling the agricultural market.

We should let the farmer build his market and encourage him to secure a better price in the marketplace. The Federal Government should never place a lid on farm prices till they reach 100 percent of parity.

This, I believe, is the way to fight rural poverty.

But let nobody twist my words to let it appear that I am against the consumer.

It is obvious from the facts . . . regarding the farmer that he is not the fault of the current inflation.

Nevertheless, inflation is with us and with us in a big way.

Let the consumer know it is not the farmer, however, who is the cause of this inflation.

The cause of inflation today can be placed squarely before the door of the so-called Great Society.

---

[39] Copyright (1966) by *Newsweek* (August 15, 1966), p. 22. Quotations are taken directly from an address by Orville L. Freeman presented before the City Council of New York City, August 4, 1966.

[40] Copyright (1966) by *Newsweek* (May 16, 1966), p. 89.

It is spawned by the vast spending binge of the so-called Great **277** Society on a series of wasteful and chaotic welfare schemes.[41]

The Big Issue: Changing Nature of the Farm Industry

The cost-price squeeze has never been eliminated. The farm population continues its rapid decline, and the size of the farm increases at a high rate. An agricultural revolution is indeed taking place. A way of life seems to be fading away. What does it mean? Can it be stemmed? Many believe not; but others, like the president of the American Farmers Union, say that it can and it must:

We consider the family-type farm to be the keystone in our highly successful agricultural system. We believe further that the interest and welfare of the Nation is inherent in the preservation of a family farm pattern of agriculture.

When the management of a farm is taken away from those who supply the management, labor and capital, there is loss of initiative, skill and prudent judgment which has made possible the efficiency of our family-farm agriculture and our ability to produce an abundance.

A "family farm" is an agricultural production unit, economically adequate to produce modern United States standards of living, using land and other capital investment, operated by one or more farm operator families, who provide the management, take the economic risk and do most of the work (peak seasons excepted) required to operate the unit.

Numerous studies have shown the family-operated farm to be more efficient than large industrial agricultural units. . . .[42]

Thus the Jeffersonian ideal lives on in the face of overwhelming economic and technological change. The farm issues are not now and never have been concerned merely with adaptation to changing circumstances or conditions. The farm issues, like the education issues, also involve questions about how we make the world adjust to us (rather than how we adjust to the world). These issues emphasize preservation of basic values and a seemingly revered way of life. Many farmers contend that a way of life should not be a victim of technology; rather, technology should serve to enhance and embellish an established and revered life pattern.

---

[41] The Honorable Albert H. Quie, U. S. Representative from Minnesota, Remarks on the floor of the House, *Congressional Record*, Vol. 112, 2nd sess., April 27, 1966, p. 9196.

[42] From a prepared statement by Tony T. Dechant, *Bulletin* (for presentation to U. S. Senate Committee on Agriculture and Forestry), April 3, 1968, p. 9.

Voters: Source of Governmental Powers

The elective franchise, . . . dictated by the wisdom and resting on the will of the people, . . .
is the only legitimate foundation
of any government.

Thomas Jefferson

. . . The conception of political equality
can mean only one thing — *one person,*
one vote.

Justice William O. Douglas

8

Why should there be issues about voting or the franchise? Nothing seems more settled than the privilege of every mentally competent adult to cast his ballot for persons he wants to serve him in his government. Actually, however, few political matters are so volatile as this one.

In a letter to Isaac Tiffany on August 26, 1816, Thomas Jefferson said, "My most earnest wish is to see the republican element of popular control pushed to the maximum."[1] American history has been a continuing story of efforts by one group of people after another to win the privilege of voting. One by one, and decade after decade, Americans have pushed over the barriers to voting, thus allowing a growing proportion of the population to cast ballots.

To get where we are now, it was necessary to sweep away such requirements for voting as property, religion, and unreasonably long residence qualifications. There was also the battle by women to be enfranchised. And the struggle by Black America to gain access to the ballot box has become a classic one. It took more than a century to wipe out the poll tax. During and after World War II, efforts were undertaken to lower the voting age from 21 to 18 years. More recently, a determined battle was waged over the principle of equality in voting — "one man, one

---

[1] As cited in Edward Dumbauld, ed., *The Political Writings of Thomas Jefferson* (New York: The Liberal Arts Press, 1955), p. 88.

vote." The objective of this effort was to get reapportionment of national and state legislative bodies on the basis of population. Each step toward fulfillment of Jefferson's goal has been far from easy.

Proponents of extension of suffrage almost always won. It sometimes took several decades or even a century, but they won. Why? Well, political parties and candidates have usually been anxious to tap new reservoirs of voters for added support. Then, too, the Americans have long been committed to an overriding democratic ideology which stresses equality. Finally, the persons and groups fighting the suffrage battles were tenacious and determined.

The story of suffrage, its steady expansion and the accompanying issues, began in colonial times, when the voting privilege was claimed on the same grounds that a stockholder today would claim a vote in the corporation. Early colonies in several instances were essentially "business corporations;" hence, the landed-property qualification became a universal requirement. Of course property did not entitle minor children, women, or the mentally incompetent to vote. They were excluded on other grounds. Nor was there any thought of granting suffrage on the basis of mere residence, since it was deemed necessary that a voter have a stake in the enterprise. When the colonies ceased to be corporations and became strictly political domains, the "stake-in-society" notion endured.

South Carolina was typical of the seven states that required a voter to own property and that specifically disfranchised Negroes (free or slave) and Jews. Most of the new states entering the union after 1790 did not require a voter to own property or pay taxes. Vermont, for example, required no more than one year of residence and "quiet and peaceable behavior." With the decline and disappearance of the property qualification, other requirements were imposed, allegedly to protect society from "unsafe elements."

The Early Issue: Property Qualification

As the issues evolved and people became engaged in the debate, it soon became apparent that the opponents of expansion relied on a familiar and well-used stock of arguments. They never failed, for example, to demonstrate the so-called "inability" of the prospective voter to carry the great responsibility required of him. The words of the brilliant English leader, Robert Lowe, were to become a popular refrain in the wars to expand suffrage:

If you want venality, ignorance, drunkenness; if you want impulsive, unreflecting, and violent people, where do you look for them in the constituencies? Do you go to the top or the bottom?[2]

---

[2] As quoted in Charles Seymour and Donald Frary, *How the World Votes* (Springfield, Mass.: C. A. Nichols Company, 1918), p. 136.

Some would be more polite in making their inferences, but the argument would appear again and again. The aspirants to suffrage were viewed as unfit for the responsibility, whether they were landless men, women, Negroes, nineteen-year-olds, eighteen-year-olds, paupers, members of select religious faiths, the insane, newly established residents, convicts, or exconvicts.

In its enactment of a statute, the Maryland Colony's Upper House said:

The freeholders are the strength and only strength of this province, not the freemen. It is their persons, purses, and stocks that must bear the burden of the government, and not the freemen who can easily abandon us.[3]

Compare the arguments made all of the way through this chapter to those of the eminent jurist Chancellor Kent, who was an early 19th-century leader of the opposition to liberalization of the property qualification. At the Albany Convention of 1821, he said:

The small farmers are the surest guardians of property, and they form the firmest basis of national power and grandeur. The Senate should be the representative of the landed interest and its security against the caprice of the motley assemblage of paupers, emigrants, journeymen, manufacturers, and those undefinable inhabitants which a state or city like ours is calculated to invite. Universal suffrage jeopardizes property and puts it into the power of the poor . . .[4]

But Kent and his following were destined to lose. By the time of the Civil War, the property qualification had disappeared. Dominion and sovereignty no longer followed land. The spirited frontier farmer and storekeeper established the principle that the "people were the fountainhead of power." Group after group, such as the Democratic Society of Kentucky and the Constitutional Society of Boston, called for election of senators by the people. They would wait three quarters of a century, but they would win. Their reasoning was simple. As the Constitutional Society of Boston put it:

Till this period, the art of government has been but the study and benefit of the few, to the exclusion and depression of the many . . . all sovereignty must be vested in the breast of every individual.[5]

---

[3] *Ibid.*, p. 210.

[4] *Ibid.*, p. 234; see also N. H. Carter, *et al., Reports of the Proceedings and Debates of The Convention of 1821* (Albany, 1821), pp. 215–221.

[5] Seymour and Frary, *How the World Votes*, p. 231.

Female suffrage was a delicate issue, especially from the male's point of view. The 19th-century author Francis Parkman described the extreme sensitivity of the issue:

> . . . If it could be treated like other subjects, and discussed fully and freely, the cause of the self-styled reformers would have been hopeless from the first. It is happy for them that the relations of women to society cannot be so discussed without giving just offense. Their most important considerations can be touched but slightly; and even then offense will be taken.[6]

Again, it should be stressed that Parkman and other opponents of women's suffrage dredged up the usual antisuffrage arguments, particularly the lack of competence and preparation to shoulder such a heavy responsibility.

> The female vote would enormously increase the evil, for it is often more numerous, always more impulsive and less subject to reason, and almost devoid of the sense of responsibility. Here the bad politician would find his richest resources. He could not reach the better class of female voters, but the rest would be ready to his hand. Three fourths of them, when not urged by some pressing need or contagious passion, would be moved, not by principles, but by personal predilections.[7]

To this, Parkman added some salty observations:

> In reckoning the resources of the female politicians, there is one which can by no means be left out. None know better than women the potency of feminine charms aided by feminine arts. The woman "inside politics" will not fail to make use of an influence so subtle and strong, and of which the management is peculiarly suited to her talents. If — and the contingency is in the highest degree probable — she is not gifted with charms of her own, she will have no difficulty in finding and using others of her sex who are. If report is to be trusted, Delilah has already spread her snares for the congressional Samson; and the power before which the

---

[6] Francis Parkman, "Some of the Reasons against Woman Suffrage," in Albert Wolfe, ed., *Readings in Social Problems* (Cambridge: Harvard University Press, 1916), p. 478; taken from a pamphlet released by the Massachusetts Association Opposed to the Further Extension of Suffrage to Women, 1876.

[7] *Ibid.,* p. 481.

wise fail and the mighty fall has been invoked against the sages and heroes of the Capitol. When "woman" is fairly "inside politics," the sensation press will reap a harvest of scandals more lucrative to itself than profitable to public morals. And, as the zeal of one class of female reformers has been, and no doubt will be, largely directed to their grievances in matters of sex, we shall have shrill-tongued discussions of subjects which had far better be let alone.[8]

To Parkman's views should be added the words of Theodore Roosevelt's Secretary of State and 1912 Nobel Peace Prize winner, Elihu Root:

Woman rules today by the sweet noble influences of her character. Put woman into the arena of conflict and she abandons these great weapons which control the world, and she takes into her hands, feeble and nerveless for strife, weapons which she is unable to wield. Woman in strife becomes hard, harsh, unlovable, repulsive; as far removed from that gentle creature to whom we all owe allegiance and to whom we confess submission.[9]

Women's suffrage, said Root, would destroy womanhood. Sweet things were not meant for the "rough and tumble" world of politics. Women were, moreover, neither physically nor psychologically able or prepared for the responsibility. However, Root, unlike Parkman, did not see women as wily and clever masters of charm in the political arena.

Edward Cope portrayed the woman as "incapable of carrying into execution any law she may enact."[10] On the other hand, he feared the political skills of women, believing that they would band together and form a separate political party, which would oppose the parties of the males.

The suffragettes remained undaunted. They were, in fact, equally salty in their literary efforts:

When, in the course of human events, it becomes necessary for one portion of the family of man to assume among the people of the earth a position different from that which they have hitherto occupied, but one to which the laws of nature and of nature's God entitle them, a decent respect to the opinions of mankind requires that they should declare the causes that impel them to such a course.

---

[8] *Ibid.,* p. 482.

[9] Elihu Root, in an address presented to the New York State Constitutional Convention, August 15, 1894.

[10] Edward Cope, "Relation of the Sexes to Government," (pamphlet distributed by New York State Association Opposed to Woman Suffrage, *n.d.*), pp. 1–10.

284   We hold these truths to be self-evident: that all men and women are created equal; that they are endowed by their Creator with certain inalienable rights; that among these are life, liberty, and the pursuit of happiness; that to secure these rights governments are instituted, deriving their just powers from the consent of the governed. Whenever any form of government becomes destructive of these ends, it is the right of those who suffer from it to refuse allegiance to it, and to insist upon the institution of a new government, laying its foundation on such principles, and organizing its powers in such form, as to them shall seem most likely to effect their safety and happiness. . . .

The history of mankind is a history of repeated injuries and usurpations on the part of man toward woman, having in direct object the establishment of an absolute tyranny over her. To prove this, let facts be submitted to a candid world.

He has never permitted her to exercise her inalienable right to the elective franchise.

He has compelled her to submit to laws, in the formation of which she had no voice.

He has withheld from her rights which are given to the most ignorant and degraded men — both natives and foreigners.

Having deprived her of this first right of a citizen, the elective franchise, thereby leaving her without representation in the halls of legislation, he has oppressed her on all sides.

He has made her, if married, in the eye of the law, civilly dead.[11]

This was the famous Seneca Declaration, but two decades passed before the Territory of Wyoming first broke the barrier and granted women universal suffrage. It took another 50 years before the 19th Amendment was ratified, giving women the ballot on the same basis as men.

The Challenging Issue: Votes for Hyphenated Americans

Part of the story here was told earlier in a chapter devoted exclusively to Afro-American issues. However, other hyphenated Americans (for example, the Hispanic-Americans) have also encountered considerable difficulty with the franchise.

The Afro-American's struggle is classic. The 15th Amendment, which

---

[11] Elizabeth Stanton *et al.*, "Declaration of Sentiments," First Woman's Rights Convention, 1848, as cited in Wolfe, *Readings in Social Problems*, pp. 441–442.

became a part of the U. S. Constitution in 1870, prohibited any state from denying or abridging the voting privilege "on account of race, color, or previous condition of servitude," but it proved to be inadequate for the job. Beginning late in the 19th century, Southerners developed a whole battery of devices to exclude Afro-Americans from the polls. The infamous "Grandfather clauses" denied the vote to anyone whose ancestors could not vote before 1866. Other devices included stiff educational requirements, prior registration, literacy tests, white primaries, poll taxes, and a host of informal techniques, such as keeping the blacks ignorant of polling hours and places, tying a vicious dog to an entrance which blacks were required to use, or threatening black persons who dared to register or vote. Between 1915 and 1965, most of these barriers were toppled by the U. S. Supreme Court, lesser federal courts, or by efforts of the U. S. Attorney-General. Under the 1957 Civil Rights Act, the Attorney-General's office was empowered to file injunction proceedings against a state electoral official who was depriving a person of his voting privilege.

Knocking down the visible barriers did not overcome the more subtle ones, such as keeping Afro-Americans ignorant and deprived. Regardless of the color of a man's skin, if he is denied information and educational opportunity, and if he is near poverty, he will not acquire vital political skills very readily. In fact, the probability is high that he will not exercise his franchise at all.

Probably the most effective of all deterrents to the free exercise of suffrage by Afro-Americans and other hyphenated Americans was their exceptionally low economic and social condition. For one thing it provided opponents of suffrage for minorities with a set of reasons. It was argued that many Afro-Americans had not demonstrated that they deserved the vote. It was the same old argument — the potential voters were presumed to be incapable of shouldering the responsibility. This viewpoint was typically expressed by Senator James K. Vardaman of Mississippi:

The negro as a race, in all ages of the world, has never shown sustained power of self-development. He is not endowed with the creative faculty. . . .

. . . He has never created for himself a civilization. He has never risen above the government of a club. . . . In truth, he has never progressed, save and except when under the influence and absolute control of a superior race. . . .

If in the providence of God the negro may make progress sufficient to justify the American people in giving him the franchise, that time has not yet arrived. . . .

God Almighty never intended that the negro should share with the white man in the government of this country; and you cannot improve upon the plans of God Almighty or defeat His purposes. . . .

286   I am not the negro's enemy. I know what is best for him. I think I can measure his productive capacity.[12]

Let us permit one of the Senator's own contemporaries to reply. Speaking in 1913, Ray Stannard Baker said:

First we shall find many negroes, and indeed hundreds of thousands of white men as well, who might vote, but who through ignorance, or the inability or unwillingness to pay poll taxes, or from mere lack of interest, disfranchise themselves.

The second difficulty is peculiar to the negro. It consists in open or concealed intimidation on the part of the white men who control the election machinery. In many places in the South to-day, no negro, no matter how well qualified, would dare to present himself for registration. . . .

Thus we have to meet a vast amount of apathy and ignorance and poverty on the one hand, and the threat of intimidation on the other.[13]

As long as the Afro-American was kept ignorant, sent to inferior schools, forced to live in a ghetto, kept on a poverty plane, it would be difficult for him to prove himself capable of shouldering the so-called responsibilities. As late as 1966, there were many in the United States, both North and South, who made claims very similar to those made by Vardaman a half century before. Consider the charges of Commander George Lincoln Rockwell, leader of the American Nazi Party until his violent death in 1967:

We're talking about niggers — and there's no doubt in my mind that they're basically animalistic. . . . When I speak at colleges, they often ask me the same question [Can he document his generalization that Negroes are inferior?]. I always answer with a question of my own: How do colleges determine the superior and inferior students? By *perform-ance,* that's how! Look at history; investigate the different races. The Chinese perform; they've created a great civilization. And the white races certainly perform. But the nigger race, until very recently, has done absolutely nothing.[14]

---

[12] The Honorable James K. Vardaman, U. S. Senator from Mississippi, *Speech* to the U. S. Senate (February 6, 1914), as reprinted in Wolfe, *Readings in Social Problems,* pp. 704–709.

[13] Ray Stannard Baker, "Problems of Citizenship," in Wolfe, *Readings in Social Problems,* p. 759.

[14] Interview with George Lincoln Rockwell, *Playboy* (April 1966), p. 74.

The point that needs to be stressed here is that until Afro-Americans and other hyphenated peoples are given the opportunity to acquire skills and to participate in society on an equal basis with other citizens, views like those of Vardaman and Rockwell will continue.

Obtaining the ballot is also essential to the progress and development of Afro-Americans, say the Black Power leaders Stokely Carmichael and Charles Hamilton.

The act of registering to vote does several things. It marks the beginning of political modernization by broadening the base of participation. It also does something the existentialists talk about: it gives one a sense of being. The black man who goes to register is saying to the white man, "No." He is saying: "You have said that I cannot vote. You have said that this is my place. This is where I should remain. You have contained me and I am saying 'No' to your containment." . . . That is what the first act does. The black person begins to live. He begins to create his own existence. . . .[15]

It is a first step, but only a first step, say Carmichael and Hamilton, in the defeat of institutionalized "racism," as distinguished from individual "racism" and prejudice.

Institutional racism relies on the active and pervasive operation of anti-black attitudes and practices. A sense of superior group position prevails: whites are "better" than blacks; therefore blacks should be subordinated to whites. This is a racist attitude and it permeates the society, on both the individual and institutional level, covertly and overtly.

"Respectable" individuals can absolve themselves from individual blame: *they* would never plant a bomb in a church; *they* would never stone a black family. But they continue to support political officials and institutions that would and do perpetuate institutionally racist policies. Thus *acts* of overt, individual racism may not typify the society, but institutional racism does — with the support of covert, individual attitudes of racism.[16]

Thus, Hamilton and Carmichael contend that registering and voting are necessary steps in the process of Afro-American advance up the social and economic ladder. While it is only the first step, it is more significant than a constitutional phrase or a right established by statute. It

---

[15] Stokely Carmichael and Charles V. Hamilton, *Black Power* (New York: Vintage Books, 1967), pp. 104–105.

[16] *Ibid.*, p. 5.

288   involves the *actual* exercise of registering and voting. Participation in this initial step is of vital importance for all hyphenated Americans.

The Languid Issue: The Eighteen-year-old Vote

We might expect college-age people to show a lot of interest in this issue, but only occasionally have young people beat this particular drum. The issue did not arise until World War II, when men under 21 were drafted in large numbers by the Selective Service. Then, a great many Americans took the position that if a young man was able to and required to fight, he should be mature enough to vote. This was the position of the U. S. Senate Judiciary Committee:

Several reasons have been advanced for the adoption of this constitutional amendment. First and foremost probably is the argument that since persons between 18 and 21 years are old enough to be drafted they are old enough to exercise the franchise. In addition, it is argued that at 18 years of age, or near the age, young people are enthusiastic in their desire to participate in political decisions, especially those which vitally affect their existence. It was contended at the hearings on this resolution that if the right to vote is withheld until attainment of the age of 21 years this enthusiasm diminishes. This diminishing enthusiasm represents a loss to the United States as well as a loss to the individual himself.

Some persons may argue that young people between the ages of 18 and 21 years lack sufficient maturity to exercise the right to vote. Senator Moody, the sponsor of this resolution, answered that argument when in his appearance before the subcommittee in support of this resolution he stated:

'If they are old enough to fight, if they have sufficient maturity to be entrusted with jet airplanes and assigned to foxholes to defend our liberties, then they are old enough to vote; they are mature enough to assume their responsibilities and rights as full-fledged citizens.'[17]

One of the elders of the House of Representatives, Emanuel Celler of New York, objected vigorously. The reader will note that a large portion of his position rests on the stock historical arguments: the teenager is unprepared and unfit to assume the responsibility of voting.

Youth is usually emotional and expresses his passionate convictions more than does the adult. The youth is like a white paper; it will take any impression.

---

[17] U. S. Senate, Committee on the Judiciary, *Report* No. 2036, S. J. Res. 127, 82nd Cong., 2nd sess. (July 1, 1952).

We have some glaring examples of evils of youthful voting or teenage voting in Germany, in Spain and in Italy, as well as in Russia. You'll find that the dictators, those dictators in those countries; to wit, Stalin, Mussolini, Hitler and Franco, deliberately reduced the voting age to 18, the time when they could be drafted and fight, and those dictators goose-stepped all those youths into receptivity and acceptance of the ideas of totalitarianism. I don't think that we want any such manipulation of youth. Youth can't evaluate as can its elders, and for that reason, I think it would be baneful to have teenage voting. . . .

The age of 21 has been time tested through the centuries, as the age of maturity for voting. We only get our wisdom teeth after 20.

Our youths haven't had hard knocks; they haven't been tested with the problems they have to face in life. For that reason, they are uncertain; they are unsure. They do not understand the complexities of life. A man, for example, doesn't understand very much about taxes unless he pays taxes, and the youth usually hasn't got his home; he is unmarried; the teenager is unmarried; he doesn't pay the taxes; he can't understand the complexities of labor problems. One never does until one is an employer oneself, or an employee, or a professional man.

In Georgia, which is the only state where they have teenage voting, they have great difficulty in making the youth understand the complexities of the political problems. I questioned a number of the members of the House from the State of Georgia. Almost to a man, they said if we had to do it over again, Georgia would not accept the teenage voting. . . .

To my mind, the draft age and the voting age are as different as chalk is from cheese. The thing called for in a soldier is uncritical obedience, and that is not what you want in a voter.

To say that he who is old enough to fight is old enough to vote is to draw an utterly fallacious parallel. No such parallel exists. The ability to choose, to separate promise from performance, to evaluate on the basis of fact, are the prerequisites to good voting. Eighteen to twenty-one are mainly formative years where youth is reaching forward to maturity. His attitudes shift from place to place. These are the years of the greatest uncertainties, a fertile ground for the demagogues. Youth attaches itself to promises, rather than to performance. These are rightfully the years of rebellion rather than reflection. We will be doing a grave injustice to democracy if we grant the vote to those under 21.

Leaders of radical movements understand that patience is not a particular virtue of the young. . . .[18]

---

[18] The Honorable Emanuel Celler, U. S. Representative from New York, *Statements* taken from a debate presented by American Forum of the Air, Washington, D. C., January 31, 1954, as reprinted in *Congressional Digest,* Vol. 34 (1954), pp. 77–79.

290   U. S. District Judge, George W. Williams, was even more pointed in his attack:

. . . The science of politics is the only science, and it is a science even though it is an inexact science, that does not require any qualifications to engage therein. It now appears that, in the opinion of some people, many of whom are in high place, no background, even, is required. Callow youth is to be accorded the same privilege as grown-ups, at a time when we already have a mass of ignorance in the voting area. To me, it is preposterous that any sensible man would say, as his excuse, that if a child is old enough to fight, he is old enough to vote. There is, in fact, little, if any, relation between the two public duties.

The above is not to say that there are not some who are well qualified to vote, but it is to say that the great mass of the youth of this country is absolutely unfitted. . . .[19]

Hubert Humphrey, then a U. S. Senator, did not agree:

I believe this proposal is amply justified as an attempt to broaden and extend the base of our democratic Government. Extending the suffrage to 18 year olds will broaden that base of democracy not only by the number of young people which it immediately adds to our voting population; but also by encouraging the participation of these people at an age when they are enthusiastic and interested in government and politics. This will enable us to make real inroads on voter apathy in the United States.

I do not have to tell the Senate that there are many potential voters in our country who do not take an interest in elections, and do not exercise their right to vote. I think it is fair to say that many people are more interested in politics and political issues and are better informed on those matters when they are between the ages of 18 and 21 than they are later on when they have been longer out of school, have become more absorbed in the everyday business of earning a living, and have become subject to the political apathy which affects so many of our citizens.

There is no better civic training than the exercise of the vote. Without the vote, all other forms of civic training are lacking in meaning and effectiveness. It is essential that our young people take on political responsibility as soon as they are ready to do so, for the real value of education comes from its association with responsibility.

The young people of this generation are better prepared educationally

---

[19] U. S. Senate, Committee on the Judiciary, Subcommittee on Constitutional Amendments, Statement by the Honorable George W. Williams, U. S. District Judge, Virgin Islands, submitted for inclusion in *Hearings* on S. J. Res. 53 and S. J. Res. 64 (June 3, 1953).

for political responsibility at the age of 18 than were the Americans of previous generations. . . .

The whole trend of this tense period in international affairs is to throw increasing responsibilities upon 18-year-olds, and to threaten interruption of their careers as well as jeopardy to life itself. Surely we have small right to place this onerous immediate future before our youth, and at the same time ask them to forego the rights and duties of full citizenship.

Youth ought to have a voice in determining its own future. What is more, youth has a definite contribution to make to the future of our whole country. I hope that the Congress will now act to grant the suffrage — the most essential right of citizenship — to the youth of America.[20]

Senator Wayne Morse punctuated Humphrey's final remarks in a manner that made the case for the eighteen-year-old vote difficult to rebut.

Here again I think there is also involved a moral principle. I do not believe we can justify asking 18 year olds to die for the country and at the same time not permit them to exercise their right to vote in the determination of its policies.[21]

Senator Kenneth Keating raised the interesting point that the enlarged numbers of older voters due to the extended life span should be balanced by increases in the numbers of young voters.

You can't dictate to the young people the way you can to some of the older people. They have more independence of judgment. They are more apt to decide things on the issues. But I don't think it is a political matter. I think it is a matter of fair play. I think that as the life span gets longer in this country, as it is doing, people are living longer, there are more people in the older ages voting, and to offset that, to give a fair balance, to determine the great issues of the day and to determine who shall govern the country, it seems we have to open it up at the lower end, and balance the thing out so that we get a fair expression of all the people of this country.[22]

---

[20] The Honorable Hubert H. Humphrey, U. S. Senator from Minnesota in a statement during Senate debate, April 1, 1953, as quoted in *Congressional Digest,* Vol. 34 (1954), pp. 76–78.

[21] The Honorable Wayne Morse, U. S. Senator from Oregon in a statement made during Senate Debate, July 18, 1953, as quoted in *Congressional Digest,* Vol. 34 (1954), pp. 78.

[22] The Honorable Kenneth Keating, U. S. Senator from New York, *Statement* during a debate presented by American Forum of the Air, Washington, D. C., January 31, 1954, as quoted in *Congressional Digest,* Vol. 34 (1954), p. 80.

The big suffrage issue of the century is How many votes should one man have? That is the question at the base of reapportionment efforts. As stated in a pamphlet published by the Twentieth Century Fund, "The central fact is that any basis of representation other than population gives one citizen's vote greater value than another."[23] The pamphlet concludes that this situation is not justified in terms of our democratic heritage.

The situation under discussion is called malapportionment — a condition in which one man's vote is worth several votes of other men. In Montana and New Mexico, for example, there have been instances when a rural dweller's vote has been worth 75 to 80 times an urban dweller's; that is, one man would represent $\frac{1}{75}$ as many people as another man in a house of a state legislature. Probably the worst situation in recent years was in Vermont, just a short time ago, when one man in the state's lower house (which is supposed to be based on population) represented less than 50 people and another had a constituency of some 33,000. A similar condition exists in both houses of Congress, where the ratio between an Alaskan's vote and a New Yorker's vote is approximately 76–1 in U. S. Senate representation — or, to put it another way, an Alaskan's vote is worth 76 times that of a New Yorker. Nor has the lower house of Congress been free of malapportionment. A short time ago a lumberjack's vote from the upper peninsula of Michigan was worth 4 to 5 times as much as a Detroit executive's vote. The Twentieth Century Fund pamphlet argued:

. . . no basis of representation other than population is defensible if candidly stated and examined for what it is. There is talk, for example of "area representation." But acres do not vote; nor do trees. When a sparsely settled area is given as many representatives as one much more populous, it simply means that the people in the sparse area have more representation. No matter how stated, it is people who choose the representatives.

And now any forthright statement of a nonpopulation theory of representation must rest on one or two propositions: Either there must be an implication that the residents of sparsely populated areas are more virtuous than other Americans and hence deserve more representation in legislatures, or else a contention that they have special needs which can only be met by giving them greater representation than that afforded others.

Belief in rural virtue does exist, but that is not likely to be advanced seriously as a reason for nonpopulation apportionments. Not many legislators would stand up and argue openly that their constituents are so much more honest and intelligent than others that each should have two

---

[23] From a Twentieth Century Fund pamphlet, as reprinted in *St. Louis Post-Dispatch* (September 23, 1962), p. 2C.

or three or ten votes. In any case, it is impermissible in a mature democracy to start comparing the merits of different population groups for purposes of weighting their votes.

The principal reliance, then, of those who advanced something other than population as a basis for representation must be on the argument that certain classes of citizens have special problems that justify giving them more than proportionate power in the legislature. This contention is indeed made in behalf of the rural areas which are now so generally over-represented in state legislatures; it is often said that the rural population is a minority with special needs that would be neglected in a legislature faithfully representing the state's population as a whole. But surely the problems of cities and suburbs, and their need for government aid, have been as great as those of rural areas in recent decades; yet no one has been heard to argue that city and suburban voters should therefore have been given disproportionate weight in legislatures. . . .

Our constitutional system protects minorities by other means than giving them majority control of legislatures (as rural minorities now have in many states); and the claim that such legislative control is needed by the rural minority leads to some absurd results. In Maryland rural counties containing less than 15 per cent of the state's population elect a majority of the members of the state senate. This apportionment has been defended against legal attack on the ground that the rural counties must have such control for protection of their minority rights. But of course it is not and logically cannot be true.

Regionalism remains a factor within states, but regional interests can be recognized without distortion of voting power. It is desirable to consider regional characteristics when drawing up districts for a state legislature, but it is neither necessary nor proper to give any one regional population group greater voting power than some other group. It is good for dairy farmers in New York, for example, to have a voice in the legislature through one or more members from dairy areas; it does not follow that the votes of dairy farmers should carry greater weight than those of businessmen or union members.[24]

The debate over this condition first arose in earnest when the Supreme Court got into the act in 1962. Beginning in 1962, the Court went all the way within six years, as the following account indicates.

It was in 1962 that the U. S. Supreme Court first poked its way into what the late Felix Frankfurter termed "the political thicket": it ruled that Federal courts have the responsibility for ordering reapportionment

---

[24] *Ibid.*

294   of state legislatures to achieve more equitable representation. Two years later, the Court pushed on to the national level and proclaimed a sweeping one-man, one-vote standard for redrawing Congressional district lines. As a result, virtually every state has striven to make significant adjustments, and despite predictions of insoluble chaos, the results have been surprisingly salutary. Last week, in a final mopping-up operation, the Court voted 5-to-3 that the principle of one man, one vote should be applied as well to the nation's more than 80,000 county and local legislative bodies.[25]

The opening gun was fired by the Supreme Court of the United States on March 26, 1962, in the famous decision, *Baker* v. *Carr*.[26] Donald Herzberg outlines events which led the Court to accept jurisdiction in this controversial area.

For a long time the Court had consistently avoided involvement in reapportionment cases. In the leading case of *Colegrove v. Green*, 328 U. S. 549 (1946) the Court, in an opinion written by Justice Frankfurter, held that it was powerless to remedy the failure of the Illinois legislature to redistrict since questions involving the reapportionment of districts for congressional representation were "political" and therefore not subject to judicial determination. However, in the case of *Gomillion v. Lightfoot*, 364 U. S. 339 (1960), the Court seemed to weaken the *Colegrove* rule, for it held unconstitutional an Alabama state law redefining the boundaries of the city of Tuskegee so as to exclude nearly all the Negro voters without removing a single white voter. Though the *Gomillion* case was concerned chiefly with racial discrimination rather than with reapportionment, it has been viewed as a steppingstone for the reexamination of *Colegrove v. Green*. This occurred in the now famous case of *Baker v. Carr*, 369 U. S. 186 (1962), where it was held that the federal courts have jurisdiction to scrutinize the fairness of legislative apportionments under the Fourteenth Amendment and to take steps to assure that inequities are wiped out. However, the Court did not give any guidance on the critical question of what constitutes a "fair" apportionment. Justice Frankfurter, writing his last opinion for the Court, dissented sharply as did Justice Harlan who, in the last paragraph of his opinion, summarized well the basic conflict. Said Harlan:

> Those observers of the Court who see it primarily as the last refuge for the correction of all inequality or injustice, no matter what its nature or source, will no doubt applaud this decision and

---

[25] Copyright (1968) by *Newsweek* (April 15, 1968), p. 50.
[26] *Baker* v. *Carr*, 369 U. S. 186 (1962).

its break with the past. Those who consider that continuing national respect for the Court's authority depends in large measure
upon its wise exercise of self-restraint and discipline in constitutional adjudication, will view the decision with deep concern.

Despite the dissenting opinions it is now readily apparent that *Baker
v. Carr* is here to stay. The *Baker* ruling is in the process of deeply
affecting the governmental power structure by shifting legislative control
from the more conservative rural areas to the cities and surrounding
metropolitan areas, where voters are more sympathetic toward social
change. Thus *Baker v. Carr* "is not only an obviously important case. It is
a critically different kind of case *because it calls upon the courts to sit in
judgment on the possession and distribution of political power.* In the
context of more than a century and half of judicial review this is
something distinctly new in the function of constitutional interpretation
and application."

Unlike most Supreme Court decisions, *Baker v. Carr* had an almost
immediate impact. In fact, never before, after an assertion of expanded
jurisdiction by the Court, has there been such a flurry of widespread
political and judicial activity. Almost within hours of the decision, litigation was begun in state and federal courts challenging the existing
schemes of legislative representation. . . .

. . . In *Gray v. Sanders*, 372 U. S. 368 (1963), the Supreme Court
agreed with the lower court. Moreover, the highest court further held
that the equal protection clause of the Fourteenth Amendment requires
that every voter be equal to every other voter in the state when he casts
his ballot in a statewide election. Speaking for the Court over the lone
dissent of Justice Harlan, Justice Douglas concluded that "the conception
of political equality can mean only one thing — *one person, one vote.*"[27]

The Court left no question about its position and justification in the
great debate when Chief Justice Warren wrote his eloquent majority
opinion in 1964:

Legislators represent people, not trees or acres. Legislators are
elected by voters, not farms or cities or economic interests. As long as
ours is a representative form of government, and our legislatures are
those instruments of government elected directly by and directly representative of the people, the right to elect legislators in a free and

---

[27] Donald Herzberg, ed., *American Government Annual, 1965–66* (New York:
Holt, Rinehart, 1965), pp. 35–36. Copyright © 1965 by Holt, Rinehart and Winston,
Inc. Reprinted by permission of Holt, Rinehart and Winston, Inc.

unimpaired fashion is a bedrock of our political system. . . . We are told that the matter of apportioning representation in a state legislature is a complex and many-faceted one. We are advised that States can rationally consider factors other than population in apportioning legislative representation. We are admonished not to restrict the power of the States to impose differing views as to political philosophy on their citizens. We are cautioned about the dangers of entering into political thickets and mathematical quagmires. Our answer is this: a denial of constitutionally protected rights demands judicial protection: our oath and our office require no less of us. . . . To the extent that a citizen's right to vote is debased, he is that much less a citizen. The fact that an individual lives here or there is not a legitimate reason for overweighting or diluting the efficacy of his vote. The complexions of societies and civilizations change, often with amazing rapidity. A nation once primarily rural in character becomes predominantly urban. Representation schemes once fair and equitable become archaic and outdated. But the basic principle of representative government remains, and must remain, unchanged — the weight of a citizen's vote cannot be made to depend on where he lives. *Population is, of necessity, the starting point for consideration and the controlling criterion for judgment in legislative apportionment controversies.*[28]

The positive arguments having been presented, what of the opposition in the debate? Since the Court precipitated the issue, let us consider the points made by the dissenting justices:

What is done to-day deepens my conviction that judicial entry into this realm is profoundly ill-advised and constitutionally impermissible. . . . I believe that the vitality of our political system, on which in the last analysis all else depends, is weakened by reliance on the judiciary for political reform; in time a complacent body politic may result. . . .

. . . [No] thinking person can fail to recognize that the aftermath of these cases, however desirable it may be thought in itself, will have been achieved at the cost of a radical alteration in the relationship between the States and the Federal Government, more particularly the Federal Judiciary. . . . Finally, these decisions give support to a current mistaken view of the Constitution and the Constitutional function of this Court. This view, in a nutshell, is that every major social ill in this country can find its cure in some constitutional "principle," and that this Court should "take the lead" in promoting reform when other branches of government

---

[28] *Reynolds* v. *Sims*, 377 U. S. 533 at 562 (1964) as quoted by Herzberg, *American Government Annual, 1965–66*, pp. 37–38.

fail to act. The Constitution is not a panacea for every blot upon the public welfare, nor should this Court, ordained as a judicial body, be thought of as a general haven for reform movements. The Constitution is an instrument of government, fundamental to which is the premise that in a diffusion of governmental authority lies the greatest promise that this Nation will realize liberty for all its citizens. This Court, limited in function in accordance with that premise, does not serve its high purpose when it exceeds its authority, even to satisfy justified impatience with the slow workings of the political process. For when, in the name of constitutional interpretation, the Court adds something to the Constitution that was deliberately excluded from it, the Court in reality substitutes its view of what should be so for the amending process. . . .[29]

Thus to Justice Harlan, the Supreme Court's attempt to force states to reapportion legislatures was a violation of the "sacred" federal relationship between the national and state governments. Looking at the decision from another angle, Chairman Howard Smith of the House Rules Committee, one of the most powerful men in the House of Representatives at the time, seemed absolutely certain that the Constitution was about to be junked and that the United States was heading for dictatorship.

In recent years and in recent months, millions of people in this country who love that Constitution and who believe in our institutions have been deeply alarmed and concerned over decisions of the Supreme Court which seem to go far beyond the powers granted to the Supreme Court under the Constitution.

If you have read the history of the formation of this country — and I am sure all of you have — one of the great arguments made during the formation of the Constitution was, and particularly Jefferson was very profound on this, that if we gave the Supreme Court power enough the first thing we knew we would have an autocratic government, because there is no appeal from the Supreme Court. There must be some check on the unlimited power of the Supreme Court, because if the Supreme Court can say anything is the law and then go by this false doctrine some people have put out, that the Supreme Court writes 'the law of the land,' then, my friends, we are drifting into an autocracy of the courts. . . .

This decision of the Supreme Court in this legislative apportionment matter is the first case that I have ever been able to discover where the Federal courts of the United States have just set out deliberately and with malice aforethought to invade the province of the Congress and to

---

[29] Justice John Marshall Harlan in dissent in *Reynolds* v. *Sims,* 377 U. S. 533 at 624 (1964).

themselves actually write legislation that is to be inscribed in the books of the States. Do you realize that? Do Members understand the depth of that? I have never known the Federal courts to say, 'If you do not write this legislation, we are going to write it for you.' . . .

Do you all realize the seriousness of that? Do Members understand what that means? That in any subject where the Supreme Court chooses to do it, since they have assumed the power which is not given to them in the Constitution, assumed the power to write the 'law of the land' — and where do they find that in the Constitution? — they cannot do so. Can any of you find it in the Constitution? The law of the land is not used but one place in the Constitution, and that says that the law as made by the Congress of the United States pursuant to the Constitution shall be the 'supreme law of the land.'

Think about what this Court can do to you. You can come to live under just as much of a dictatorship — and I hate to say this — as any European country which has gone through the regimes of Hitler and Khrushchev. I do not say these men mean to do this. I think they take so much jurisdiction now that I am afraid they do not have time to sit down and read this Constitution and see what is meant when it says the Federal courts shall only have such jurisdiction as is not excepted by the Congress of the United States. . . .[30]

Senator Wallace Bennett of Utah was far less of an alarmist, but he argued vigorously in opposition to the Court's action.

It is deeply to be regretted that the Supreme Court majority in its State legislature reapportionment decisions deliberately chose to abandon time-honored constitutional doctrine. A majority of the Court held in these decisions that both houses of State legislatures must be apportioned on a population basis and that virtually no factors other than population may be considered in determining representation in these legislative bodies. By so holding, the Supreme Court majority in effect amended the Constitution of the United States and thereby arrogated to itself the authority to legislate, a power hitherto reserved to the Congress. This is true since there is no authority whatever in the Constitution giving the Court the power to impose on the States any particular standard of representation in legislatures so long as the State government is republican in form.

The only claimed authority cited by the Court majority in its deci-

---

[30] The Honorable Howard W. Smith, U. S. Representative from Virginia, Statement made in House floor debate of H.R. 11926, the "Tuck bill" (August 19, 1964), as reported in *Congressional Digest,* Vol. 44 (1965), pp. 18–20.

sion is the equal protection clause of the 14th amendment. But the Court completely ignores section 2 of the 14th amendment as well as the 15th and 19th amendments which clearly make the Court's novel interpretation of the equal protection clause untenable.

By embarking on a course of judicial lawmaking to implement its own political and social theories, the Court majority totally avoids not only the plain meaning of the Constitution, but also ignores constitutional history. Two-thirds of the legislatures of the 23 so-called 'loyal States' which by 1870 ratified the 14th amendment had apportionments of their legislatures which would not coincide with the new equality of population theory of the Court. Surely these State legislatures would not have ratified the amendment had they believed it might render their own State constitutions unconstitutional. Furthermore, Congress did not require equality of legislative districts in the constitutions of the 10 'reconstructed States' of the South which it required to ratify the 14th amendment before they were admitted to the Union. To make the argument completely conclusive, the legislative history of the 14th amendment in Congress fails to provide one scintilla of evidence to support the Court's interpretation, but rather to the contrary. Thus it is perfectly obvious that the framers and ratifiers of the 14th amendment had no intention whatever of requiring the apportionment of legislatures solely on a population basis. . . .

Our constitutional fathers were proccupied with the feared trampling of minority rights by a tyranny of the majority. The Constitution reveals their concern. Moreover, they wisely permitted State legislatures to consider other factors than population in determining representation, recognizing that the rights and liberties of minorities are worthy of consideration and protection in our form of Government.

Thomas Jefferson made quite clear his distrust of unqualified democracy and majority rule. The Virginia Senate, Jefferson thought, was constructed too much like the House of Delegates. The result was that the very purpose of having two Houses of legislation, 'to introduce the influence of different interests or different principles,' was frustrated. To Jefferson, Virginia did not receive from the separation of the two houses, 'its benefits which a proper complication of principles is capable of producing.'

A foundation theory of our Constitution is to achieve a consensus among all the people by a process of accommodating group interests through our democratic representative institutional arrangements. . . .

The effect of this arbitrary ruling is to sap local initiative both at the State and local level. It will encourage party gerrymandering. It stifles the value of local individuality and initiative by compelling all legislatures to be poured into a common mold. It likely will result in the neglect

300   of rural areas, small cities, and suburbs of large cities throughout a large majority of our States. . . .

In many of our large industrial States the effect of the Court decision will be to throw the control of State legislatures into the hands of corrupt political machines and party bosses. Once in power, these corrupt machines then can both gerrymander the State legislative districts and the House districts for Congress. Surely it is not irrational for State legislatures to require either its senate or house to be based in part on factors other than population to prevent this from happening.[31]

Senator Wayne Morse, who always fancied himself as the watchdog of the U. S. Constitution disagreed sharply.

Politicians at the State and the local level, who hold their offices under a rotten-borough system in the United States, see that time has caught up with them and that at long last the Supreme Court has caught up with them. They are putting on a terrific political power drive to prevent reapportionment on the basis of the sound, democratic principle that one person should have one vote.

His vote should be weighted as one vote and not weighted as four, five, or six votes, which is exactly the case in those areas in which the city dweller is allowed much less weight as far as his voting influences are concerned than the rural dweller.

Will we support the decision of the Supreme Court on constitutional grounds or will the Congress of the United States be a party to weakening the prestige for and the respect of the American people in the Supreme Court?

I should like to say to the American people: "If you permit yourselves to be victimized by this propaganda, you will deserve exactly what you get."

I should like to say to the people in the rural areas of America: "You have as much of a precious right at stake in seeing to it that the decisions of the Supreme Court are upheld by the defeat of this vicious proposed legislation that seeks to undercut the judicial authority of the Supreme Court as any citizen voting in any metropolitan area of the Nation."

If the time ever comes when we cease to have a government based on three coordinate and coequal branches of government, but in contrast thereto have a government in which either the executive or the legisla-

---

[31] The Honorable Wallace Bennett, U. S. Senator from Utah, statement made in floor debate in U. S. Senate, August 15, 1964, as quoted in *Congressional Digest*, Vol. 44 (1965), pp. 14–16.

ture becomes supreme, it will only be a question of time before the
American people will cease to be the masters of their Government. That
means that the liberty and the freedom of the individual will soon
degenerate and wither away.

I say to the American people: "Please bear in mind that the reapportionment cases, like the civil rights cases, have arisen from that portion of
the 14th amendment to the Constitution which requires that each State
must give its citizens equal protection of the law."[32]

Senate Minority leader Everett Dirksen responded somewhat differently. He had a concrete proposal to amend the Constitution. His proposed amendment was dedicated to the federal principle in that it would
have given the states specific permission to apportion one house of their
legislatures on some criterion other than population. In support of his
amendment Dirksen asserted:

We are confronted with a basic issue of free government here. . . .
The right of the people to determine for themselves the manner in which
they will be governed is at stake. They may make mistakes in the exercise
of their fundamental authority but it is their mistake. It will be made by
them and not for them, and herein, I think, lies the principle so often
overlooked in the current debate on reapportionment of state legislatures.

Shall the people themselves be allowed the right to determine the
organic structure of their state government? That is what we here in the
first instance are called upon to decide. If the people are not permitted to
make this decision then who is to make it for them? If we deny this right
then a major step in the process of fragmenting freedom has begun.
When a type of government is fashioned or an organic structure is
created, not by the people or their delegate, but by someone else, then a
deprivation of freedom has occurred. Freedom will flourish and can only
flourish when the people retain free exercise of the powers of government.

What specifically would Senate Joint Resolution 2 permit the people
of each state to do that they cannot now do? It would only permit them
the right to base one house of their state legislature on factors other than
population. But this decision, under the procedure provided in the
proposed amendment, could only be made by a majority of the people of

---

[32] The Honorable Wayne Morse, U. S. Senator from Oregon, Statement during
Senate floor debate, August 21, 1964, as quoted in *Congressional Digest,* Vol. 44
(1965), p. 15.

a state at a state-wide election. Clearly the principle of "one man, one vote" would be adhered to in this process. That is all that the amendment would do, nothing more. . . .

. . . Probably forceful expression came in the State of Colorado. There the people in a state-wide election, voting purely on a "one man, one vote" basis, were given a clear choice between legislative districts in which each house was apportioned strictly on the basis of population or a legislature patterned on the federal system. What choice did they make? The "populations" formula was rejected by a vote of two to one and the federal formula was approved by a similar vote of two to one! In fact the federal formula was approved by the voters in every county in the state.[33]

The Colorado situation to which Senator Dirksen referred was one in which the voters resoundingly endorsed a "Federal Plan" in a popular referendum in 1962. Colorado's "Federal Plan" called for a districting formula that used population for allocating seats in the lower house and nonpopulation factors, especially geographic area, in the Senate. The arguments advanced in behalf of the plan stressed the diverse nature of the state, its interests, and its population. The need to balance four principal regions of the state was underlined. The plan's proponents claimed that the regions represented identifiable and widely varied economic interests that would be deprived of adequate representation in proportion to their value to the state if numbers of people were the only basis for districting the state legislature. To put it another way, areas with a sparse population but containing extremely important economic interests would be deprived of a sufficient voice in the legislature if that body was apportioned solely on the basis of population.

But in this case the state vote was not conclusive in the matter. Proponents of the "Federal Plan" argued vehemently that the people themselves had overwhelmingly endorsed two bases for districting the Colorado legislature — one basis by population, a second by geography and area. However, the *Colorado Democrat,* a political party publication, retorted that the electorate voted for reapportionment and received in return a plan by which the Republican party could "hang on to a majority in the state legislature." In 1964, the U. S. Supreme Court declared the outcome of the 1962 referendum unacceptable and gave the General Assembly of Colorado until July 15th of that year to reapportion.[34] If reapportionment was not accomplished by that time, the federal courts would do the job. A former Democratic governor and U. S. Senator from

---

[33] The Honorable Everett Dirksen, U. S. Senator from Illinois, Statement before the Senate Subcommittee on Constitutional Amendments, March 3, 1965.

[34] *Lucas* v. *Colorado,* 377 U. S. 713 (1964).

Colorado, Edwin C. Johnson, responded in acid tones, "The federal courts in *Lucas* v. *Colorado General Assembly* have burned down a barn to get rid of a couple of mice."[35]

---

[35] U. S. Senate, Subcommittee of the Committee on the Judiciary, *Hearings, Reapportionment of State Legislatures,* 89th Cong., 1st sess. (1965), p. 497.

Radicals, Extremists, Protesters: Left and Right

For some, not to be a martyr is martyrdom.

St. Just

Americans have an extraordinary talent for compromise in politics and for extremism in morality.

Daniel Bell

9

Americans not only cherish their freedoms, they exercise them. Almost daily, the press reports events and incidents that involve the broad exercise of the so-called basic rights, such as freedom to speak, print, protest, and even challenge the basic beliefs that undergird the American social system. For example, two incidents were reported in the July 16, 1968, issue of *The New York Times*. On the East Coast, the actions of a "right-winger" prompted a New Jersey prosecutor, a grand jury, a governor, and a state legislature to seek means for protecting the public.

Guy W. Calissi, the Bergen County Prosecutor, said today that a so-called vigilante group known as PRE-ARM (People's Rights Enforced Against Riots and Murder) was a one-man organization consisting of its chairman, Ernest T. Bradow.

Mr. Calissi told newsmen in the county courthouse here that the conclusion was "based on the Prosecutor's investigation."

His comments followed a brief appearance by Mr. Bradow, a 26-year-old former automobile salesman, before the Bergen County grand jury.

Mr. Bradow, who is a member of the John Birch Society and state organizer for George Wallace's American Independent party, said last week that his organization patrolled 11 municipalities in Bergen and Hudson Counties to help police curb "a rising tide of insurrection."

Mr. Calissi, who has denounced such vigilante activities, said in an interview today that "everything Bradow has told the newspapers is a rotten lie."

Then, repeating what he had said on a recent radio broadcast, he asserted: "This is the era of the exaltation of jerks."

Mr. Bradow had claimed his organization had 319 members and 30 "citizens patrol cars," but shortly thereafter he said he had suspended the patrols following a conversation with a member of the staff of Gov. Richard J. Hughes.

He said today that the organization now would be an arm of the American Independent party.

Governor Hughes has said that he might call a special session of the Legislature to complete passage of a law banning vigilante groups, such as PRE-ARM and the militantly white North Ward Citizens Committee in Newark.

The Senate has passed the bill, but the Assembly failed to act on it before the Legislature adjourned for the summer.[1]

Appearing in the same issue of *The New York Times* was the report of an official response to the public activities of a "left-wing" group some 3,000 miles from New Jersey in Oakland, California.

Twenty-five hundred chanting, sign-carrying demonstrators ringed the courthouse where a leader of the Black Panther party, Huey P. Newton, went on trial today on charges of murdering a policeman.

Heavily armed sheriff's deputies stared impassively as the marchers, half of them Negroes, chanted "Free Huey" and waved signs saying, "Anything happens to Huey, the sky's the limit."

Marchers who tried to gain access to the courthouse were turned back at the entrances. Armed guards watched over lobbies and passage-ways and sealed off the seventh floor, where the trial is being held, to everyone except those with seat passes.

Inside the packed courtroom, Newton sat beside his attorney, Charles R. Garry, as the lawyer began a series of arguments designed to stop the proceedings.

Mr. Garry told Alameda County Judge Monroe Friedman that Newton could not get a fair trial in Oakland because the list of prospective jurors "does not reflect the community." He said the list from which jurors were picked was "loaded with white racism.". . .

---

[1] *The New York Times* (July 16, 1968), p. C-22.

The public was not allowed at the opening session. Of the 62 seats, 28 were reserved for newsmen and the rest were filled by the prospective jurors.

Newton, 26 years old, is charged with shooting to death patrolman John Frey, 23, during a street battle last Oct. 28. The Panthers say that the police were "out to get Huey" because of the militant stance of his organization and that the police "harassed" Newton into shooting.

During the court proceedings, the Panthers lined up 250 men in black leather jackets and turtleneck sweaters alongside the building, all at parade rest. Previous estimates had put their membership at 60.

Newton formed the Black Panther Party for Self-Defense less than two years ago and chose the cat as a symbol because "it is not in the panther's nature to strike first, but when he is attacked and is backed into a corner he will respond viciously and wipe out the aggressor."

The Panthers argue that Negroes are "held in bondage" by an "oppressive, colonialist mother country — epitomized by white policemen."[2]

Although such incidents occur almost daily somewhere in America, and despite the large number of groups on the far left or the far right who exist in this country at any moment, the activities of such groups never fail to excite some opposition or concern. But deep concern, controversy, and issues are sharpest when the "middle-of-the-road" American feels threatened or is aroused by the activities of either wing. One can always expect one wing to react vigorously to the other; but general public issues take shape in terms of the reactions of the more moderate, compromising type of citizen — the "fuzzy or woolly" type of American, as Arthur Koestler pictures him below.

I like to imagine an instrument which would enable us to break up patterns of social behaviour as the physicist breaks up a beam of rays. Looking through this sociological spectroscope we would see spread out under the diffraction grating the rainbow-coloured spectrum of all possible human attitudes to life. The whole distressing muddle would become neat, clear and comprehensive.

On one end of the spectrum, obviously on the infra-red end, we would see the Commissar. The Commissar believes in Change from Without. He believes that all the pests of humanity, including constipation and the Oedipus complex, can and will be cured by Revolution, that is, by a radical reorganization of the system of production and distribution of goods; that this end justifies the use of all means, including violence, ruse, treachery and poison; that logical reasoning is an unfailing

---

[2] *Ibid.*, p. C-14.

compass and the Universe a kind of very large clockwork in which a very large number of electrons once set into motion will forever revolve in their predictable orbits; and that whosoever believes in anything else is an escapist. This end of the spectrum has the lowest frequency of vibrations and is, in a way, the coarsest component of the beam; but it conveys the maximum amount of heat.

On the other end of the spectrum, where the waves become so short and of such high frequency that the eye no longer sees them, colourless, warmthless but all-penetrating, crouches the Yogi, melting away in the ultra-violet. He has no objection to calling the universe a clockwork, but he thinks that it could be called, with about the same amount of truth, a musical-box or a fishpond. He believes that the End is unpredictable and that the Means alone count. He rejects violence under any circumstances. He believes that logical reasoning gradually loses its compass value as the mind approaches the magnetic pole of Truth or the Absolute, which alone matters. He believes that nothing can be improved by exterior organisation and everything by the individual effort from within; and that whosoever believes in anything else is an escapist. He believes that the debt-servitude imposed upon the peasants of India by the money lenders should be abolished not by financial legislation but by spiritual means. He believes that each individual is alone, but attached to the all-one by an invisible umbilical cord; that his creative forces, his goodness, trueness and usefulness can alone be nourished by the sap which reaches him through this cord; and that his only task during his earthly life is to avoid any action, emotion or thought which might lead to a breaking of the cord. This avoidance has to be maintained by a difficult, elaborate technique, the only kind of technique which he accepts.

Between these two extremes are spread out in a continuous sequence the spectral lines of the more sedate human attitudes. The more we approach its centre, the more does the spectrum become blurred and woolly. On the other hand, this increase of wool on the naked spectral bodies makes them look more decent, and intercourse with them more civilised. You cannot argue with a naked Commissar — he starts at once to beat his chest and next he strangles you, whether you be friend or foe, in his deadly embrace. You cannot argue with the ultra-violet skeleton either, because words mean nothing to him. You can argue with post-war planners, Fabians, Quakers, liberals and philanthropists. But the argument will lead nowhere, for the real issue remains between the Yogi and the Commissar, between the fundamental conceptions of Change from Without and Change from Within.

It is easy to say that all that is wanted is a synthesis — the synthesis between saint and revolutionary; but so far this has never been achieved. What has been achieved are various motley forms of compromise — the blurred intermediary bands of the spectrum — compromise but not synthesis. Apparently the two elements do not mix, and this may be one of the reasons why we have made such a mess of our History. The Commissar's emotional energies are fixed on the relation between individual and society, the Yogi's on the relation between the individual and the universe. Again it is easy to say that all that is wanted is a little mutual effort. One might as well ask a homosexual to make a little effort towards the opposite sex, and vice versa.[3]

Most of us reside in the middle of Koestler's spectrum. But there are always quite a number who do not fit into this middle grouping. If the reader will turn to the chapter covering educational issues, he will note that members of the Students for a Democratic Society (SDS) and supporters of "Student Power" normally reside somewhere between the middle of the spectrum and the Yogi's end. Like the Yogi, many students are asking about the relation between man and the universe. They are asking ultimate questions, such as: "What is the purpose of life?" They want to know where they are going and why. On the other hand, the segregationist, the John Birch Society member, and the Christian Crusader are less likely to ask questions. They are more inclined to believe that they know the answers. For example, they contend that they know what America should do as a nation. Many are also convinced of what will happen if other Americans pay them no heed. *The Blue Book of the John Birch Society,* for instance, has the answers.

The greatest enemy of man, is and always has been, government. And the larger, the more extensive that government, the greater the enemy. . . .

. . . And you have a society in which *fault* of government . . . is held to be a *benefit* and a desirable part of the framework of life.[4]

It seems quite evident that persons located near the center of the political spectrum will frequently deem activities by persons at the extremes as ominous and threatening. If such activities do appear to threaten us, we may lash out at the extremists as did the Bergen County prosecutoᵢ whom we cited earlier. When enough people in the middle of the spectrum become aroused, issues emerge and sharpen. If a controversy spreads, as it has on many occasions throughout American history, the issues become national in scope, and Congress may be a vital center of the debate, if not of vituperation and invective.

---

[3] Arthur Koestler, *The Yogi and the Commissar* (New York: Macmillan, 1945), pp. 3–5.

[4] *Blue Book of the John Birch Society,* sixth imprint (Belmont, Mass.: The John Birch Society, 1961), p. 138.

310   Whether it is the anti-communist crusades or the draft card burnings of the 1960s, the anti-Masonic movement of the early 1800s, or the antics of agrarian radicals during the Great Depression of the 1930s, group actions were and are called into question and debated. In some instances, the very privilege of a group to exist may be questioned; the group's life may become an issue. Several times during his term as president, Lyndon Johnson publicly questioned the right of the Ku Klux Klan to exist. Men rally around other men who agree with them and organize in some fashion to pursue common goals and interests. The rallying points, as well as the goals and activities, have often been an issue. As movements that appear radical develop and grow, they stimulate opposition and controversy. Once the issues are engaged, the action or even the existence of the radical group becomes an issue in itself.

What, then, are the special conditions which spawn seemingly radical groups and their activities? What is the nature of *radicalism* or *extremism* and what undergirds it? What sorts of people engage in the activities that generate such controversies and issues? To what degree are extremist activities threatening and dangerous? Finally, what is to be done?

A Central Issue: What Is Extremism?

Ambrose Bierce, a master of the art of cynicism, defines extremism or radicalism as "the conservatism of tomorrow injected into the affairs of today."[5] Many times in the past, an originally revolutionary and dangerous position has later caught on and is staunchly defended by conservatives. Our own social security program was once believed to be socialistic. On the other hand, there have been many seemingly radical programs which have faded away without having their goals fulfilled. So Bierce's salty remark is "catchy" but only partially true.

Koestler's spectrum indicates that radicalism involves diametrically opposed ideologies (systems of beliefs). However, he notes elsewhere that true believers at one pole may shed those beliefs at a moment's notice and become devotees at the opposite pole. For example, the fascist dictator Benito Mussolini was once a devout socialist, as was Pierre Laval, Hitler's puppet in Vichy France during World War II.[6] In America, too, there have been many examples of strong leftists who have swung to arch-conservative positions. Governor Ronald Reagan of California is one; the author James Burnham is another. Former Senator Harry Cain of Washington is an example of a right-winger who ended up on the liberal side of the spectrum.

We can infer that persons at both poles of the spectrum may share common personality traits. Indeed, as we shall see later, many observers believe that it takes a special type of personality to espouse either

---

[5] Ambrose Bierce, *The Devil's Dictionary* (Mount Vernon, N. Y.: The Peter Pauper Press, 1958), p. 50.

[6] Koestler, *The Yogi and the Commissar*, pp. 3–16.

extreme. However, what makes radicals an issue in American politics is **311**
the extent to which their views, beliefs, and demands differ from the
outlooks, ideas, and demands that are generally acceptable to the great
majority of Americans who have positions closer to the center of Koestler's spectrum. Consider for a moment the words of Thomas Kuchel,
minority whip of the U. S. Senate in 1963. He depicted the so-called
radical rightist as a "fright peddler" and went on to say:

I rise today to speak of another danger we confront, not as dread or
as foreboding, but equally offensive and evil to all reasonable, rational,
free American citizens.

It is the danger of hate and venom, of slander and abuse, generated
by fear and heaped indiscriminately upon many great Americans by
another relative handful of zealots, in the ranks or clutches of self-styled
"I am a better American than you are" organizations.

It results from a strange intellectual strabismus which professes to
see our government crawling with Communists and which, abandoning
the processes of reason, pours its spleen upon anything or anybody
which does not meet its own queer and puzzling dogmas.[7]

Later that year, Kuchel's fellow senator from the majority party,
Stephen Young, spoke out in agreement but used harsher language.

Who are the people who believe this propaganda? They are the
frightened and the frustrated; the bitter and the vindictive; the twisted
zealots and well-meaning cranks; the malicious cynics and confused
innocents; the people who have nightmarish fears of a radical bogey,
who suspect eggheads, who hated and still hate the New Deal or who
hate anyone who differs with their extremist views.

Who are the leaders of the radical right-wing groups? Many are
sincere believers in their causes of hate. Others typified by Robert
Welch, founder and fuehrer of the John Birch Society, are cold oppor-
tunists who have carved lucrative careers by playing on the prejudices of
their adherents.[8]

On the other hand, Senator Barry Goldwater of Arizona speaks much
more positively about the goals and behavior of arch-conservatives. In
1961, he said, "A lot of people in my home town have been attracted to

---

[7] The Honorable Thomas Kuchel, U. S. Senator from California in the *Congressional Record*, 88th Cong., 1st sess. (May 2, 1963), p. 7636.

[8] The Honorable Stephen Young, U. S. Senator from Ohio, *Congressional Record*,
88th Cong., 1st sess. (August 15, 1963), p. 15179.

312 the [John Birch] society, and I am impressed by the type of people in it. They are the kind of people we need in politics."[9] Later, when he was the 1964 Republican presidential candidate, he objected to the tendencies to label members of the Birch Society as "extremist."[10]

Clearly, Senators Kuchel and Young are located closer to the center of the spectrum and are thus further removed from the polar right wing than Senator Goldwater. So, as could be expected, the observer's own belief system and his location along the political spectrum make a big difference in his assessments of the actions, policies, and positions of others. One is reminded of a nearly forgotten cartoon by Frank Interlandi depicting an American tourist and his Italian guide viewing the famous leaning tower of Pisa. The guide tells the American that the tower is "like politics." Whether it leans left or right and how far it leans in one direction or the other depends upon where one stands.

However, the distance between the observer's position and the position of another person or group on the political spectrum is just one of several factors that affects his reaction to the other party and his tendency to call it radical or nonradical. Another factor is the degree to which another person's or group's action or position is visible and significant to the observer. The so-called radical right was quite visible to Senator Kuchel. He stressed the number of letters he received from "peddlers of fright," as he called them — some two hundred a day when the mail ran heavy.[11] Alan Westin, a student of radicalism, notes that in recent times the right wing has been quite visible. This high visibility has generated at least three rather popular explanatory descriptions of right-wing activities, all of which are rather unsatisfactory in Westin's view.

. . . Last spring, most Americans, including most of the nation's political leaders, had never heard of the John Birch Society, or its kissing kin such as We The People, the Liberty Lobby, The Christian Crusade of the Reverend Billy Hargis, the Circuit Riders, or Freedom-in-Action. Today there are some twenty-five major national organizations and over one hundred local or regional groups in this camp of the Radical Right. Its terrain lies between the right wing of American conservatism — which the Radical Right considers "soft" — and the frank "hate groups" in the Gerald L. K. Smith pattern — which the Radical Right avoid as "bigotry."

Radical Right organizations have by now attracted over 300,000 members; their annual budgets run to more than $20 million; and they have won priceless national publicity by featuring extremist charges in their literature, films, and indignation rallies.

While everyone now agrees that the Radical Right exists, there is far

---

[9] *Time* (April 7, 1961), p. 19.

[10] Richard Hofstadter, *The Paranoid Style in American Politics and Other Essays* (New York: Alfred Knopf, 1964), p. 111.

[11] Thomas Kuchel, *Congressional Record*, 88th Cong., 1st sess. (May 2, 1963), p. 7636.

from universal agreement as to its origin, its prospects, or its meaning for **313** American politics. At least three main analyses of the Radical Right have been suggested by leading commentators.

The first and most unruffled view, typified by the columnist William S. White, is that the Radical Right is a temporary boil on the body politic, like earlier fringe groups in American history. War fevers of 1960–61 brought the infection to a head and it is clearly an irritation. However, the healthy, conserving processes of American life will push the sore off if only the sensation-seeking press and what White calls "ultra-Liberals" will cease spreading the infection by overexcited rubbing.

A second, more anxious reaction, typified by comments in *The Nation* and in some leading foreign newspapers, views the Radical Right as a classic proto-fascist threat. Supported by reactionary big business, Southern racists, fundamentalist religious leaders, and angry military men, the Radical Right is crying "betrayal of the nation" and is attacking the capacity of democracy to cope with the Cold War. It is thus a kind of French "ultra" movement, lobbing ideological plastic bombs into the national marketplace.

A third analysis, and probably the most widely held one, sees the Radical Right as a regrouping of the old McCarthyite forces. Between 1950 and 1954, these forces used the charge of "internal Communist conspiracy" not to expose real Communists in government but to harass liberals within the Democratic and Republican parties, to discredit social reform, and to advance a neo-isolationist position in world affairs. Today, the same forces are seeking to regain influence by capitalizing on national unrest over Cold War setbacks.[12]

Why are these descriptive explanations unsatisfactory? Westin finds no compelling analogies, and he feels that the real dangers of radicalism are not stressed. These criticisms tell the reader that Westin's position on the scale is quite a distance from that of the John Birch Society or the Liberty Lobby. But Westin's other points are the crucial ones. First, if we dwell on movements that are of immediate concern, we are apt to forget or overlook movements that arise in other corners from time to time and could arise again. That is, too many of the descriptions and explanations of extremism focus on the radicalism being expressed at the moment and forget to compare these movements with others out of our past. As a result our views are likely to be distorted. We should remember that it was the "Radical Left" that was disturbing persons in the middle of the

---

[12] Alan Westin, "The Deadly Parallels: Radical Right and Radical Left," *Harper's,* Vol. 224 (April 1962), pp. 25–26. Copyright © 1962 by Harper's Magazine, Inc. Reprinted from the April 1962 issue of Harper's Magazine by permission of the author.

314   spectrum during the 1940s, the "Radical Right" in the early 1960s, and the Radical Left again in the late 1960s.

But even more crucial is the failure of Westin's three explanations above to focus on the common features or parallels that are characteristic of extremist movements throughout history, whether they happen to be leftist or rightist. What did they have in common, historically speaking? This question generates a great deal of heat in the lively debate over the true nature of extremism. Both left and right groups object promptly and sharply to efforts that point up similarities between them.

One thing the new left and far right agree on is that Gordon Hall is Way Out.

Robert Welch, leader of the John Birch Society, calls Hall a "slimy character." The late Malcom X dubbed him a "white mercenary." American Nazi George Lincoln Rockwell says Hall is "the lowest and vilest man I know." Viet Cong sympathizers at Berkeley hooted him off the platform.

The object of this abuse is a tall, mild-seeming Bostonian who has spent nearly half his 44 years investigating and lecturing on extremist groups.

Hall's career on the political fringes has led him to form some pithy judgments on the nature of extremism and some of its foremost practitioners.[13]

Why do both extremes dislike a person such as Gordon Hall so intensely? Well, who likes being told that he looks and acts like his own worst enemy? Moreover, such comparisons are mirrors that tell us how we look. No doubt many extremists do not appreciate the traits or characteristics reflected in the mirror. For example, Welch doubtlessly does not relish being called a "true believer," which is a polite synonym for a fanatic, even if Hall calls him a sincere one. Nor does he like to be accused of tactical errors.

Hall considers Welch a "sincere, true believer. If he was not he wouldn't commit such unbelievable tactical errors as labeling Eisenhower a tool of the Communist conspiracy. I know he is sincere because every time he sees me, he turns white, quivers and screams."[14]

But what are the factors that distinguish extremists from nonextremists, whether they be left or right? One is that American radicals borrow heavily from a rich religious heritage and approach political questions in a

---

[13] *The Denver Post* (October 26, 1966), p. 5.
[14] *Ibid.*

manner that is deadly serious and dedicated to principles — treating such principles in a way that is similar to the manner that religious folk treat their religious principles and symbols. At this point let us allow some of the groups that have been labeled radical to speak for themselves. Consider, first, the behavior of a leftist group of recent times, Students for a Democratic Society.

The scene might have been written by Genet; it was worthy of filming by Fellini. A young man, well clothed and well groomed but with his shirt collar open now, and his tie pulled down, shouted to the audience like an old-fashioned revivalist.

"Come up," he cried, "come up and confess. Put some money in the pot and be saved!"

And they came. The first youth, clutching the green pieces of paper in his hand, recited for all to hear: "My father is a newspaper editor. I give twenty-five dollars." His penitence brought cheers from the assembly. The sin of the next young man was a father who was assistant director of a government bureau. He gave forty dollars. "My dad is dean of a law school," confessed another, as he proffered fifty dollars for indulgence.

The occasion was not a rehearsal for the theater of the absurd but a convention of Students for a Democratic Society. The "sins" which the students confessed were the occupations or the social classes of their fathers. Their origins placed these students in the elite, the high-status group of any community, and yet here they were, exuberantly adopting a political stance and a style of life which they believed to be the very antithesis of those origins.

Why this should be so frankly puzzled me and led to research which has confirmed and refined my earliest impression of the social make-up of today's youth in dissent. They are of the middle- and upper-middle class. They are the core of the student movement. They are the dissenters.[15]

For comparable behavior on the "student right," one of the authors observed several "sing-outs" of the Moral Rearmament group. Following each of the long song sessions, three or four members would confess their misdeeds to the remainder of the group. On one occasion, for example, a boy confessed that he had treated his little brother cruelly. He was especially repentant for having neglected his studies in school, drinking with his buddies, and having had sexual relations with four girls before joining M.R.A.

Also consider the words of the Reverend Billy James Hargis of the *Christian Crusade:*

---

[15] Richard Flacks, "Student Activists: Result, Not Revolt," *Psychology Today,* Vol. 1 (October 1967), p. 18. Copyright © Communications/Research/Machines, Inc.

316   Patriotism and Christianity are very close to each other. It is impossible to be a true Christian and not be a true patriot. One who loves God also loves his country. Our forefathers believed in Jesus Christ and in His atoning blood. They talked about their faith in their homes, taught it in the schools as well as in the churches, and sang of it in wilderness brush arbors, tabernacles and camp-meetings. . . .

Communism, however, has come along with insistence that America no longer look toward God, but instead toward government. Communism, through its associates, liberalism, progressivism, socialism, and modernism is creating class warfare within America, fomenting hatred, stirring up various so-called "social crises," destroying love of country, perverting morals of young and old, casting aside beloved traditions, banning the Bible from American schools, and in general reducing the proud and free American citizenship to an insignificant, helpless, hopeless pawn of giant government.[16]

Hargis indicates that he is a man strongly wedded to principle. Thus, it is not surprising that many observers argue that the extremist is one who eschews the slightest compromise of principle. He is said to be contemptuous of political bargainers, compromisers, and brokers. A compromiser or broker of issues, such as Lyndon Johnson or Everett Dirksen, should not be admired for his capacity to arrive at solutions which satisfy few completely but give most people some measure of satisfaction. To meet demands partially and try to satisfy many competitors in the political market-place means that principles are sacrificed. This is the mark of an amoral man, says Robert Welch of the John Birch Society.

The most terrible result of this collapse of the rock of faith on which our morality was built is the rise of the amoral man — of which the usual Communist himself is the most illustrative example. For an amoral man, like Stalin, is infinitely worse, from the point of view of a humanitarian civilization, than an immoral one like Hitler. An immoral man may lie, steal, and murder; the worst of them even without any seeming limit or hesitation. But it hurts his conscience. He is, at least potentially, susceptible to humanitarian or moral considerations, to some extent, and if they are presented cogently enough to him. There is even the possibility always that he may sometime, or in some ways, repent and make what amends he can for his crimes.

An amoral man, however, has simply wiped out his conscience, along with any reason for its existence. He is not immoral, even when performing coldblooded mass murders, because to him there is no such thing as

---

[16] Billy James Hargis, *Communist America: Must It Be?* (Tulsa: Christian Crusade, 1960), pp. 31–32.

either morality or immorality. There is only the pragmatic consideration of the advantages or disadvantages to himself, for his own personal desires or plans, in any action — whether it be the building of a monument or the murder of his wife. And these amoral men, the products of a materialistic and sophomoric disillusionment, who have not yet gone on in their thinking to deeper and more permanent truths, now stalk in our midst in greater numbers than ever before in history. Such men, among the Communists, and they are plentiful and highly placed, have no real dedication even to Communism. They regard it merely as an expedient means to satisfy their personal ambitions more nearly than would any other star to which they might hitch their wagons.

But on our own side of the fence, among the millions who either are, or pretend to be, non-Communists, the amoral man, who has no slightest inner concern with right or wrong, is one of the greatest causes of our constant retreat, and one of the greatest dangers to our survival. And he doesn't wear any label. He usually lives up to the appearance of excellent morals, because it is expedient for his purposes, and you will usually find him in church on Sunday morning, maybe even a Catholic church. But as a member of the United States Senate, running for the presidency, and smart enough to know the strong Communist support behind-the-scenes which he will have to get in order to have any chance of being nominated in 1960, such an amoral man can do a tremendous amount of ball-carrying on behalf of the Communist aims here in the United States; and he can do an almost equal amount of damage to anti-Communist morale in other parts of the world, by his well-publicized speeches against Chiang Kai-shek or in favor of the Algerian rebels. Or an amoral man, as the head of a great so-called Republic, may have no slightest scruples or concern about its fate or the fate of other nations, in the face of Communist conquest and of the cruel tyranny of their rule. And any similarity of characters in this story to any living persons is not coincidental.[17]

In the above statement and many others, Welch sounds as if he believes that he has a corner on truth. He will tell you precisely what is moral, immoral, and amoral. Moreover, politics is a matter of principle, not an enterprise for the adjustment of social differences. As such, politics is a deadly serious business. All of the gamesmanship and fun is gone. One of the authors here recalls a remark made by the Honorable Walter Sales, State Representative from Gallatin County, Montana, in 1961. Sales is a strong enough conservative to be called radical right by some of his adversaries; yet he emerged from a John Birch organizer's meeting

---

[17] *The Blue Book of the John Birch Society,* sixth imprint, pp. 64–66. Reprinted with permission.

saying, "I can't buy that stuff. They take all of the fun out of being a politician."

Of far greater moment, however, is the widely expressed observation that extremists exhibit at least mild forms of paranoia. In a sense, this says that they are sick people. Of all contentions, this one has, by far, the most impressive mass of documentation. This documentation depends heavily upon the radical's tendency to find a conspiracy underlying the political outcomes he detests. Again, Alan Westin notes the similarity between left and right on this score.

The Radical Left of 1946–48 and the Radical Right today [1962] both derive, of course, from the stream of American fundamentalism which goes back to the Know-Nothings of the 1850s, the Populists of the 1890s, and the Coughlinites of the 1930s. All these movements share a common belief in betrayal of the American dream by hidden conspiracies and the possibility of total solutions by the aroused masses of the nation. The two contemporary groups, however, must be seen in the unique setting of our contemporary situation. Since 1945, for the first time, the United States has consciously accepted leadership in international affairs. For the first time, the United States must live with the undeniable possibility of physical destruction by a self-declared enemy nation. For the first time, the American public has developed a high concern for foreign policy in "peacetime," though most Americans are still unskilled in the realities of international relations. It is against this backdrop of public instability that the two great challenges to the national anti-Communist consensus of our era should be examined. . . .

In 1946, the Radical Left saw its wartime hopes for a perfect world — for total disarmament, an economy of abundance, a harmonious United Nations, and fraternal U. S.-Soviet relations — shattered by the rise of severe tensions between the United States and Russia. The cause of these tensions, the Radical Left concluded, was not Soviet imperialism or the "natural" conflicts of nation-states but a "fascist conspiracy" within the United States. The danger was basically *internal.* "Nazis are running the American government," Henry Wallace declared at one passionate moment in 1948. Our two major parties had "rotted" and Wall Street, the military clique, labor "misleaders," "red-baiting" intellectuals, and even the churches had become part of a program to "betray" peace and progress. Unless "the people" rose and shook off this conspiracy, the Radical Left warned, the country faced an imminent fascist take-over and American foreign policy would serve only dictator regimes and the former-fascist nations.

Compare this ideological image with that of the new Radical Right. Its dream of perfection was that a Republican Administration in 1952 (preferably led by MacArthur or Taft rather than Eisenhower) and a green light for Senators McCarthy and McCarran would bring an end to the "appeasement" and "defeats" of the "Yalta-Acheson" decades. (This attitude was of course shared by many Democrats at the state and local levels who rejected the party's New Deal and Fair Deal leadership.) American prestige would soar upward, the Soviet empire would be pushed back to the borders of Russia, and the Soviet regime itself would probably collapse. All this would be accomplished while we were "restoring free enterprise" at home, erasing the "Socialist" measures of the New and Fair Deals, and balancing the budget.

However, when Soviet power rose rather than fell in the middle 1950s, when the forces of nationalism and neutralism increased, and when "Socialist" measures like TVA and Social Security remained and were even extended, the Radical Right exploded. Beginning about 1958, when the Birch Society was organized and other Radical Right groups began to expand, the cause of our troubles was perceived: a vast "Communist conspiracy" at home, even under the Eisenhower Administration. Our major parties, with their "Left-wing tendencies" and reliance on "minority groups," the "Socialist" unions, Communist-infiltrated churches, even leaders of American business — all had been saturated with Communist ideas and were in the hands of Communist conspirators.[18]

Richard Hofstadter, an eminent historian, sees paranoia as a recurring historical phenomenon.

. . . One of the most impressive facts about the paranoid style . . . is that it represents an old and recurrent mode of expression in our public life which has frequently been linked with movements of suspicious discontent and whose content remains much the same even when it is adopted by men of distinctly different purposes. Our experience suggests too that, while it comes in waves of different intensity, it appears to be all but ineradicable.[19]

Hofstadter quotes from former Senator Joseph McCarthy to illustrate his point.

How can we account for our present situation unless we believe that men high in this government are concerting to deliver us to disaster? This must be the product of a great conspiracy, a conspiracy on a scale so immense as to dwarf any previous such venture in the history of man.

---

[18] Westin in *Harper's* (April 1962), pp. 26–27.
[19] Richard Hofstadter, *The Paranoid Style in American Politics and Other Essays*, p. 6.

320   A conspiracy of infamy so black that, when it is finally exposed, its principals shall be forever deserving of the maledictions of all honest men. . . .[20]

Utterances that appear to spring from paranoia abound in the right and left wing literature. Consider this sample from *Common Sense,* a publication that was once widely read by persons of a right wing persuasion:

. . . *Common Sense* states positively that the NAACP is a Communist dominated, agitation group which has never had a Negro as head. . . .

The NAACP derives its real power from the Anti-Defamation League of B'nai B'rith which is the Jewish F.B.I. Twenty-four years study of the world Marxist conspiracy enables us to state that the U. S. is being brain-washed and prepared to give up its freedom. AWAKE! BEFORE IT IS TOO LATE!![21]

For examples of conspiratorial outlooks on the left of the political spectrum, we can turn to some of the more violent outbursts in the student power movement.

University administrators and my home town high school superintendent are simply establishment lackeys who knowingly or innocently carry out the goals of a gigantic cultural and business world conspiracy to deprive us young people of what is rightfully ours. I am personally not going to wait until I am fifty and grey to get the goodies out of the system. I refuse to jump through all those little hoops they put in front of me while they are smiling hypocritically about their "cushy" jobs and salaries. If schools are nothing more than a way of keeping us off the streets and out of the labor market, I say, "Burn 'em, Baby, Burn 'em." If a university is to be used as an instrument of suppression, then we are better off without them. We got to teach some of these self-righteous_____ that their conspiracies are just as criminal as theft or murder. And that is why I don't care if this multiversity never holds another class.[22]

Robert Welch of the John Birch Society sees an entirely different sort of conspiracy.

---

[20] The Honorable Joseph McCarthy, U. S. Senator from Wisconsin, *Congressional Record,* 82nd Cong., 1st sess. (June 14, 1951), p. 6602.

[21] *Common Sense* (August 1, 1957), p. 2.

[22] From a private interview by Duane W. Hill with a student activist from Los Angeles, California, March 3, 1969.

Communism is not a political party, nor a military organization, nor an ideological crusade, nor a rebirth of Russian imperialist ambitions, though it comprises and uses all of these parts and pretenses. Communism, in its unmistakable present reality, is wholly a conspiracy, a gigantic conspiracy to enslave mankind; an increasingly successful conspiracy controlled by determined, cunning and utterly ruthless gangsters, willing to use any means to achieve its end.[23]

Now consider Welch's indictment of President Dwight D. Eisenhower:

For the sake of honesty, however, I want to confess here my own conviction that Eisenhower's motivation is more ideological than opportunistic. Or, to put it bluntly, I personally think that he has been sympathetic to ultimate Communist aims, realistically willing to use Communist means to help them achieve their goals, knowingly accepting and abiding by Communist orders, and consciously serving the Communist conspiracy, for all his adult life.[24]

But this is not something new in American history, as Hofstadter illustrates. The following words appeared in the Populist party's manifesto of 1895:

As early as 1865–66 a conspiracy was entered into between the gold gamblers of Europe and America. . . . For nearly thirty years these conspirators have kept the people quarreling over less important matters, while they have pursued with unrelenting zeal their one central purpose. . . .[25]

And now to a statement that appeared in the *Texas State Times,* September 15, 1855:

. . . It is a notorious fact that the Monarchs of Europe and the Pope of Rome are at this very moment plotting our destruction and threatening the extinction of our political, civil, and religious institutions. We have the best reasons for believing that corruption has found its way into

---

[23] *The Blue Book of The John Birch Society,* sixth imprint, pp. 30–31.

[24] Welch as quoted by The Honorable Milton Young, U. S. Senator, North Dakota, *Congressional Record,* 87th Cong., 1st sess. (September 25, 1961), p. 18,126.

[25] As reprinted in Frank McVey, "The Populist Movement," *Economic Studies,* Vol. 1 (August 1896), pp. 201–202.

322   our Executive Chamber, and that our Executive head is tainted with the infectious venom of Catholicism. . . .[26]

But we really should not neglect the Marxists who also saw conspiracy. Religion was considered the opiate of the people or a mechanism which the oppressors used to lull the proletariat to sleep. It was V. I. Lenin who advocated the recruitment of a hard core of top communist leaders — dedicated fanatics or godless Jesuits — who would be cleansed and steeled so as never to become capitalistic lackeys or dupes of a capitalistic conspiracy.

Here, too, Alan Westin sees a similarity running through left and right extremists. They tend not only to harass their arch or polar adversaries but also the people in the middle of the spectrum. On the left, radical student groups (at Berkeley and Columbia, for example) have, at times, brought effective university administration and policy nearly to a halt. On the right, as Alan Westin notes, radicals have eroded the effective democratic processes in a number of American communities.

Anonymous and threatening phone calls are being made to liberal teachers, ministers, and school principals; to dentists who support flouridation; or to Quakers supporting disarmament.

Private meetings of churches, civic groups, and community forums are being packed by Radical Rightists who harass the speakers and provoke violence.

On the eve of liberal gatherings, anonymous telephone calls are warning that a bomb is planted in the hall, thus causing the police to cancel the meeting.

Vicious falsehoods are being circulated from the platform and in print about such responsible groups as the National Council of Churches of Christ, the Foreign Policy Association, and the Anti-Defamation League.

To restore these communities to the climate of free debate, to turn the concern of Americans over the dynamics of communism into constructive channels, businessmen, conservatives, and the Republican party must rise to defend the basic ideals of American democracy, as labor, liberal groups, and the Democratic party did in the late 'forties. . . .[27]

Finally, Westin argues that programs, strategy, and tactics of left and right have many parallels.

---

[26] Quoted by Sister Paul of the Cross, *Political Nativism in Texas, 1825–1860* (Washington, 1930), pp. 114–115, from *Texas State Times* (September 15, 1855).

[27] Westin, in *Harper's* (April 1962), p. 32.

The Radical Left attacked the basic international programs of the **323**
United States in the late 1940s as *too* "anti-Communist." It opposed
American policy toward the UN as based upon Cold War power politics,
and demanded that we abandon the regional "war pacts" in which we
were supposedly engaging as contrary to the UN charter. The Radical
Left opposed what it called the "Martial Plan" for Europe — as well as
military aid to Greece, Turkey, and Iran — warning that we were shoring
up decadent regimes and that "the people" in these countries would not
be bought for our "Cold War mercenaries." Defense spending and rearmament were violently denounced as warlike, costly, and the death
knell for domestic reform. To meet the might of Soviet power, the Radical
Left urged us to rely on our overpowering moral example as a peace-
loving nation and to trust the prospects of Soviet reasonableness at the
conference table.

In its own terms, the Radical Right is mounting an identical attack
on the nation's international position today. Now our policies are not
"anti-Communist" enough. Our participation in the UN is rejected because we cannot use the world body as a Cold War spear. The Radical
Right rejects American alliances and friendly relations with all governments which are not "firmly anti-Communist," a list which includes
Mexico, India, Ghana, Burma, and others which are "playing along with
the Communists." Foreign aid is bitterly assailed as "pouring money
down Communist ratholes.". . .

Both Radical Left and Radical Right add a muted chord of prejudice
to their positions, clear enough to draw the money and support of some
of the bigoted but not loud enough to open the groups to charges of
being full-dress "hate movements." The Radical Left in 1946–48 attacked
the "Vatican conspiracy" which was pushing us toward a "holy war"
against Russia. A Radical Left magazine, *The Protestant,* said that Catholicism wanted "a fascist world hegemony." . . .

On the Radical Right some well-known anti-Semitic spokesmen have
already appeared, such as Allen Zoll, a staff member of the Christian
Crusade, and Merwin K. Hart, a chapter leader of the Birchers. The
presence of powerful anti-Semitic currents in the audiences of the Radical Right's public meetings has been noted by careful observers from the
Anti-Defamation League. Openly segregationist and anti-Negro positions
are evident in the Christian Crusade, and the White Citizens Councils in
the South have close ties with many national Radical Right groups.
Leading anti-Semitic publications such as Gerald Smith's *The Cross and
the Flag* and Conde McGinley's *Common Sense* are recommended in
Radical Right literature.

In terms of basic strategy, the Radical Left's top leadership in
1946–48 aimed at winning influence within two key sectors of American
civic life which were considered to be ripe for penetration — the labor

324 movement and organized liberalism. Communists and Progressives had secured important positions in the union movement between 1935 and 1945; they hoped to operate outward from unions controlled by the Radical Left such as the United Electrical Workers, the International Longshoremen's Union, and the Mine, Mill, and Smelter Workers to bring the "left-leaning" unions such as the United Auto Workers and then the CIO itself into the "Progressive camp."

The Radical Left had control of Communist-front groups such as the Joint Anti-Fascist Refugee Committee. Within organized liberal groups such as the American Veterans Committee, the Radical Left was already attempting to secure positions of influence, and a concious drive was planned to move into liberal [groups]. . . .

Radical Left strategists reasoned that control of the CIO and organized liberalism would give them access to power in the Democratic party. . . .

As for the established conservative groups, the themes of the Radical Right have been echoing in such conservative strongholds as the National Association of Manufacturers, the National Association of Real Estate Boards, the American Legion, and the Daughters of the American Revolution. Other conservative groups, such as the American Medical Association, American Bar Association, and American Farm Bureau Federation, are now facing ideological penetration.

If it can rally enough business and conservative group support, the Radical Right can look forward to influence in the Republican party. . . .

Unlike Senator McCarthy and the loose apparatus of "McCarthyism," the Radical Right is fervently organizational today. Once people attending Radical Right rallies have been alarmed by tales of Communist betrayal in Washington and imminent collapse of the nation — as those of the Radical Left were alarmed by tales of impending fascism — the organizers carefully follow up by leading the new recruits into a total "life-way" apparatus. Followers are put to work in "Americanist" cadres. In the Birch Society, there are home "study groups" where tape recordings and films are played. . . .

In a lovely parallel with the American Communist party, there are now bookstores throughout the nation which serve as nerve centers for local Radical Right activity: the Betsy Ross Bookshop in Los Angeles; the Pro-Blue Patriotic Book Store in Torrance, California; and the Anti-Communist Bookstore in Fort Lauderdale, Florida, are only a few of the dozens now in existence. The functions of such places were recently described by a *New York Times* report on Radical Right bookstores in California: Radical Right books and pamphlets are sold, speakers' names listed, rallies advertised, petitions left for signing, and membership and mailing lists traded among various local groups.

Like the Radical Left, the Radical Right knows how to manipulate the appeals of martyrdom. The Radical Right begins with Senator McCarthy, the patron saint driven to his death by the Communists, and moves on to "Americanists" such as General Edwin A. Walker who are "hounded" from positions in the military, the colleges, the communications media, and government because they dare to tell "the Truth." Thus a leading article in *American Opinion,* the Birch organ, could have cribbed a paragraph from a Radical Left organ of 1946 in its lament that today America sees "witch-hunting of patriots . . . , character assassination, and wild accusations against anybody who dares ask questions and insist upon answers." It is also an article of faith for both movements that all of these powerful persecuting forces can be wiped out in a flash by revealing "the Truth" to an "angry people.". . .[28]

Thus the basic issue concerning the true nature of extremism frequently involves more invective than enlightenment. In fact, the willingness of extremists to dismiss the whole subject by calling a participant "a slimy character," as they did Gordon Hall, illustrates the utter contempt they have for the issue itself.

The Torrid Issue: How Dangerous Is Extremism?

Just how threatening is extremism? Any group which is labeled extremist might logically reply that those who fear them are really the ones suffering from paranoia. In certain instances, this could be the case.

It should be clear by this time that the far left and the far right view each other with some alarm and foreboding. We could expect this. It is when people in the middle of the political spectrum become aroused that sparks fly. Impending violence brings a swift and sharp reaction by those who represent the middle of the spectrum — the government.

Police say they have arrested 20 members of the super-secret, right-wing Minutemen organization, seizing tons of ammunition and weapons and breaking up what they called a plot to blow up three private camps in New York State, New Jersey and Connecticut.

In lightning predawn raids Sunday in Queens, Westchester County, on Long Island, and at Syracuse, more than a hundred state, county and local police went into action. They said they confiscated arsenals that included mortars, bazookas, machine guns, semiautomatic rifles, home-

---

[28] *Ibid.,* pp. 26–29.

326   made bombs, machetes, crossbows, garroting nooses, and a million rounds of ammunition.

The raids were announced by Queens Dist. Atty. Nat H. Hentel. He would not disclose the identity of the target camps, but added that the Minutemen group is dedicated to destroying "Communist, left-wing and liberal installations of any kind."

Hentel said the camps were slated for destruction Sunday, a few days after the start of the hunting season.

Six of the men, all dressed in hunting garb, were seized in a Queen's diner. Officers said guns, ammunition and bombs were found in the car of one of them. Another man was arrested in his Katonah, Westchester County home.

Hentel charged the men with conspiracy to commit arson and most received additional charges of violation of the antiweapons law and unlawful assembly.

During an investigation which began last January, police said they learned the following about the Minutemen:

That they tried to infiltrate the Army Reserve's 11th Special Forces — the "Green Berets" — at Miller Field, Staten Island, to learn guerrilla tactics.

That members of the group distributed racist literature in Queens, purporting to be from Negro extremists and urging Negroes to "kill white devils."

Robert B. DePugh of Norborne, Mo., who established the Minutemen six years ago, was not available for comment. DePugh also is national chairman of the newly organized Patriotic party.

Membership in the Minutemen has been estimated from a few thousand to 100,000.

As Dist. Atty. Nat H. Hentel talked to reporters in his Queens office, agents streamed in carrying armloads of guns, boxes of ammunition and radio equipment.

"Lots more equipment is coming in by the truckload," Hentel said, adding:

"This is the biggest haul of weapons and death-dealing material seized in this area in the memory of law-enforcement officers."

Members of the organization are supposed to train themselves in guerrilla warfare. They are organized into small bands of from five to 15 and the membership is so secret that there is no apparent way for one Minuteman to recognize another unless they are from the same band.[29]

It is when there are no caches of arms or evidence of violence that debate ensues. Does mere advocacy of violence, for example, constitute

[29] *The Denver Post* (October 26, 1966), pp. 1, 5.

a sufficient threat to warrant action that would put a group out of business or its leaders in jail? Gordon Hall doesn't consider the nonviolent extremist to be a great threat, although he acknowledges the possibility of danger on the right and left.

"I don't feel that we're about to be engulfed by either the Marxist left or the know-nothing right," he said during an interview.

"On the other hand, I don't think there's anything in our system that insures that we never will be. If we should have a really bad economic collapse, the country could go either way, left or right.

"Should the left ever get control, at least they would know what to do with power. They have a general program, with China and Castro and the Soviet Union for models.

"But a right-wing coup would be something else entirely. I've studied and talked with the rightist leaders enough to know that they don't have a glimmer of what they would do about running the country. If Welch ever took over, he'd probably be toppled an hour later by the Minutemen."

Hall estimates that about seven million Americans are involved in fringe politics. He counts about 1,000 organizations on the ultra-right and about 150 on the far left.

Of them all, the Birch Society is most likely to endure, he says, mainly because of the personality of Welch.

"He is a poor speaker — I call him the Casey Stengel of American radicalism. Yet he is a man who spent 35 years of his adult life in the mainstream of American business, and he has brought to the society all of the dynamics of a modern corporation."[30]

Senator Stephen Young, however, finds certain groups extremely dangerous, especially the John Birch Society.

When I express my conviction that the John Birch Society is the most dangerous organization in America, I perhaps give it an importance it does not merit. I do not think so.

The John Birch Society has introduced a new intelligence to the lunatic fringe by developing a formal structure more sophisticated than any other right-wing group. It has evolved secretive community-level cells, just as the Communists did. Its leader — its "little Hitler" — Robert Welch, maintains rigid control of programs and activities. Because of its secret nature, the society has drawn into its ranks and into its leadership ultra-respectable business and industrial leaders who shun participation in the more clamorous right-wing groups. They have money and influ-

---

[30] *The Denver Post* (October 26, 1966), p. 5.

328   ence and are willing to use both for the organization. The monetary support of these business leaders, plus that of the ordinary John Birch Society members, brings the society an estimated income of more than $1,500,000 a year. Since its founding in 1958 the society is believed to have attracted more than 60,000 members.

Mr. President, America has enough headaches in finding a course of action to meet the encroachments and challenges of international communism and Soviet and Red Chinese imperialism. We do not need the radical right to complicate matters. Every picture of a race riot, North or South, fomented by right-wing extremists, every American smeared by fellow Americans for his political beliefs, every reckless charge against responsible government officials by the demagogues of the right does more to serve the aims of international communism than 5,000 American Communists could hope to do.[31]

The question of whether extremism is dangerous is inextricably intertwined with the issues concerning proper action toward extremist individuals and groups. Hence, in the remainder of the chapter about the nature of extremist perils, we shall consider the set of issues that concern appropriate action in regard to extremist activity.

The Action Issue: What Do We Do About Extremism?

These issues take us "down to where the action is." The right to speak and print freely are cherished rights of every American. Extremists are Americans, too. This means that we must deal with some very "sticky" questions. Can a democratic nation, for example, be permitted to use democratic processes to vote themselves a dictatorship? At what point are utterances and assemblages sufficiently dangerous to warrant denial of the exercise of speech or advocacy? The courts have faced these questions for years. So have Congress, the president, and the U. S. Attorney-General.

J. Edgar Hoover of the Federal Bureau of Investigation called for education of the misled:

Today far too many self-styled experts on communism are plying the highways of America giving erroneous and distorted information. This causes hysteria, false alarms, misplaced apprehension by many of our citizens. We need enlightenment about communism — but this information must be factual, accurate and not tailored to echo personal idiosyncrasies. To quote an old aphorism, we need more light and less heat.[32]

---

[31] Senator Young in *Congressional Record*, 88th Cong., 1st sess. (August 15, 1963), p. 15177.

[32] J. Edgar Hoover, *Law Enforcement Bulletin* (April 1961), p. 2.

Somewhat in the same vein, Senator Kuchel proposed a program of **329**
persuasion, which would presumably include reeducation:

I am concerned about right-wing extremists, not because of the noise
they make, which, as with the vile Communists, is out of proportion to
their size. I am concerned because they are, after all, Americans, not
agents sworn to allegiance to a foreign power.

Astonishingly to me, I sometimes get letters from avowed Birchers
who furiously deny their leader has ever charged the Central Intelligence Agency is Communist-controlled, or that Dulles was a Communist,
or that NATO is a Communist-planned hoax.

And I find it equally hard to believe that the followers of the fright
peddlers are all wholly oblivious to the anti-Semitism, anti-Catholicism,
and outright racism of many of their "saviors.". . .

Can these cruelly swindled victims of the fright peddlers be shocked
into a reappraisal of their swindlers and be reclaimed as valuable and
effective contributors in the fight against the real enemy? I do not know.
But I believe it is time such an attempt be made.

Perhaps I am naive about this. Yet I feel there must be some — and
they belong to both political parties — who can be persuaded to join the
ranks again of sensible and decent anti-Communist, proAmericans. . . .[33]

Senator Young proposed that radical groups be prevented from using
tax loopholes, and he further suggested that their activities and propaganda be exposed for what they really are.

Mr. President, unfortunately today all American taxpayers are indirectly financing many of these vicious organizations. Although our laws
do not grant tax-exempt status to an organization, a substantial part of
whose activities is carrying on propaganda, there is increasing evidence
. . . that dozens of these groups are masquerading as educational and
religious organizations, flooding the country with partisan political
propaganda, and are financed by tax-free contributions from businessmen. . . .

I do not propose that committees of Congress caravan about the
country conducting investigations into the activities of the radical right. I
believe we have had enough investigations into the political beliefs of
free American citizens. However, I do propose that corrective action be
taken to close this tax loophole favoring these book-burners and witch-
hunters. . . .

. . . If they are to be restrained and to be prevented from giving

---

[33] Senator Kuchel, *Congressional Record*, 88th Cong., 1st sess. (May 2, 1963), p.
7640.

330   further solace and comfort to our Communist adversaries, they must be
subjected to constant exposure and relentless publicity. We must continue to show them as the demagogues they are. America is last with
them.[34]

> Senator Jacob Javits would engage the extremists in direct confronta-
> tion.

It should be pointed out that this danger is creeping up on the blind
side of Americans. Almost every American is opposed to communism.
However, it is important that we do what the Senator from California
has done in speaking out against those who would spread hate and plant
the seed of suspicion in the hearts of men. The thing to do is to take on
the rascals frontally, as the Senator has done, and speak out against
organizations like the Birch Society — and not every member of the Birch
Society necessarily feels that way — and speak out, not only here on the
floor of the Senate, unchallenged, but also in campaigns, as he has done,
where it can be a political danger to do so. That is where it counts. The
Senator from California has done that, as have the Senator from Colorado, the Senator from Minnesota, and others, including myself.

In speaking out in this way, we are ready to take the consequences.
That is where it really counts. It is a dramatic demonstration of our unity
in opposition to this kind of imposition on the feelings of the American
people, by people who might just as well have as their goal the destruction of our society.[35]

> Senator Young's and Senator Javits' demands for confrontation, ad-
> vertisement, and exposure did not meet with approval from all of those
> who shared their antipathy toward extremism. They claimed that such
> measures function only to sensationalize the group's activities and in-
> crease its prestige, standing, and even its membership.

Almost ever since they first started attracting national attention some
two years ago, the organizations of the so-called New Left had lacked the
one thing no radical political movement can really prosper long without
— someone to persecute them. The nation as a whole largely shrugged off
the New Left.

Then, two weeks ago, the Justice Department decided it would try
to force one of the New Left's noisier outfits, the W. E. B. Du Bois Clubs,
to register as a Communist front under the controversial Subversive

---

[34] Senator Young in *Congressional Record,* 88th Cong., 1st sess. (August 15, 1963),
p. 15178.
   [35] The Honorable Jacob Javits, U. S. Senator from New York, *Congressional
Record,* 88th Cong., 1st sess. (May 2, 1963), p. 7641.

Activities Control Act of 1950. The Du Bois Clubs, launched on cam- puses three years ago to promote militant civil-rights action, are Marxist oriented. The department's action put the clubs smack on the front pages, and overnight, the picture changed completely. In New York, some 200 neighborhood toughs descended on a Du Bois Club headquar- ters in Brooklyn, pelted the members with eggs and garbage cans and pummeled as many as they could get their hands on. In San Francisco, a massive dynamite charge shattered the Du Bois Club headquarters in what could have been a major tragedy.

By now, the radicals' response was in full swing. At Du Bois Club headquarters in Manhattan, a chalk-scrawled slogan proclaimed, "De- mocracy Lives!" and club officials reported that membership applications and contributions were rising steadily. In San Francisco, executive secre- tary Terence Hallinan (who said he thought the bombing might have been the work of a local motorcycle gang) denounced Attorney General Nicholas deB. Katzenbach and insisted that the whole thing was "an attempt to intimidate us and keep us from speaking out against the Vietnam war."

Strong support for the clubs was forthcoming from the American Civil Liberties Union, which wired Attorney General Katzenbach pro- testing the attempt to list the clubs as a Communist front, and labeled it "an effort to intimidate the organization from carrying on its unpopular program."[36]

Now, let's move from where the action is to the courts and the offices of the prosecutors. One thing has to be remembered about a court. It needs evidence. When there is clear evidence of attempts to overthrow the government, or conspiracy to do so, judicial remedy is quite swift and certain. This is also true of evidence of actual violence or acts that lead to violence. But when there is no evidence of actual violence or of a demonstrated attempt to overthrow the government as a result of the exercise of some basic freedom or right, court convictions are difficult to obtain.

Earlier in this century, after much wrangling and debate, the courts arrived at a crude measure for determining the presence of a serious or threatening danger flowing from the exercise of our basic freedoms. This was the famous "clear and present danger" test. The test required the existence of a "clear and present danger" before basic liberties and rights could be infringed by government action. In one case, Mr. Justice Holmes, speaking for the majority of the U. S. Supreme Court, said:

The question in every case is whether the words used are used in such circumstances and are of such a nature as to create a clear and

---

[36] Copyright (1966) by *Newsweek* (March 21, 1966), p. 35.

332   present danger that they will bring about substantive evils that Congress has a right to prevent. It is a question of proximity and degree.[37]

During the next thirty years, the "clear and present danger" test was applied in various ways by the Court. Twenty years later, however, Congress enacted the famous Smith Act, which was to raise questions about the test that Holmes enunciated. Among other things, the Smith Act said:

Sec. 2. (a) It shall be unlawful for any person —

(1) to knowingly or wilfully advocate, abet, advise, or teach the duty, necessity, desirability, or propriety of overthrowing or destroying any government in the United States by force or violence, or by the assassination of any officer of such government;

(2) with intent to cause the overthrow or destruction of any government in the United States, to print, publish, edit, issue, circulate, sell, distribute, or publicly display any written or printed matter advocating, advising, or teaching the duty, necessity, desirability, or propriety of overthrowing or destroying any government in the United States by force or violence;

(3) to organize or help to organize any society, group, or assembly of persons who teach, advocate, or encourage the overthrow or destruction of any government in the United States by force or violence; or to be or become a member of, or affiliate with, any such society, group, or assembly of persons, knowing the purpose thereof. . . .

Sec. 3. It shall be unlawful for any person to attempt to commit, or to conspire to commit, any of the acts prohibited by the provisions of . . . this title.[38]

As construed in Schenck and later cases, the "clear and present danger" test meant roughly that Congress and other governmental agencies could not infringe the exercise of a basic freedom if such exercise, say a speech or the printing of a pamphlet, did not result in some substantive evil. You could teach or preach the overthrow of the government, or you could advocate the burning of a church; but if neither you nor anyone else did anything subsequently about what you advocated or taught, governments could not infringe your right to say it or print and circulate it. The situation changed, however, when the Smith Act came up for interpretation in 1951. Speaking for the Court, Chief Justice Vinson referred to the Schenck case and then went into the "clear and present danger" test. He first pointed out that in the Schenck case:

---

[37] *Schenck* v. *United States*, 249 U. S. 47 at 52 (1919).
[38] 54 *Stat.* 671 (1939).

. . . The charge was causing and attempting to cause insubordination in the military forces and obstruct recruiting. The objectionable document denounced conscription and its most inciting sentence was, "You must do your share to maintain, support and uphold the rights of the people of this country." 249 U. S. at 51. Fifteen thousand copies were printed and some circulated. This insubstantial gesture toward insubordination in 1917 during war was held to be a clear and present danger of bringing about the evil of military insubordination.[39]

The Dennis case, on the other hand, involved several members of the American Communist party, including its national chairman, Gus Hall. All members were indicted for conspiring to overthrow the American government. Vinson first pointed out the following:

The obvious purpose of the statute is to protect existing Government, not from change by peaceable, lawful and constitutional means, but from change by violence, revolution and terrorism. That it is within the *power* of the Congress to protect the Government of the United States from armed rebellion is a proposition which requires little discussion. Whatever theoretical merit there may be to the argument that there is a "right" to rebellion against dictatorial governments is without force where the existing structure of the government provides for peaceful and orderly change. We reject any principle of governmental helplessness in the face of preparation for revolution, which principle, carried to its logical conclusion, must lead to anarchy. No one could conceive that it is not within the power of Congress to prohibit acts intended to overthrow the Government by force and violence. The question with which we are concerned here is not whether Congress has such *power*, but whether the *means* which it has employed conflict with the First and Fifth Amendments to the Constitution.[40]

Then Vinson spoke to the Holmes test:

In this case we are squarely presented with the application of the "clear and present danger" test, and must decide what that phrase imports. We first note that many of the cases in which this Court has reversed convictions by use of this or similar tests have been based on the fact that the interest which the State was attempting to protect was itself too insubstantial to warrant restriction of speech. . . . Overthrow of the Government by force and violence is certainly a substantial enough

---

[39] *Dennis* v. *United States,* 341 U. S. 494 at 504 (1951).
[40] *Ibid.* at 501.

334   interest for the Government to limit speech. Indeed, this is the ultimate value of any society, for if a society cannot protect its very structure from armed internal attack, it must follow that no subordinate value can be protected. If, then, this interest may be protected, the literal problem which is presented is what has been meant by the use of the phrase "clear and present danger" of the utterances bringing about the evil within the power of Congress to punish.

Obviously, the words cannot mean that before the Government may act, it must wait until the *putsch* is about to be executed, the plans have been laid and the signal is awaited. If Government is aware that a group aiming at its overthrow is attempting to indoctrinate its members and to commit them to a course whereby they will strike when the leaders feel the circumstances permit, action by the Government is required. The argument that there is no need for Government to concern itself, for Government is strong, it possesses ample powers to put down a rebellion, it may defeat the revolution with ease needs no answer. For that is not the question. Certainly an attempt to overthrow the Government by force, even though doomed from the outset because of inadequate numbers or power of the revolutionists, is a sufficient evil for Congress to prevent. The damage which such attempts create both physically and politically to a nation makes it impossible to measure the validity in terms of the probability of success, or the immediacy of a successful attempt. In the instant case the trial judge charged the jury that they could not convict unless they found that petitioners intended to overthrow the Government "as speedily as circumstances would permit." This does not mean, and could not properly mean, that they would not strike until there was certainty of success. What was meant was that the revolutionists would strike when they thought the time was ripe. We must therefore reject the contention that success or probability of success is the criterion. . . .[41]

The result was this: The connection of American communists with a foreign power and their advertised goal of overthrow of the American government by force of arms created a "clear and probable" danger, if not a present danger. If the probability of danger was high, Congress and other authorities could act to prevent the danger. This was toned down a bit in the *Yates Case* in 1957, when Justice John Marshall Harlan, speaking for a majority of the Court, said that preaching or advocating overthrow of the government *in the abstract* is a crime only if it urges people to do something rather than believe something.[42]

The question of "danger" arose again during the Vietnam war. This

---

[41] *Ibid.* at 508.
[42] *Yates* v. *United States*, 354 U. S. 298 (1957).

time the challenge came from an internationally distinguished pediatrician and expert on child care, Dr. Benjamin Spock, as well as from a host of other draft card burners. Spock was sentenced to two years in jail for encouraging and supporting evasion of the Selective Service System's draft of young men. Interference with the draft was not unlike attempts of Schenck to encourage military insubordination. "Rebellion against the law is in the nature of treason," said the trial judge.

"Every week in this court, young men are sentenced to three years in prison for evading the draft," said Judge Ford. "It would be preposterous to sentence those young men and allow those who incited them to escape punishment."

Spock chose not to comment in the courtroom, but he wasted no time in demonstrating his determination to continue an outspoken opposition to the Vietnam war and the Selective Service System that helps fuel it. Leaving the courthouse, he joined 200 peace pickets in a march to a demonstration on Boston Common. Later he made a passionate political appeal in a news conference at the Parker House hotel, "I am not convinced I broke any law," said Spock. "I will continue working against the war . . . The killing [of] American young men at the rate of 1,000 a month or 2,000 a month . . . could go on for years . . . This war could be stopped if a hundred million Americans stood up and said, 'Let's stop it.' "[43]

Is Spock an extremist? Are the editors of *Ramparts*?

The Government is considering the prosecution of four top editors of Ramparts magazine for alleged violations of the Selective Service laws.

The editors were taken before a special Federal grand jury in New York last month to testify about the magazine's cover of December, 1967, which depicted flaming draft cards bearing the names of four men. They were informed by the Government attorney that they were the "targets" of the investigation. . . .

"An indictment of the Ramparts editors," the 29-year-old president said in an interview yesterday, "must be interpreted as a direct and unmistakable attempt to close down the leading organ of dissent in the American press."

The disclosure of the investigation recalled the 1917 prosecution of The Masses, a Socialist journal that opposed the draft during World War I. The charges against the magazine and seven of its editors, including

---

[43] Copyright (1968) by *Newsweek* (July 22, 1968), p. 30.

336   Max Eastman and John Reed, were dismissed after two trials in which the juries were deadlocked.

One of the earliest cases involved Mathew Lyon who was arrested under the Alien and Sedition Act for an editorial comment about President John Adams. The President was dedicating a cannon and Mr. Lyon said that he hoped it would backfire and "blow his backside off."

Mr. Hinckle said that if the Government proceeded to indict the editors, "we can only conclude that they seek retribution."

"It doesn't take much imagination to understand why they'd want to put us out of business," he said. "We've exposed the C.I.A.'s undercover relationship with the National Student Association, we've consistently attacked the Vietnam war, we ran a piece charging that Johnson took payoffs from a gambler during his Senate tenure and we published portions of a book attacking Hubert Humphrey."[44]

Is Robert Shelton of the United Klans an extremist as he talks about the civil rights marchers in Selma, Alabama, and the trial of a Klan member for the murder of Mrs. Liuzzo, a marcher from Detroit?

Shelton: . . . Those beatniks, tennis-shoe wearers, sex perverts at Selma were carrying the United Nations flag for anybody to see.

Playboy: Well, it's not a crime to carry a UN flag, of course. But even if your description of the Selma marchers were accurate, how is it relevant to the innocence or guilt of the Klansmen accused of Mrs. Liuzzo's murder?

Shelton: It is further evidence of the pressure of the influx of these outsiders, of the Federal Government, of the whole international conspiracy to break the back of the Klan. They will stoop to any level. They were offering only the word of a pimp, Gary Rowe [Rowe was the F.B.I. witness at the trial]. He is not a real informer; he is a political prostitute. I have letters from relatives of his in Savannah, Georgia, saying he is the lowest scum on earth. Why, just two days before the shooting, he pistol-whipped a man in Birmingham, beat him senseless to the ground with the butt of his pistol.

Playboy: What was the man's name?

Shelton: The man was a religious member of a sect that doesn't permit violence, so he just held his arms. . . .[45]

---

[44] *The New York Times* (July 18, 1968), p. C4.
[45] Interview with Robert Shelton, *Playboy* (August 1965), p. 48.

Are all of the above speakers prototypes of extremism or not? Again, **337** in each case, it depends considerably upon where you, the observer, stand politically and upon what you believe. On the other hand, it is not so simple as that because there may be a limit to what the political and social system can withstand. Severe outbreaks of violence and extremism do pose threats to political and social stability; extremist activity might at some moment combine with the right circumstances and forces to produce results that not even an extremist would desire.

Soldiers: The Widening Front

Let men everywhere . . . know that a
strong, confident, vigilant
America stands ready to seek an
honorable peace . . . and to
defend an honored cause, whatever
the price, whatever the burden, whatever
the sacrifices that duty may require.

Lyndon B. Johnson

Hell no! We won't go!

Students

The Cold War

A "cold war" began after World War II. Before that time, our military objectives had been fairly clear. Armies confronted each other, fought, and finally one side capitulated and the conflict ended with a formal surrender. The identity of the enemy was obvious, there was a definite beginning and ending of hostilities, and there was no doubt as to who won and who lost.

Since World War II, we have been engaged in military actions that are less clear cut and more difficult to understand. The identity of the real enemy is not always obvious. The conflict has continued with various degrees of intensity (hotness and coldness) and with no sharply defined beginning and ending. There have been no formal declarations of war, and there have been no surrenders or peace treaties in the traditional sense. Neither have there been any obvious winners or losers. Finally, our objectives have sometimes been obscure or at least not clearly understood by "the man in the street."

The concept of "limited wars" for "limited objectives" has received little popular support. Probably most Americans, in any given conflict situation, tend to react in terms of "Let's win or get out."

This chapter will sketch the major international events during the decade 1945–1954, provide a chronology of United States involvement in

340 Vietnam since 1954, and conclude with a discussion of the issues surrounding the Vietnam conflict.

It is the opinion of the authors that Vietnam cannot be lifted out of the context of international affairs and considered in isolation, apart from the trends of recent history. It is for this reason that we have made an attempt to place Vietnam in historical perspective.

The Reich that was to have lived a thousand years crashed to ruin on May 7, 1945, when the German army collapsed. On September 2 of the same year, Japan signed an unconditional surrender on the decks of the U.S.S. Missouri.

In the meantime forty-eight nations met on April 25, 1945, at San Francisco, to debate the Dumbarton Oaks plan for a United Nations Organization. The UN came into being on October 24, 1945. The UN Charter, as finally drafted, was approved by the Senate 89–2. Apparently the United States was no longer an isolationist nation. In his fourth inaugural address, President Roosevelt had said:

We have learned that we cannot live alone, at peace; that our own well-being is dependent upon the well-being of other nations far away. We have learned that we must live as men and not as ostriches, nor as dogs in the manger. We have learned to be citizens of the world, members of the human community.

Perhaps most Americans agreed with him. At any rate the United States came to think of itself as the guardian of the "free world." The old great powers (Britain, France, Germany, and Japan) were exhausted. Only Russia and the United States remained strong — and Russia had taken a hard beating. Colonial peoples throughout the world rebelled against their old masters, who in many cases did little to prevent them from leaving "the empire."

The Russians quickly indicated that they had no intention of leaving the areas they had overrun during the war. All of Eastern Europe came to be Russian-dominated; and as early as March 1946, Winston Churchill denounced Russian aggression in the now famous "Iron Curtain" speech at Fulton, Missouri.

The Truman Doctrine, the Marshall Plan, and the Berlin Blockade

The Germans had been cleared out of Greece in 1944 by the British, who then attempted to keep order. By early 1947, however, Britain notified the United States that it had to withdraw its forces. At that time, Communists in Bulgaria, Albania, and Yugoslavia were assisting Greek rebels in a civil war, and it appeared that they would be successful. In the meantime, Russia had been menacing Turkey and Iran.

In this crisis, President Truman enunciated what came to be called the Truman Doctrine: "The seeds of totalitarianism are nurtured by misery and want," he said. "They reach their full growth when the hope of a people for a better life has died. We must keep that hope alive." Congress responded by appropriating $300 million to aid Greece and $100 million for Turkey. These two countries did not come under Russian domination, presumably because of American military and economic aid.

Two years after the end of the fighting with Germany, all of Eastern Europe was closed off behind the Iron Curtain, and Western Europe was torn by internal strife and low productivity. To reverse the trend, Secretary of State George Marshall proposed a joint program of recovery, subsidized by the United States, but with the recipient countries assessing their needs and providing the labor force.

Sixteen countries — none from behind the Iron Curtain — asked to participate, and they received some $12 billion in mutual assistance during the next four years. By the end of 1951, the Marshall Plan countries had raised their industrial production index to a level that was 50 percent higher than it had been in the prewar period 1936–38.

On April 1, 1948 (two days before President Truman signed the Marshall Plan bill), the Russians blockaded the city of Berlin. At the close of the war, Germany had been divided into four zones occupied by the United States, Britain, France, and Russia respectively, except that the capital city of Berlin (in the Russian zone) was jointly occupied by the four powers. Berlin was thus an "island" within Russian-occupied Germany. The response of the United States and Britain to the Russian blockade was to establish the "Berlin Airlift," which at its peak carried three thousand tons of food and medicines per day, in planes that were landing at three-minute intervals. Eventually the blockade was lifted without an armed confrontation.

In the meantime, Czechoslovakia had been nudged over into the Russian bloc.

The Formation of NATO, Russian A-Bombs, and the Collapse of Nationalist China

On April 4, 1949, the foreign ministers of the United States, Britain, France, and nine other countries signed the North Atlantic Treaty Organization (NATO) and agreed that "an armed attack against one . . . shall be considered an armed attack against all." Not long afterward, in September 1949, President Truman announced: "We have evidence that . . . an atomic explosion has occurred in the U.S.S.R."

World War II interrupted a long conflict between the Chinese Communists and the Chinese Nationalists. During the war, the United States provided substantial assistance to Nationalist China as part of the resistance to Japan. When the war ended, the civil conflict resumed, and the United States continued to support the Nationalist forces under Chiang Kai-shek. Despite United States assistance, the Communist forces swept through China in 1949, and the remnants of General Chiang's army were forced to escape to Formosa.

Korea

NATO had been organized to contain Russia in Europe, but the next blow fell on the opposite side of the world in Korea, a former Japanese colony. At the close of the war with Japan, Korea had been occupied by Russia in the North and the United States in the South. Eventually, the dividing line came to be recognized as the 38th parallel. On June 26, 1950, the North Korean army, equipped with Russian tanks and other matériel, broke across the 38th parallel and moved toward the ancient gates of Seoul. The next day, President Truman announced that he was sending air and naval units to Korea, and the UN Security Council (with Russia absent) called on member nations to help repel aggression in Korea. UN troops were first forced to retreat to the southeast corner of Korea, but later they moved back north beyond the 38th parallel toward the Yalu River. At that point, large numbers of Chinese "volunteers" came across the border to assist the North Koreans. After three years and 400,000 UN casualties, a truce was signed on June 27, 1953, with the boundary line approximately where it had been when the conflict started.

Vietnam: A Chronology

One year after the Korean truce, the French in Vietnam were defeated at Dien Bien Phu, ending 70 years of French rule. It was also the end of a 9-year struggle for independence started by Ho Chi Minh in 1945.

The Declaration of Independence of the Democratic Republic of Vietnam (September 2, 1945) began with these familiar words:

All men are created equal. They are endowed by their Creator with certain inalienable rights, among these are Life, Liberty, and the pursuit of Happiness.

During the war years, an independence movement called the "Vietminh" had been formed. The Vietminh had as their slogan "Neither the French nor the Japanese as masters: For the Independence of Vietnam." After the surrender of Japan, this group assumed power over all of Vietnam — but only very briefly.

France Returns to Vietnam

Under the terms of the Potsdam Conference, the British were to occupy southeastern Asia; but they divided the occupation of Vietnam with China. For occupation purposes, the dividing line was set at the 16th parallel, with Nationalist China in the north and Britain in the south. The principal mission of both the Chinese and British was presumed to be to disarm and repatriate the defeated Japanese.

The Chinese recognized the *de facto* government of the Vietminh in Hanoi and, after some months of selective looting, they withdrew. The British, however, did not recognize the Vietminh; they established a system of military government. In the process, they also invited, or permitted, the French to return. By Christmas (1945), there were 50,000 French troops in South Vietnam, and the British prepared to withdraw.

In 1948 the French installed former emperor Bao Dai as chief of state in Saigon to unify the nation and to weaken the forces of Ho Chi Minh. Apparently Bao Dai's return accomplished neither purpose.

The Beginnings of U. S. Involvement

By 1950 the Ho Chi Minh government had been recognized by both Communist China and the Soviet Union. These recognitions prompted Secretary of State Dean Acheson to say that this ". . . should remove any illusion as to the 'nationalist' character of Ho Chi Minh's aims and reveals Ho in his true colors as the mortal enemy of native independence in Indochina."[1] At this point in history, the United States had been involved for five years in resisting Russian expansionist moves and had witnessed the communist victory in China. Then in 1950, the North Koreans had launched their attack across the 38th parallel. The war against the French in Vietnam seemed to fit the same pattern — to be part of the same design of relentless communist expansion. On June 27, 1950 (after the outbreak of war in Korea), President Truman announced ". . . acceleration in the furnishing of military assistance to the forces of France and the associated states in Indochina and the dispatch of a military mission to provide close working relations with these forces."[2]

From June 1950 to May 1954, when the French were defeated at Dien Bien Phu, the United States provided $2.6 billion worth of military and economic aid to the French in Vietnam, no less than 80 per cent of the total cost of the French war effort.[3]

The Geneva Conference

The agreements reached at the Geneva Conference (May to July 1954) formally ended the French-Indochinese War. The Geneva Conference produced two documents. The first provided for a cessation of hostilities, divided the country along the 17th parallel pending reunification through general elections, granted 300 days for Vietnamese to move

---

[1] Department of State *Bulletin* (February 13, 1950), p. 244.
[2] Department of State *Bulletin* (July 5, 1950), p. 5.
[3] Theodore Draper, *Abuse of Power* (New York: Viking Press, 1967), p. 26.

344   either north or south as they pleased, prohibited any increase in military forces or equipment in either zone, and created an International Control Commission (India, Canada, Poland) to ensure compliance with the agreement. This document was signed by France and North Vietnam only.

The second document expressed approval of the first one and fixed July 1956 as the date for the general elections. This document was *not* signed by any of the members of the conference (Britain, the Soviet Union, France, Communist China, Cambodia, Laos, North Vietnam, South Vietnam and the United States), but they all supported it verbally except South Vietnam and the United States.

The Geneva Agreement also established Laos and Cambodia as independent states. France's role in Indochina was ended.

Dominoes and SEATO

On April 7, 1954, President Eisenhower said:

Finally, you have broader considerations that might follow what you would call the 'falling domino' principle. You have a row of dominoes set up, you knock over the first one, and what will happen to the last one is a certainty that it will go over very quickly.[4]

Secretary of State John Foster Dulles followed up on the "domino theory" by unsuccessfully attempting to convince the British that if Vietnam fell, Thailand, Malaya, Burma, and the rest of Indochina would go next.

Admiral Radford, Chairman of the Joint Chiefs of Staff, supported this view but was opposed by the Army's General Gavin and Army Chief of Staff General Ridgway. General Ridgway is purported to have said that if two million troops were sent to Vietnam, they would be "swallowed up." The Army's point of view prevailed and there was no direct military intervention in Vietnam in 1954.

Even though the United States decided against military intervention in 1954, it did attempt to gain some support for such an eventuality through the formation of the Southeast Asia Treaty Organization (SEATO). The signatories to SEATO were Australia, France, New Zealand, Pakistan, the Philippines, Thailand, Britain, and the United States. SEATO was billed as another NATO, but it was considerably less than that. It was, in fact, a rather vague and permissive document. Perhaps the most significant language appeared in Article 4, Sections 1 and 2, which are reproduced below:

Article 4. 1. Each party recognizes that aggression by means of armed attack in the treaty area against any of the parties or against any

---

[4] Quoted by Draper, *Abuse of Power,* p. 30.

State or territory which the parties by unanimous agreement may hereafter designate would endanger its own peace and safety, and agrees
that it will in that event act to meet the common danger in accordance
with its constitutional processes. Measures taken under this paragraph
shall be immediately reported to the Security Council of the United
Nations.

2. If, in the opinion of any of the parties, the inviolability or the
integrity of the territory or the sovereignty or political independence of
any party in the treaty area or of any other State or territory to which the
provisions of paragraph 1 of this Article from time to time apply is
threatened in any way other than by armed attack or is affected or
threatened by any fact or situation which might endanger the peace of
the area, the parties shall consult immediately in order to agree on the
measures which should be taken for the common defense.

American Aid

The Geneva Agreement was signed on July 20, 1954; the SEATO
treaty was concluded on October 14; and on October 23, President
Eisenhower wrote President Diem:

I am . . . instructing the American Ambassador to Vietnam
[Donald R. Heath] to examine with you in your capacity as Chief of
Government, how an intelligent program of American aid given directly
to your Government can serve to assist Vietnam in its present hour of
trial, provided that your Government is prepared to give assurances as to
the standards of performance it would be able to maintain in the event
such aid were supplied.

The purpose of this offer is to assist the Government of Vietnam in
developing and maintaining a strong, viable state, capable of resisting
attempted subversion or aggression through military means.

The United States Military Assistance Advisory Group assumed responsibility for training the South Vietnamese Army in 1955 with a few
advisers. This number rose slowly to 685 men in 1960. Richard N. Goodwin, Assistant to Presidents Kennedy and Johnson, continues:

Next, as terror and attack mounted — though still on a small scale —
under President Kennedy, the American military presence began to
increase. It consisted of advisers, instructed to train, help, counsel, but
not to fight. Late in 1961, we suffered our first military casualty. By the
end of that year, there were three thousand American troops in South
Vietnam; by the end of the next year, eleven thousand; by the end of
1963, sixteen thousand.

346   At every step, it seemed to many that the struggle was almost won. Who, in good conscience, and in the interests of the United States, could refuse the small additional help that did not seem to risk major conflict yet might prevent a Communist takeover?[5]

President Kennedy had originally been opposed to the use of American combat forces in Vietnam. Arthur Schlesinger quotes him as saying, "It's like taking a drink. The effect wears off, and you have to take another." Nevertheless, on the advice of General Maxwell D. Taylor, Walt W. Rostow of the State Department, and others, Kennedy did authorize modest increases in military personnel "with combat capabilities." But, as we have noted, there were only 16,000 American troops in Vietnam by the end of 1963.

The turning point of the Vietnam conflict occurred on August 2, 1964, when three North Vietnamese torpedo boats fired on the United States destroyer *Maddox* in the Gulf of Tonkin about 30 miles off the coast. Two days later, enemy torpedo boats again fired at the *Maddox* and another destroyer, the *C. Turner Joy,* this time about 65 miles off the coast of North Vietnam. That same day (August 4), President Johnson ordered retaliatory air attacks on North Vietnamese torpedo boat bases and their oil storage depots. The President also asked for congressional approval to use whatever military measures he deemed necessary in Vietnam. By a vote of 88–2 in the Senate (only Senators Morse and Gruening dissented) and a vote of 416–0 in the House, Congress passed the so-called Gulf of Tonkin Resolution (P.L. 88–408, August 10, 1964). This resolution read in part:

That the Congress approves and supports the determination of the President, as Commander in Chief, to take all necessary measures to repel any armed attack against the forces of the United States and to prevent further aggression. . . .

. . . the United States is, therefore, prepared, as the President determines, to take all necessary steps, including the use of armed force, to assist any member or protocol state of the Southeast Asia Collective Defense Treaty requesting assistance in defense of its freedom.

On February 7, 1965, air attacks on North Vietnam began; and by the end of 1965, some 150,000 American troops had been committed. The war continued to escalate, despite the consistently optimistic reports of military commanders, until there were over half a million American troops in or near Vietnam by 1968.

---

[5] Richard N. Goodwin, *Triumph or Tragedy: Reflections on Vietnam* (New York: Vintage Books, 1966), p. 29.

On March 31 of that year, a president who had been elected by the **347** largest popular majority in American history just four short years earlier, declined to run for another term mainly because of public dissatisfaction with the Vietnam War.

In Dubious Battle

The selections that follow include representative statements from some of the most influential policy-makers involved with Vietnam.

Students: "Hell No! We Won't Go!"

Students, like the rest of the population, were divided in their reactions to Vietnam. ROTC registrations went up but so did draft card burning, the number of escapes to Canada, and student protests generally. The following letter to *Grope*, a student publication, catches the mood of the students who were opposed to Vietnam.

Editor:

My ancestors arrived in this great country nineteen years before the American Revolutionary War, just in time to join in the fight and help the cause of freedom. Although I have no records to prove it, family legend has it that one of my great great great grandfathers was decorated for valor at Bunker Hill.

We have always been poor and uneducated, but we love our country and we have always pitched in the battle when the time came. We have always known our duty, and when it calls, and our country and the cause of freedom must be defended, we have always answered.

When the War of 1812 came along, we were there, fighting along side the others against the dirty British. Then the Mexican War started up and we fought bravely against the dirty Mexicans. One of my great great uncles personally met Sam Houston.

During the Civil War just about our whole family was killed off; half our family fought against the dirty northerners, and half our family fought against the dirty southerners. Then came that great time of peace, and my family restored itself, and was ready for action in the Spanish-American War.

My grandfather was right there riding with old Colonel Roosevelt up San Juan Hill, killing those dirty Spaniards right and left.

Then the dirty Northerners and the dirty Southerners and the dirty British and the dirty Mexicans and the dirty Spaniards all joined together in a wonderful gesture to kill off the dirty Germans.

We thought we had them whipped, but a generation later (my

348   father this time) it was necessary to join with the dirty Russians (they quit on us in World War I) and whip those dirty Germans again.

Then we were ready as my brother bravely defended us against the dirty Chinese in the Korean War, joining hands with the dirty Germans, dirty British, dirty Spaniards, etc.

Yes, we may be poor and uneducated, but we have always been there when our leaders said our nation was in trouble.

Now we are involved in a great conflict in Vietnam, and your publication has been telling us it does not serve the cause of peace. It is you un-American unpatriotic types who are destroying freedom and the great traditions of our country. My family has always served the cause of peace. Where are your principles?

Freedom Lover[6]

Ho Chi Minh

For over forty years, Ho Chi Minh (born in 1890) was the acknowledged leader of the revolutionary communist forces in Vietnam. In his report to the Second National Congress of the Vietnam Workers' Party in February 1951, Ho Chi Minh gave his version of the history of World War II and the events that followed it. At the time of this speech, Vietnam was at war with France. Brief excerpts from this lengthy report are reproduced below.

On January 6, 1930, our Party came into being.

After the success of the Russian October Revolution, Lenin promoted the setting up of the Communist International. Since that time, the international proletariat and the world revolution have become a great family, and our Party is one of its youngest members.

Marx, Engels, Lenin, and Stalin are the common teachers for the world revolution. Comrade Mao Tse-tung has skillfully "Sinicized" the ideology of Marx, Engels, Lenin, and Stalin, correctly applied it to the practical situation of China, and has led the Chinese Revolution to complete victory.

Owing to geographical, historical, economic, and cultural conditions, the Chinese Revolution exerted a great influence on the Vietnamese revolution, which had to learn and indeed has learned many experiences from it.

Thanks to the experiences of the Chinese Revolution and to Mao Tse-tung's thoughts, we have further understood the ideology of Marx, Engels, Lenin, and Stalin and consequently scored many successes. This

---

[6] *Grope,* an occasional publication of the Colorado State University *Collegian* (March 29, 1966), p. 2.

the Vietnamese revolutionaries must engrave on their minds and be grateful for. . . .

Period from 1939 to 1945. The great events in this period in our country and in the world occurred only ten years ago. Many people witnessed them and they are still fresh in the memory of many of us. I shall recall only some principal ones:

In 1939, World War II broke out. At first, it was an imperialist war between the German, Italian, and Japanese fascist imperialists on the one side and the British, French, and American imperialists on the other.

In June, 1941, the German fascists attacked the Soviet Union, the fortress of the world revolution, and the latter had to fight back and to ally with the British and Americans against the fascist camp. Henceforward, the war was waged between the democratic camp and the fascist camp.

Owing to the enormous forces of the Red Army and the Soviet people, and Stalin's correct strategy, in May, 1945, Germany was crushed and in August, 1945, Japan surrendered. The democratic camp won complete victory. . . .

Thanks to the clear-sighted and resolute leadership of our Party and the solidarity and enthusiasm of the entire people within and without the Viet Minh Front, the August Revolution was successful.

Not only the toiling classes and people but also the oppressed people in other countries can be proud that this is the first time in the revolutionary history of colonial and semicolonial peoples in which a party only fifteen years of age has led the revolution to success and seized power throughout the country.

On our part, we must bear in mind that our success was due to the great victory of the Soviet Red Army which had defeated fascist Japan, to the friendly assistance of international solidarity, to the close unity of our entire people, and to the heroic sacrifice of our revolutionary predecessors. . . .

On September 2, 1945, the Government of the Democratic Republic of Viet-Nam declared to the world that Viet-Nam had the right to be independent, and put into practice democratic freedoms in the country. . . .

The Difficulties of the Party and Government. As soon as the people's power came into existence, it met with great difficulties.

Due to the policy of ruthless exploitation by the Japanese and the French, within only half a year (end of 1944 and beginning of 1945) more than 2 million people in the North died of starvation.

We were independent for hardly one month when the British troops entered the South. They allegedly came to disarm the Japanese army, but were in reality an expeditionary corps helping the French colonialists in their attempt to reoccupy our country.

The Kuomintang troops entered the North under the same pretext, but actually they had three wicked aims: (1) to annihilate our Party, (2) to smash the Viet Minh Front, and (3) to help the Vietnamese reactionaries overthrow the people's power in order to set up a reactionary government under their sway. . . .

When the French deliberately provoked war, we could no longer put up with them, and the nation-wide war broke out.

The Long-term Resistance War. The enemy schemed a lightning war. As they wanted to attack swiftly and win swiftly, our Party and Government put forth the slogan "Long-term Resistance War." The enemy plotted to sow dissension among us, so our slogan was "Unity of the Entire People." Therefore, right from the start, our strategy prevailed over the enemy's. . . .

At the beginning of the Resistance War our army was young. Though full of heroism, it lacked weapons, experience, officers, everything.

The enemy army was well known in the world. They had navy, infantry, and air forces. Moreover, they were supported by the British and American imperialists, especially by the latter.

The difference between our forces and the enemy's was so great that there were at the time people who likened our Resistance War to a "locust fighting an elephant."

It was so if things were seen from the material side, in their actual conditions and with a narrow mind. We had then to oppose airplanes and cannons with bamboo sticks. But guided by Marxism-Leninism, our Party did not look only at the present but also at the future and had firm confidence in the spirit and forces of the masses, of the nation. Therefore we resolutely told the wavering and pessimistic people that "Today the locust fights the elephant, but tomorrow the elephant will be disemboweled." . . .

New Situation and New Tasks. As is well known, the present world is divided into two distinct camps: the democratic camp and the antidemocratic camp.

The democratic camp is headed by the Soviet Union, including the socialist countries, and the new democracies in Europe and in Asia. It also embraces the oppressed nations which are struggling against aggressive imperialism and the democratic organizations and personalities in the capitalist countries. . . .

The antidemocratic camp is headed by the United States. Immediately after the end of World War II, the United States became the ringleader of imperialists and world reactionaries. Britain and France are its right and left hands and the reactionary governments in the East and the West its henchmen.

Aspiring to world hegemony, the United States brandishes dollars in one hand to lure the world people and an atomic bomb in the other to menace them.

Fourteen years later, his approach had not changed noticeably, as these excerpts from a speech to the National Assembly in April 1965 indicate.

Our National Assembly is holding the present session in a very urgent situation but full of enthusiasm and confidence. The movement to oppose the United States and save the country is seething everywhere. Many great successes have been recorded in both North and South Viet-Nam.

Over the past ten years, the U. S. imperialists and their henchmen have carried out an extremely ruthless war and have caused much grief to our compatriots in South Viet-Nam. Over the past few months, they have frenziedly expanded the war to North Viet-Nam. In defiance of the 1954 Geneva Agreements and international law, they have sent hundreds of aircraft and dozens of warships to bomb and strafe North Viet-Nam repeatedly. Laying bare themselves their piratical face, the U. S. aggressors are blatantly encroaching upon our country. They hope that by resorting to the force of weapons they can compel our 30 million compatriots to become their slaves. But they are grossly mistaken. They will certainly meet with ignominious defeat.

Our Vietnamese people are a heroic people. Over the past ten years or more, our 14 million compatriots in the South have overcome all hardships, made every sacrifice and struggled very valiantly. Starting with their bare hands, they have seized guns from the enemy to fight against the enemy, have recorded victory after victory, and are launching a continual attack inflicting upon the U. S. aggressors and the traitors ever greater defeats and causing them to be bogged down more and more deeply. The greater their defeats, the more frantically they resort to the most cruel means, such as using napalm bombs and toxic gas to massacre our compatriots in the South. It is because they are bogged down in South Viet-Nam that they have furiously attacked North Viet-Nam.

As the thief crying "stop, thief!" is a customary trick of theirs, the U. S. imperialists, who are the aggressors, have impudently slandered North Viet-Nam as committing "aggression" in South Viet-Nam. The U. S. imperialists are precisely the saboteurs of the Geneva Agreements, yet they have brazenly declared that because they wished to "restore peace" and "defend the Geneva Agreements" they brought U. S. troops to our country to carry out massacres and destruction. The U. S. imperialists are precisely those who are devastating our country and killing our people, yet they hypocritically declared that they would give $1 billion to the people in Viet-Nam and the other Southeast Asian countries to "develop their countries and improve their life."

U. S. President Johnson has also loudly threatened to resort to violence to subdue our people. This is a mere foolish illusion. Our people will definitely never be subjugated.

The Taylor plan has been frustrated. The MacNamara plan has also gone bankrupt. The "escalation" plan which the U. S. imperialists are now endeavoring to carry out in North Viet-Nam will certainly fail, too. The U. S. imperialists may send in dozens of thousands more U. S. officers and men and make all-out efforts to drag more troops of their satellite countries into this criminal war, but our army and people are resolved to fight and defeat them. . . .

Our people are very grateful to and highly value the fraternal solidarity and devoted assistance of the socialist countries, especially the Soviet Union and China, of the people in all continents who are actively supporting us in our struggle against the U. S. imperialist aggressors, the most cruel enemy of mankind. . . .

The Government of the Democratic Republic of Viet-Nam once again solemnly declares its unswerving stand: to resolutely defend Viet-Nam's independence, sovereignty, unity, and territorial integrity. Viet-Nam is one, the Vietnamese people are one, no one is allowed to infringe upon this sacred right of our people. The U. S. imperialists must respect the Geneva Agreements and withdraw from South Viet-Nam. That is the only way to solve the problem of war in Viet-Nam, to carry out the 1954 Geneva Agreements, to defend the peace in the Indochinese and Southeast Asian countries. There is no other solution. That is the answer of our people and Government to the U. S. imperialists.[7]

Senator Wayne Morse

Senator Wayne Morse was one of two senators who opposed the Gulf of Tonkin Resolution (the vote was 88–2) in 1964. Senator Morse had been in the minority on many issues and rather frequently had annoyed other senators by his belief in his own infallibility. At the same time he was respected (and sometimes feared) as "one of the best minds" in Congress. Reproduced below are excerpts from a Morse speech of 1965, when he stood almost alone in opposition to the Vietnam war. In the years that followed, he did not alter his position, and many congressmen and other Americans eventually came to agree with him.

---

[7] Address to the National Assembly, as printed in the *Vietnam Courier* (Hanoi) (April 15, 1965).

The daily American air raids on North Viet-Nam which began on February 7 and the landing of American troops, now numbering 45,000, on the mainland of Asia, are markers in the tragic failure of the Viet-Nam policy begun by this country in 1954. At that time, the many American voices who wanted the United States to join France in re-establishing French dominion over its old colony of Indochina were deterred by President Eisenhower's precondition that we would do so only if joined by Britain. British Prime Minister Churchill declined to embark on the venture, and after the French defeat at Dien Bien Phu, a peace conference was held at Geneva which produced the Geneva Accord of 1954.

Right up to the minute of that defeat, official French sources remained optimistic about the final outcome. French airpower was unchallenged; French armor and equipment were the best that American aid could furnish, and we furnished more material for her forces than France spent herself on the war.

Nonetheless, after eight years of fighting and after 240,000 casualties, the French people had had enough of war. Mendès-France became the premier on the promise to end it.

As the peace conference progressed among representatives of France, Britain, the United States, Russia, China, the Viet-Minh, Laos, Cambodia, and Viet-Nam, many Americans expressed a deep bitterness at what they viewed as a triumph for the Chinese Communists. The head of the U. S. military mission, General John W. O'Daniel, said on July 8, 1954, in a classic statement of the blindness to reality in Viet-Nam that has characterized an entire generation of French and later American military officers: "The war in Indochina can still be won without bringing in one single American soldier to fight. The Vietnamese have ample manpower and even today outnumber the enemy by 100,000 with superior firepower at least in a ratio of two to one and probably more. And we are ready to assist them in training an adequate national army for the security of their homeland."

The Senate Majority Leader at the time was Senator William Knowland of California. He called the Geneva Conference a step toward bringing China into the U. N., and declared he would resign his position as party leader in the Senate if Red China were admitted. For a time, it appeared that the United States representatives at Geneva would withdraw from the conference due to what was called "great Congressional pressure."

In the end, our Secretary of State did return home before the conference ended, leaving only an undersecretary to represent this country. And we did not sign the final product. We issued a statement saying only that we would regard the Accord as binding on all parties and "would view any renewal of the aggression in violation of the aforesaid agreements with grave concern." But in a separate statement in Washington, the President said: "The United States has not itself been party to or bound by the decisions taken by the Conference," attributing this position to the questionable contention that we were not a co-belligerent. . . .

The 1954 agreement provided for the withdrawal from Indochina of France, and the division of the country into three parts — Laos, Cambodia, and Viet-Nam. Each was to be free of military alignment and military aid from outside. Viet-Nam was divided into two zones for purposes of military occupation — North and South. In July of 1956, general elections to reunite the country under one government were to be held under the supervision of an International Control Commission.

Historical evidence of who began violating the agreement first is hard to come by. But it is certain that the most significant violation was the refusal of South Viet-Nam, now headed by Diem, to proceed with the elections. He pointed out that like the U. S., his "government" had not signed the agreement and was not bound to it.

Undoubtedly, the Viet-Minh under Ho Chi Minh would have won such a free election. President Eisenhower declares in his *Mandate for Change* that all the experts he talked to in that period believed Ho would get at least 80 per cent of the vote. Ho was the nationalist patriot of Viet-Nam who had our favor and our help in World War II when he organized local resistance to the Japanese occupation. Thereafter, he led the resistance to the effort of France to resume its prewar colonial dominion in Indochina. A Moscow-trained and avowed Communist, Ho had reflected the ancient Vietnamese hostility to the Chinese and was considered closer to Moscow than to Peking.

Our aid to South Viet-Nam ran about $200 million a year after 1954, in a country of only 14 million people. Even so, by 1963, Diem had become so remote from the general population and had allowed so much arbitrary power to be exercised by his family that more and more elements of the population went into opposition against him. The raids of the security police upon the Buddhists' pagodas, the suicide by fire of the monks, and the reaction against the terror of the police finally led to an overthrow of the Ngos that had at least the tacit support of the United States.

We made it quite clear that our interest was in the prosecution of the war against the rebels. What hindered that effort was bad and what helped it was good. When Diem no longer suited the American purpose, he was deposed.

Since then, the internal situation in Viet-Nam has steadily deteriorated. Putting together a government in Saigon became a major challenge to the U. S. embassy. The Viet-Cong have come to control more and more of the people and territory of the South.

With a regularity that was laughable in Western capitals that had abandoned colonialism years earlier, our top government officials went back and forth from Washington to Saigon, repeating the time-worn phrases that things never looked better, and that these additional "advisers" and these helicopters, and this new civic-action program in the hamlets, and then air raids on the North, would finally do the job of defeating the Viet-Cong.

Not once has any of these predictions proved accurate. The total of all the increments in aid has brought the cost of aid to South Viet-Nam alone to over $700 million a year, exclusive of the $700 million the President asked to pay the cost of the U. S. military operations. The original 600-man military mission of 1954 has grown to 45,000 in May, 1965. . . .

Over this whole dreary picture hangs China. At what point she may consider her territory to be threatened is anyone's guess. We found out in Korea that there are limits to where Western powers can conduct military operations on her near borders without drawing in Chinese manpower.

Altogether too many American officials brush aside all this recital of what went before. They insist that even if it was a mistake to take up where the French left off, that is all water over the dam and now we can do nothing but keep on fighting, else we will lose "face" and no one anywhere will believe we mean what we say.

But it is unthinkable to me that the United States should be talking about backing up a policy with full-scale war, if that is what it takes, when that policy admittedly was a mistake when it was started! How can any nation consider making war for reasons so many of its leaders agree were unsound?

How can a policy that was unsound to begin with ever be made to work? Are Americans so confident of the miracles to be wrought with nuclear bombs and billion-dollar aid programs that we think they will make a success of anything, no matter how badly conceived? I fear this is our assumption.

Considered on the facts of what it has cost so far and what it has achieved, the Eisenhower-Kennedy-Johnson policy in Viet-Nam has been a total failure. It has not saved the area from communism, nor from war. Its fruits today are: (1) the unifying of the large non-Communist nations of Asia — India, Japan, Pakistan, Indonesia — *against* the United States; (2) the exposure of the United States as the only foreign power engaging in the war in Viet-Nam, and a white Western power, at that; (3) the revelation that the overwhelming force of the United States is ineffective

356   when it operates through a "front" government against indigenous revolutionary forces. . . .

In my opinion, our effort to "save face" has lost us not only face in
Asia but much more. It is making enemies and frightened neutrals out of
people who once respected us. It is making the Communists look like
people whose main purpose is to rid Asia of unwanted white domination,
a purpose behind which the vast bulk of Asians are united. . . .

We must get over the idea that whoever we do not control in Asia is
against us. A modern epigram has been coined which says: "He who
would save face in Asia should keep his body in his own country." Some
form of neutralism for Viet-Nam would probably emerge from third-
party intervention. But a neutralism guaranteed by many nations, especially those of Asia itself, would do more to further our long-term
objective of containing communism in Asia than a war which comes
down to one of white man versus Asian. In that kind of war only
communism will prosper.[8]

Senator J. William Fulbright

Senator Fulbright, Chairman of the Senate Foreign Relations Committee, has been critical of American actions in Vietnam. In the passage that
follows, he points out some of the reasons for that criticism and his fears
for the United States.

When all the official rhetoric about aggression and the defense of
freedom and the sanctity of our word has been cited and recited, we are
still left with two essential reasons for our involvement in Vietnam: the
view of communism as an evil philosophy and the view of ourselves as
God's avenging angels, whose sacred duty it is to combat evil philoso-
phies.

The view of communism as an evil philosophy is a distorting prism
through which we see projections of our own minds rather than what is
actually there. Looking through the prism, we see the Viet Cong who cut
the throats of village chiefs as savage murderers but American flyers who
incinerate unseen women and children with napalm as valiant fighters
for freedom; we see Viet Cong defections as the rejection of communism
but the much greater number of defections from the Saigon Army as
expressions of a simple desire to return to the farm; we see the puritan
discipline of life in Hanoi as enslavement but the chaos and corruption
of life in Saigon as liberty; we see Ho Chi Minh as a hated tyrant but
Nguyen Cao Ky as the defender of freedom; we see the Viet Cong as

---

[8] Senator Wayne Morse, Remarks at St. Mary's University, San Antonio, Texas,
May 14, 1965. Printed with permission of Senator Morse.

Hanoi's puppet and Hanoi as China's puppet but we see the Saigon government as America's stalwart ally; and finally, we see China, with no troops in South Vietnam, as the real aggressor while we, with hundreds of thousands of men, are resisting foreign intervention.

These perceptions are not patently wrong but they are distorted and exaggerated. It is true that whatever the fault may be on our side, the greater fault is with the communists, who have indeed betrayed agreements, subverted unoffending governments, and generally done a great deal to provoke our hostility. It is *our* shortcoming, however, that we have the power to overcome and, in so doing, to set a constructive example for our adversaries. As the more powerful belligerent by far, we are better able to take the initiative in showing some magnanimity, but we are not doing so. Instead we are treading a strident and dangerous course, a course that is all but unprecedented in American history. . . .

Our search for a solution to the Vietnamese war must begin with the general fact that nationalism is the strongest single political force in the world today and the specific fact, arising from the history to which I have referred, that in Vietnam the most effective nationalist movement is communist-controlled. We are compelled, therefore, once again to choose between opposition to communism and support of nationalism. I strongly recommend that for once we give priority to the latter. The dilemma is a cruel one, and one which we must hope to avoid in the future by timely and unstinting support of non-communist nationalist movements, but it is too late for that in Vietnam. I strongly recommend, therefore, that we seek to come to terms with both Hanoi and the Viet Cong, not, to be sure, by "turning tail and running," as the saying goes, but by conceding the Viet Cong a part in the government of South Vietnam. . . .

The war in Southeast Asia has affected the internal life of the United States in two important ways: it has diverted our energies from the Great Society program which began so promisingly, and it has generated the beginnings of a war fever in the minds of the American people and their leaders.

Despite brave talk about having both "guns and butter," the Vietnamese war has already had a destructive effect on the Great Society. The 89th Congress, which enacted so much important domestic legislation in 1965, enacted much less in 1966, partly, it is true, because of the unusual productivity of its first session but more because the Congress as a whole lost interest in the Great Society and became, politically and psychologically, a "war Congress."

There is a kind of Gresham's Law of public policy: fear drives out hope, security precedes welfare, and it is only to the extent that a country is successful in the prevention of bad things that it is set free to concentrate on those pursuits which renew the nation's strength and

bring happiness into the lives of its people. For twenty years beginning
in 1940 America was greatly preoccupied with external dangers and
accordingly neglectful of those aspects of domestic life which require
organized public programs and sizable public expenditures. The reason
for this, of course, was the exacting demands of two world wars and an
intractable cold war, which required the massive diversion of resources
from community life to national security. We felt ourselves compelled to
turn away from our hopes in order to concentrate on our fears and the
public happiness became a luxury to be postponed to some distant day
when the dangers besetting us would have disappeared. . . .

The turning away from constructive pursuits after so brief an inter-
lude is the first and at present more conspicuous fallout effect of the war
on American life. The second, no less damaging, is the stirring up of a
war fever in the minds of our people and leaders. It is only just now
getting under way, but as the war goes on, as the casualty lists grow
longer and affect more and more American homes, the fever will rise and
the patience of the American people will give way to mounting demands
for an expanded war, for a lightning blow that will get it over with at a
stroke. The American people have already registered their approval, if
the polls are to be believed, of the bombing of oil installations in Hanoi
and Haiphong, not, I think, out of bellicosity but in the vain hope that
these air strikes would shorten the war. If the war continues for a long
time, the demand for expanded hostilities will rise, first perhaps for a
blockade of the North Vietnamese ports; then, if that does not work, for
an all-out attack on the North Vietnamese air bases; then, if the North
Vietnamese withdraw their planes to Chinese bases, for a strike against
China; and then we will have a general Asian war if not a global nuclear
war. . . .

Under normal circumstances most people would immediately and
instinctively say "no" if asked whether they were proud of their country's
ability to kill and destroy. But in a war all that changes, and in the
course of dehumanizing an enemy — and this is the ultimate fallout from
any war — a man dehumanizes himself. It is not just the naturally belli-
cose, the thwarted or the twisted personalities, that become dehuman-
ized in a war. It is everyman: the good and decent citizen who looks
after his children, who is considerate of his neighbors and kind to
animals. It is he who ultimately prays the obscene "War Prayer" of Mark
Twain:

> . . . O Lord our God, help us to tear their soldiers to bloody
> shreds with our shells; help us to cover their smiling fields with
> the pale forms of their patriot dead; help us to drown the thunder
> of the guns with the shrieks of their wounded, writhing in pain;
> help us to lay waste their humble homes with a hurricane of fire;
> help us to wring the hearts of their unoffending widows with

unavailing grief; help us to turn them out roofless with their little children to wander unfriended the wastes of their desolated land in rags and hunger and thirst, sports of the sun flames of summer and the icy winds of winter, broken in spirit, worn with travail, imploring Thee for the refuge of the grave and denied it — for our sakes who adore Thee, Lord, blast their hopes, blight their lives, protract their bitter pilgrimage, make heavy their steps, water their way with their tears, stain the white snow with the blood of their wounded feet! We ask it, in the spirit of love, of Him Who is the Source of Love, and Who is the everfaithful refuge and friend of all that are sore beset and seek His aid with humble and contrite hearts. Amen.

Behind the "War Prayer" is the arrogance of power, the presumption of the very strong who confuse power with wisdom and set out upon self-appointed missions to police the world, to defeat all tyrannies, to make their fellow men rich and happy and free. Great nations in the past have set out upon such missions and they have wrought havoc, bringing misery to their intended beneficiaries and destruction upon themselves.[9]

General Maxwell D. Taylor

Perhaps the most influential military commander in formulating Vietnam policy was General Maxwell D. Taylor. General Taylor was chief military adviser to President Kennedy and Chairman of the Joint Chiefs of Staff. He was the principal architect of the Kennedy-Johnson doctrine of "flexible response," which replaced "massive retaliation" as the official U. S. military strategy. He also served as ambassador to Vietnam, and his reports and recommendations undoubtedly carried considerable weight. The comments which follow are from his statement to the Senate Committee on Foreign Relations in 1966:

For the purpose of providing a basis for our subsequent discussion, with your permission I would like to make a continuous statement which will undertake to answer three basic questions.

First, what are we doing in South Vietnam?

Secondly, how are we doing it?

And, finally, can we improve upon what we are doing?

A simple statement of what we are doing in South Vietnam is to say that we are engaged in a clash of purpose and interest with the militant wing of the Communist movement represented by Hanoi, the Vietcong and Peiping. Opposing these Communist forces, in the front rank stand

---

[9] J. William Fulbright, *The Arrogance of Power* (New York: Vintage Books, 1966), pp. 107–108, 119, 131–132, 135, 137–138. Mark Twain's "War Prayer" is cited from Mark Twain, *Europe and Elsewhere* (New York: Harper and Brothers, 1923), p. 398.

the Government and people of South Vietnam supported primarily by the United States but assisted in varying degree by some 30 other nations.

The purpose of the Hanoi camp is perfectly clear and has been since 1954. It is to absorb the 15 million people of South Vietnam into a single Communist state under the leadership of Ho Chi Minh and his associates in Hanoi. In the course of accomplishing this basic purpose, the Communist leaders expect to undermine the position of the United States in Asia and to demonstrate the efficacy of the so-called war of liberation as a cheap, safe, and disavowable technique for the future expansion of militant communism.

Our purpose is equally clear and easily defined. In his Baltimore speech of April 7, 1965, President Johnson did so in the following terms:

> Our objective is the independence of South Vietnam and its freedom from attack. We want nothing for ourselves — only that the people of South Vietnam be allowed to guide their own country in their own way.

This has been our basic objective since 1954. It has been pursued by three successive administrations and remains our basic objective today.

Like the Communists, we have secondary objectives derived from the basic one. We intend to show that the "war of liberation," far from being cheap, safe, and disavowable is costly, dangerous, and doomed to failure. We must destroy the myth of its invincibility in order to protect the independence of many weak nations which are vulnerable targets for "subversive aggression" — to use the proper term for the "war of liberation." We cannot leave while force and violence threaten them.

The question has been raised as to whether this clash of interests is really important to us. An easy and incomplete answer would be that it must be important to us since it is considered so important by the other side. Their leadership has made it quite clear that they regard South Vietnam as the testing ground for the "war of liberation" and that after its anticipated success there, it will be used widely about the world. Kosygin told Mr. Reston in his interview last December:

> We believe that national liberation wars are just wars and they will continue as long as there is national oppression by imperialist powers.

Before him, Khrushchev, in January 1961, had the following to say:

> Now a word about national liberation wars. The armed struggle by the Vietnamese people or the war of the Algerian people serve

as the latest example of such wars. These are revolutionary wars. Such wars are not only admissible but inevitable. Can such wars flare up in the future? They can. The Communists fully support such wars and march in the front rank with peoples waging liberation struggles.

General Giap, the commander in chief of the North Vietnamese forces, has made the following comment:

> South Vietnam is the model of the national liberation movement of our time. If the special warfare that the U. S. imperialists are testing in South Vietnam is overcome, then it can be defeated anywhere in the world.

The Minister of Defense of Communist China, Marshal Lin Piao, in a long statement of policy in September 1965, described in detail how Mao Tse-tung expects to utilize the "war of liberation" to expand communism in Latin America, Africa, and Asia.

These testimonials show that, apart from the goal of imposing communism on 15 million South Vietnamese, the success of the "war of liberation" is in itself an important objective of the Communist leadership. On our side, we can understand the grave consequences of such a success for us. President Eisenhower in 1959 stressed the military importance of defending southeast Asia in the following terms. He said:

> Strategically, South Vietnam's capture by the Communists would bring their power several hundred miles into a hitherto free region. The remaining countries of southeast Asia would be menaced by a great flanking movement. The loss of South Vietnam would set in motion a crumbling process which could as it progresses have grave consequences for the forces of freedom.

Now, this view has often been referred to as the "domino theory." I personally do not believe in such a theory if it means belief in a law of nature which requires the collapse of each neighboring state in an inevitable sequence, following a Communist victory in South Vietnam. However, I am deeply impressed with the probable effects worldwide, not necessarily in areas contiguous to South Vietnam, if the "war of liberation" scores a significant victory there. President Kennedy commented on this danger with moving eloquence:

> The great battleground for the defense and expansion of freedom today is the southern half of the globe — Asia, Latin America, Africa, and the Middle East — the lands of the people who harbor the greatest hopes. The enemies of freedom think they can

destroy the hopes of the newer nations and they aim to do it before the end of this decade. This is a struggle of will and determination as much as one of force and violence. It is a battle for
the conquest of the minds and souls as much as for the conquest
of lives and territory. In such a struggle, we cannot fail to take
sides.

Gentlemen, I think a simple answer to the question, what are we doing
in South Vietnam, is to say that for more than a decade we have been
taking sides in a cause in which we have a vital stake.

My second question was, How are we doing in the pursuit of our
objectives in South Vietnam? Both sides in the struggle have over the
years developed the current strategies which are now in confrontation.

During 1964 and 1965, the Hanoi leadership attempted to exploit
the political turbulence which followed the fall of President Diem in
November 1963. Greatly encouraged by the disorder which marked the
political scene in Saigon, the Communist leadership made a massive
effort to press on to victory. To meet the growing needs in military
manpower, they began the infiltration of personnel of the North Vietnamese Army, first as individual replacements, later as formed tactical
units. Utilizing this new strength, they intended to make the monsoon
offensive of 1965 a major drive for significant military victories.

Concurrently, they increased the sabotage directed at the land
communication system in South Vietnam for the purpose of hampering
the distribution of commodities and thus adding to the economic stresses
in the south.

Terrorism was stepped up and directed with added frequency at
U. S. personnel and installations. They apparently hoped to be able to
seize and hold politically important localities such as district and provincial capitals, to demoralize the Vietnamese people and Government and
to demonstrate to the United States that we were backing a cause which
must inevitably fail.

Faced with this growing threat, the Vietnamese Government and
our American officials were obliged to develop a counter strategy to
blunt and defeat the intensified efforts of our adversaries. It evolved out
of the experience of the preceding months and years and assumed its full
form with the critical decisions in 1965 to introduce U. S. ground forces
and to initiate the bombing campaign against military targets in the
north. Both of these courses of action had been under consideration at
least since November 1961, when I presented my report to President
Kennedy following a visit to Saigon to appraise the growing criticality of
the situation there.

We did not take either action at that time but my report contained
the following comment with regard to the possible necessity of using air

power against the source of the Vietcong support in North Vietnam: I   **363**
quote:

> While we feel that the program recommended represents those
> measures which should be taken now, I would not suggest that
> it is the final word. If the Hanoi decision is to continue the irreg-
> ular war declared on South Vietnam in 1959 with continued
> infiltration and covert support of guerrilla bands in the territory
> of our ally, we will then have to decide whether to accept as
> legitimate the continued guidance, training, and support of a
> guerrilla war across an international boundary.
>
> Can we admit the establishment of the common law that the
> party attacked and his friends are denied the right to strike the
> source of the aggression after the fact that external aggression is
> clearly established?

By February, 1965, it became clear that we could no longer tolerate
this clandestine support from the immune sanctuary in North Vietnam
which served as the external base for the Vietcong insurgency.

In brief, the strategy which we have been and are pursuing consists
of four components. The first includes the many activities directed at
increasing the effectiveness of our ground combat against the Vietcong
and North Vietnamese units in South Vietnam. For this purpose, we have
made the utmost efforts to increase the indigenous forces of South
Vietnam, always mindful that this is a Vietnamese war in which we
should do only those things which the Vietnamese cannot do for themselves or cannot do in time to avert defeat.

From July 1964 to July 1965 the armed forces and police of South
Vietnam were increased by some 140,000 trained men, a very creditable
effort on the part of this small country where military leadership and
administrative experience are inevitably in short supply. As of today, the
overall military strength in South Vietnam is approaching 700,000, the
largest military force in being among all of our allies, worldwide.

Encouraging though the results have been in increasing the Vietnamese strength, during the year cited, our intelligence authorities believed that the Vietcong increased their total strength by some 60,000. In
other words, we were advancing at a rate only a little better than 2 to 1
in our favor.

Since history has shown that the Government forces successfully
opposing a guerrilla insurgency in the past have required a much greater
preponderance of strength, 10 to 1 or 12 to 1 for example, it was quite
clear the Vietnamese could not raise forces fast enough to keep pace with
the growing threat of the Vietcong in time. It was this sobering conclusion that led to the decision to introduce American ground forces with
their unique mobility and massive firepower to compensate for the

deficiency in Vietnamese strength. With such forces available, it was felt that the ratios of required strength cited above would lose much of their validity.

I am thoroughly, Mr. Chairman, aware of the concern of this committee over the growing requirement for American troops in South Vietnam. Is this an endless requirement in an open-ended war? I do not believe that anyone can give a completely satisfactory reply to this question but I can suggest the consideration of certain limiting factors which have a bearing on the matter.

First, on our side, we are not setting as an objective for our ground forces the occupation of all South Vietnam or the hunting down of the last armed guerrilla. We are in Vietnam to safeguard the people who are the real target of the enemy. Terrain has little meaning except insofar as it supports people. Thus the extent of control and protection of population is the true measure of progress rather than control of territory. By the former indicator we are not doing too badly.

Senator Mansfield estimates, in his recent report, that the Government controls about 60 percent of the population, the Vietcong about 22 percent, leaving 18 percent contested. When I left Saigon last July, those figures were 53 percent, 25 percent, 22 percent.

The point I wish to make is that when one expresses our military objective in terms of securing a high proportion of the population, the troops requirement loses some of its impression of open-endedness. Under this concept, the prime target of our U. S. forces becomes the main-line enemy units which constitute the greatest threat to population — not the entire guerrilla force wherever found.

Another limiting factor is the logistic difficulty of the Vietcong in supporting increased numbers of troops in combat. The combination of air attacks on their lines of supply and of increasing ground attacks on their units which must then consume supplies at an increased rate places some kind of ceiling on the forces they can maintain in South Vietnam.

I wish I knew exactly where that ceiling is but our basic data on Vietcong logistics are too uncertain to permit precision. But the point is that there are factors which tend to keep our troop requirement finite and limit the capability of Hanoi to support large numbers of additional forces in the south.

The second component of our strategy relates to the use of airpower against military targets in North Vietnam. It is well to remind ourselves the reasons which impelled us to this decision. There were three which we recognized perfectly at the time of the decision and which remain valid today. The first was to give the people of South Vietnam the assurance for the first time of imposing a direct penalty on the source of the aggression. For 11 years they had suffered the depredations of the

Vietcong without exacting any price from the country which provided the direction and support. The morale of the people and that of the armed forces in Vietnam received an inestimable lift from the decision to use the air forces of both our countries against military targets in the homeland of the enemy — a lift which has certainly contributed to sustaining their will to continue to fight.

The second reason for the decision was to use airpower, insofar as it could be effective, to limit and render more difficult the infiltration of the men and supplies from North Vietnam to South Vietnam. It was perfectly clear from the start as it is clear today that airpower would not be able to stop infiltration. We were quite sure, however, that it could impose a ceiling on the forces which could be sustained in combat in South Vietnam. I do not believe that anyone who has reflected on the effect of the destruction of bridges, ports, railyards and similar facilities, and on the effect of the limitation of daylight movement on the roads throughout a large part of North Vietnam can avoid the conclusion that the air campaign has had an important effect in slowing down infiltration and in raising its price. A testimonial to its effectiveness was the feverish activity in North Vietnam during the bombing pause to repair bomb damage and to move transport in daylight.

The third reason for the decision to use our airpower was to provide a sobering reminder to the leaders in Hanoi that progressively they must pay a mounting price for the continuation of their support of the Vietcong insurgency.

In spite of their defiant statements of determination to endure these attacks forever, I for one know from experience that no one derives any enjoyment from receiving incoming shells and bombs day after day and I have no doubt that the warning message is getting through to the leadership of Hanoi. In a very real sense, the objective of our air campaign is to change the will of the enemy leadership.

We hope that, in due course, the combination of the Vietcong failure to win victory on the ground in South Vietnam and the effect of continued air attacks will present to the Hanoi leadership a situation so disadvantageous that they will decide that it is in their interest to halt their aggression, redefine their aims, and join with us in discussing ways and means of improving the lot of all Vietnam.

The third component of our current strategy includes all of those nonmilitary activities which are so important but which receive too little public attention. It is not that our leaders have been unaware of the importance of better government, better living conditions, and the promise of a better future for the people of this country. Unfortunately, lack of security and governmental instability were for a long time factors limiting the effectiveness of the many programs for development and

366   reconstruction. But now, with the growing military effectiveness of our forces on the ground and the slowly developing maturity of the civil leadership in Saigon and in the provinces, I hope that conditions will permit much greater progress than in the past in bringing the benefits of a comparatively normal life to this war-weary people.

As you know, the recent Honolulu Conference devoted most of its time to a consideration of these nonmilitary activities. If we are to leave a country after the end of the Vietcong insurgency, it is essential that we make progress even under the conditions of war in stabilizing the government, the society, and the economy.

The fourth component of our strategy is that which relates to our political and diplomatic efforts to initiate the discussion of a peaceful settlement of this conflict.

The so-called peace offensive is so well known as to require no discussion at this time, as is also the discouraging lack of response from the other side.

I am obliged to feel that the Hanoi leadership is not yet convinced that it must mend its ways. Perhaps they still hope for some kind of military victory in the South. Certainly, they are not convinced that in some way the United States cannot be detached from the support of South Vietnam. They hope against hope that through international or domestic pressures our Government can be forced off course.

They have not forgotten that the Vietminh won more in Paris than in Dienbienphu and believe that the Vietcong may be as fortunate in Washington. They doubt the will of the American public to continue the conflict indefinitely. In a contest of patience, they expect to win even though North Vietnam like the South has been constantly at war for over 20 years. Until it becomes perfectly clear to them that we are going to stay on course regardless of anything they can do, I am afraid we are not likely to see them at a conference table. Or if they come unconvinced of the inevitability of the failure of their present course, we can expect them to stall, delay, and maneuver just as they did at Panmunjom in Korea for over 2 years.

In summary then, our four-point strategy consists of a complex but coherent package of measures designed to improve the effectiveness of our forces on the ground in South Vietnam, to exploit our air superiority by attacking military targets in North Vietnam, to stabilize the political, social, and economic systems in South Vietnam, and to seek an honorable negotiated settlement of the conflict.

It is limited as to objective, as to geographical scope, as to weapons and forces employed, and as to targets attacked.

All parts of it are interrelated; all parts are indispensable; we must be successful on all fronts. The key, I believe, is inexorable pressure at all points, directed at the will, the ability, and the means of the Communist aggressors.[10]

Secretary of State Dean Rusk

Almost as much as the president, the Secretary of State speaks for the United States on matters of foreign policy. Dean Rusk served under two presidents and was intimately involved in the policy decisions on Vietnam. In the following news conference (October 12, 1967), he sets forth his views on the central issue.

I should like to begin with a brief comment on the current public discussion of Viet-Nam.

I find no significant body of American opinion which would have us withdraw from Viet-Nam and abandon Southeast Asia to the fate which Asian communism has planned for it. Similarly, I find no serious opinion among us which wishes to transform this struggle into a general war.

We Americans are therefore debating variations on a theme — but the theme is a central position resting upon: (a) the need to meet our commitments and defend our vital national interests; (b) the pursuit of our limited objectives by limited means; and (c) our earnest desire to bring this conflict to a peaceful conclusion as soon as possible. Hanoi particularly should not misunderstand the character of this debate.

Our commitment is clear, and our national interest is real. The SEATO treaty, approved with only one dissenting vote by our Senate, declares that "Each Party recognizes that aggression by means of armed attack in the treaty area . . . would endanger its own peace and safety, and agrees that it will in that event act to meet the common danger . . ." The treaty says "each party" will act. The fidelity of the United States is not subject to the veto of some other signatory — and five signatories have engaged their forces alongside Korean and South Vietnamese troops. Indeed, the proportion of non-U. S. forces in South Viet-Nam is greater than non-U. S. forces in Korea.

In August 1964 the Congress by joint resolution declared, with only two dissenting votes, that "The United States regards as vital to its national interest and to world peace the maintenance of international peace and security in southeast Asia." This was not a new idea in 1964. It was the basis for the SEATO treaty a decade earlier. It is no less valid in 1967. Our several alliances in the Pacific reflect our profound interest in

---

[10] U. S. Senate, Committee on Foreign Relations, *Supplemental Foreign Assistance Fiscal Year 1966 — Vietnam,* Hearings on S. 2793, Part 1, January 28; February 4, 8, 10, 17 and 18, 1966, pp. 432–438.

peace in the Pacific and in Asia, where two-thirds of the world's people live, no less vital to us as a nation than is peace in our own hemisphere or in the NATO area.

I have heard the word "credibility" injected into our domestic debate. Let me say, as solemnly as I can, that those who would place in question the credibility of the pledged word of the United States under our mutual security treaties would subject this nation to mortal danger. If any who would be our adversary should suppose that our treaties are a bluff, or will be abandoned if the going gets tough, the result could be catastrophe for all mankind.

It is not easy for our people to wage a struggle by limited means for limited objectives. We Americans are an impatient people, a quality which has helped to build a great nation. The present impatience about Viet-Nam is thoroughly understandable and is shared by those who carry official responsibility. But our overriding object is — and must be in this modern world — the establishment of a reliable peace. It is easy to rush into total catastrophe. It requires courage and determination to act with both firmness and restraint in the interest of peace. An examination of all the crises in which we have been involved since 1945 will show, I think, the supremacy of the objective of a reliable peace.

President Johnson has emphasized time and time again his interest in a prompt and peaceful settlement of the present struggles in Southeast Asia. Just 2 weeks ago, in San Antonio, he said:

> The United States is willing to stop all aerial and naval bombardment of North Viet-Nam when this will lead promptly to productive discussions. We, of course, assume that while discussions proceed, North Viet-Nam would not take advantage of the bombing cessation or limitation.

Can there be a more reasonable proposal? Is there anything unfair about such a simple proposition? Is it not clear that if Hanoi is interested in peace it could say, "Yes," publicly or privately, to the President's offer?

A rejection, or a refusal even to discuss such a formula for peace, requires that we face some sober conclusions. It would mean that Hanoi has not abandoned its effort to seize South Viet-Nam by force. It would give reality and credibility to captured documents which describe a "fight and negotiate" strategy by Viet Cong and the North Vietnamese forces. It would reflect a view in Hanoi that they can gamble upon the character of the American people and of our allies in the Pacific.

Earlier I referred to variations on a theme. The debate in which we are now involved is essentially a debate about detail — this or that military move, this or that diplomatic step, this or that formulation of what is in fact a common middle position. If that be true, precision is important. People at least should make it clear whether they are arguing with Washington or with Hanoi.

When people talk about a pause in the bombing, they should know that Hanoi calls a pause an "ultimatum." When a Senator says that he wants to stop the bombing but of course wishes to continue to bomb in support of our Marines south of the DMZ [demilitarized zone], he should know that Hanoi categorically rejects any such notion. When people say "Negotiate now" they should know that the President would meet with Ho Chi Minh and other chiefs of state concerned tomorrow — and that I would depart today for any mutually convenient spot if I could meet a representative of North Viet-Nam with whom I could discuss peace in Southeast Asia.

Chairman Thieu and Prime Minister Ky have repeatedly offered to meet with the authorities of Hanoi to arrange a cease-fire and a peaceful settlement. They and we both responded affirmatively to U Thant's proposals of last March. Had there been a similar response from Hanoi, there would have been discussions to arrange a military standstill, preliminary conversations, and a convening of the Geneva conference. Literally dozens of proposals made by ourselves, other governments, or groups of governments have been rejected by Hanoi.

I cannot tell you when peace will come. I am encouraged by progress toward peace in South Viet-Nam, but I cannot name a date. But we shall continue our effort both by resisting those who would impose their solutions by brute force and by an unremitting exploration of every path which could lead to peace.

I am ready for your questions. . . .

Q. Mr. Secretary, in a speech in the Senate yesterday, Senator [J. W.] Fulbright asserted that the United Nations is being deterred from action concerning Viet-Nam more by the failure of the United States to encourage it to act than by the opposition of the Soviet Union. What are your views on that, sir, and what role do you think the United Nations can play?

A. Well, I don't have his statement in front of me. I — relying upon the way you stated it —

Q. Would you like for me to get it verbatim?

A. — would say that it is not true. The United States would be glad to have the United Nations take up this question and deal with it responsibly. We have pending in the Security Council a resolution which the Security Council does not wish to act upon.

I think the general attitude in the United Nations seems to be that since Hanoi and Peking and Moscow are saying that this is not appropri-

370   ate for the United Nations, that an effort by the United Nations to resolve this problem might get in the way of the use of other machinery, such as the Geneva machinery or quiet bilateral diplomatic exploration.

Now, I have said many times that we ourselves do not share this view, because we believe that the United Nations has a responsibility for general peace and security in the world, and we'd be glad to see them take it up. But on the other hand, there are some problems about going through an exercise of futility, if that is what it appears to be, to satisfy some critics among our own people. . . .

Q. Mr. Secretary, may I ask, in view of a widely published report, whether in your non-public appearances around the country you are denouncing the intellectual critics of the war, including Arthur Schlesinger, and whether as reported you have dismissed Roger Hilsman?

A. No; I am not going to comment on third-hand reports on what I was alleged to have said in a private meeting. These things get out of context very quickly.

It is not true that I have any generic attitude toward all those people who call themselves or are called intellectuals.

I've been around them a good deal in my time.

I do recall once in a while — perhaps you will forgive me for this — as friends used to say of Einstein, that he was a genius in mathematical physics, an amateur in music, and a baby in politics.

Now, I think that an idea stands or falls on its own merits and the fact that a man knows everything there is to know about enzymes doesn't mean that he knows very much about Viet-Nam or how to organize a peace or the life and death of nations. . . .

Q. Mr. Secretary, I'm not clear yet on your explanation of the President's statement in San Antonio. Is that intended to modify, reduce, or leave ambiguous our terms, our conditions for a bombing pause in North Viet-Nam?

A. Well, I think we ought to just read the statement for what it says and reflect upon the absence of a response from Hanoi.

Now, you may wonder about the details of this expression that they will not take advantage of a bombing halt. There's no point, as I have said before in these conferences, no point in my negotiating the details of that with you, because you can't stop the bombing. We are prepared to discuss the details of that with Hanoi. They know it—they know it. But the point I was making is this: It seems to me that this is an essentially reasonable and fair proposal for anyone who is interested in peace. And it seems to me that it is hard for anyone to reject this proposal without confessing at the same time that they are not interested in peace and that they propose to continue their effort to move in on Southeast Asia.

This is not, by the way, just a question of Viet-Nam. I have never subscribed to the domino theory; it's much too esoteric. There are North Vietnamese regiments today fighting in South Viet-Nam. There are North Vietnamese armed forces in Laos being opposed by Laotian forces. There are North Vietnamese-trained guerrillas operating in northeast Thailand. There are Communist dissident elements in Burma who are being aided, encouraged, and helped from outside Burma across the Chinese frontier.

There was a major Communist effort in 1965 to pull off a coup d'etat against Indonesia. You don't need the domino theory. Look at their proclaimed doctrine, and look at what they're doing about it.

Now, we would like to see peace in South Viet-Nam and in Southeast Asia just as quickly as possible. It takes two to make a peace; and we would like to see some indication from the other side that they accept the notion that all countries, large and small, as the U.N. Charter puts it, have a right to live in peace without molestation from across their frontiers.

When that moment comes, there can be peace very quickly indeed; and the United States will be no obstacle whatever in making a peace on that basis. . . .

Q. Mr. Secretary, one of the elements in the public discussion over stopping the bombing, particularly in Congress, seems to be senatorial worries about how the United States is regarded abroad. Senators have heard the opening debate in the General Assembly, where foreign minister after foreign minister has urged the United States to stop the bombing. When you are confronted with a concern like that — I think almost 30 foreign ministers asked for a pause in the bombing — how do you reply to that concern? And linked with that is Senator [John Sherman] Cooper's proposal to stop bombing except on the infiltration routes above the DMZ.

A. Well, on the last point, a proposal to stop the bombing except on the infiltration routes would be categorically rejected by Hanoi; and not move us one inch toward peace, unless Hanoi makes a major change in its position. Your count on foreign ministers is a little higher than mine, in terms of stopping the bombing.

You know, I haven't found anyone in the world — private citizen or public official, in this or other governments — who has come to me and said, "If you stop the bombing and there is no response from Hanoi, then our attitude would change."

I had a group of private citizens in not long ago to talk about this, and they wanted us to stop the bombing. I said, "All right, if we stop the bombing" — we have stopped it on a number of occasions — "If we stop the bombing and Hanoi does not respond, will you then change your view?" They said, "No, of course not."

I could only say "Well, if we can't influence you by stopping the bombing, how do you expect us to influence Hanoi by stopping the bombing?"

Now, I would be glad to hear from any of these foreign ministers what their governments will do if we stop the bombing and there is no response from Hanoi. And I want to hear that. I haven't heard it from anybody.

I do know what the British co-chairman would do if we stopped the bombing: make a maximum effort to get this matter moved toward peace.

But if Hanoi is saying "No" all the time, then he has very little chance. And if the other co-chairman won't cooperate, there is very little chance. . . .

For us to say, "We will stop, you go right ahead with your war; you live there safely and comfortably without being disturbed while you send your men and arms into South Viet-Nam for the next 50 years," where would be the incentive for peace?

Now, we are interested in peace; we are not interested in a sanctuary which will let them carry on these operations against South Viet-Nam and Laos for eternity, while they sit there in a sanctuary taking their own time, paying no price, trying to seize their neighbors by force. Now, let's not be children.

Q. Mr. Secretary, one of the questions — basic questions — that seems to be emerging in this Senate debate is whether our national security is really at stake in Viet-Nam and whether Viet-Nam represents an integral part of our defense perimeter in the Pacific. Your earlier statement indicates that you think our security is at stake in Viet-Nam. I think it would help in this debate if you would perhaps elaborate and explain why you think our security is at stake in Viet-Nam.

A. Within the next decade or two, there will be a billion Chinese on the mainland, armed with nuclear weapons, with no certainty about what their attitude toward the rest of Asia will be.

Now, the free nations of Asia will make up at least a billion people. They don't want China to overrun them on the basis of a doctrine of the world revolution. The militancy of China has isolated China, even within the Communist world, but they have not drawn back from it. They have reaffirmed it, as recently as their reception of their great and good friend, Albania, 2 days ago.

Now, we believe that the free nations of Asia must brace themselves, get themselves set, with secure, progressive, stable institutions of their own, with cooperation among the free nations of Asia stretching from Korea and Japan right around to the subcontinent, if there is to be peace in Asia over the next 10 or 20 years. We would hope that in China there would emerge a generation of leadership that would think seriously about what is called "peaceful coexistence," that would recognize the pragmatic necessity for human beings to live together in peace rather than on a basis of continuing warfare.

Now, from a strategic point of view, it is not very attractive to think of the world cut in two by Asian communism reaching out through Southeast Asia and Indonesia, which we know has been their objective, and that these hundreds of millions of people in the free nations of Asia should be under the deadly and constant pressure of the authorities in Peking, so that their future is circumscribed by fear.

Now, these are vitally important matters to us, who are both a Pacific and an Atlantic power. After all, World War II hit us from the Pacific, and Asia is where two-thirds of the world's people live. So we have a tremendous stake in the ability of the free nations of Asia to live in peace; and to turn the interests of people in mainland China to the pragmatic requirements of their own people and away from a doctrinaire and ideological adventurism abroad. . . .

Q. Mr. Secretary, would you describe the net objective here then as the containment of Chinese Communist militancy?

A. No. The central objective is an organized and reliable peace.

Now, if China pushes out against those with whom we have alliances, then we have a problem; but so does China. If China pushes out against the Soviet Union, both China and the Soviet Union have a problem.

We are not picking out ourselves — we are not picking out Peking as some sort of special enemy. Peking has nominated itself by proclaiming a militant doctrine of the world revolution and doing something about it. This is not a theoretical debate; they are doing something about it.

Now, we can live at peace — we have not had a war with the Soviet Union in 50 years of coexistence since their revolution. We are not ourselves embarked upon an ideological campaign to destroy anybody who calls themselves Communist. But we are interested in the kind of world structure sketched in articles I and II of the United Nations Charter, in which all nations, large and small, have a right to live in peace. And the aggressors nominate themselves — we don't choose them — the aggressors nominate themselves by what they say and do. And when they do, then those who are genuinely interested in peace have a problem on their hands, and sometimes it gets tough; and sometimes we are tested and we find out what kind of people we are. And I think one of the most important historical facts in this postwar period has been that the almost unbelievable power of the United States has been harnessed to the simple notion of organizing a peace in the world.

Q. Thank you, Mr. Secretary.[11]

President Johnson

As commander-in-chief of the nation's military forces, President Johnson ordered the bombing of North Vietnam and the build-up of American forces from a few thousand to over half a million men. Presumably, these decisions were taken on the advice of the best minds in the Pentagon and the State Department, and with the consent of the Congress.

President Johnson outlined his Vietnam policies in this speech at Johns Hopkins University in the spring of 1965, and generally maintained the same views throughout the rest of his term of office.

I have come here to review once again with my own people the views of the American Government.

Tonight Americans and Asians are dying for a world where each people may choose its own path to change. This is the principle for which our ancestors fought in the valleys of Pennsylvania. It is the principle for which our sons fight tonight in the jungles of Vietnam.

Vietnam is far away from this quiet campus. We have no territory there, nor do we seek any. The war is dirty and brutal and difficult. And some 400 young men — born into an America that's bursting with opportunity and promise — have ended their lives on Vietnam's steaming soil.

Why must we take this painful road?

Why must this nation hazard its ease and its interests and its power for the sake of a people so far away?

We fight because we must fight if we are to live in a world where every country can shape its own destiny. And only in such a world will our own freedom be finally secure.

This kind of a world will never be built by bombs or bullets. Yet the infirmities of man are such that force must often precede reason — and the waste of war the works of peace.

We wish that this were not so. But we must deal with the world as it is, if it is ever to be as we wish.

The world as it is in Asia is not a serene or peaceful place. The first reality is that North Vietnam has attacked the independent nation of South Vietnam: its object is total conquest.

Of course, some of the people of South Vietnam are participating in

---

[11] *Department of State Publication 8313,* East Asian and Pacific Series 168, Press release 227 (October 12, 1967).

attack on their own government, but trained men and supplies, orders and arms flow in a constant stream from north to south. This support is the heartbeat of the war and it is a war of unparalleled brutality.

Simple farmers are the targets of assassination and kidnapping; women and children are strangled in the night because their men are loyal to their government. And helpless villages are ravaged by sneak attacks. Large-scale raids are conducted on towns, and terror strikes in the heart of cities.

The confused nature of this conflict cannot mask the fact that is: it is the new face of an old enemy.

Over this war and all Asia is another reality: the deepening shadow of Communist China. The rulers in Hanoi are urged on by Peking. This is a regime which has destroyed freedom in Tibet, which has attacked India and has been condemned by the United Nations for aggression in Korea.

It is a nation which is helping the forces of violence in almost every continent. The contest in Vietnam is part of a wider pattern of aggressive purposes.

Why are these realities our concern?

Why are we in South Vietnam?

We are there because we have a promise to keep.

Since 1954 every American President has offered support to the people of South Vietnam. We have helped to build, and we have helped to defend. Thus, over many years we have made a national pledge to help South Vietnam defend its independence. And I intend to keep that promise.

To dishonor that pledge, to abandon this small and brave nation to its enemies, and to the terror that must follow, would be an unforgivable wrong.

We are also there to strengthen world order. Around the globe, from Berlin to Thailand, are people whose well-being rests in part on the belief that they can count on us if they are attacked. To leave Vietnam to its fate would shake the confidence of all these people in the value of an American commitment; and in the value of America's word.

The result would be increased unrest and instability — and even wider war.

We are also there because there are great stakes in the balance. Let no one think for a moment that retreat from Vietnam would bring an end to conflict. The battle would be renewed in one country and then another. The central lesson of our time is that the appetite of aggression is never satisfied.

To withdraw from one battlefield means only to prepare for the next. We must say in Southeast Asia, as we did in Europe, in the words of the Bible, "Hitherto shalt thou come; but no further."

There are those who say that all our efforts there will be futile; that China's power is such that it is bound to dominate all Southeast Asia. But there is no end to that argument until all of the nations of Asia are swallowed up.

There are those who wonder why we have a responsibility there. Well, we have it there for the same reason that we have a responsibility for the defense of Europe. World War II was fought in both Europe and Asia and when it ended we found ourselves with continued responsibility for the defense of freedom.

Our objective is the independence of South Vietnam, and its freedom from attack. We want nothing for ourselves — only that the people of South Vietnam be allowed to guide their own country in their own way.

We will do everything necessary to reach that objective. And we will do only what is absolutely necessary.

In recent months attacks on South Vietnam were stepped up. Thus it became necessary for us to increase our response and to make attacks by air. This is not a change of purpose. It is a change in what we believe that purpose requires.

We do this in order to slow down aggression.

We do this to increase the confidence of the brave people of South Vietnam who have bravely borne this brutal battle for so many years with so many casualties.

And we do this to convince the leaders of North Vietnam, and all who seek to share their conquest, of a very simple fact:

We will not be defeated.

We will not grow tired.

We will not withdraw, either openly or under the cloak of a meaningless agreement.

We know that air attacks alone will not accomplish all of these purposes. But it is our best and prayerful judgment that they are a necessary part of the surest road to peace.

We hope that peace will come swiftly. But that is in the hands of others besides ourselves. And we must be prepared for a long-continued conflict. It will require patience as well as bravery, the will to endure as well as the will to resist.

I wish it were possible to convince others with words of what we now find it necessary to say with guns and planes. Armed hostility is futile. Our resources are equal to any challenge because we fight for values and we fight for principles rather than territory or colonies. Our patience and our determination are unending.

Once this is clear, then it should also be clear that the only path for reasonable men is the path of peaceful settlement.

Such peace demands an independent South Vietnam — securely

guaranteed and able to shape its own relationships to all others, free from outside interference, tied to no alliance, a military base for no country.

These are the essentials of any final settlement.

We will never be second in the search for such a peaceful settlement in Vietnam.

There may be many ways to this kind of peace: in discussion or negotiation with the governments concerned, in large groups or in small ones, in the reaffirmation of old agreements or their strengthening with new ones.

We have stated this position over and over again 50 times and more to friend and foe alike. And we remain ready, with this purpose, for unconditional discussions.

And until that bright and necessary day of peace we will try to keep conflict from spreading. We have no desire to see thousands die in battle — Asians or Americans. We have no desire to devastate that which the people of North Vietnam have built with toil and sacrifice. We will use our power with restraint and with all the wisdom that we can command.

But we will use it.

This war, like most wars, is filled with terrible irony. For what do the people of North Vietnam want? They want what their neighbors also desire — food for their hunger, health for their bodies, a chance to learn, progress for their country, and an end to the bondage of material misery. And they would find all of these things more readily in peaceful association with others than in the endless course of battle.

These countries of Southeast Asia are homes for millions of impoverished people. Each day these people rise at dawn and struggle through until the night to wrestle existence from the soil. They are often wracked by disease, plagued by hunger, and death comes at the early age of forty.

Stability and peace do not come easily in such a land. Neither independence nor human dignity will ever be won, though, by arms alone.

It also requires the work of peace.

The American people have helped generously in times past in these works, and now there must be a much more massive effort to improve the life of man in that conflict-torn corner of our world.

The first step is for the countries of Southeast Asia to associate themselves in a greatly expanded cooperative effort for development.

We would hope that North Vietnam would take its place in the common effort just as soon as peaceful cooperation is possible.

The United Nations is already actively engaged in development in this area, and as far back as 1961 I conferred with our authorities in Vietnam in connection with their work there. And I would hope tonight that the Secretary General of the United Nations could use the prestige of his great office and his deep knowledge of Asia to initiate as soon as possible with the countries of that area a plan for cooperation in increased development.

For our part I will ask the Congress to join in a billion-dollar American investment in this effort as soon as it is under way.

And I would hope that all other industrialized countries, including the Soviet Union, will join in this effort to replace despair with hope and terror with progress. The task is nothing less than to enrich the hopes and the existence of more than 100 million people, and there is much to be done.

The vast Mekong River can provide food and water and power on a scale to dwarf even our own TVA.

The wonder of modern medicine can be spread through villages where thousands die every year from lack of care.

Schools can be established to train people in the skills that are needed to manage the process of development.

And these objectives, and more, are within the reach of a cooperative and determined effort. I also intend to expand and speed up a program to make available our farm surplus to assist in feeding and clothing the needy in Asia.

We should not allow people to go hungry and wear rags, while our own warehouses overflow with an abundance of wheat and corn and rice and cotton.

So I will very shortly name a special team of outstanding patriotic distinguished Americans to inaugurate our participation in these programs. This team will be headed by Mr. Eugene Black, the very able former president of the World Bank.

In areas that are still ripped by conflict, of course, development will not be easy. Peace will be necessary for final success. But we cannot and must not wait for peace to begin this job.

This will be a disorderly planet for a long time. In Asia, as elsewhere, the forces of the modern world are shaking old ways and uprooting ancient civilizations. There will be turbulence and struggle and even violence.

Great social change, that we see in our own country now, does not always come without conflict.

We must also expect that nations will on occasion be in dispute with us. It may be because we are rich or powerful, or because we have made some mistakes, or because they honestly fear our intentions.

However, no nation need ever fear that we desire their land or to impose our will or to dictate their institutions.

But we will always oppose the effort of one nation to conquer another nation. We will do this because our own security is at stake. But there is more to it than that. For our generation has a dream. It is a very old dream. But we have the opportunity to make that dream come true.   **379**

For centuries, nations have struggled among each other. But we dream of a world where disputes are settled by law and reason. And we will try to make it so.

For most of history, men have hated and killed one another in battle. But we dream of an end to war. We will try to make it so.

For all existence, most men have lived in poverty, threatened by hunger. But we dream of a world where all are fed and charged with hope. And we will help to make it so.

The ordinary men and women of North Vietnam and South Vietnam, of China and India, of Russia and America, are brave people. They are filled with the same proportions of hate and fear, of love and hope. Most of them want the same things for themselves and their families. Most of them do not want their sons to ever die in battle; or to see their homes, or the homes of others, destroyed.

Well, this can be their world yet. Man now has the knowledge — always before denied — to make this planet serve the real needs of the people who live on it.

I know this will not be easy. I know how difficult it is for reason to guide passion, and love to master hate. The complexities of this world do not bow easily to pure and consistent answers.

But the simple truths are there just the same. We must all try to follow them as best we can.

We often say how impressive power is. But I do not find it impressive at all. The guns and the bombs, the rockets and the warships, are all symbols of human failure. They are necessary symbols. They protect what we cherish. But they are witness to human folly.

A dam built across a great river is impressive.

In the countryside where I was born, and where I live, I have seen the night illuminated and the kitchens warmed and the homes heated where once the cheerless night and the ceaseless cold held sway. And all this happened because electricity came to our area along the humming wires of the R.E.A.

Electrification of the countryside — yes, that too is impressive. A rich harvest in a hungry land is impressive.

The sight of healthy children in a classroom is impressive. These, not mighty arms, are the achievements which the American nation believes to be impressive.

And if we are steadfast, the time may come when all other nations will also find it so.

Every night before I turn out the lights to sleep I ask myself this question: "Have I done everything that I can do to unite the world, to try to bring peace and hope to all the peoples of the world? Have I done enough?"

380   Ask yourselves that question in your homes and in this hall tonight. Have we, each of us, all done all we could? Have we done enough? We may well be living in the time foretold many years ago when it was said:

"I call heaven and earth to record this day against you; that I have set before you life and death, blessing and cursing. Therefore choose life that both thou and thy seed may live."

This generation of the world must choose: destroy or build, kill or aid, hate or understand.

We can do all these things on a scale that's never been dreamed of before. Well, we will choose life. And so doing we will prevail over the enemies within man and over the natural enemies of all mankind. . . .[12]

On February 8, 1967, President Johnson sent a letter to Ho Chi Minh:

Dear Mr. President:

I am writing to you in the hope that the conflict in Vietnam can be brought to an end. That conflict has already taken a heavy toll — in lives lost, in wounds inflicted, in property destroyed and in simple human misery. If we fail to find a just and peaceful solution, history will judge us harshly.

Therefore, I believe that we both have a heavy obligation to seek earnestly the path to peace. It is in response to that obligation that I am writing directly to you.

We have tried over the past several years, in a variety of ways and through a number of channels to convey to you and your colleagues our desire to achieve a peaceful settlement. For whatever reasons, these efforts have not achieved any results.

It may be that our thoughts and yours, our attitudes and yours, have been distorted or misinterpreted as they passed through these various channels. Certainly that is always a danger in indirect communication.

There is one good way to overcome this problem and to move forward in the search for a peaceful settlement. That is for us to arrange for direct talks between trusted representatives in a secure setting and away from the glare of publicity. Such talks should not be used as a propaganda exercise but should be a serious effort to find a workable and mutually acceptable solution.

In the past two weeks, I have noted public statements by representatives of your government suggesting that you would be prepared to enter into direct bilateral talks with representatives of the U. S. government, provided that we ceased "unconditionally" and permanently our bomb-

---

[12] Address by President Lyndon B. Johnson at Johns Hopkins University, April 7, 1965.

ing operations against your country and all military actions against it. In the last day, serious and responsible parties have assured us directly that this is in fact your proposal.

Let me frankly state that I see two great difficulties for this proposal. In view of our public position, such action on our part would inevitably produce worldwide speculation that discussions were under way and would impair the privacy and secrecy of those discussions. Secondly, there would inevitably be grave concern on our part whether your government would make use of such action by us to improve its military position.

With these problems in mind, I am prepared to move even further toward an ending of hostilities than your government has proposed in either public statements or through private diplomatic channels. I am prepared to order a cessation of bombing against your country and the stopping of further augmentation of U. S. forces in South Vietnam as soon as I am assured that infiltration into South Vietnam by land and by sea has stopped. These acts of restraint on both sides would, I believe, make it possible for us to conduct serious and private discussions leading toward an early peace.

I make this proposal to you now with a specific sense of urgency arising from the imminent new year holidays in Vietnam. If you are able to accept this proposal I see no reason why it should not take effect at the end of the new year or Tet holidays. The proposals I have made would be greatly strengthened if your military authorities and those of the government of South Vietnam could promptly negotiate an extension of the Tet truce.

As to the site of the bilateral discussions, I propose, there are several possibilities. We could for example, have our representatives meet in Moscow where contacts have already occurred. They could meet in some other country such as Burma. You may have other arrangements or sites in mind, and I would try to meet your suggestions.

The important thing is to end a conflict that has brought burdens to both our peoples, and above all to the people of South Vietnam. If you have any thoughts about the action I propose, it would be most important that I receive them as soon as possible.

Sincerely,

Lyndon B. Johnson[13]

Ho Chi Minh replied on February 15, in a message that was broadcast by the official North Vietnamese News Agency:

---

[13] As reported in the *Chicago Sun-Times,* (March 22, 1967), by permission of Associated Press.

382   To his excellency Mr. Lyndon B. Johnson,
         President, United States of America,
     Your Excellency:

     On February 10, 1967, I received your message. This is my reply.

     Vietnam is thousands of miles away from the United States. The Vietnamese people have never done any harm to the United States. But contrary to the pledges made by its representative at the 1954 Geneva conference, the U. S. government has ceaselessly intervened in Vietnam, it has unleashed and intensified the war of aggression in South Vietnam with a view to prolonging the partition of Vietnam and turning South Vietnam into a neo-colony and a military base of the United States. For over two years now, the U. S. government has, with its air and naval forces, carried the war to the Democratic Republic of (North) Vietnam, an independent and sovereign country.

     The U. S. government has committed war crimes, crimes against peace and against mankind. In South Vietnam, half a million U. S. and satellite troops have resorted to the most inhuman weapons and the most barbarous methods of warfare, such as napalm, toxic chemicals and gases, to massacre our compatriots, destroy crops, and raze villages to the ground. In North Vietnam, thousands of U. S. aircraft have dropped hundreds of thousands of tons of bombs, destroying towns, villages, factories, schools. In your message, you apparently deplored the sufferings and destruction in Vietnam. May I ask you; who has perpetrated these monstrous crimes? It is the U. S. and satellite troops. The U. S. government is entirely responsible for the extremely serious situation in Vietnam.

     The U. S. war of aggression against the Vietnamese people constitutes a challenge to the countries of the Socialist camp, a threat to the national independence movement, and a serious danger to peace in Asia and the world.

     The Vietnamese people deeply love independence, freedom and peace. But in the face of the U. S. aggression, they have risen up, united as one man, fearless of sacrifices and hardships. They are determined to carry on their resistance until they have won genuine independence and freedom and true peace. Our just cause enjoys strong sympathy and support from the peoples of the whole world, including broad sections of the American people.

     The U. S. government has unleashed the war of aggression in Vietnam. It must cease this aggression. That is the only way to the restoration of peace. The U. S. government must stop definitively and unconditionally its bombing raids and all other acts of war against the Democratic Republic of Vietnam, withdraw from South Vietnam all U. S. and satellite troops, recognize the South Vietnam National Front for Liberation and let the Vietnamese people settle themselves their own affairs. Such is the basic content of the five-point stand of the government of the Democratic Republic of Vietnam, which embodies the essential principles and provisions of the 1954 Geneva agreement on Vietnam, it is the basis of a correct political solution to the Vietnam problem.

In your message, you suggested direct talks between the Democratic Republic of Vietnam and the United States. If the U. S. government really wants these talks, it must first of all stop unconditionally its bombing raids and all other acts of war against the Democratic Republic of Vietnam. It is only after the unconditional cessation of the U. S. bombing raids and all other acts of war against the Democratic Republic of Vietnam that the Democratic Republic of Vietnam and the United States could enter into talks and discuss questions concerning the two sides.

The Vietnamese people will never submit to force, they will never accept talks under the threat of bombs.

Our cause is absolutely just. It is to be hoped that the U. S. government will act in accordance with reason.

Sincerely,

Ho Chi Minh[14]

On Sunday evening, March 31, 1968, the President made a dramatic offer to North Vietnam and an even more dramatic announcement that he would not be a candidate for the presidency. Excerpts from the speech follow:

Good evening my fellow Americans.

Tonight I want to speak to you on peace in Vietnam and Southeast Asia.

No other question so preoccupies our people. No other dream so absorbs the 250 million human beings who live in that part of the world. No other goal motivates American policy in Southeast Asia.

For years, representatives of our government and others have traveled the world — seeking to find a basis for peace talks.

Since last September, they have carried the offer I made public at San Antonio.

That offer was this:

That the United States would stop its bombardment of North Vietnam when that would lead promptly to productive discussions — and

---

[14] *Chicago Sun-Times,* (March 22, 1967), by permission of the Associated Press.

that we would assume that North Vietnam would not take military advantage of our restraint.

Hanoi denounced this offer, both privately and publicly. Even while the search for peace was going on, North Vietnam rushed their preparations for a savage assault on the people, the government, and the allies of South Vietnam.

Their attack — during the Tet holidays — failed to achieve its principal objectives.

It did not collapse the elected government of South Vietnam or shatter its army — as the Communists had hoped.

It did not produce a "general uprising" among the people of the cities. The Communists were unable to maintain control of any city. And they took very heavy casualties.

But they did compel the South Vietnamese and their allies to move certain forces from the countryside, into the cities.

They caused widespread disruption and suffering. Their attacks, and the battles that followed, made refugees of half a million human beings.

The Communists may renew their attack. They are, it appears, trying to make 1968 the year of decision in South Vietnam — the year that brings, if not final victory or defeat, at least a turning point in the struggle.

This much is clear:

If they do mount another round of heavy attacks, they will not succeed in destroying the fighting power of South Vietnam and its allies.

But tragically, this is also clear: many men — on both sides of the struggle — will be lost. A nation that has already suffered 20 years of warfare will suffer once again. Armies on both sides will take new casualties. And the war will go on.

There is no need for this to be so.

There is no need to delay the talks that could bring an end to this long and bloody war.

Tonight, I renew the offer I made last August — to stop the bombardment of North Vietnam. We ask that talks begin promptly, and that they be serious talks on the substance of peace. We assume that during those talks Hanoi would not take advantage of our restraint.

We are prepared to move immediately toward peace through negotiations.

Tonight, in the hope that this action will lead to early talks, I am taking the first step to de-escalate the conflict. We are reducing — substantially reducing — the present level of hostilities.

And we are doing so unilaterally, and at once.

Tonight, I have ordered our aircraft and naval vessels to make no attacks on North Vietnam, except in the area north of the demilitarized zone (DMZ) where the continuing enemy build-up directly threatens allied forward positions and where movements of troops and supplies are clearly related to that threat.

The area in which we are stopping our attacks includes almost 90 per cent of North Vietnam's population, and most of its territory. Thus there will be no attacks around the principal populated areas, and in the food-producing areas of North Vietnam.

Even this limited bombing of the north could come to an early end — if our restraint is matched by restraint in Hanoi. But I cannot in conscience stop all bombing so long as to do so would immediately and directly endanger the lives of our men and our allies. Whether a complete bombing halt becomes possible in the future will be determined by events.

Our purpose in this action is to bring about a reduction in the level of violence that now exists.

It is to save the lives of brave men — and of innocent women and children. It is to permit the contending forces to move closer to a political settlement. Tonight. I call upon the United Kingdom and the Soviet Union — as co-chairmen of the Geneva Conferences, and as permanent members of the United Nations Security Council — to do all they can to move from the unilateral act of de-escalation I have just announced toward genuine peace in Southeast Asia.

Now, as in the past, the United States is ready to send its representatives to any forum, at any time, to discuss a means of bringing this war to an end.

I am designating one of our most distinguished Americans, Ambassador Averell Harriman, as my personal representative for such talks. In addition, I have asked Ambassador Llewellyn Thompson, who returned from Moscow for consultations, to be available to join Ambassador Harriman at Geneva or any other suitable place just as soon as Hanoi agrees to a conference.

I call upon President Ho Chi Minh to respond positively and favorably to this new step toward peace.

But if peace does not come now through negotiations, it will come when Hanoi understands that our common resolve is unshakeable and our common strength is invincible.

Tonight, we and other allied nations are contributing 600,000 fighting men to assist 700,000 South Vietnamese troops in defending their country.

Our presence there has always rested on this basic belief: the main burden of preserving their freedom must be carried out by them — by the South Vietnamese themselves.

We and our allies can only help to provide a shield — behind which

the people of South Vietnam can survive and develop. On their efforts —
on their determination and resourcefulness — the outcome will ultimately
depend.

And there may come a time when South Vietnamese — on both sides
— are able to work out a way to settle their differences by free political
choice rather than by war.

As Hanoi considers its course, it should be in no doubt of our
intentions. It must not miscalculate the pressures within our democracy
in this election year.

We have no intention of widening this war.

But the United States will not accept a fake solution to this long and
arduous struggle and call it peace.

No one can foretell the precise terms of an eventual settlement.

Our objective in South Vietnam has never been the annihilation of
the enemy. It has been to bring about a recognition in Hanoi that its
objective — taking over the South by force — could not be achieved.

We think that peace can be based on the Geneva accords of 1954 —
under political conditions that permit the South Vietnamese — all the
South Vietnamese — to chart their course free of any outside domination
or interference, from us or from anyone else.

Tonight I also reaffirm the pledge we made at Manila — that we are
prepared to withdraw our forces from South Vietnam as the other side
withdraws its forces to the North, stops infiltration, and the level of
violence thus subsides.

Our goal of peace and self-determination in Vietnam is directly
related to the future of Southeast Asia — where much has happened to
inspire confidence during the past 10 years. We have done all that we
knew how to do to contribute and to help build that confidence.

One day, my fellow citizens, there will be peace in Southeast Asia.

It will come because the people of Southeast Asia want it — those
whose armies are at war today, and those who, though threatened, have
thus far been spared.

Peace will come because Asians were willing to work for it—to
sacrifice for it — to die for it.

But let it never be forgotten: peace will come also because America
sent her sons to help secure it.

It has not been easy — far from it. During the past four and a half
years, it has been my fate and responsibility to be commander-in-chief. I
have lived — daily — with the cost of this war. I know the pain it has
inflicted and the misgivings it has aroused.

Throughout this period, I have been sustained by a single principle:
that what we are doing now, in Vietnam, is vital not only to the security
of Asia, but to our own security.

Surely we have treaties which we must respect, and commitments we must keep. Resolutions of Congress testify to the need to resist aggression in Southeast Asia.

But the heart of our involvement in South Vietnam has always been America's security.

And the larger purpose of our involvement has always been to help the nations of Southeast Asia become independent, self-sustaining members of the world community, at peace with themselves, and with all others.

With such an Asia, our country — and the world — will be far more secure than it is tonight.

I believe that a peaceful Asia is far nearer to reality, because of what America has done in Vietnam. I believe that the men who endure the dangers of battle there are helping the entire world avoid far greater conflicts than this one.

The peace that will bring them home will come. Tonight I have offered the first in what I hope will be a series of mutual moves toward peace.

I pray that it will not be rejected by the leaders of North Vietnam. I pray that they will accept it as a means by which the sacrifices of their own people may be ended.

With America's sons in the field far away, with America's future under challenge here at home, with our hopes — and the world's hopes — for peace in the balance every day, I do not believe that I should devote an hour of my time to any personal partisan causes or to any duties other than the awesome duties of this office.

Accordingly, I shall not seek — and will not accept — the nomination of my party for another term as your president. Let men everywhere, however, know that a strong, confident, vigilant America stands ready to seek an honorable peace and to stand ready to defend an honored cause, whatever the price, whatever the burden, whatever the sacrifices that duty may require.

Thank you for listening.

Good night and God bless all of you.

After a month of haggling with Washington over possible conference sites and other matters, the Foreign Ministry of North Vietnam issued the following statement on May 3, 1968.

As is known, for a correct solution of the Viet Nam problem, the Vietnamese people have adopted an unswerving position, namely the four points of the Government of the Democratic Republic of Viet Nam and the Political Programme of the South Viet Nam National Front for Liberation.

388   On March 31, 1968, U. S. President L. B. Johnson announced the
"limited bombing" of North Viet Nam, and once again expressed a desire
to enter into talks with the Democratic Republic of Viet Nam.

On April 3, 1968, the Government of the Democratic Republic of
Viet Nam issued a statement making clear its stand and attitude on this
subject, and its readiness to appoint its representative to contact the U. S.
representative.

But due to the lack of a serious attitude on the part of the U. S.
Government, contacts which are to lead to talks between the two sides
have not begun as yet. After professing "readiness to go anywhere" for
talks with Hanoi, the U. S. President has put forward conditions after
conditions for the choice of a site with a view to rejecting Phnom Penh
and Warsaw, suggested by the Democratic Republic of Viet Nam. The
U. S. side has also proposed places inconsistent with its own conditions.
Of late, it raised a new question suggesting that the two parties hold
private discussions on the place and time of the contacts; and they
should accordingly choose one more place for those private discussions.
To show its good will, the Government of the Democratic Republic of
Viet Nam instructed its ambassador to Warsaw to stand ready to enter
into discussions with the U. S. ambassador on the place and time of the
talks. But the U. S. side also refused.

In the meantime, the United States has kept intensifying its air and
naval bombardments on an important part of the territory of the Democratic Republic of Viet Nam, and has pursued other acts of war against
North Viet Nam; it has also made every effort to step up its war of
aggression in South Viet Nam, perpetrating new crimes of utmost bar-
barity against the Vietnamese people.

One month has elapsed since the Government of the Democratic
Republic of Viet Nam issued the above-mentioned statement. Preliminary contacts which are to lead to talks between the two sides should
have been held. But the U. S. government has deliberately resorted to
dilatory manoeuvres.

In face of such a situation, the Government of the Democratic
Republic of Viet Nam is of the view that formal talks between Hanoi and
Washington should be held without delay. The Government of the
Democratic Republic of Viet Nam has decided to appoint Minister Xuan
Thuy as its representative to enter into formal talks with the U. S.
government's representative, with a view to ascertaining with the U. S.
side the unconditional cessation of the U. S. bombing raids and all other
acts of war against the Democratic Republic of Viet Nam, and then
discussing other problems of concern to the two sides. The Government
of the Democratic Republic of Viet Nam welcomes the French Government's willingness to let Paris serve as site for talks between the Democratic Republic of Viet Nam and the United States, as stated by the

French Foreign Minister Mr. Couve de Murville on April 18, 1968. The   **389**
Government of the Democratic Republic of Viet Nam considers that
Paris, like Phnom Penh or Warsaw, is a suitable place for formal talks
between the two sides. These formal talks will begin on May 10, 1968 or
a few days thereafter.

The U. S. government must positively respond to the goodwill attitude of the Government of the Democratic Republic of Viet Nam, and
stop all dilatory manoeuvres so that formal talks may start at an early
date.

Progressive American opinion and world opinion resolutely demand
that the U. S. government unconditionally stop the bombing raids and all
other acts of war on the whole territory of the Democratic Republic of
Viet Nam, and bring its aggression in Viet Nam to an end.

So long as the United States obdurately pursues its war of aggression, the Vietnamese people will close their ranks, determined to fight till
total victory for the independence and freedom of the fatherland, for
peace in South-East Asia and the world.[15]

The Paris talks began with Averell Harriman representing the United
States and with Xuan Thuy acting as the negotiator for North Vietnam.
Apparently both sides came to the conference table under the impression
that the other side had had enough and was ready to make concessions.
As the weeks dragged on, it became obvious that both were wrong. Thuy
argued that the United States must stop the bombing before any other
matters could be considered. Harriman demanded that North Vietnam give
assurances of substantial reciprocal deescalation before the bombing
would be stopped. The following article from the *Vietnam Courier* is
typical of Hanoi's response.

The D.R.V.N.'s proposal to hold official talks threw Mr. Johnson's
Democratic Administration into utter confusion. Coming after that
American avowal of defeat: the decision to carry out "limited bombing"
of the North, it caused such surprise in Washington that for the whole
month of April, Messrs. Johnson, Rusk and Co. left no stone unturned to
try to free themselves from their own pledge to go "anywhere, any time"!
Again it was only thanks to D.R.V.N. good will that meetings could be
arranged in Paris between Mr. Xuan Thuy and Mr. Harriman.

Recalling these circumstances will give the reader an idea of the
state of mind in which the White House's delegates arrived [at] Rue
Kléber. In its April 3 statement, the Foreign Ministry of the D.R.V.N.,
while insisting on the fact that Mr. Johnson's "limited bombing" was an
important victory for the Vietnamese people, did not forget to point out

---

[15] *Vietnam Courier* (Hanoi), No. 163 (May 6, 1968), p. 1.

the perfidious manoeuvres behind that U. S. measure. As stressed in the Western press, the Americans' acceptance of the Paris meeting was merely a time-gaining and time-biding move.

Fifteen sessions so far. And no progress has been recorded. The American delegates have kept beating about the bush and eluding the main subject: "to ascertain the unconditional cessation of the bombing and all other acts of war over the whole territory of the D.R.V.N." Arrogating to themselves the right to infringe on an independent and sovereign country, they have been harping on the "San Antonio formula," which they have presented in the most various forms. At the 13th session, Mr. Harriman declared straight away: "It would not be enough to simply say: Stop the bombing!" One can't more overtly ask for a ransom in exchange for a cessation of one's criminal action! It is evident that the Vietnamese people, with their sense of self-respect and conscious of their international duties, will not permit the creation of such a precedent: putting a premium on violation of laws governing relations among States![16]

Finally, after six months of haggling, the United States capitulated. A weary president announced on nation-wide television, "I have now ordered that all air, naval, and artillery bombardment of North Vietnam cease as of 8 A.M. Washington time, Friday morning" [November 1, 1968]. As Ho Chi Minh understood it, the President's action meant that the United States had been "compelled" to stop the bombing "unconditionally" and that the bombing halt represented a "glorious victory" for North Vietnam.

But the Paris talks and the now-limited but still bloody war dragged on, with both sides stalling for time, awaiting the inauguration of the President-elect, Richard M. Nixon.

---

[16] *Vietnam Courier* (Hanoi), No. 176, (August 5, 1968).

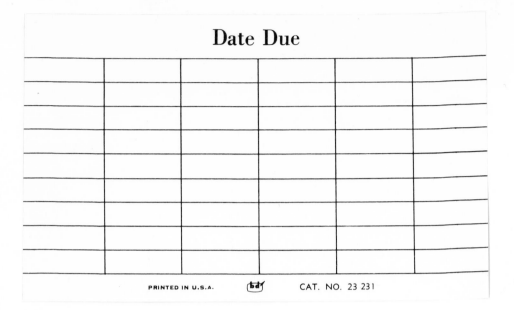